Mastering Adoption
Law and Policy

CAROLINA ACADEMIC PRESS MASTERING SERIES

Russell Weaver, Series Editor

Mastering Administrative Law
William R. Andersen

Mastering Adoption Law and Policy
Cynthia Hawkins DeBose

Mastering Alternative Dispute Resolution
Kelly M. Feeley & James A. Sheehan

Mastering American Indian Law
Angelique Townsend EagleWoman & Stacy L. Leeds

Mastering Appellate Advocacy and Process, Revised Printing
Donna C. Looper & George W. Kuney

Mastering Art Law
Herbert Lazerow

Mastering Bankruptcy
George W. Kuney

Mastering Civil Procedure, 2d e
David Charles Hricik

Mastering Constitutional Law, 2d e
John C. Knechtle & Christopher J. Roederer

Mastering Contract Law
Irma S. Russell & Barbara K. Bucholtz

Mastering Corporate Tax
Reginald Mombrun, Gail Levin Richmond & Felicia Branch

Mastering Corporations and Other Business Entities, 2d e
Lee Harris

Mastering Criminal Law, 2d e
Ellen S. Podgor, Peter J. Henning & Neil P. Cohen

Mastering Criminal Procedure, Volume 1: The Investigative Stage, 2d e
Peter J. Henning, Andrew Taslitz, Margaret L. Paris,
Cynthia E. Jones & Ellen S. Podgor

Mastering Criminal Procedure, Volume 2: The Adjudicatory Stage, 2d e
Peter J. Henning, Andrew Taslitz, Margaret L. Paris,
Cynthia E. Jones & Ellen S. Podgor

Mastering Elder Law, 2d e
Ralph C. Brashier

Mastering Employment Discrimination Law
Paul M. Secunda & Jeffrey M. Hirsch

Mastering Adoption Law and Policy

Cynthia Hawkins DeBose
PROFESSOR OF LAW
STETSON UNIVERSITY COLLEGE OF LAW

CAROLINA ACADEMIC PRESS
Durham, North Carolina

Library of Congress Cataloging in Publication Data

DeBose, Cynthia Hawkins, author.
  Mastering adoption law and policy / Cynthia Hawkins DeBose.
      pages cm. -- (Carolina Academic Press Mastering Series)
  Includes bibliographical references and index.
  ISBN 978-1-59460-619-9 (alk. paper)
  1. Adoption--Law and legislation--United States. 2. United States. Indian Child Welfare Act of 1978. I. Title.
  KF545.D43 2015
  344.7303'2734--dc23
                                    2015021361

Carolina Academic Press
700 Kent Street
Durham, NC 27701
Telephone (919) 489-7486
Fax (919) 493-5668
www.cap-press.com

Printed in the United States of America

My sincere thanks and appreciation to my immediate and extended family members who have supported and encouraged me throughout the lengthy process from the germination of my initial idea to final publication.

We Did It With God's Help!
Cynthia Hawkins DeBose

Contents

Series Editor's Foreword

The Carolina Academic Press Mastering Series is designed to provide you with a tool that will enable you to easily and efficiently "master" the substance and content of law school courses. Throughout the series, the focus is on quality writing that makes legal concepts understandable. As a result, the series is designed to be easy to read and is not unduly cluttered with footnotes or cites to secondary sources.

In order to facilitate student mastery of topics, the Mastering Series includes a number of pedagogical features designed to improve learning and retention. At the beginning of each chapter, you will find a "Roadmap" that tells you about the chapter and provides you with a sense of the material that you will cover. A "Checkpoint" at the end of each chapter encourages you to stop and review the key concepts, reiterating what you have learned. Throughout the book, key terms are explained and emphasized. Finally, a "Master Checklist" at the end of each book reinforces what you have learned and helps you identify any areas that need review or further study.

We hope that you will enjoy studying with, and learning from, the Mastering Series.

Russell L. Weaver
Professor of Law & Distinguished University Scholar
University of Louisville, Louis D. Brandeis School of Law

Mastering Adoption
Law and Policy

Chapter 1

History of Adoption

Roadmap

- History of adoption worldwide
- How adoption evolved throughout the United States
- Ways in which modern adoption compares to early adoption practices

---

I. Babylonia and Rome

Adoption is a legal process that severs the ties of one's biological parent(s) and reassigns those familial ties—along with all rights and responsibilities of parenthood—to the adoptive parent(s). The concept of adoption is nearly timeless. Adoption is found in the ancient Babylonian Codes of Hammurabi (2285 B.C.), which stated:

> Section 185. If a man has taken a young child from his waters to sonship and has reared him up, no one has any claim against the nursling.
> Section 186. If a man has taken a young child to sonship and when he took him his father and mother rebelled, that nursling shall return to his father's house.

The rules of adoption were further regulated in Ancient Rome. In Rome, the purpose of adoption was to further the patrilineal line and to continue the practice of ceremonial ancestor or family religious worship—particularly to tend to the grave of the deceased. As such, adoptees were customarily adults and male. Under Roman law, two types of adoption were recognized, namely the Latin terms of *adrogatio* and *adoptio*. Under the process of adrogation, a person who had been *sui juris* and independent lost his independence and came under the *patria potestas* of the adopting father—the *adrogans*. Adrogation was accomplished either by special act of the patrician assembly—the *comitia curiata*—and, in later times, through imperial rescript. Alternatively, under

3

the process of *adoptio,* a person who had been *alieni juris* and a dependent was removed from their *paterfamilias* and was placed under the *patria potestas* of a new family head. Under both forms of adoption, the adoptee (almost always male) became the child and the heir of the adopter—regardless of the age of the adoptee. *Adoptio* was affected only after the father fictitiously sold his son three times or sold his daughter and grandchild once. The head of the new family demanded absolute loyalty and the adoptee's rights were strictly controlled.

By 500 A.D., pursuant to the Code of Justinian, a proceeding before a magistrate was introduced. The adopter, adoptee, and the head of the adoptee's natural family were required to participate in the process. Even after adoption, the adoptee retained his inheritance rights from his birth father. Under the Code of Justinian, the adoption was required to resemble nature. As such, the adoptee had to be at least eighteen years younger than the adopter. Both the abrogated and adopted person took the last name of his new father, and kept his birth family's name as a surname. Until 291 A.D., women were disallowed from adopting.

II. Ancient Greece and Egypt

The Ancient Greeks and Egyptians also recognized the concept of adoption. In Greece the procedure involved certain ceremonies and occurred in concert with proscribed festivals. During the reign of the Egyptian kings, the informal adoption of Moses was recorded in the Bible in Exodus 2:10 ("And she adopted him for a son and called him Moses, saying I took him out of water.").

III. The Western Continent

France recognized adoption even before the Napoleonic Code, although the Code did not allow for an absolute change of family: it recognized an officious tutorship. Ancient Italy, Spain and Germany all recognized the concept of adoption.

IV. The "New World" and the United States

Notably, adoption law was never part of either the Scottish or the English common law:

> The law of England knows nothing of adoption. Its theory is that the
> father, as legal guardian — and the same principle applies to the
> mother — cannot abdicate by any contract the position of parental re-

sponsibility, or rid himself irrevocably of the sacred duties of fatherhood. He may purport to do so, but the law will not recognize any such promise as binding; it allows him to retract and repudiate at any time. Cyc. 1371–72.

Significantly, legal adoption was not recognized in England until the passage of the Adoption of Children Act of 1926 (Great Britain Statutes, 16 & 17 Geo. 5. c. 29 (1926)).

It has been opined that the English feudal practice of apprenticeship, indenture and/or "putting out" of children (both male and female) from the young age of six or nine years old until the age of twenty-one undermined a need for the process and practice of adoption within the English society and common law. The apprenticeship system continued full force into the sixteenth century—with vestiges still existing into the nineteenth century. Under this practice, children were shifted out of their homes to other families to work, learn a trade, and/or learn the proper manners of a more well-off family.

The practice of "putting out" children migrated to the New World with the Puritans. Although this was often a voluntary parental choice, the 1648 Laws of the Massachusetts Colony allowed the state to require such placement. If a child became rude, stubborn, and unruly, the state could act to remove the child and place him or her into another family (presumably for proper guidance and correction). Notably, Colonial law concurrently allowed the death penalty for a rebellious son or any child who would "smite or curse" their parents.

Early Colonial law allowed the implementation of wills whose terms included the disposition of children. The common practice was to have the child adopted by a relative who was detailed in a will. Orphaned children with no relatives were "bound out" (as opposed to "put out") which meant that they were placed into orphanages.

During this time period, adopted children had no right to inheritance— thus, any intended inheritance was required to be detailed in the appropriate will. In 1692, the then-Governor of Massachusetts Sir William Phips executed his last will and testament, which included his adopted son (Spenser Phips, alias Bennett) and his heirs. Sir William and Lady Mary Phips were a childless couple who "adopted" her nephew Spenser Bennett. In 1716, the General Court passed a private act officially changing Spenser's surname from Bennett to Phips—"as if … he had descended from the said Sir William Phips any Law[,] usage[,] or Custom to the contrary Notwithstanding." This is the earliest recorded adoption in Massachusetts.

Further, in the early years of colonization, the mandate of communal living led to the creation of artificial or contrived families. For example, a 1638

Massachusetts law ordered that every town "dispose of all single persons and inmates within their towne to servise or otherwise." Subsequently, individuals discovered to be living alone were ordered to "remove and settle themselves in some orderly family in the town, and be subject to the orderly rules of family government." Refusal would lead to arrest and jailing.

From 1781 through 1851, the General Court of Massachusetts enacted 101 private acts to change the names of the individuals so listed. The acts were the result of terms in individual last wills and testaments whereby the testator stated that he was "adopting him for his son." During that same time period 309 persons were adopted via petitions to the General Court of Massachusetts.

Therefore, unlike the majority of U.S. laws, adoption law is not derived from the English common law. U.S. adoption laws were based upon the Roman principles and processes as described above; however, while the purpose of Roman adoption was to meet the needs of the adoptive father, U.S. adoption law eventually sought to protect the welfare of the adopted child.

In 1851, Massachusetts was the first Commonwealth to pass a comprehensive adoption statute which regulated the public process. The law required that the adoption be of a younger person who was neither the wife, husband, brother, sister, uncle or aunt, of whole or half-blood, of the adopter. Further, the Act required: (1) written consent of the child's married parents, unwed mother, or the child's legal guardian if orphaned; (2) the child's consent if 14 years of age or older; (3) both the adopter and his or her spouse (if any) was required to join in the petition; and (4) a finding by a probate judge that the petitioners have the sufficient ability to raise the child and that it is "fit and proper" for the adoption to take place.

The statute called "An Act to Provide for the Adoption of Children" was revolutionary because it transformed adoption from a parent-centered process to a child-centered process. The statute also set forth more specific procedures for the adoption process. An older child's consent and his or her biological parents' or guardians' consent for the adoption were required. Prospective parents had to be certified before they could adopt a child. Prospective parents' rights and responsibilities toward the adoptee were described. Furthermore, judges had to be persuaded that the adoption was in the child's best interests. In part, the Massachusetts statute provided:

> If both or either parent of such child shall be living, they or the survivor of them ... shall consent in writing to such adoption....
> If the child be of fourteen years or upwards, the adoption should not be made without his or her consent.

No petition by a person having a lawful wife shall be allowed unless such wife shall join therein, and no woman having a living husband shall be competent to present and prosecute such petition.

...

If, upon such petition ... the judge of probate should be satisfied of the identity and the relations of the persons, and that the petitioner(s) ... are of sufficient ability to bring up a child, and furnish suitable nurture and education, having reference to the degree and condition of its parents, and that it is fit and proper that such adoption should take place, such adoption should take effect, he shall make a decree setting forth the said facts, and ordering that, from and after the date of the decree, such child should be deemed and taken, to all legal intents and purposes, the child or the petitioner or petitioners....

The natural parent or parents of such child shall be deprived, by such decree of adoption, of all legal rights whatsoever, as respects such child; and such child shall be freed from all legal obligations of maintenance and obedience, as respects such parent or natural parents.... Massachusetts Adoption of Children's Act of 1851, Act of May 24, 1851, Mass. Act 816, Ch.324.

Notably, the first mention of an adoption in the New World was in the Commonwealth of Massachusetts in 1693 — nearly 150 years before the first comprehensive adoption act was passed.

V. The Orphan Train Era

By 1850, New York City had an estimated 10,000 orphaned, vagrant, homeless children who were said to wander the streets committing crimes. In 1863, the Reverend Charles Loring Brace founded the Children's Aid Society and developed the first U.S. child placement system whereby he "placed-out" New York City orphans to families and farms in the West—although Reverend Brace and others were motivated by their attempts to "save the souls" of impoverished and orphaned children, the children sent West were mainly used as cheap labor, although not indentured. Reverend Brace stated early on:

The demand [in the West] for children's labor is practically unlimited. A child's place at the table of the farmer is always open; his food and cost to the family are of little account.... The chances, too, of ill treatment in a new [part of the] country, where children are petted and favored, and every man's affairs are known to all his neighbors, are far less than in an old [part of the country]. *The Best Method of Disposing of Pauper and Vagrant Children* (1859)

To appreciate the circular nature and the somewhat sordid beginnings of modern adoption in general and trans-racial adoption specifically, it is necessary to delve briefly into the history of the phenomenon. In the Arizona territory in 1904, an interracial foster care placement of White children with Hispanic families nearly transpired. The manner in which the case unfolded caused the incident to gain folklore status; the fact that the case was appealed to the United States Supreme Court is not its most notable attribute.

The incident began when the New York Foundling Hospital, a Catholic institutional home founded in 1870 by the Sisters of Charity as an alternative to the Protestant institutions that were predominant at the time, endeavored to place Catholic children in Catholic homes. By paying foster mothers thirty-eight cents per day to care for its charges, the Foundling Hospital established New York's first system of paid foster care. After twenty-four years, the sisters "had admitted 26,000 children and placed out 10,000, about 39 percent [of the total]."

By 1879, the Sisters of Charity had emigrated one thousand children. By 1904, they were handling approximately 1,900 children per year and emigrating between 450 and 475 of those children annually. By 1919, a total of almost 25,000 orphans had been emigrated to the Midwest and West by the Foundling Hospital. These planned exoduses — referred to as the "orphan trains" — were generally romanticized by the adults involved.

In the fall of 1904, arrangements were made to send thirty-five to forty children from New York City to two small towns in the southeastern Arizona Territory, approximately ninety miles from the Mexican border. The inquiring priest explained that the waiting families were "not wealthy people, but all had work at good wages, had comfortable homes, were mostly childless and could well take care of the little ones, that they were all good, practicing Catholics." What the priest failed to mention was that all of the couples were either Mexican or so-called Anglos interracially married with Mexicans. In comparison, the orphans sent to Arizona were all of Irish-American descent.

When the Anglo townsfolk in the Arizona Territory discovered that the Irish orphans were being placed with Mexican families, a vigilante posse was formed, and the children were forcibly removed from their foster homes within twenty-four hours of their arrival. The crux of the matter for the White townsfolk was that these were innocent White children in the care and custody of people perceived to be swarthy, unfit caretakers who would mistreat them. Although twenty-one of the children returned to New York with the nuns and nurses who had accompanied them to the West, nineteen children were virtually kidnapped and held by Anglo residents.

Through a writ of habeas corpus, the resulting civil suit sought the return of one of the children to the custody and control of the Foundling Hospital (*N.Y. Foundling Hosp. v. Gatti*, 79 P. 231 (Ariz. 1905), *appeal dismissed* 203 U.S. 429 (1906)). The suit alleged that "on or about the second day of October, 1904, the respondent unlawfully, and by means of force and violence, took possession of said child from the person to whom it was entrusted by the petitioner, and has ever since retained possession of the same."

The case's recitation of facts described the Mexican foster parents as:

> wholly unfit to be intrusted [sic] with [the children]; that they were, with possibly one or two exceptions, of the lowest class of half-breed Mexican Indians; that they were impecunious, illiterate, unacquainted with the English language, vicious, and in several instances, prostitutes and persons of notoriously bad character; that their homes were of the crudest sort, being for the most part built of adobe, with dirt floors and roofs; that many of them had children of their own, whom they were unable properly to support. *N.Y. Foundling Hosp. v. Gatti*, 203 U.S. 429 (1906).

The court also referred to the original foster parents as "degraded half-breed Indians." Interestingly, the vigilante mob that summarily took the children from their legal wards was described as consisting of "persons of some means and education from the day when, with humanitarian impulse, and actuated by motives of sympathy for their pitiful condition, they assisted in the rescue of these little children from the evil into which they had fallen." Stating that it was in the children's best interest to remain with the White families, the court dismissed the writs.

The New York Foundling Hospital appealed the case to the United States Supreme Court. After referring to the original foster parents as "half-breed Mexican Indians of bad character," the Court dismissed the appeal for lack of jurisdiction. Justice Day determined that a writ of habeas corpus for personal freedom does not apply to children. In addition, the Court's description of the events ignored the fact that the children had been violently taken from their legal guardians under threat of force. The Court stated:

> [i]n the present case there was no attempt to illegally wrest the custody of the child from its lawful guardian while temporarily in the territory of Arizona. The [Sisters of Charity] voluntarily took the child there with the intention that it should remain. Through imposition the

child was placed in custody of those unfit to receive or maintain control over it, and, as above stated, came into the custody and possession of the respondent. *N.Y. Foundling Hosp. v. Gatti*, 203 U.S. 429, 441 (1906).

Although Reverend Brace's program successfully placed tens of thousands of children throughout the Midwest and West, the program was criticized.

VI. Modern Adoption Practices and the Child Welfare System

From the 1850s through the 1950s, adoption became a legal process and a child welfare service in which the child's best interests were taken into account. An overarching public policy was that law was to mirror, or reflect, biology. In general, state law dictated that the process encompass the following elements: (1) voluntary, non-coerced consent of the birth parent; (2) an investigation of the proposed adoptive parents by the placement agency to determine their suitability—a home study; (3) the child was placed into the adoptive home for a preliminary, trial period; (4) a final adoption decree issued by a Judge or Magistrate; and (5) the proceeding remained secret and a new birth certificate was issued.

During the first half of the nineteenth century, approximately eighty private agencies for the care of dependent children were founded nationwide. Approximately fifty more were founded in the 1850s, and another eighty in the 1860s. Beginning in the 1850s, the stated purpose of these private agencies was to place orphaned younger children into a familial atmosphere.

From 1863 through 1883, Brace's Children's Aid Society of New York placed over 20,000 children into homes outside of New York City. However, by 1910, the Children's Aid Society had placed over 106,000 children into 47 states, the District of Columbia, and Indian Territories. In response to several factors— namely, the rising hostility of western states against the mass exportation of indigent and often criminal children, and the decrease in the need for child labor in the West—the orphan train era ended in 1929.

In contrast to the first one hundred years of adoption when biological similarity was a concern, inter-country adoptions began to take place during the middle part of the twentieth century. In the 1940s and 1950s, Americans responded to the orphan crisis caused by war in Europe and then in Korea by adopting children. In the 1980s, the birthrate in the United States declined and this decline led to Americans looking abroad to adopt. This decline was due to several factors, such as use of birth control, the availability of abortion, focusing on careers first, and the increased acceptance of single parenthood (Brumble and Kampfe, 159).

The 1851 Massachusetts Act transferred jurisdiction over adoptions to the probate court and codified customary practices. This Act was a model for similar legislation within the U.S. common law states. Directing a court to determine whether "the petitioner(s) ... are of sufficient ability to bring up a child, and furnish suitable nurture and education, having reference to the degree and condition of its parents, and that it is fit and proper that such adoption should take place" was a precursor to the "best interests of the child" standard of modern adoption law and policy. Unlike Roman, Egyptian, and English practice and policies of *adrogatio, adoptio,* apprenticeship and indenture, modern U.S. adoption law focuses on the dualities of the creation of a parent-child relationship and the welfare of the child — as opposed to the child as the parent's chattel.

Checkpoints

- The definition of adoption is a legal process that severs the ties of one's biological parent(s) and reassigns those familial ties to the adoptive parent(s).

- Early adoptions in England were considered apprenticeships, and this process followed the first settlers to America.

- Orphaned children were placed in orphanages, churches, and charities in early American history.

- U.S. adoption law evolved from Roman practices and not English common law; the welfare of the child was most important and was reflected in early laws.

- Public policy shaped adoptions by requiring voluntary consent, an investigative home study, a trial period with foster care, approval of an adoption decree by a judge, and new birth certificates issued.

Chapter 2

The History of the Child Welfare System and Foster Care

Roadmap

- How child welfare changed throughout the United States
- The importance of Child Protection Services in shaping foster care
- The effect of nongovernmental charities on foster care
- The history of how governmental foster care evolved in the United States

---

I. Child Welfare Prior to the Enactment of Child Protection Services

Before 1875, there were no child welfare agencies or organizations designed to protect children. People that egregiously abused children in some manner were usually criminally prosecuted within the criminal justice system. However, the state generally did not interfere in the family and child-rearing measures. Aside from protecting seriously abused children by imprisoning their abusers, some states allowed courts to intervene in the parental home and remove the child from an abusive or neglectful situation. These states enacted laws that authorized magistrates to remove children from their parents when the parents did not raise their children properly. Massachusetts was a commonwealth that enacted a similar law in 1642.

Improper child-rearing included providing no education for their child or when parents were considered to be criminals, drunks, or had unsavory vices. Court intervention and removal of a child from the parental home was rare prior to 1875, but it did occur.

When children were removed in the Colonial era, it was often for an apprenticeship. During such time, children would learn necessary skills to become productive members of society. In the 1700s, many dependent children were sent to the South to work on large plantations. In the early nineteenth century, the Industrial Revolution and a large influx of immigrants from European countries left many children on the streets. When a child was removed from his home, he was often placed with a wealthy family. However, he was often seen as an indentured servant rather than as a member of the family. During the mid-1800s, dependent children were often placed in orphanages or poorhouses. If a child was placed in an orphanage, it was often the goal of the orphanage to place the child with biological relatives. During this time period, critics of orphanages often noted their harsh disciplinary measures, the expense to run an orphanage, and the inability of orphanages to help the children become independent.

II. Child Welfare and Nongovernmental Protection Societies

Throughout the mid-to-late nineteenth century, child care reformers sought to place children in homes as opposed to orphanages and poorhouses. Massachusetts enacted the first adoption law in 1851. In 1853, the New York's Children's Aid Society was established in an effort to place dependent children in homes in the midwestern and western United States. Westerners were viewed as honest and hardworking people. From 1853 to 1893, 84,000 children were sent on "orphan trains" to western states in the hopes of being adopted into homes. Some reformers believed these adoptions were the best method of "child saving," by turning these children from misfits into "upstanding" citizens. In part, due to the volume of children sent to the West during the mid-1800s, states began enacting adoption statutes.

During the mid-1800s, "the best interests of the child" standard was created, as well as four general principles of family law. The first was the tender years doctrine, in which young children should be placed in the care of the mother. The second principle was that fathers should take care of older boys. Third, the courts should respect any attachments and affections the child formed with its caretakers. Finally, if a child is capable to exercise "reasonable discretion," the court should consider the child's wishes on the location of its placement.

The first organization designed to protect children was the New York Society for the Prevention of Cruelty to Children, which was created in 1875. The society was created by Henry Bergh, a founder of a society that protected animals from abuse, and his attorney, Elbridge Gerry. Bergh and Gerry created the society when a woman sought to protect a child from abuse and local authorities refused to investigate the matter. At that time, there were no agencies with the authority to intervene to remove a child from a home. As such, Bergh and Gerry sought to create the first nongovernmental charitable society solely to protect children from abuse and neglect. By 1922, approximately 300 nongovernmental societies in the United States were devoted to protecting children from abuse.

As more and more nongovernmental child protection societies were created, the juvenile court system emerged. In 1899, Chicago created the first juvenile court. By 1919, all but three states had implemented juvenile courts. Initially, the primary purpose of these courts was to deal with delinquent children. However, the courts were also given the jurisdiction to intervene in child abuse and neglect cases.

Due to the growth of these children's societies and the creation of the juvenile court system, the state's role expanded to regulate adoption procedures. States established procedures for gaining proper consent from a biological parent, for investigating the prospective adoptive family's homes, and for the confidentiality of records. In implementing new procedures, states were acting under the theory of *parens patriae*. Under this theory, the state thought of itself as "the parent" of the child. As a parent of the child, the state was the ultimate guardian of the children within the state. Thus, any state intervention was seen as a means to protect the child, but not to punish the parent.

Although the number of private protection agencies was growing, many urban and rural children did not have access to these organizations. A growing belief among welfare scholars was that the government needed to create public agencies in order to provide child welfare protection across the nation.

III. Child Welfare and Government-Sponsored Child Protection Services

In the early twentieth century, child protection gradually came under the hand of government agencies. In 1908, President Theodore Roosevelt held the first White House Conference on Dependent Children. At this conference, states got the idea to create a system where they could provide stipends to mothers, mostly widows, in an effort to help support and care for their children. All but two states had so-called "Mothers' Pensions" by 1935.

During that time, many state departments of health, labor, social services, and welfare were created. In 1912, the federal government created the Children's Bureau. From 1921 to 1929, federal money was granted to provide mothers and their babies with health services under the Sheppard-Towner Act.

In 1921, the Child Welfare League of America was established. This private, nonprofit organization implemented standards for both public and private adoption agencies. These standards were eventually published in 1938.

President Franklin D. Roosevelt's focus on social welfare during the New Deal era also created provisions to protect dependent children. The Federal Emergency Relief Act of 1935 and the Social Security Act of 1935 both provided federal funding to child welfare agencies.

As part of the Social Security Act, the Children's Bureau was authorized to assist state agencies in creating and strengthening child welfare services in order to protect and care for children that were homeless, dependent, neglected, or in danger of becoming delinquent. These provisions were extremely valuable to the child welfare system because most nongovernmental societies that protected children were closed as a result of the Great Depression (which lasted from 1929 through the late 1930s and by many estimates into the 1940s). To comply with new federal regulations, states either enacted or revised adoption laws. By 1937, forty-four states had done just that. One such provision was the investigation into the prospective adoptive homes prior to any court hearing.

By 1956, eighty-four of the private, nongovernmental child welfare societies were closed and thirty-two states didn't have any nongovernmental societies that were designed to protect children. Further, by 1967, only ten nongovernmental child protective agencies remained in the entire United States. By that time, the majority of states enacted statutes that placed the responsibility of child welfare in the hands of the government. Yet, for the first half of the twentieth century, there were not enough agencies to meet the needs of the entire United States. State services were not available statewide and did not provide for twenty-four hour coverage.

A collective, nationwide interest in protecting children from child abuse did not arise until physicians began writing about the epidemic. In 1946, pediatrician John Caffey published an article about six children who suffered from subdural hematoma and fractures as a result of abuse. The article sparked more doctors to write on the subject of child abuse. However, it was not until 1962, when pediatrician Henry Krempe wrote *The Battered Child Syndrome*, that the topic of child abuse became mainstream. As doctors wrote about specific cases, the media also began to cover stories about child abuse. As the media drew more attention to child abuse, the public became more aware of the issue. Congress took notice and amended the Social Security Act in 1962. The amendment required all states to have child welfare services available throughout the entire state. As a result, beginning in the early 1960s, government child welfare services grew and expanded. By 1967, every state had laws that required doctors to report anything they thought might be child abuse to the police or a child welfare agency.

The number of adoptions rose as the news coverage of dependent children grew. For example, in 1937, there were 16,000 adoptions; in 1945, there were 50,000 adoptions; in 1955, there were 93,000 adoptions; and by 1965, there were 142,000 adoptions.

Prior to World War II, adoption agencies did not accept children with physical and mental handicaps because social workers believed these children were "unadoptable." This view changed after the war, and for the first time, agencies tried to place children that were handicapped, older, a racial minority, or foreign-born. In the 1950s, adoption agencies sought to create the "picture perfect" family. To that end, adoption agencies insisted that prospective adoptive parents be married, not over the age of forty, and must not be homosexual. Adoption agencies also preferred a woman to be a stay-at-home mom instead of a "career woman."

The view of creating a "picture perfect" family deteriorated, and by 1971, transracial adoptions were the highest they had ever been. Transracial adoption is the adoption of a child from a different ethnic or racial group than the adoptive parents. Notably, the vast majority of transracial adoptions are of African American or Black children by Caucasian or White parents. In 1971, 468 agencies made a total of 2,574 transracial placements. In 1972, the National Association of Black Social Workers denounced the idea of transracial adoption. The NABSW believed that Black children were best served when placed with and adopted by Black families. After the NABSW released their collective opinion, the practice of transracial adoptions began to wane in the mid-to-late 1970s—however, the practice would see an upturn in the 1990s and beyond.

During the 1980s, open adoption became a new trend in adoption law. Birth parents and adoptive parents became more open with each other, and more welcoming of the idea that the adoptive child benefits from post-adoption contact with their biological parents. As a result, in an open adoption, birth parents received updates on their birth children and the adoptive family and child were able to reach out to the birth parents with relevant questions. In a California-based study during 1988 and 1989, 55% of adoptive families kept in contact with the adopted child's birth families. Also, during the 1980s, adults who had been adopted began advocating for their rights. These adults advocated for the unsealing of birth records—to receive medical, social and personal information about their birth families.

As child welfare continued to be a nationwide headline, the number of reported incidents of abuse and neglect rose. Sixty thousand incidents of child abuse were reported in 1974. In 1980, over 1 million incidents were reported. Over 2 million incidents were reported by 1990 and approximately 3 million incidents were reported in 2000. During 2012, an estimated 3.4 million referrals involving in the alleged maltreatment of approximately 6.3 million children, were received by Child Protective Services agencies nationwide. Of the 2.1 million reports that were screened in and received a CPS response, 62% were investigated. Of the 3,184,000 reports that were investigated, about 214,917 were substantiated; and 1,448,840 were found to be unsubstantiated.

As of January 2013 (based upon available data), it was estimated that the child poverty rate was 22% (16.1 of 72 million children living in the United States).

IV. Foster Care in the United States

The roots of foster care in the United States relate back to the informal English practice of boarding orphaned or out-of-wedlock children with relatives or "legal strangers," or indentured servitude. In the eighteenth century, children of all socio-economic classes could be indentured to families so that they could learn a trade. By the nineteenth century, the foster-care system began focusing on poor children, orphaned children, or children with unfit parents, and indentured them to families to learn a trade. Eventually, the system evolved into placing children with families who either agreed to provide free homes or were paid to board needy children. The philosophy of this early system was "child rescue" and focused on providing safe living environments for children. However, in time, the philosophy shifted toward one of rehabilitation and reunification, states then began to focus on returning children to their biological families rather than permanent placement elsewhere.

The Federal Government defines foster care as a "24-hour substitute care for children outside their own homes." Foster care settings include, but are not limited to, family-foster homes, relative/kinship care, group homes, emergency shelters, residential facilities, child-care institutions, and pre-adoptive homes.

Several federal agencies are responsible for regulating and operating the foster care system and states have various reporting requirements. First, within the U.S. Department of Health and Human Services (DHHS), Administration for Children and Families (ACF) is responsible for data collection concerning the foster-care system. Second, the Adoption and Foster Care Analysis and Reporting System (AFCARS) is the repository for case-level information on all children in foster care for whom state child welfare agencies have responsibility, including those children adopted through the individual state's system. Third, states must file biannual reports covering the periods October 1 through March 31 and April 1 through September 30th—the so-called Fiscal Year (FY). To understand the fiscal magnitude of the U.S. foster-care system, it is crucial to note that for FY 2008, Congress allocated nearly $7.9 billion for child-welfare funding—down from $12.4 billion for FY 2006.

As previously stated, throughout the 1800s and early 1900s, children who were abused or neglected were placed in orphanages or poorhouses. Foster homes did not become prevalent until the mid-1900s. During the latter part of the 1900s, foster homes and the foster care system were widely criticized. Critics argued that in general, children were often mired in the system (called "foster care drift"); and specifically, Black children were statistically overrepresented within the foster care system.

The number of children in the foster care system decreased nationally by approximately 28% in 2012, as compared to the number of children in foster care in 2000. As of September 30, 2012, there were 397,122 children in foster care nationwide, as compared to the 552,000 children in foster care in September of 2000. The number of children entering foster care also decreased during that same time period: in 2000, 293,000 children entered foster care; whereas, 251,764 children entered foster care in 2012.

In 1974, Congress passed the Child Abuse Prevention and Treatment Act (CAPTA), which gave federal funds to states that improved its response to child abuse and neglect. The goal of CAPTA was to improve each state's investigation and reporting system as well as provide funding for training. The National Center on Child Abuse and Neglect was created to administer the enforcement of CAPTA and to fund various research efforts about child abuse.

As the government began to enact federal laws, state agencies had to reform their agencies in order to meet federal guidelines and obtain federal funds. Also, for the first time, states were allowed to subcontract to private, nonprofit companies. To that end, the government finances the services while the private nonprofit provides the services. For example, after the state agency has stepped in and the agency and family has agreed upon a case plan, the private agency provides those services to the family.

The Indian Child Welfare Act (ICWA) was enacted by Congress in 1978. The 1978 House Report on ICWA stated that as many as one in four (some estimated up to 35%) of Native American children under the age of one had been adopted. Estimates showed that 85–90% of the removed children were placed with non-Native American families. The vast majority of the removals were based on vague grounds such as "neglect," "social deprivation," or unsupported allegations of "emotional damage" from living with their natural or biological parents. Nationwide, at the time of H.R. Rep. No. 1386, more than 17% of school-age Native American children lived in Bureau of Indian Affairs institutional facilities or homes. The rate of outplacements for Native American children far outpaced that of the general population.

In its findings for the ICWA, Congress stated that "an alarmingly high percentage of Indian families are broken up by the removal, often unwarranted, of their children from them by nontribal public and private agencies and that an alarmingly high percentage of such children are placed in non-Indian foster and adoptive homes and institutions." The effect of this trend was identified as a form of "cultural genocide."

Congress' stated purpose for the ICWA, as a reflection of United States policy, was "to protect the best interests of Indian children and to promote the stability and security of Indian tribes and families...." This goal was to be achieved "by making sure that Indian child welfare determinations are not based on 'a white, middle-class standard which, in many cases, forecloses placement with [an] Indian family.'" Congress found "that the States, exercising their recognized jurisdiction over Indian child custody proceedings through administrative and judicial bodies, have often failed to recognize the essential tribal relations of Indian people and the cultural and social standards prevailing in Indian communities and families."

The Act applies to any "Indian" child involved in a child custody proceeding in state court. The Act establishes the "minimum Federal standards for the removal of Indian children from their families" and seeks to ensure "the placement of such children in foster and adoptive homes which will reflect the unique values of Indian culture...."

The ICWA specifically and explicitly gives custody and adoption preference to members of the "Indian" child's extended "Indian" family, other "Indian" families, or members of the child's tribe. Unless there is a showing of good cause to the contrary, foster placements are to be made to either: (1) a member of the Indian child's extended family; (2) a foster home (either Indian or non-Indian) licensed by the Indian child's tribe; or (3) a tribe-approved children's institution.

The ICWA additionally requires that—prior to either foster care placement (even if temporary) or the termination of parental right—remedial and rehabilitative programs be provided to prevent the breakup of an Indian family. Further, the state must prove beyond a reasonable doubt that it made active efforts to prevent the breakup of the family. Placing the child with a member of its extended tribal family is considered a remedial effort under the Act. Such a placement must be proven to have failed prior to any outplacement. Under the ICWA, the burden of proof for the termination of parental rights is proof beyond a reasonable doubt that serious emotional or physical harm to the child will occur if the custody situation continues.

Tribes must be notified of a proceeding and have the right to intervene in a state court child custody proceeding. Tribal courts have sole jurisdiction over cases involving Indian children who reside on the reservation and retain concurrent jurisdiction with state courts for Indian children not domiciled on the reservation. Moreover, all courts in the United States are required to give full faith and credit to the child custody determinations of tribal courts.

The application of the ICWA is far-reaching. In *Mississippi Band of Choctaw Indians v. Holyfield*, 490 U.S. 30 (1989), the United States Supreme Court expressly held that the Act does not permit Native American parents to circumvent the Act by going off the reservation to give birth when the parents are domiciled on the reservation. Thus, a parent cannot voluntarily consent to adoption by a non-Native American to avoid having the child raised in an Indian environment or to frustrate the purposes of the Act.

The Act has rather onerous provisions for valid voluntary consent by Native American parents for either foster care placements or the termination of parental rights. Specifically, the act requires that: (1) written consent be obtained; (2) the consent be recorded before a judge; (3) the judge certify that (a) the terms and consequences of the consent were explained and understood, and (b) either English or the parent's native language was used; and (4) the consent may be given within ten days after the "Indian" child's birth. Consent to foster care placement may be withdrawn at any time and consent to parental rights termination may be withdrawn prior to the entry of a final adoption or termination decree.

By 1980, Congress enacted the Adoption Assistance and Child Welfare Act (AACWA). This was the first time in which the federal government increased its effort to gain control over family law issues. In effect, AACWA was a major over-haul of the child welfare system.

The goal of AACWA was to preserve families. The Act required that a state make "reasonable efforts" to prevent the removal of children from their parents, even if they were abused. When children had to be removed, the state had to create a plan to reunite the child with its family. If that was impossible, parental rights were to be terminated and children were to be placed for adoption. AACWA also brought a new source of funding if states used "reasonable efforts" to reunify families. Title IV-E provided uncapped funds based upon a federal-state matching formula. These funds included capped grants that reimbursed states for preventative services up to a predetermined level. Eventually, AACWA was criticized for keeping children in peril—rather than removing them from their abusive and/or neglectful families.

AACWA also provided reimbursement by the federal government to states making adoption assistance payments to parents who adopted children with special needs. To be eligible for an adoption subsidy, a child must qualify for AFDC, TANF or SSI and meet the state's definition of a "special needs child." Although the specific state definitions vary, the broad federal guidelines require that the child meet certain factors or conditions which make it reasonable to conclude that the child cannot be placed without assistance. In general, these factors are: ethnicity; age; race; part of a sibling group; and mental, physical or emotional conditions or handicaps.

During the 1990s, there were approximately 500,000 children languishing in foster care, the media sensationalized tales of family reunification that ultimately led to children's deaths, and class action suits were brought against the welfare system.

The Multi-Ethnic Placement Act (MEPA) was enacted in 1994. It prohibited agencies from denying or delaying adoptive placements because of a child's or a potential adoptive family's race. Prior to MEPA, agencies often implemented same-race placements, meaning Black children could only be placed in Black adoptive homes and White children in White adoptive homes.

Between World War I and the 1980s, adoption agencies strived to create families that looked alike, came from the same background, and had the same race and religion. Critics of this policy stated that these race matching placements often delayed the placement of children into adoptive homes, and as a result, children languished longer in foster care.

MEPA was intended to end race-matching practices. However, the Act did allow race to be considered as a factor in deciding a permanent placement for the child. Therefore, in a 1996 amendment (the Interethnic Placement Act (IEPA)), race could only be considered a factor if the needs of a specific child require that race be considered. IEPA was meant to help place minority children in permanent homes and get them out of the foster care system faster.

In 1996, although Black children were 15% of the United States child population, Black children comprised 41% of the foster care population. Alternatively, white children were 61% of the child population and only 40% of the foster care population. At the same time, Native American children were 2%, while representing only 1% of the general child population.

In response to the failure of AACWA, Congress enacted the Adoption and Safe Families Act of 1997 (ASFA). In passing ASFA, Congress intended to promote stability and permanency for the 500,000 children then in the U.S. foster-care and child-welfare system. ASFA was a change in scope from the law in effect in 1997 where the goal was reunification for children in foster care.

When signing the ASFA bill into law on November 11, 1997, President Bill Clinton reiterated ASFA's intent, stating that, "[t]he new law will help us to speed children out of foster care and into permanent families by setting meaningful time limits for child welfare decisions, by clarifying which family situations call for reasonable reunification efforts and which simply do not." As stated, this emphasis was a shift away from AACWA's reunification promotion.

While Congress passed the ASFA in late 1997, states took two years to enact and fully implement state legislation that complied with ASFA's requirement. Therefore, ASFA did not take effect until 1999. At the end of 1996, prior to ASFA, an estimated 531,311 children resided in "out-of-home" care nationwide—nearly 20% of that year's U.S. child population. By September 30, 1997 (FY 1998), approximately 559,000 children were in foster care, nearly twice as many children than were in the system in 1982. These children spent an average of almost three years in foster care. For about 100,000 of these children each year, reunification with family members was not an option. Furthermore, only 38,221 children were adopted from foster care in 1998.

By September 30, 1999, the number of children in foster care nationwide had risen to 567,000. This figure reflects statistics compiled from forty-seven states, Washington, D.C. and Puerto Rico. At that time, only 113,400 of the 567,000 children (20%) were available for adoption. Before ASFA, approximately 15,000 children "aged-out" of foster care annually without being adopted.

Under ASFA, the foster-care system is based on "permanency planning," in which states mainly focus on providing children with familial relationships within a limited time frame. Permanency planning is balanced against the state's primary goal of child placement in the most stable and permanent living arrangement and to provide the child with the care, custody, and discipline that the biological parents should have given. State agencies place children with foster parents who supervise the day-to-day activities of the child and provide the child's daily needs, such as food, clothing, and shelter. They also strive to reunite children with their biological families or place them with adoptive families within a year.

Child safety was the ASFA's main concern, although it did also stress the importance of family preservation where it was safe to do so. ASFA stressed that a child's permanence was key to a successful welfare system. States are given financial incentives for promoting ASFA's goals. Unlike AACWA, the funds are not for states using "reasonable efforts" for family reunification. Instead, states are afforded money when it promotes adoption when family reunification is not the goal of the case plan.

ASFA seeks to promote and facilitate permanency through adoption and shortened foster-care stays. After all, the legislature intended for foster care to be temporary. To this end, ASFA has changed the waiting time for a child entering foster care. Under the AACWA of 1980, a child "entered" foster care when a case went to disposition, which could last two months to two years after the child actually came into care. Under ASFA, the child "enters" foster care at the date of fact-finding regarding abuse or neglect, or a maximum of sixty days after the State removes the child from the home. This change amounts to a substantial temporal difference.

ASFA stresses that the child's health and safety and a permanent plan for the child are the paramount concerns of the legislation, rather than the parents' right to have a child returned to them. Thus, the statute pressures parents to work diligently to get their children back because of the greater risk under ASFA that their children will be permanently placed elsewhere if parents do not meet the statutory time limits.

ASFA requires states to utilize "cross-jurisdictional" resources to facilitate adoptions or permanent placements. Thus, states must focus their child placement efforts nationally, not just locally. Premised on President Clinton's "Adoption 2002 Initiative" from 1996/1997, a stated goal of ASFA was to "double the number of domestic adoptions annually to 54,000 by the year 2002."

Two of the more significant criticisms of ASFA are:

(1) The ASFA requirement to file a TPR petition for any child who has been in foster care for fifteen of the most recent twenty-two months. Arguably, this has been the most controversial provision. Filing a TPR petition does not bring children permanency. Regrettably, this provision has created "legal orphans" where no adoption is pending.

(2) ASFA's bonus incentives have become a significant "cash cow" to the states. Critics fear that these bonuses may result in hasty child placement and adoption. For example, on September 10, 2001, California "earned" over $4 million by increasing its adoptions by 31%. That same year, 35 states plus the District of Columbia received a total of $11 million. Originally, Congress authorized incentive payouts of up to $20 million per year. Continuing the trend, President Bush proposed $20 million in incentives in the Federal Budget for FY 2009. Further, the Fostering Connections to Success and Increasing Adoptions Act of 2008 (FCSIAA) authorized funding of $43 million for the Adoption Incentives Program. In FY 2011, $36 million in incentives were awarded to various states (Texas "earned" $7.9 million); in FY 2012, the total reached $44 million (Texas "earned" $10 million); and in FY 2013, payouts had to be prorated because the total amount of funds "earned" by states exceeded the amount of funds available. Therefore, in FY 2013, $26.5 million in incentives

represents approximately 57% of the true total (Texas "earned" a prorated amount of $7.1 million).

The DHHS reporting system (AFCARS) is reliable only to the extent that the states report their data. To address this problem, Congress has considered allowing DHHS to assess fines to states who fail to file or submit inaccurate information for AFCARS.

In 1999, Congress enacted the Foster Care Independence Act to help those foster children who aged out of the system without ever being adopted.

The Keeping Children and Families Safe Act of 2003 (KCFSA) was signed into law on June 25, 2003 after languishing in Congress the previous term. The purpose of KCFSA was to reauthorize a number of child and family-related statutes, such as the Adoption Opportunities Act and the Child Abuse Prevention and Treatment Act (CAPTA). One of CAPTA's provisions increases the number of older children in foster care placed into adoptive homes by adding a grant program to facilitate interstate placements. CAPTA, which KCFSA reauthorizes and updates, makes the necessary connection between the child-welfare system and issues of domestic violence that result in child abuse.

Despite the reforms made over the past few decades, most states are still not in compliance with federal requirements. Every state has taken part in the federally mandated Child and Family Services Reviews ("CFSRs"), which are used to assess whether states meet its goals of providing safety, permanence, and the well-being of children in foster care as well as in-home services. However, no state has passed the federally mandated CFSRs. As of 2012, 28% of foster children were in kinship care, 47% were in foster care with non-relatives, 17% were in institutions or group homes, 4% were in pre-adoptive homes, 1% was runaway, and the remaining children were at other various placements.

In an effort to better reform the child welfare system, the PEW Commission on Children in Foster Care made various recommendations to Congress in 2004. Members of the PEW Commission consisted of persons involved in the child welfare system — members ranged from judges and legislators to social workers, psychologists, foster and adoptive parents, and former foster youth. The Commission primarily focused on improving federal financing mechanisms and the dependency court system in order to place children in permanent families faster and reduce the overall number of children in foster care.

The PEW Commission also sought to improve the CFSRs. It recommended a three-phase process. Phase One required states to conduct a self-assessment of its child welfare system — to be submitted to the federal government. Phase Two required an on-site assessment of the state's system by the federal government. Under this review process, representatives of the federal government would assess cases, interview parents, foster children, foster parents, adoptive parents, caseworkers, and other service providers. If the state does not meet federal mandates, as Phase Three, the state must submit an improvement plan. This plan must include how the state will meet the federal requirements; and the state's plans to correct any weaknesses in its child welfare system.

As much as the United States has reformed its child welfare system, surprisingly, it is one of two members of United Nations that did not ratify the U.N. Convention on the Rights of the Child ("CRC") in 1989. Not only does the CRC protect anyone under the age of eighteen from abuse and exploitation, but it also gives minors a right to participate in matters that affect them—including dependency and/or foster care proceedings.

The CRC mandates that governments ensure the youths involved in such matters have a voice in the proceedings. In the United States, the Supreme Court has never given foster children a right to be heard or present in his or her own proceeding, nor has it given foster children a right to legal representation. Approximately 400,000 children that were abused or neglected are in state custody. Many others are involved in the system through investigations or in-home supervision programs, but not actually in state custody. If the United States ratified the CRC, these children would have a legal right to voice their opinions in proceedings that affect them. Some states do provide for children of a certain age to be present at such proceedings, but if the CRC was ratified, all children in foster care would be allowed this right.

In 2006, Congress enacted the Child and Family Services Improvement Act (FSIA). FSIA requires states receiving federal money for child welfare to make sure the dependency courts consult with the child involved about the proposed plans for permanency in an age appropriate manner. Although Congress recognized the importance of children's voices being heard, states are not required to follow the provision and it is not a guaranteed right of children. Children themselves are taking initiative to make their voices heard, especially with the growth of the Internet. Foster children have created blogs about the foster care system and even created advocacy groups—however, this advocacy is not a legal and absolute right.

In October of 2008, President George W. Bush signed into law the Fostering Connections to Success and Increasing Adoptions Act of 2008 (FCSIAA). This Act was a bi-partisan measure that passed unanimously in both the House and Senate. Christine James-Brown, President and Chief Executive Officer of the Child Welfare League of America, heralded the passage of this Act as:

> an historic moment for foster children and families. Not since the Adoption Assistance and Child Welfare Act of 1980 ["AACWA"] has

this country had a bill that speaks directly to the more than 513,000 children in foster care.

Further, Jack Kroll, Executive Director of the North American Council on Adoptable Children [NACAC] opined: "Though child welfare policy was reformed in 1997 with the Adoption and Safe Families Act [of 1997 ("ASFA")] it has been 28 years since there was any meaningful child welfare financing reform."

As previously stated, FCSIAA will influence wide-ranging change within the child welfare system. In pertinent part, the Act extends federal funding to some kinship care families and requires—upon removal of a child—a 30-day search for, and notification of, adult relatives of the child's availability. It also provides direct access to federal funds to tribal governments and extends foster care and support to youth in need up to the age of 21 years. Over time, the Act seeks to de-link AFDC eligibility from special needs adoption when implementing the Adoption Assistance Program. In doing so, the FCSIAA expands access to federal child welfare training funds by private agencies and courts, increases access to education for foster children, and increases monitoring and access to health care for foster children. Lastly, the Act makes changes to the Federal Adoption Incentives Program by doing the following: (i) extending the program through FY 2013; (ii) changing the base year for computation to FY 2007; (iii) doubling the incentive payment amounts for special needs children from $2,000 to $4,000 per child and for older children adoptions from $4,000 to $8,000 per child; (iv) authorizing Federal funding to the states to increase to $43 million for the AIP; and (v) requiring states to make reasonable efforts to place siblings together for adoption, foster care and/or guardianship.

The most recent statistics, as of September 30, 2012, show that 397,122 children were in the United States foster care system. As previously mentioned, that is a national decrease of 28% from September 30, 2000 when there were 552,000 children in foster care. The number of children entering foster care has also decreased. By September 30, 2000, there were 293,000 children entering foster care as opposed to the 251,764 children entering foster care by September 30, 2012. From 2000 to 2012, almost every state has both increased and decreased in the number of foster care children in its system each year. California and Illinois are the only states to have decrease their total number of foster children each year.

Checkpoints

- During the mid-1800s, public policy demanded orphans be placed in homes versus orphanages with the movement towards the "best interest of the child."

- The first adoption law was enacted in Massachusetts in 1851.

- "The best interests of the child" standard was created with four principles: the tender years doctrine; fathers should take care of older boys; the courts should respect any attachments and affections the child formed with its caretakers; and the court should consider the child's wishes on placement (with mother, father, or both).

- Public policy demanded regulation of adoptions and protection of child welfare through laws and agency control. In 1922, 300 organizations in the U.S. were in place to protect child welfare, and numerous acts had been passed for child protection.

- Foster care did not become prevalent until the mid-1900s and was based on permanency planning.

- The ICWA was enacted to prevent the cultural genocide that was occurring with adoptions from Native American tribes in the United States.

- The U.S. Supreme Court has never given a foster child the right to be heard in court proceedings or the right to legal counsel; therefore, many foster children are left in state care.

Chapter 3

Types of Adoption: Public Agency (Foster Care), Private Agency, and Independent (Non-Agency)

Roadmap

- The three types of adoption — public agency, private agency, and non-agency
- The history and parameters of each of the types of adoption
- Fees associated with the three types
- Legal issues and regulations among the three types

The majority of states recognize three types of adoption: public agency adoption, private agency adoption, and independent (non-agency) adoption. Independent adoptions are also called private adoptions.

There are six characteristics — variously combined and emphasized — that are attributable to the modern adoption process: (1) consent by the biological parent(s); (2) the permanent and complete legal usurpation of the biological parent(s) by the adoptive parent(s); (3) the confidentiality of the adoption proceedings and records; (4) the judicial application of the "best interest of the child" standard; (5) the unilateral, gratuitous, and non-contractual nature of the process; and (6) the correlation between the age of the child at adoption and the long-term success of the adoption.

An agency adoption involves either an official state agency with an adoption from the foster care system or a private, state-licensed agency with an adoption that is not from the foster care system. These agencies are designed to place children with adoptive parents. Birth parents typically surrender their parental rights to the agency. Agencies investigate or conduct a home study of the adoptive parents to ensure the couple is fit to parent and that the child will be placed in an adequate, safe and loving home. If the couple is approved, they are placed on a waiting list until the agency finds a match with an available child. The agencies are then required to conduct a post-placement investigation to ensure the adoption is in the best interests of the child. If the agency finds the placement is in the child's best interests, it files the adoption petition with the court for approval. If the placement is not in the child's best interests, the process begins once more.

In general, the adoption placement process consists of three steps:

- The pre-placement evaluation of the prospective adoptive parents—including the home study (discussed below);
- The placement of the child with the adoptive parents; and
- The post-placement evaluation and study—prior to finalization of the adoption.

For a detailed recitation of the adoption process, there are numerous "how to" guides for adoptive parents—this book is not a "how to" guide; rather, it is a desk reference on adoption law and policy.

Public and private agencies and independent intermediaries place restrictions on who will be deemed "acceptable" adoptive parents. To varying degrees and in combination, here are some of the most prevalent characteristics: age, religion, race, marital status, and sexual orientation.

I. Public Agency Adoption (Foster Care)

It has been estimated that approximately 10–12% of all adoptions are of children over the age of two who are adopted by foster parents with whom the children have resided for two or more years.

As discussed in Chapter 2, "The Child Welfare System and Foster Care," prior to the passage of the Adoption and Safe Families Act of 1997 (ASFA), the normative case plan goal for children in the foster care system was family preservation and reunification. This led to literally hundreds of thousands of dependent children within the child welfare system spending years in numerous temporary foster care placements (perhaps) punctuated by periods of family reunification—until their biological parents' rights were ultimately terminated due to unabated abuse and/or neglect. This phenomenon is called "foster care drift."

The process of foster care adoption can be fraught with pitfalls for even the most experienced adoption professional. The most prevalent pitfalls for adoption professionals and adoptive parents alike are: (a) inadequate, fraudulent, or coerced "voluntary" consent from the birth parents; (b) incomplete involuntary termination of parental rights (TPR); (c) lack of knowledge regarding available federal and/or state subsidies for "special needs" children; (d) lack of, incomplete, or misleading information about the child; and (e) the length and complexity of the process—including the home study (see discussion below).

If adopting as a foster parent or through a public agency, the likelihood of finding and being matched with a child far outpaces that of private agency or independent adoption. According to The AFCARS Report (21), the preliminary estimates for FY 2013 (July 2014) reveal that there were 402,378 children in foster care in the United States on September 30, 2013. Of those children, 101,840 were "waiting to be adopted"—namely, children who have a goal of adoption and/or their parental rights have been terminated (not including children 16 years of age and older with the goal of emancipation).

These waiting children had been in foster care for a mean of 33.5 months; had a mean age of 4.9 years upon entry into foster care; were a mean of 7.7 years old on September 30, 2013; 25% (25,640) of the children were less than 1 year old upon entry into foster care; and 58,887 of the waiting children had had their parental rights terminated for all living parents as of September 30, 2013.

In FY 2013, 50,608 children were adopted through public agency adoption. These adopted children were a mean age of 6.2 years when adopted; 93% (47,172) received an adoption subsidy; over 58% of the children were adopted by foster parents; and after the parental rights were terminated, it took a mean of 12.3 months for the children to be adopted. Adopting a child from the foster care system can cost from $0 to $2,500.

II. Private Agency Adoption

As there are significantly more potentially adoptive parents than children privately placed for adoption, the process can take a number of years to successfully complete (particularly if the perspective adoptive parents are seeking to adopt a healthy infant). The uncertainty of the agency adoption process has led parents to pursue independent, non-agency adoptions (see the discussion below).

As adoption is a state-defined and regulated concept, the definition of a private adoption agency (or even the use of that particular term) is not universal. For the purposes of this reference manual, an adoption agency is a state licensed entity that is authorized by the laws and/or regulations by the State to place individuals for adoption.

Agencies are licensed or certified by the state when they meet minimum standards—however, the state does not subject agencies to state accreditation. Licensing of an agency in one state does not provide reciprocity for licensure and child placement in another state. In addition, some states require that placement agencies be non-profit organizations, while other states prefer that the agencies be for-profit entities. The amount of state regulation—through administrative rules, standards, and regulation—of these licensed placement agencies varies from state-to-state as well. Finally, some states will not allow an individual to be licensed as an adoption "agency." (Note: In those states, independent adoptions (see discussion below) are highly unlikely to be legitimate if they occur.)

Many of these private agencies are denominational or sectarian. Others have a special purpose such as finding homes for "special needs" children—namely, children over the age of eight years, sibling groups, and minority children of any age.

In both public and private agency adoptions, an exhaustive home study of the prospective adoptive parents shall be conducted by the adoption agency. Although the exact requirements of the home study vary from state-to-state, some of the areas to be studied are as follows:

- The applicant's motivation for adoption;
- Autobiographical information of the applicant—including education and employment;
- The strengths and weaknesses of each household member (primarily adults);
- The attitudes and feelings of the household members, extended family regarding being accepting of adopted children and parenting children who are not biologically related to them;
- The attitudes of the applicant towards the biological parent(s);
- The applicant's views about child behavior and discipline/punishment;
- The applicant's physical, mental, and emotional health and stability;
- The applicant's lifestyle and acceptance in the community;
- The child-rearing skills of the applicant (and the ability and desire to seek additional skills, if the need arises);
- The applicant's ability to provide for the child's physical, emotional, and financial needs;
- The current adjustment, maturity and stability of birth children or previously adopted children, if any;
- The applicant's views on age-appropriate discussion of adoption with the child;
- The applicant's criminal record (other than minor traffic violations), if any;
- The location and physical environment of the home;

- The applicant's personal character references;
- Type of child/children the applicant prefers; and
- Determination regarding the number, age, sex, special needs of a child or children who would be best served by a placement with this particular applicant.

Note that this is a non-exhaustive list of factors for consideration and the agency may consider these factors in any combination thereof.

For the time period post-placement and prior to finalization, in most jurisdictions, the agency retains legal responsibility for the child. During this period, states require a variety of post-placement supervisory visits with the adoptive parent and the child. The agency has the ability to remove the child under varying conditions—primarily if the child is at risk; the placement no longer serves the child's needs; or the placement becomes unsatisfactory. Again, the requirements vary from state-to-state.

Finally, it must be noted that adoption utilizing a private agency is costly— nation-wide such adoptions cost from $5,000 to $40,000+.

III. Independent Adoption (Non-Agency)

A. General Information

Independent adoptions do not involve any public or private agency, and those involved do not have to follow rigid placement procedures. The vast majority of healthy (non-sibling-group) infants are placed utilizing an independent adoption process.

There are two methods for independent adoptions. The first is a direct private placement adoption, which only involves the birth parents and the prospective adoptive parents. In that case, the birth parents choose who they want to be the adoptive parents of their child. There is not a third party to assist them in completing the adoption. The second is a private placement adoption which involves a third party, commonly referred to as an intermediary. An intermediary assists the birth parents and prospective adoptive parents with the adoption of the child. The intermediary is typically an attorney who specializes in adoptions, although states may restrict who may be an intermediary. In either kind of independent adoption, no agency is involved in the adoption process.

Independent adoptions are becoming increasingly popular in the United States. This type of adoption is popular with birth parents because they have control over where their child is placed. Birth parents can choose who the adoptive parents will be and they can do so for any reason. Birth parents also may prefer this type of adoption because they may be able to receive financial assistance from the prospective adoptive parents. Also, if birth parents want to remain in their child's life, this type of adoption is more likely to produce an open adoption where the birth parent has future contact with the child through letters or visitation.

Independent adoption is popular with prospective adoptive parents because they can bring the child immediately into their home and there are no risks of foster care placement. Prospective adoptive parents also do not have to meet certain requirements laid out by agencies, such as the length of their marriage or any religion or age requirements. Historically, California and New York prohibited adoption placements by unlicensed intermediaries — including attorneys.

There are also risks with independent adoptions. Such risks include the lack of safeguards that are implemented with agency adoptions — such as pre-placement home studies; a full and accurate social and medical history of the birth family and child; and/or post-placement studies. Risks for the birth parents include a lack of confidentiality, the possibility that the child will go to a couple that was not approved of by an agency for legitimate reasons, or the unavailability of counseling. Risks for prospective adoptive parents include a possibility of a custody dispute with the birth parents prior to the adoption being finalized, the possibility of the birth parent changing their mind about the adoption before their consent became irrevocable, the high fees associated with independent adoptions, and the possibility of being extorted for additional monies in order to continue to keep their child of choice. As a result of these risks, states have implemented regulations of independent adoption.

B. The Regulation of Independent Adoptions

States vary on how they choose to regulate independent adoptions. In most states, independent adoptions are not regulated by statute but by administrative rules, regulations, and standards.

Some states prohibit these types of adoptions outright due to the lack of agency safeguards and lack of a screening process and counseling. Another reason some states do not allow this type of adoption is because it is seen as closely related to baby selling on the black market. On the black market, birth parents receive money for their child in excess of what is permitted by state law. Opponents of independent adoptions often refer to it as "the gray market" because — arguably — the only difference between independent adoptions and the black market is the amount of money birth parents receive.

Despite state regulations to the contrary, there are ways to avoid a state's prohibition of independent adoptions. For example, the birth parents and adoptive parents can seek each other out first and then arrange the placement through an agency as an "afterthought." This is often referred to as a "directed agency" adoption.

In states that permit independent adoptions, other restrictions and regulations might include disclosure of expenses paid by the adoptive parents, a limitation on certain types of fees, a requirement that the birth parent retain independent counsel, a requirement that a home study be completed, a requirement that the adoptive parent files a report with a state agency before or after the adoption, or a criminal sanction if a profit is made by either the birth parent or adoptive parent. Some states limit prospective adoptive parents in independent adoptions to be people who are closely related to the birth parents.

1. Regulation of Intermediaries

Some states regulate the use of intermediaries during independent adoptions. Intermediaries are either a person or an organization that matches or sets up a meeting between prospective adoptive parents and birth parents that want to place their child. Some states prohibit intermediaries in independent adoptions and only allow birth parents and prospective adoptive parents to work through a licensed or state agency.

Intermediaries are used to ensure that the birth parents' parental rights are properly and timely terminated to avoid any legal issues with the placement of the child. Intermediaries should be knowledgeable adoption professionals and expected to understand: the time period in which the birth parent can revoke consent; the costs the birth parents can recover; the length of time it takes for the adoption to become finalized; and the degree of enforceability of any agreements made between the birth parents and adoptive parents. Intermediaries also make certain that medical and social history is exchanged, and provide contact information for adoption counselors. Due to the legal knowledge involved, attorneys are most commonly used intermediaries.

Traditionally, attorneys have not been able to represent both the birth parents and the prospective adoptive parents in the adoption proceedings. The rationale for this limitation is that dual representation goes against the ethics of the profession due to the inherent conflict of interest.

Attorneys that act as intermediaries can find themselves amidst conflict. An attorney that represents the prospective adoptive parents must be sure not to give an unrepresented birth parent the idea that they are also being represented. The Model Rules of Professional Conduct (MRPC) caution such an attorney to not give any advice to the unrepresented birth parent. The MRPC also advise attorneys that they may not accept fees from another party other than the client unless the client consents. In independent adoptions, adoptive parents typically pay for some expenses, including attorney fees. If the attorney represents the birth parent, he must be careful to get the client's full consent to accept fees on the client's behalf.

Historically, only two states expressly allowed dual representation in independent adoptions—namely, California and Kansas. With dual representation, the intermediary/attorney is allowed to represent both the birth parents and the prospective adoptive parents. Outside this area of law, attorneys typically cannot represent two opposing parties in the same proceeding. The difference in this case is that these intermediaries are treated as though they were private adoption agencies who work on behalf of the birth parents as well as the adoptive parents. States that allow dual representation specify how it must be effectuated. Usually, separate representation must be offered first, and only after both parties have consented to dual representation can the attorney represent both parties. In addition, if there is any sign of a conflict between the parties, the attorney must withdraw and advise both parties to hire independent counsel.

2. Regulation of Fees and Expenses

States have regulated expenses to ensure that neither the birth parents nor the intermediary profits from the adoption of a child. However, adoptive parents are often expected to cover certain expenses in an independent adoption. These expenses may include: the placement costs; attorney fees for both the adoptive and birth parents; and some expenses to the birth mother during the pregnancy. As of 2014, only Hawaii, Rhode Island, and Wyoming had not statutorily addressed adoption expenses. Some states require an accounting of all expenses that were paid in relation to the adoption to be filed with the court. The accounting must take place prior to the adoption proceeding or it can be attached to the affidavit in the form of an affidavit or a sworn statement. Some states require all receipts to be attached to the statement, and if there is an itemized expense that is not proven by receipt, that expense may be disallowed. In other states, it is up to the court's discretion whether to review the adoption expenses. Additionally, in some of those states, any expense can be modified or denied if the court finds it to be unreasonable, unnecessary, or unauthorized by law.

i. Expenses to Birth Parents

When examining expenses paid to birth parents, courts typically apply a "reasonable and customary" standard. Most states itemize exactly what adoptive parents can pay for in relation to the birth mother's pregnancy. The expenses usually include any maternity-related medical and hospital costs, the birth mother's living expenses during the pregnancy, counseling fees, attorney fees, and travel costs — food and lodging, if court appearances necessitate these costs. Some states limit the time period for which payments may be made and/or the amount of money to be paid. The time period varies from state to state: from 30 days to 6 months after the child's placement or birth.

Some states specify what adoptive parents are not permitted to pay. These limitations could include the cost of: education; vehicles; vacations; permanent housing; and/or anything that could be seen as paying the birth parent in exchange for their child. Idaho is the only state that mandates reimbursement of these expenses if the birth parent decides not to place the child with the adoptive parents. However, since the cost of an independent adoption can range from $10,000 to more than $40,000, some states allow families to take out adoption cancellation insurance to protect them from incurring these expenses when an adoption is not successful.

Excessive fees may not be discovered until after the child is already in their adoptive placement. Even if they are found, a court may still conclude that the adoptive placement is in the best interests of the child and leave punishment up to the authorities. These "consequences" might encourage prospective adoptive parents to provide further financial incentives to birth parents in order to have the child.

ii. Agencies as Intermediaries — Fees and Costs

Where agencies act as intermediaries between prospective adoptive and birth parents, agencies will itemize birth parent expenses, collect the money from the prospective parents, and disburse the monies to the birth parent. Some states allow agencies to place some of their administrative costs into their placement fees. The fees and costs must be whatever is "reasonable and customary." Fees for agency services could include pre- and post-home studies of the adoptive parents, a social and medical history of the birth parents, and counseling. Independent agency adoption is costly — the nationwide range is from $10,000 to $40,000+.

3. Regulation of the Exchange of Information

In an independent adoption, the birth parents and adoptive parents must decide on how open they want the adoption. Most states require that non-identifying information be exchanged, although some states require the exchange of identifying information as well. The concept of openness has been a growing trend since the 1990s.

If the parties choose not to be completely open with one another, a problem of confidentiality could arise with an attorney acting as an intermediary. As an attorney, he or she is bound by the code of professional ethics. This includes the duty of confidentiality. For the most part, an attorney cannot disclose information that his client wishes to remain confidential. The problem arises in independent adoptions when the attorney represents both the birth parents and the adoptive parents, and one party expresses something meant to be confidential to the attorney.

C. Baby Broker Acts

Some states enacted "baby broker acts" in an effort to address black market adoptions. These acts penalize the person or entity who, without a license, places a child for adoption. Depending upon the statute, the range of penalties include: civil sanctions, criminal sanctions, or both. Since states vary in what is a permissible payment and what is an illegal payment, it can be hard to distinguish lawful payments from unlawful payments. When a court determines a payment was unlawful, it has the authority to refuse an adoption petition.

Critics have found that some of these acts are too vague and/or contradictory. If no one can profit from an independent adoption, how are the intermediaries to be paid for their services? Intermediaries can be seen as baby brokers, as the sole reason for their involvement in the proceeding is to make money from the adoption. If a court draws that conclusion, it could refuse the concomitant adoption petition.

D. Advertising

States also differ on whether birth parents can place advertisements to search for prospective adoptive parents and whether prospective adoptive parents can place advertisements to seek birth parents looking to adopt. Some states allow advertisements while others do not. Opponents of such advertisements look to other ways to place children—through crisis pregnancy centers, doctors, hospitals, or school guidance counselors.

A state's professional rules of ethical conduct for attorneys will also play a part in whether advertising is allowed. These rules restrict how, where, what, and by what means an attorney may advertise. One such rule is that attorneys may not target specific people. In that case, an attorney acting as an intermediary could not seek out people he knows are looking to adopt a child or give up a child.

IV. Additional Legal Issues

A. Birth Father Rights and Putative Father Registries

Some birth mothers choose independent adoptions to avoid having to provide the birth father's name. An adoption cannot be completed if either the birth father's parental rights were not properly terminated or he did not legally consent to the adoption. In an attempt to make an "end run" around a birth father's legal rights, birth mothers misinform the adoptive parents of the birth father's identity. As a result, the true birth father never has a chance to voluntarily terminate his parental rights or consent to the adoption.

In an Iowa Supreme Court case, a two-and-a-half-year-old child was removed from the only home it knew after the birth father proved he was the biological father and had not terminated his parental rights. *In re B.G.C.*, 496 N.W.2d 239 (Iowa 1992). In that case, the birth mother misidentified the birth father, and together they terminated their parental rights. *Id.* at 240–241. When the real birth father found out about this, he contested the adoption and the adoption petition was dismissed. *Id.* at 246.

The same result happened in an Illinois Supreme Court case. *In re Petition of Doe to Adopt Baby Boy Janikova*, 638 N.E.2d 181 (Ill. 1994). In that case, the birth mother lied to the birth father about their child's death and she subsequently placed the child up for adoption. *Id.* at 349–350. She would not give the birth father's name to the attorney or the adoptive parents. *Id.* After three years of the child living with the prospective adoptive parents, the court ruled that the child must be removed from the home and placed with the birth father since he never terminated his parental rights. *Id.* at 351.

B. Birth Parent Revokes Consent

Even after the birth parents surrender their child to the adoptive parents, the birth parents still have the legal right to change their mind and revoke their consent within a certain period of time. Nationwide by statute, the timespan for allowable parental revocation of consent for a variety of reasons is from zero days, i.e., it is irrevocable, unless due to fraud or duress, to six months after placement and before finalization. This is a relatively small window of opportunity for birth parents who doubt their decision to place their child for adoption before their decision becomes irrevocable. In addition, generally there is no recourse for the adoptive parents to seek reimbursement for any expenses or fees they provided if the birth parent revokes his or her consent.

C. Birth Parent Contests the Adoption and Sues to Regain Custody

With an independent adoption, if the birth parent contests the adoption, a court will look at the termination of parental rights with greater scrutiny. This is because the parents, for the most part, did this on their own with no agency involvement. As a result, this type of adoption involves an inherently greater risk for prospective adoptive parents when the court becomes involved.

D. Internet Adoption — Caveat Emptor

With the rising pervasiveness of the internet and global connectivity, there has been an increase in illegal adoption-related practices. Adam Pertman, Director of the Evan Donaldson Adoption Institute has stated that "the internet and adoption is like the Wild West … [Adoption] is about helping the child find a family, not casting a net and seeing what you can pull in." Further, critics state that the internet has allowed agencies to skirt state laws.

In response to illegal, contested adoption practices by unlicensed agencies (and intermediaries), states have passed laws requiring agencies to be both licensed and tax exempt, which takes monetary gain out of the adoption process; and prohibits unlicensed agencies located out-of-state from advertising within its boundaries. An example is the Illinois Adoption Reform Act of 2005. This act was passed in response to the "Baby Tamia" case involving a 3-month-old infant taken from Illinois to Utah by her mother (suffering from long-term bipolar disorder and post-partum depression) in response to the agency's newspaper advertisement. The for-profit agency paid for the mother's plane ticket, and its workers allegedly threatened the birth mother when she attempted to renege upon her arrival in Utah. A judge later voided the adoption placement citing the agency's failure to comply with the Interstate Compact for the Placement of Children (ICPC) standards. The purpose of the ICPC is to provide protections to children placed across state lines for purposes of foster care and adoption. In addition, after passing all of the Utah state-required background checks and investigation, the prospective adoptive parents were later convicted for misdemeanor drug possession.

Checkpoints

- The six characteristics of the modern adoption process are: consent of the biological parents; permanent legal usurpation of the biological parents by the adoptive parents; confidential proceedings; judicial process is in the best interest of the child; the non-contractual nature of the process; and the correlation of the age of the child with long-term success.

- The three types of adoptions are through a public agency, a private agency, or an independent agency.

- The process of adoption usually involves a pre-placement evaluation, placement of the child in the home, and a post-evaluation.

- Both public and private adoptions usually involved an exhaustive home-study to be completed, and private adoptions are normally more costly than public adoptions.

- Independent adoptions do not have to follow the same procedures and are usually done between the birth parent(s) and the adoptive parent(s).

- Even if a valid adoption procedure is followed, birth parents can revoke their consent to adoption within a certain time frame mandated by state law.

Chapter 4

Consent

Roadmap

- The varying circumstances surrounding consent and adoption
- The effect on biological and adoptive parents with respect to consent
- Putative father's rights and consent
- The issues surrounding surrogacy and consent

I. Who May Give Consent

In any adoption, a person or an agency that has custody over a child to be adopted must consent to the adoption. In doing so, they no longer have any rights over or duties to the child. Generally, the consent must be written and executed before a judge, or witnessed and notarized.

A. Biological Parent(s)

Courts have long held that biological parents have a right to family privacy and parental autonomy. This includes the right to decide how to raise their child so long as it does not interfere with a compelling state interest. Biological parents are presumed to be fit parents. Therefore, parental consent to a petition to an adoption is a prerequisite for an adoption to be finalized.

In some cases, courts do not need the consent of a biological father to finalize an adoption. This will be discussed in the section on unwed fathers. In other cases, consent is not needed where a parent's parental rights have been terminated in a court proceeding brought by the state.

B. Child's Legal Guardian or Custodian

In cases where a parent's rights have been terminated, where the birth parents have died, or where they are unable to give consent, the person or agency who has custody over the child must give consent to the adoption. Consent to the adoption can also come from the child's guardian or guardian *ad litem*, the court that has jurisdiction over the child, a close relative of the child, or a person close to the child that was appointed by the court.

II. When Consent Can Be Executed

The majority of states do not allow a woman to consent to an adoption prior to the birth of the child. The reason for this is that women tend to grow attached to the child that they have carried and often realize this once they give birth to the child. In one study, approximately half of the women who thought they would give their child up for adoption changed their minds once they gave birth to the child. Most state statutes specify when a parent may give consent to an adoption. The few states that allow a woman to consent to an adoption prior to the birth of that child also require that the consent be reaffirmed after birth. Some states allow the mother to consent at any time after the birth, while other states required a minimal waiting period before the mother can consent. Some states require as little as twelve hours while other states allow up to fifteenth days for the parent to consent. The most common amount of time before a mother can consent is three days after the birth of the child.

During the waiting period, the biological parent is able to visit, hold, feed, and care for the child. In allowing this, states ensure that biological mothers do not rush into a decision at a time when they are under an incredible amount of physical and emotional stress. However, in limiting the waiting period, states also ensure that the child finds a permanent home as soon as possible.

Some states require the birth parents to attend counseling sessions prior to consenting to an adoption. Of those states, some mandate the amount of time the biological parent must receive counseling. Other states require that birth parents be informed that they are entitled to counseling.

III. Termination of Parental Rights

When the state removes a child from his birth parents for abuse, abandonment, or neglect, the child is often placed in foster care. Prior to 1997, with the passage of the Adoption and Safe Families Act, the ultimate goal of the state was to reunify these children with their parents. However, these children could not be reunified with their family until the parents completed their case plans that ensured that they could take adequate care of their children. Until the parents completed their case plan, the children were in limbo for an indefinite period of time, often bouncing from foster home to foster home. This is a condition often referred to as "foster care drift." For the state to terminate a parent's rights over the child, the state had to go through the lengthy process of trying to reunify the family (which could take years), and prove that reunification was unsuccessful.

The Adoption and Safe Families Act of 1997 sought to expedite this process. It dictated circumstances where a parent's rights could be terminated without going through the process of having the parents complete a case plan in order to reunify them with their children. This brought children into permanent, adoptive homes faster. The Act also provided a time limit for the state to file a petition for the termination of parental rights. The state could file such a petition where the child was in foster care for fifteen of the last twenty-two months. Pursuant to ASFA, the parents can either voluntarily relinquish their parental rights or they may be forced to do so after a termination of parental rights hearing before a court.

Once a parent either voluntarily gives up their parental rights, or is forced to do so by a court, the child is usually placed under the custody of an agency or guardian to facilitate an adoption. However, in most states, the parents must have their rights terminated before the agency or custodian can consent to an adoption. The process of terminating parental rights differs from state to state. Some states require a judicial proceeding, while other states do not. Of those states that require a judicial proceeding, some states require that the relinquishment and adoption take place in a single proceeding. Some states allow a birth parent to relinquish parental rights before birth, although the termination of parental rights proceeding cannot be completed until after the child is born. When a parent voluntarily relinquishes their rights to the child, they are able to do so only after the child is born or they may have to wait a few days, depending on state law. If only one biological parent relinquishes their rights to the child, the court must terminate the other parent's rights before the child can be adopted. Once the parental rights are terminated, the birth parents generally do not have a right to be notified about the child's adoption.

IV. Revocation of Consent

Over the past ten years, adoptions in the United States have greatly increased. With the rate of adoptions increasing, so does the rate of failed adoptions. Depending on the state, adoptions have failed before the adoption has been finalized between 3% and 53%. The rate of adoptions that failed after adoptions were finalized is unknown.

In order to rescind or revoke a finalized adoption, the parent must petition the court. The court follows the process set out in state statutes that specify how to revoke an adoption. Most states have their own specific time requirements that a parent who contests an adoption must abide by. Other states do not statutorily provide for a revocation of consent. If the parent opposing the adoption meets the time requirements, courts generally hold a hearing to determine what is in the best interests of the child. Some states allow a birth mother to revoke days after the birth, while other states allow a birth mother to revoke up until the time the court approves of the consent after a hearing. The courts generally disfavor a revocation of a finalized adoption.

When a birth parent has voluntarily terminated their parental rights, some states allow that parent to revoke the relinquishment after a few days. Other states give the birth parents months to decide whether or not to revoke. If they do revoke, the parents often have to refund any money that was received from the adoptive parents or agency. Birth parents can also revoke when consent was obtained through fraud, duress, or misrepresentation.

If state statutes do not guarantee an absolute right to revoke consent to an adoption, the birth parent may revoke before the adoption is finalized if the parent can prove that the revocation is in the child's best interest. The court would hold a hearing on the child's best interests where the birth parent must show his or her parental fitness. Another way for a birth parent's revocation to be granted is if the consent was not valid at the time of its execution. In that case, the birth parent must prove there was fraud, duress, or an undue influence at the time of the execution.

Alternatively, consent can be revoked when procedural requirements were not complied with; if the birth parent did not know what it was signing and the effect of such a signing; if the consent was conditional; or if there was payment to the birth parents that was abnormal or in addition to pregnancy and birth expenses.

In general, adoptive parents have several arguments available with which to rebut the birth parents' request for revocation: some revocations are impermissible after consent was executed; other revocations are impermissible after the statutory time requirements ran out, during which time there was an absolute right to revoke consent; some states do not allow revocation after a certain time period—namely, after the child was placed in the adoptive home, after a court recognized the consent, or after the adoption was finalized; and finally, the adoptive parents can argue that it is in the best interests of the child to be adopted because the birth parents are unfit to raise the child.

V. Unwed Biological Parents

A. Unwed Biological Mothers

Prior to the 1960s, children born out of wedlock were considered to be illegitimate, and laws did not protect an illegitimate child's relationship with its biological parents. However, two United States Supreme Court (USSC) cases issued in 1968 changed that position—namely, *Levy v. Louisiana*, 391 U.S. 68 (1968), and *Glona v. American Guar. & Liab. Ins. Co.*, 391 U.S. 73 (1968).

In *Levy v. Louisiana*, 391 U.S. 68 (1968), a representative of five children born out of wedlock sued to recover on the children's behalf pursuant to a wrongful death statute after the death of their mother. The claim was dismissed by the lower court because the children were not covered under the statute. The U.S. Supreme Court reversed, holding that under the equal protection clause, the children could not be discriminated against. Since their being born out of wedlock was in no way related to the wrongful death of their mother, the children were allowed to bring such a suit.

That same year, the U.S. Supreme Court case heard a wrongful death action brought by a mother for the death of her illegitimate son—*Glona v. American Guar. & Liab. Ins. Co.*, 391 U.S. 73 (1968). The state's reason for not allowing the mother to be compensated by the statute was the mere fact that the child was born out of wedlock. The USSC disagreed with the state and held that where the claimant is clearly the mother and the state withheld relief merely because the son, who was wrongfully killed, was born to her out of wedlock, the state violated the equal protection clause.

Levy and *Glona* both reached the conclusion that the mother-child relationship is Constitutionally protected, whether the mother is married or single (and the child(ren) were legitimate or illegitimate).

B. Unwed Biological Fathers

Unlike unwed biological mothers, unwed biological fathers do not have a guaranteed, Constitutionally-protected relationship with their biological child. In fact, prior to a series of USSC opinions issued in the 1970s and 1980s entitled "the unwed father cases," most state laws ignored the unwed father and the possibility of his right to notice and consent to adoption.

Under common law, the unwed father was seen as a stranger to his child and could not establish an action for paternity. Furthermore, if the biological mother was married, it was presumed her husband was the child's biological father. It was not until "the unwed father cases" that unwed fathers established some parental rights. In those cases, the U.S. Supreme Court ruled that the biological relationship between an unwed father and his child—without more—is not enough to be constitutionally protected. There must be more to the relationship than just biology.

The first of the series of unwed father cases was *Stanley v. Illinois*, 405 U.S. 645 (1972). Mr. Stanley lived with his girlfriend (who was the mother of his children) for eighteen years prior to her death. The couple never married. When the mother died, the state declared the children dependents of the state pursuant to Illinois statute. In Illinois, like most states at that time, unwed fathers were presumed unfit parents. Mr. Stanley argued that he was denied his Fourteenth Amendment rights when the state never held a hearing on his fitness as a parent. The U.S. Supreme Court agreed.

The Court held that under the due process clause, Mr. Stanley was entitled to a parental fitness hearing before his children were taken away from him. Absent a prevalent countervailing interest (because Mr. Stanley had lived with and helped raise his children), he was entitled to some protections. In reaching its decision, the USSC weighed the unwed father's private interest in his father-child relationship against the state's interest in protecting children's welfare by avoiding unnecessary parental fitness hearings. This was the first case in which the U.S. Supreme Court, by power of the due process clause, protected a family unit that was something other than a marital unit.

The *Stanley* decision affected adoption statutes nationwide. As a result of that decision, many states enacted registration statues that provided a process to give notice of an impending adoption to unwed fathers through a Putative Father Registry. The father, usually before the child's birth, gave the registry his name and address and would be notified of any adoption proceeding. Thus, it became the father's burden to take the initiative to register in the hopes of establishing a father-child relationship. *Stanley* was an important case for unwed fathers and their children nationwide, but the following unwed father cases limited the rights "bestowed upon" them by the Court in *Stanley*.

In *Quillon v. Walcott*, 434 U.S. 246 (1978), the mother had custody over her child born out of wedlock, and later married a man who was not the child's father. Her husband sought to adopt the child and the mother consented to the adoption. The biological father attempted to block the adoption by challenging the applicable Georgia statute. Under the statute, only the mother of an illegitimate child was recognized as the parent. Thus, the mother had sole authority over the child and his or her adoption.

In its holding in *Quillon*, the U.S. Supreme Court issued an exception to *Stanley*. The Court determined that because the biological father had not sought actual or legal custody during the eleven years of the child's life, he was not entitled to a fitness hearing. Furthermore, during those eleven years, the father never took any responsibility in providing for the supervision, education, or care for the child. Therefore, the father was not deprived of his asserted rights to a parental fitness hearing under the Due Process and Equal Protection clauses.

In *Caban v. Mohammed*, 441 U.S. 389 (1979), a mother and father of two children lived together, but were never married. After a few years, the father moved out and the mother married another man who sought to adopt the children. The father objected to the petition for the adoption because he still had substantial contact with his children. The U.S. Supreme Court held that where a father established a substantial relationship with his children and admitted paternity, the state should not preclude him from vetoing the adoption.

In *Lehr v. Robertson*, 463 U.S. 248 (1983), the mother and father lived together before their child was born and the father visited the child when it was born in the hospital. After the birth, the father moved out, his name was never placed on the birth certificate, and he never financially supported his child. The mother later married another man, and that man sought to adopt the child. The court granted the adoption without notifying the biological father. The U.S. Supreme Court held that the unwed father was neither guaranteed an absolute right to notice nor an opportunity to be heard before the child may be adopted. An unwed father only *earns* protection under the due process clause when he makes a full commitment to his responsibilities as a father and helps to raise the child. A biological link alone does not give rise to constitutional protection. The biological link only gives him an opportunity to develop a relationship with his child(ren), and if he takes that opportunity to establish a parent-child relationship, he will be provided constitutional protection.

The final case in this series of USSC cases involving unwed fathers is *Michael H. v. Gerald D.*, 491 U.S. 110 (1989). In that case, a married woman had an affair, and out of that affair, a child was born. Soon after the child's birth, the mother consented to a paternity test—the purported biological father was beyond statistical doubt determined to be the child's biological father. During the first years of the child's life, the mother and child alternatively lived with the biological father and the mother's husband. Both men held themselves out to be the child's father. The biological father sought to be declared the father of the child even though, in California, the husband is statutorily presumed to be the father of a child born to the wife during a marriage. The U.S. Supreme Court upheld the state law.

In analyzing these decisions, it is clear that the U.S. Constitution protects an unwed father's opportunity interest in developing a relationship with his child. If the father fails to use that opportunity to develop a substantial parent-child relationship, there is no constitutional protection. The exception to this constitutionally protected opportunity interest involves an unwed man who fathers a child with a married woman. In that instance, if the married couple wants to raise the child without the unwed father, that unwed father has no liberty interest to be protected even if he established a substantial parent-child relationship.

Since these USSC decisions, there has been a push to create a National Putative Father Registry. Not all states have putative father registries, and importantly those states that do have registries have varied policies. Supporters of a national registry contend that the registry would be beneficial because it would ensure putative fathers notice of any legal proceeding involving their child. When an unwed mother moves out of state and attempts to give the child up for adoption, the national registry would protect unwed fathers by providing them notice of the adoption process. However, a putative father would still have the responsibility of properly and accurately placing his name on the national registry — there is a presumption that any registry would apply only to unwed mothers.

In 2009, Senator Mary Landrieu (D-LA) introduced a bill entitled "The Promoting Adoption and Protecting Responsible Fatherhood Act (PAPRFA) (S.939)" which provided for a national putative father registry. Representative Laura Richardson (D-CA) introduced the companion bill in the U.S. House of Representatives (H.R. 6298). The drafters stated that in instances where unwed mothers are unable or unwilling to provide the identification of a child's father, the children need protection to prevent the disruption of adoptions and to provide them with a safe and permanent home, while ensuring the rights of unmarried and unknowing fathers.

PAPRFA established and maintained a National Putative Father Registry (NPFR) to be administered by the U.S. Department of Health and Human Services. The registry would contain contact information submitted by putative fathers. Upon registering, a putative father would secure the right to notice of any proceedings related to a pending or planned adoption of the child, a proceeding to terminate the putative father's rights, a proceeding related to the entry of the child into state custody, and the opportunity to establish paternity. Registry access would be limited to state agencies maintaining the database and to any state agencies or entities involved in the placement of children for adoption. The bill also established grants for states to enhance legal protections for putative fathers, assist mothers in planning for a child's future, and protect the privacy of birthparents.

In 2009, more than half of U.S. states had putative father registries. By establishing a national paternity database, PAPRFA increased a state's capacity to prevent a father's efforts to take responsibility for his child from being undermined. In introducing the bill, Senator Landrieu identified the need for the U.S. adoption system to balance the rights of fathers and the privacy of mothers, while ultimately working in the best interests of children. Although both bills were considered by Congress, neither bill passed. As of January 2013, 35 states had putative father registries. Of these 35 states, some only have limited forms of notice and more rigid time restrictions for filing.

In June 2013, Ann Kuster (D-NH) proposed a similar bill to the House of Representatives regarding the application of a Responsible Fatherhood Act. (H.R. 2439) This proposition mirrored many of Senator Landrieu's suggestions in PA-PRFA. Kuster's act did not pass in either house. But this act, among many others, continue to knock at the door of Congress indicating a nationally accepted putative father registry and adoption reform are in the near future.

VI. Surrogacy and Consent

When a couple asks a woman to be their surrogate, they may encounter legal problems when it comes to parenting that child. The traditional surrogate may have a biological connection with the child (if the surrogate is biologically related to the child through the use of the surrogate's ovum, but also has a nine month physical relationship with the child by carrying the child to term) compared with a gestational surrogate who is not biologically related to the child.

Although it might be analogized that, in accordance with the holdings of the USSC unwed father cases, this biological and caretaker relationship gives the surrogate a claim to parental rights. Courts have come to different conclusions regarding surrogacy and the parental rights of surrogates.

In *Johnson v. Calvert*, 19 Cal. Rptr. 2d 494 (Ca. 1993), a couple had their sperm and egg fertilized and implanted the embryo in a gestational surrogate mother who bore the child. The surrogate then claimed she should be found to be the child's legal mother. The court denied the surrogate mother's claim, likening her to a foster mother. The court opined that since the biological parents were also the (ultimate) intended parents, they should be the child's legal parents.

In a New Jersey Supreme Court case, a husband and wife used the husband's sperm and the surrogate's egg to create a child—*In re Baby M*, 109 N.J. 396 (NJ 1988). Once the baby was born, the wife sought to adopt the baby and have the biological surrogate's legal rights as the mother terminated. The court, in determining the best interests of the child, gave custody to the father but denied the adoption to the wife, voided the surrogacy contract, and granted the surrogate limited visitation since she was the legal mother. Notably, in cases where the surrogate was the biological mother, no court has allowed the wife of the biological father (the "intended mother") to adopt the child without the surrogate mother's consent.

Disputes also arise when a fertility clinic mistakenly implants an embryo in the wrong woman. In *Perry-Rogers v. Fasano*, 276 A.D.2d 67 (2000), a couple's embryo was mistakenly implanted into another patient. The implanted mother gave birth to twins. In a highly unlikely turn of events, the twins were fraternal and of different racial backgrounds. At the birth of these twins, the clinic realized their mistake since the two sets of parents were of different races. The patient voluntarily surrendered custody of the one child to its biological parents, provided that she be allowed visitation. When the biological parents did not allow her to visit, she sought to enforce the agreement in Court. The Court held that the patient (in effect a gestational surrogate) was a stranger to the child and the biological parents were the legal parents.

A surrogacy agreement coupled with a subsequent parenting agreement that terminates any parental rights depicts another difficult situation in surrogacy. In *Rosecky v. Schissel*, 349 Wis. 2d 84 (2013), the biological father used his sperm with their best friend's egg under a surrogacy agreement for the friend to carry the child; the parenting agreement stipulated the friend relinquish all parent rights to the biological father and his wife upon birth of the child. The court ruled the parenting agreement named the friend as a surrogate which terminated her future parenting rights, even in lieu of the friend using her own egg as a donor. The parenting agreement was viewed as a proper adoption agreement that was in accordance with the surrogacy agreement.

The USSC has not yet heard a case involving gestational or biological surrogacy.

Checkpoints

- Written consent terminating parenting rights must be obtained from the biological parent(s) or person(s) who have legal custody of the child before adoption can proceed.
- Most states prohibit the biological mother from consenting to adoption prior to birth; some states have a specific waiting period post-birth before consent is allowed.

- Consent can be revoked, but states differ on the time period after the birth of the child.
- Children can be removed from a home if there is abuse, abandonment, or neglect, or the threat of any of those three things. Depending on the state, parental rights can be terminated upon findings of these elements through agency investigations and court proceedings.
- The ASFA was created to protect the best interests of the child and its goal is to move the child toward permanent placement.
- Historically, unwed biological fathers have not been given the same rights as the mothers and therefore gave rise to the National Putative Father Registry. Most states offer this registry now, but differ on time periods for filing.
- Recent case law depicts the legal issue of consent with surrogacy and adoption. Surrogacy contracts should have a written termination of any parental rights of the surrogate(s) to give full parental rights to the adoptive parent(s).

Chapter 5

Open Adoption

Roadmap

- The history and definition of open adoption
- The procedures encompassing open adoption
- How states offer different levels of confidentiality
- The benefits and risks to birth parents, adoptive parents, and adoptees in open adoptions

---

I. History of Record Keeping Regarding Adopted Children

When adoption statutes were first created in the nineteenth century, birth certificates and records from adoption proceedings were not sealed. During that time period, privacy of the birth parents was not of primary concern since these proceedings tended to be informal. In the early 1900s, states began enacting legislation that barred public access to birth records of adopted children. However, the parties involved were not denied access to the relevant records.

In 1916, New York passed the first state statute sealing adoption records from the public. In 1917, Minnesota became the first state to bar not only the public from these records, but also the birth parents, the adopted child, and the adoptive parents. Thus, the birth and adoption records became totally sealed. The main reason for the complete denial of access was to protect the adopted child from any stigma attached to its purported illegitimacy and the birth mother from the stigma of bearing an illegitimate child.

By the 1940s, most states followed Minnesota's lead and sealed the original birth certificates of adopted children and all records from adoption proceedings. In 1941, the U.S. Children's Bureau approved the practice of issuing new birth certificates declaring that the adoptive parents were the parents who gave birth to the adopted child.

Starting in the late 1960s and continuing through the 1970s, the number of women placing their newborns for adoption began to decline sharply. History shows this decline was primarily due to three reasons: first, a lifting of the stigma against unwed motherhood and "illegitimate" children born out of wedlock; second, the legalization of abortion and the recognition of a woman's right to choose; and third, the growing access to contraception—particularly for unmarried persons.

Over time, it became increasingly clear that most women did not want secrecy, or preferred an opening of information about and/or contact with their child when placing that child for adoption. Contrarily, with fewer and fewer infants available, the forces of supply and demand provided expectant parents considering adoption increased involvement in choosing who would adopt their child. Hand-in-hand came the opportunity for the birth parents to decide what kind of ongoing contact the birth and adoptive families might have— if any.

In the 1970s, adoptees who had reached adulthood began to campaign about their "right to know" where they came from and their medical history. In response, some state legislatures enacted statutes that permitted adoptees access to their records if they could show "good cause" for gaining access. Other states only allowed access to the birth records if the birth parents had consented to the adoptee's access via an adoption registry.

II. The Advent of Open Adoption

By the 1990s, as the social stigma of illegitimacy waned, birth parents began to desire continuing, life-long contact with (at most) or information about (at a minimum) their children post-adoption. This phenomenon, in conjunction with adult adoptees' quests for information, began to effect adoption professionals' opinion of secrecy and sealed adoption records. As a result, nationwide, over the last 15 years, there has been an increase in the number of open adoptions.

Open adoptions allow birth parents, adoptive parents, and adopted children to acknowledge each other's existence and have some sort of contact with each other. In that sense, this type of adoption means many different things to many different families because the families themselves define the type and amount of contact that is to be implemented. For some, contact means birth parents solely provide identifying information and other information that will help the adoptee grow and develop as a person. For others, it means that the birth parents and new adoptive family meet only once. Others share photos and letters on an annual basis. For some, there is a continuous, ongoing relationship that could include phone calls, letters, and/or face to face contact. In open adoption the birth parent(s) and adoptive parent(s) negotiate a mutually acceptable level of birth parent involvement with the child post adoption. As such, open adoptions are growing in popularity today.

In years past, most states only allowed adopted children access to non-identifying information. This left many adoptive families without access to important medical history of the adopted child's birth family. Adoptive families did not have access to original birth certificates nor records from the adoption proceedings. Open adoptions not only provide medical history and information about the birth family, but also give the adopted child a better sense of self.

Adoptions exist along a continuum, from completely closed (sometimes called "confidential" adoptions) — meaning there is no contact between the birth and adoptive families and usually little if any knowledge about each other. At the other extreme are completely open (sometimes called "fully disclosed" adoptions) — in these cases, there is ongoing contact among those involved, including the child. Between these two extremes falls "mediated" adoptions where the adoption agency facilitates the periodic exchange of pictures and letters, but typically there is no direct contact among the affected parties and they do not receive identifying information about each other.

As stated earlier, in historical terms, absolute secrecy in adoption is a relatively recent practice; it began in the United States in 1916 and grew out of the prevailing attitudes regarding the stigma of illegitimacy. As that stigma gradually evaporated over time, the number of agencies offering open adoptions grew rapidly and, by 1999, close to 80% offered the option of some form of open adoption.

III. Statutorily Conditioned Access to Birth Records

A. "Good Cause" Statutes

Most states will release identifiable information if there is a judicial finding for "good cause" to do so. However, since these determinations are made on a case-by-case basis, courts differ on how this standard is to be applied and what adoptees must show to meet the requirement.

Generally, "good cause" for the release of information is determined when there is a medical or psychiatric necessity for such information. Few courts allow adoptees to contact their birth parents if their sole purpose is to gain more accurate and up to date information regarding the parents' health. Even fewer courts will allow adult adoptees to contact their birth parents out of mere curiosity.

Furthermore, in a "good cause" proceeding, courts never receive testimony from the birth parents. The assumption being that the birth parent(s) are opposed to the disclosure of any information.

B. Mutual Consent Registries

Some states have enacted statutes that provide for the creation of mutual consent registries. These registries give the willing parties of adoption proceedings the ability to meet. A formal consent must be filed by both the birth parents and the adult adoptee in order to disclose any identifying information. When both parties file the appropriate consent, a state administrator or adoption agency notifies each of the parties and releases the information.

The primary challenge regarding these registries is that they are not well publicized. As a result, a birth parent who is willing to release such information may be unaware of such a registry within their state or the state of the child's birth. If the birth parents have not filed a notice of consent with the registry, the adoptee must meet the "good cause" standard in order to gain any identifiable information.

C. "Search and Consent" Procedures

With the goal of reunification/contact by adult adoptees and their birth parent(s), some states provide more than the mutual consent registries. These states have enacted legislation that allows agencies to actively assist adult adoptees locate birth parents. When an adoptee has begun their search, the agencies are allowed to contact the birth parent(s) and inquire whether they are willing to be identified or even meet with the adoptee. Understandably, the agency can only divulge the type and amount of information that the birth parents have consented be divulged. Contrarily, if the birth parent(s) does not consent, the agency may not release confidential information to the adoptee unless the adoptee meets the judicial "good cause" standard.

D. Affidavits and Vetoes

Under the affidavit and veto system, birth parents are able to complete an affidavit that provides their consent to the adoptee gaining identifying information. Birth parents also are able to veto an adoptee's decision to get the birth parent's identifying information.

IV. Protecting the Privacy of Birth Parents vs. the Adoptee's Right to Know

The purpose of enacting the sealed records statutes was to protect the adopted child from any stigma regarding their illegitimacy. As a result, states sought to provide for equal treatment of adopted children and non-adopted children — both legally and socially. States also sought to nurture the adopted child's relationship with its adoptive parents by sealing the records. In essence, states believed they were protecting the adoptive relationship from the possibility of interference from the child's biological parents. In addition, states sought to protect the biological parents from any public ridicule regarding the adoption proceedings.

A. Birth Parents' Privacy Interests

Sealed records protect birth parents and their privacy interests. An argument in favor of sealed records is that birth parents relinquished their children for a reason and (unless they have listed themselves on a Contact Registry) they do not want their lives to be disturbed by the adoptee. If the birth parents were promised confidentiality when they surrendered the child and voluntarily terminated their parental rights to the child, that promise should be kept. This is their fundamental right to privacy. However, under this premise, it is assumed that birth parents intended to completely and forever sever all ties with their children. However, not all similarly situated birth parents feel this way.

Another argument that favors closed records is that more abortions would occur if the birth mother cannot be promised that her identity will be forever private and confidential. This argument presumes that a birth mother would rather terminate a pregnancy than have the possibility of the child contacting them later in life. The rationale here is that *in futuro*, if adoptees seek out their birth parents, it will be an unwanted intrusion for the birth mother.

A final argument in support of the birth parents' right to privacy is that for birth parents who relinquished their child during a difficult time in their lives, contact from the adult adoptee could resurrect those memories and perhaps deep-rooted psychological problems.

B. Adoptee's Right to Know

Adult adoptees assert many reasons why they should be allowed access to their birth and adoption records. Adult adoptees often posit that while confidentiality may be in the best interests for children, once adoptees have reached the age of majority, confidentiality is not in their best interest. At that juncture, adoptees have the ability to determine for themselves what is in their best interests, and whether they believe they should have access to such information or not. Therefore, they conclude that it should be up to each individual adult adoptee to determine whether they want to exercise their fundamental right to know.

In addition, adoptees argue that their constitutional rights to privacy, to receive pertinent information, and equal protection of the law are violated by the sealed records statutes. Adoptees claim that they have a fundamental right to know who their birth parents are because that information is necessary for their own emotional development. It is argued that since the Constitution protects one's right to privacy within familial relationships, the Constitution must protect one's right to know his or her background.

Further, by denying adult adoptees access to such records, states are denying them the opportunity to participate in and contribute to society and the democratic process. Adoptees argue, in order to fully participate within society, they need information that will give them a better sense of their self. Thus, if they know themselves more fully and where they came from, they are more readily and more intelligently able to participate in societal and governmental decision-making processes.

In regards to the equal protection claim, adoptees argue that they are a quasi-suspect class which is therefore subject to a heightened level of scrutiny. In that sense, because they cannot readily access their birth records in a manner that non-adoptees can, adult adoptees are discriminated against. The argument continues that sealed records statutes do not have a compelling state interest and, thus, would fail a heightened scrutiny test.

These arguments have not been accepted by any United States court. Courts have held that an adoptee's claims to a right to privacy and to information directly conflicts with birth parents' rights to privacy. Further, because the sealed records statutes have a rational relationship in protecting the adoption process and its integrity, the statutes have been upheld. Courts have also rejected the claim that adult adoptees are a quasi-suspect class. Further, even if they were a quasi-suspect class, the sealed records statutes would still be upheld because they substantially relate to an important state interest.

V. Enforceability of Open Adoption Agreements

A. Forms of Open Adoption

1. Informal Agreements

An informal agreement to an open adoption is a verbal agreement between the birth parents and the adoptive parents. Since the adoptive parents have legal rights to the child, the type and amount of contact involved is largely determined by the adoptive parents. As such, in a jurisdiction that does not recognize open adoption agreements, if there is ever a dispute between the birth parents and adoptive parents that requires judicial involvement, most likely the adoptive parents will not be ordered by a court to comply with their prior oral agreement to openness.

2. Post-Adoption Contact Agreements

A post-adoption contact agreement is a written agreement that provides guidelines for the type of contact between the birth parents and the adoptive family. The more detailed post-adoption contact agreements set out a visitation schedule. Some agreements go further and include contact between the adoptive family and other birth relatives, such as siblings or grandparents. The agreement could also include relevant, important medical information, the birth family's heritage, or anything that would be helpful to the child's growth and development. Twenty-two states currently have statutes that explicitly provide for enforceable post-adoption contact agreements.

Few states specifically prohibit these agreements. In North Carolina, there is case law that declares a post-adoption contact agreement not enforceable (*Quets v. Needham*, 198 N.C. App. 241 (N.C. Ct. App. 2009)). Also, there are instances where a statute gives the court leave to refuse to follow one of these post-adoption contact agreements. In a Maryland statute, the judge can decide against a post-adoption contact agreement if it is not in the best interest of the child (Md. Code Ann., Fam. Law § 5-3B-07 (West 2014)). Those parties who agree to an open adoption utilizing post-adoption contact can face a problem with enforcement. Problems arise not only when one party seeks to change part of the agreement or stop contact all together against the other party's wishes, but also where the court deems the best interest of the child is to not have contact.

In states that allow open adoption, the written agreements need to be signed by both parties and the provisions of the agreement must be approved by the court. A best interests of the child standard is typically applied by the court when reviewing the agreement.

3. Court-Imposed Open Adoption

A court-imposed open adoption is regulated by state statute and allows courts to order visits between the adoptee and a third party, even if the adoptive parents object. The third party is usually a nonparent relative but also could be a birth parent or sibling. This form of open adoption is useful when the adoptee and third party have a pre-existing substantial bond that the adoptive parents fail to recognize. However, this form of open adoption outright challenges adoptive parents' autonomy and the functioning of their new family. Most of these statutes require the adoptive parents to agree to maintain contact in order for the agreement to be enforced.

B. States With Completely Open Records

Only six states permit adult adoptees with unrestricted access to identifying information. Those states include Alabama, Alaska, Kansas, Maine, New Hampshire, and Oregon.

C. States Without Completely Open Records

Where parties to an open adoption agreement disagree over some of its terms, a judicial determination must be made in states that do not give adoptees complete access to their birth records. Courts tend to either rule that no agreement existed or that the agreement is not enforceable. In that case, it is up to the adoptive parents to determine whether they want to honor it or not, absent any statute to the contrary. In so deciding, courts often rely on public policy arguments. First, the agreements contradict the intent of adoption laws. Second, in order for an adoption to be finalized, birth parents must terminate all of their parental rights including visitation. Third, an open adoption jeopardizes the autonomy of the adoptive family.

Although most courts will side with the adoptive parents when disputes arise, one recent Minnesota Supreme Court decision held to the contrary (*C.O. v. Doe*, 757 N.W.2d 343 (2008)). In that case, the birth father sought to enforce his rights under a post-adoption contact agreement with the adoptive parents. The Supreme Court of Minnesota held that the birth father had a property interest in the post-adoption contact agreement and was entitled to an evidentiary hearing on whether the agreement should be terminated.

VI. The Benefits and Risks of Open Adoptions

A. Birth Parents

1. Benefits

For a birth parent that faces an adversarial termination of parental rights proceeding, voluntarily relinquishing their rights and agreeing to an open adoption allows the birth parent the prospect of ongoing contact with the adoptee, which they wouldn't have if their rights were involuntarily terminated. For any birth parent, an open adoption helps them to deal with the grief and loss that comes with giving up their child. With contact, birth parents can take comfort in actively seeing that the child is being well taken care of. Further, through openness, the birth parent has the ability to have a substantial relationship with the adoptee and a permanent role in the adoptee's life.

2. Risks

If an open agreement takes place in a jurisdiction that does not expressly permit these agreements, it is doubtful that the birth parent will be able to maintain contact if a problem arises and the adoptive parent objects to the contact. For example, a birth parent may want more contact as the child gets older—which might not be granted by the adoptive parent. Along the same lines, through openness, a birth parent may not be able to move on with their life.

B. Adoptive Parents

1. Benefits

Adoptive parents can benefit from having the birth family in their lives because they can gain an understanding of the adoptee's history and background. In knowing why the birth parents relinquished the child, the adoptive parents can better explain any questions the adoptee has in the future. With an open adoption, it eases the fear of adoptive parents that the birth parents will want to reclaim their child.

2. Risks

Potentially, adoptive parents could be pressured into accepting this type of agreement because they are committed to the adoption process and to that particular child. Adoptive parents have to continue to relate to and interact with the birth parents and any issues and/or problems they may have. Birth parents may want more and more contact with the child than the adoptive parents are unwilling to allow. Adoptive parents might have to deal with birth parents that either intentionally or unintentionally are undermining of the new family.

C. Adoptees

1. Benefits

Adoptees gain direct access not only to their history but to their birth parents. Thus, later in life (as an adult) there is no need for a search that could often take years to complete. As a result (it has been posited), adoptees are less likely to have self-identity issues. Adoptees will not likely suffer from any guilt in asking their adoptive parents about their birth parents. Further, adoptees who are adopted into families of a different race, heritage, or religion will be able to maintain contact with their roots, heritage and culture. Older adoptees benefit from ongoing contact with their birth parents because they already became attached and bonded with the birth parents.

2. Risks

An adoptee might not fully settle into the new adoptive family if the birth parents are still present. Further, once an open relationship has been established with the birth parents, if the birth parents stop or lessen contact in the future, the adoptee could once again feel rejected and abandoned. In addition, the adoptee may experience difficulty in balancing the two families.

VII. The Current Trend

Openness in adoptions is becoming the norm. According to the DHHS 2007 National Survey of Adoptive Parents (NSAP) (released in 2009), approximately one-third of children adopted by non-relatives have a pre-adoption agreement that relates to openness. Further, approximately one-third of adopted children have post adoption contact with their birth family, including face to face contact, letters, or emails. Finally, NSAP reveals that 67% of children who were adopted privately have pre-adoption agreements.

A nationwide survey of 100 adoption agencies (4,400 adoptions facilitated over a two-year period) conducted by the Evan B. Donaldson Institute and released in March of 2012 provides important findings regarding current trends in open adoption:

- The number of "closed" infant adoptions in the U.S. has shrunk to a tiny minority. Indeed, respondents said confidential adoptions constituted only 5% of their placements during the past two years, while 55% were fully disclosed and 40% were mediated. 95% of the agencies said they now offer open adoptions.
- In the vast majority of infant adoptions, the adoptive and expectant parents considering adoption meet each other and the expectant parents pick the new family for their baby.
- There is definite fluidity in openness levels, particularly during the first few years of an adoption, with studies showing that contact is subsequently established in some arrangements that did not start off as open, while relationships are sometimes curtailed or ended even though the initial plan had been for ongoing contact.
- Most participants in open adoptions report positive experiences, and greater openness is associated with greater satisfaction with the adoption process. Furthermore, birthmothers who have ongoing contact with their children report less grief, regret and worry, as well as more peace of mind, than do those who do not have contact.
- The primary benefit of openness is access by adopted persons—as children and continuing later in life—to birth relatives, as well as to their own medical, genealogical and family histories. Adolescents with ongoing contact are more satisfied with the level of openness in their own adoptions than are those without such contact, and they identify the following benefits: coming to terms with the reasons for their adoption, physical touchstones to identify where personal traits came from, information that aids in identity formation, positive feelings toward birthmother, and others. Youth in open adoptions also have a better understanding of the meaning of adoption and more active communication about adoption with their adoptive parents (citations omitted).

Siegel, D. and Smith, S., *Openness in Adoption: From Secrecy and Stigma to Knowledge and Connections*, available at http://www.adoptioninstitute.org/publi cations/2012_03_OpennessInAdoption.pdf.

It should be noted that of the 4400 adoptions facilitated and reported in the above study, only 5% (roughly 220) were confidential adoptions.

Importantly, the survey identified the following factors as important to achieving successful open adoption relationships:

1. **Shared understanding by birth and adoptive parents about what open adoption is and is not** (based on an ethical foundation of decision-making, a child-centered focus, clear expectations of respective roles,

and an understanding of open adoption's benefits, challenges and complexities). For instance, that it does not erase loss.

2. **Foundational relationship qualities and values** (empathy, respect, honesty, trust and a commitment to maintaining the connection) are ideals for the parties in open relationships.

3. **Ability of all parties to exercise self-determination in choosing and shaping open relationships** (exercising self-determination in the original agreement, in setting boundaries, and adaptability as the relationship changes over time).

4. **Development by all parties of "collaborative" communication in planning for contact and in conveying needs** (comfort and honesty in communicating, planning for contact and availability of post-adoption services).

In sum, the current major policies regarding access to birth records can be categorized as follows:

1. Open Records: Original birth records of adoptees are available to them upon request once they reach the age of majority (18 or 21, depending on the state). In 2014, 18 states have open access and partial restriction laws. Of these 18, 8 states are completely open access, meaning the records will be available at 18 or 21 years of age. The other 10 have partial access or restricted access that allow the adoptee to gain access to basic information, like their original birth certificate, once the adoptee reaches the age of majority. Other states, like New Jersey, will allow open access in the year 2017. Present legislation is changing the way information becomes available to the adoptee.

2. Nondisclosure Veto: A document filed by one party to the adoption expressing their right to refuse that their identifying information be disclosed to a searching party. As a result, the searching party has no access to private/personal information.

3. Contact Veto: A document filed by one party to the adoption expressing their right to refuse to be contacted. This veto may extend to varying degrees of the filing person's relatives as well.

4. Bifurcated System: A state law by which different disclosure protocols are in place before and after a specific date in time.

5. Confidential Intermediary System (an "active registry"): A system by which a party to an adoption requests information or contact with another party or parties through an intermediary—an individual or an entity—who facilitates communication. The intermediary then contacts the other party or parties to determine whether they are open to contact or the sharing of information. Information is then relayed to the requesting party through the intermediary to the extent agreed upon by the non-requesting party.

6. Mutual Consent Registry (a "passive registry"): A system allowing individuals involved in an adoption to register, stating their willingness to exchange information or make contact with another party to their adoption (or, in some cases, stating their wish *not* to be contacted).

7. Court Order Only: In every state, a procedure is in place where original birth certificates or information—including medical or identifying information—can be requested if the requester can meet the state's required standard of proof. Typically the standard is a high one, requiring an emergent need such as a severe illness that might be able to be better treated with knowledge of medical history, not simply a desire to know the information.

Checkpoints

- Early adoption proceedings did not seal records or birth certificates.

- In 1916, New York passed a statute to seal adoption records from the public. Minnesota added to this concept of confidentiality by passing a statute that kept the records sealed from all parties, including the birth parents, the child, and the adoptive parents. This was to protect the child from carrying a negative stigma of being adopted.

- This negative outlook on adoption changed as society began accepting unwed mothers. Therefore, less children were put up for adoption. And in the adoptions that did occur, the birth mothers wanted to keep the records open.

- In the 1970s, the adoptees began to demand access to their adoption records, which evolved in to the present day practice of open adoption. Adoptions can vary from completely closed, to solely medical history access, to completely open with contact between the birth parent(s), child, and adoptive parent(s).

- The "good cause" standard must be met by a child seeking access to closed records. This standard is high.

- Some states offer mutual consent registries where the parents can consent to information being accessed at a future time.

- In a sealed records adoption, the agency would have to get consent from the birth parent(s) if information or contact is requested by the adoptee. The birth parent can accept or veto this request.

- Birth parent(s) privacy is respected.

- Adoptees claim a fundamental right to know their birth parent history.

- Open adoptions can be informal, involve a detailed post-adoption contract, or be a court-imposed open adoption. Only six states offer completely open adoptions.

- Requests for documents must be done by court order.

Chapter 6

Transracial Adoption

CAN YOU IMAGINE?

Have you ever spent time *imagining*
what it would have been like
to have been raised amongst individuals who were
racially different from you?
What it would have been like
to have gone FOR YEARS never having
spoken to a person who was of the same race as you;
What it would have been like
throughout the course of a typical day
never having encountered a person
who looked like you.
What it would have been like
to have EVEN your own PARENTS be
of a different race from you?
Can you imagine?

Susan R. Harris, *Race, Search and My Baby-Self: Reflections of a Transracial Adoptee*, 9 YALE J.L. FEMINISM 5, 5–6 (1997).

I. History

A. General Background

Within the adoption process, "race-matching" describes the practice of placing children with prospective adoptive parents solely or primarily on the basis of race to achieve same-race placements. Conversely, the practice of placing children with prospective adoptive parents who are not of the same race has been denoted as a transracial adoption (TRA) or transracial placement. Transracial adoption in the United States is older than the nation itself: Christopher Columbus kidnapped and adopted a Native American boy who became his translator and guide.

Transracial adoptions in America predominantly involve the adoption of African American children by White parents. There are extremely few, if any, documented cases of African American parents adopting White children. However, the phenomenon of African Americans serving as foster parents for White children is slightly more frequent. The one-way nature of transracial adoption is demonstrated not only by the lack of adoptions of White children by African American parents, but also by other non-White parents of color, and even to the adoption of White children by interracial couples. The issue has been aptly summarized:

> Today the rapidly expanding number of "mixed-race" couples and adoptions may be reducing the anxiety about "race mixing" in the present. But mixed-race adoptions, even more than mixed-race couples, occur only in one direction: there is debate about whether whites should adopt children of color, but adoptions of white children by parents of color are so rare they are not even debated. This dimension of racial policy in child welfare suggests something of the degree to which race is about hierarchy, not difference.

Linda Gordon, THE GREAT ARIZONA ORPHAN ABDUCTION 309 (1999).

B. The 1904 Arizona Orphan Train: The Wrong Way on a One-Way Track

To appreciate the circular nature and the somewhat sordid beginnings of modern transracial adoption, it is necessary to delve briefly into the history of the phenomenon. In the Arizona territory in 1904, an interracial foster care placement of White children with Hispanic families nearly transpired. It should be noted that, at the time of the incident, legal adoption was not well-known. The manner in which the case unfolded caused the incident to gain folklore status; the fact that the case was appealed to the United States Supreme Court (which was dismissed for lack of jurisdiction) is not even its most notable attribute.

The incident began when the New York Foundling Hospital, a Catholic institutional home founded in 1870 by the Sisters of Charity, as an alternative to the Protestant institutions that were predominant at the time, endeavored to place Catholic children in Catholic homes. By paying foster mothers thirty-eight cents ($0.38) per day to care for its charges, the Foundling Hospital established New York State's first system of paid foster care. After 24 years, the sisters had admitted 26,000 children and placed out 10,000 (about 39% of the total) of the children.

During the late 1800s, a common practice in the child welfare placement "industry" was to "emigrate" orphans from eastern cities to more rural towns in the midwestern and western states and territories for foster care placement. These placements had no legal bonds—which allowed foster parents to return children who did not meet their expectations. By 1879, the Sisters of Charity had placed one thousand (1,000) children. By 1904, the Sisters were handling approximately 1,900 children per year and emigrating nearly 500 of those children annually. By 1919, a total of almost 25,000 orphans had been emigrated to the Midwest and West by the Foundling Hospital. These planned exoduses— referred to as the "orphan trains"—were for the general purpose of providing child labor.

In the fall of 1904, arrangements were made to send thirty-five to forty children from New York City to two small towns in the southeastern Arizona Territory, approximately ninety miles from the Mexican border. The inquiring priest explained that the waiting families were "not wealthy people, but all had work at good wages, had comfortable homes, were mostly childless and could well take care of the little ones, that they were all good, practicing Catholics." What the priest failed to mention was that all of the couples were either Mexican or so-called Anglos interracially married with Mexicans. In comparison, the orphans sent to Arizona were all of Irish-American descent.

When the White townsfolk discovered that the Irish orphans were being placed with Mexican families, a vigilante posse was formed, and the children were forcibly removed from their foster homes within twenty-four hours of their arrival. The crux of the matter for the White townsfolk was that these were innocent White children in the care and custody of people perceived to be swarthy, unfit caretakers who would mistreat them. Although twenty-one of the children returned to New York with the nuns and nurses who had accompanied them to the West, nineteen children were virtually kidnapped and held by White residents.

Through a writ of habeas corpus, the resulting civil suit sought the return of one of the children to the custody and control of the Foundling Hospital (*N.Y. Foundling Hosp. v. Gatti*, 79 P. 231 (Ariz. 1905), *appeal dismissed* 203 U.S. 429 (1906)). The case's recitation of facts described the Mexican foster parents as: "wholly unfit ... of the lowest class of half-breed Mexican Indians ... impecunious, illiterate, vicious, and in several instances, prostitutes and persons of notoriously bad character."

Interestingly, the vigilante mob that summarily took the children from their legal wards was described as consisting of "persons of some means and education from the day when, with humanitarian impulse, and actuated by motives of sympathy for their pitiful condition, they assisted in the rescue of these little children from the evil into which they had fallen." Stating that it was in the children's best interest to remain with the White families, the court dismissed the writs.

The New York Foundling Hospital appealed the case to the United States Supreme Court. After referring to the original foster parents as "half-breed Mexican Indians of bad character," the USSC dismissed the appeal for lack of jurisdiction. Justice Day determined that a writ of habeas corpus for personal freedom does not apply to children. In addition, the Court's description of the events ignored the fact that the children had been violently taken from their legal guardians under threat of force.

C. Transracial Adoption in Modern Times

The first documented modern transracial adoption occurred in Minneapolis, Minnesota in 1948. Transracial adoption gained momentum in the mid-1950s and then declined in the early 1960s. However, with the Civil Rights Movement in the mid-1960s, there was another rise in the number of transracial adoptions. This trend continued until the early 1970s when vocal opposition began to cause a decline in the practice.

The question of whether White parents should adopt African American children has been the subject of momentous debate in the social work and child development literature. The discussion was initiated by a 1972 position paper drafted by the National Association of Black Social Workers (NABSW), which vehemently opposed the placement of African American children with White families and referred to this type of placement as a form of "cultural genocide." This groundbreaking and controversial NABSW position paper set the tone regarding transracial adoptions and same-race placements for more than two decades.

The term "cultural genocide" was first coined in relation to the placement of Native American children outside of their tribal family, culture, and identity and into White families. Outplacement of Native American children had occurred in such large numbers throughout the 1950s, 1960s, and 1970s that Congress responded by passing the Indian Child Welfare Act of 1978 (ICWA) to stop the irreversible decimation of the Native American tribal system.

In an attempt to adhere to the tenets of the NABSW position paper, adoption agencies began to enact and enforce same-race placement policies. As a result, the number of transracial adoptions dropped drastically nationwide. While over 12,000 transracial adoptions occurred between 1960 and 1979, in 1972, the year in which the NABSW position paper was published, only 1,569 transracial adoptions occurred. The previous year had seen over 2,500 transracial placements. By 1976, the annual number of transracial adoptions had shrunk to 1,076. By 1987, despite a higher percentage of African American children in foster care, the number of transracial adoptions had increased only slightly to 1,169. In fact, even when including international adoptions, transracial adoptions account for only about 8% of all adoptions in the United States.

In 1978, the Child Welfare League of America stated that it was preferable to place a child in a family of his own racial background. In Title VI of the 1964 Civil Rights Act, Congress provided that "[n]o person in the United States shall, on the ground of race, color, or national origin, be excluded from participation in, be denied the benefits of, or be subjected to discrimination under any program or activity receiving Federal financial assistance" (42 U.S.C. §2000d (1994)).

Despite the strong, prohibitive language of Title VI, adoption law was viewed as outside the statute. In the adoption context, race could be considered as a relevant factor because of the unique aspects of the relationship between a child and his or her adoptive or foster parents. As a result, race matching existed as an unwritten policy, and most adoption agencies had internal transracial adoption placement policies.

Before the passage of federal legislation in the mid-1990s, not only did most states allow for considerations of race (for example, California, Illinois and New Jersey), but some states even favored same-race placements over transracial placements via order of preference statutes (California, Maryland, and Minnesota). These same-race policies were due, at least in part, to foster care and adoption professionals' concerns that transracial adoption did not offer optimal placements for African American children. As recently as 1987, 35 states prohibited the adoption of Black children by White families. Even in states that allowed transracial adoptions, however, state and private adoption agencies were committed to race matching.

II. The Federal Statutory Framework: The Multi-Ethnic Placement Act of 1994 (MEPA) and the Removal of Barriers to Interethnic Adoption Act of 1996 (IEAA)

A. General Background

The transracial adoption controversy continued to rage among social workers, lawyers, legislators, foster parents, and prospective adoptive parents for twenty years after the publication of the NABSW position paper. Because the debate that transpired during the 1970s, 1980s, and early 1990s raised concerns about the best interests of children who were transracially placed, race matching was regularly utilized as a determinative factor in placing African American children in adoptive homes. During this time frame, transracial adoption was considered a last-resort placement alternative.

Eventually, race matching was identified as one of the causes of foster care drift and the escalating number of children in foster care. Some estimates indicated that there was a 72% increase in the number of children in the foster care system between 1986 and the early 1990s from 276,000 children in 1985 to 494,000 children in 1994.

B. MEPA

In 1993, Texas became the first state to pass a statute prohibiting "the use of race to delay, deny, or otherwise discriminate" in child placement decisions. The following year, modeling its legislation after the Texas statute, Congress entered the transracial adoption debate by passing the Multi-Ethnic Placement Act of 1994 ("MEPA") (42 U.S.C. 622; Pub. L. No. 103–382 (1994)). The act's stated purposes were: (1) decreasing the length of time that children wait to be adopted; (2) preventing discrimination in the placement of children on the basis of race, color, or national origin; and (3) facilitating the identification and recruitment of foster and adoptive families that can meet these children's needs.

MEPA prohibited child placement agencies receiving federal funds from "categorically deny[ing] to any person the opportunity to become an adoptive or a foster parent, solely on the basis of the race, color, or national origin of the adoptive or foster parent, or the child, involved." Further, the act prohibited the delay or denial of child placements due to the race, color, or national origin of the adoptive or foster parents or of the child.

MEPA was considered a "revolutionary act in concept." MEPA allowed consideration of the following factors:

- The child's relationship to the prospective adoptive parent;
- The child's age, sex, racial, ethnic, religious, and cultural background;
- The location of the child's siblings, if any;
- The prospective adoptive parents' capacity to meet the child's needs;
- The child's physical and emotional needs;
- The child's education; and
- The continuity and stability of the child's foster care placement.

As Senators Carol Moseley-Braun and Howard Metzenbaum, the sponsors of the original legislation, stated in separate MEPA-related articles, the wording of MEPA did not allow race to be the sole factor in rejecting pre-adoptive parents, but it did allow race to be considered in adoption placements. Thus, rather than achieving the congressionally intended purpose of resolving the transracial adoption debate by limiting the basis for considering race, MEPA fueled the flames of the debate. In addition, there was evidence that, following the passage of MEPA, race matching in adoptions continued.

C. IEAA

To close the so-called loophole for race matching, Congress repealed portions of MEPA and passed Section 1808 of the Small Business Job Protection Act of 1996, entitled "Removal of Barriers to Interethnic Adoption" ("IEAA") (Pub. L. No. 104-188, § 1808, 110 Stat. 1755, 1903–04 (1996)).

IEAA's purposes were to ensure that (1) the practice of race matching ended, and (2) race was not considered at all during the adoption process — even for purposes of racial sensitivity screening or when the birth parent requested that the child be placed intra-racially. Further, IEAA contained an enforcement provision whereby federally funded state programs and private programs receiving federal funds that violated IEAA would have their funding reduced by 2% for the first violation, 3% for the second violation, and 5% for the third and each subsequent violation during any fiscal year. Therefore, Congress struck at the pocket books of state agencies and state-funded private organizations to ensure compliance with Congress's mandate that race should not be considered during the adoption process — even in transracial adoptions where, by definition, the race of the adoptive parents is different from that of the adopted child.

D. Legal Implications and Considerations for MEPA/IEAA

In evaluating the MEPA/IEAA, there are three aspects that must be considered. First, MEPA/IEAA does not explicitly incorporate the best interest of the child standard in making adoption placements. Thus, there is concern that such a standard will not be utilized in adoption placements pursuant to MEPA/IEAA. Due to the lack of a best interest standard, the adoptive parents' interests may, in some instances, weigh more heavily than the child's interests.

Second, failure to comply with MEPA/IEAA constitutes a violation of Title VI of the Civil Rights Act of 1964 (42 U.S.C. § 1996b(2)(2000 Supp. V); 45 C.F.R. §§ 80.1, 80.3 (2001)). Therefore, anyone who feels that he or she has been discriminated against on the basis of race, color, or national origin in relation to an adoption placement may file a complaint with the Office for Civil Rights for investigation and review. This is particularly relevant for parents seeking to adopt transracially since race may not be considered even in terms of the potential parents' racial sensitivity and acuity.

Further, the appropriate Constitutional standard for evaluating the use of race, color, or national origin in adoption and foster care placements is strict scrutiny under Title VI and the U.S. Constitution. This standard forbids decision making on the basis of race or ethnicity, except in the very limited circumstances where such consideration would be necessary to achieve a compelling governmental interest. The only compelling governmental interest related to child welfare that has been recognized by courts is protecting the "best interests" of the child who is to be placed. Additionally, the consideration must be narrowly tailored to advance the child's interests, and must be made as an individualized determination for each child. Even the wishes of a child's birth parents for a same-race placement in foster care or for adoption does not amount to a compelling state interest that would justify preferences for same race placements.

The third consideration in evaluating MEPA/IEAA is the potential impact of private lawsuits. In addition to lawsuits under the Civil Rights Act, MEPA/IEAA allows individuals to bring a federal cause of action in a private lawsuit for alleged violations of the Civil Rights Act or MEPA/IEAA. In certain instances, aggrieved persons have two years from the date of the alleged violation to file a lawsuit in federal court. Pursuant to MEPA/IEAA, cases alleging unlawful race-matching have been filed. *See Generally, Doe v. Hamilton County*, Ohio, No. C-1-99-281 (D.S.D. Ohio) (filed Apr. 19, 1999; case settled in 2002 (case of first impression under MEPA/IEAA)).

Curiously, while IEAA requires a color-blind approach to placements, it did not repeal section 554 of MEPA, which requires state agencies to diligently recruit potential foster and adoptive parents and families that reflect the ethnic and racial diversity of the children in foster care (Pub. L. No. 104-185, § 1808, 110 Stat. 1755, 1903–04 (1996)). This recruitment process shall not, however, cause delay or denial of placement based on race, culture, or ethnicity. As a result, caseworkers are faced with a Hobsonian choice, as demonstrated in *Doe v. Hamilton County*.

III. Arguments in Opposition to and in Support of Transracial Adoption

A. Arguments in Opposition to Transracial Adoption

1. One-Way Nature

One of the primary reasons that African Americans and organizations purporting to represent the interests of African Americans are opposed to transracial adoption is that the phenomenon of transracial adoption occurs unilaterally; the overwhelming trend in transracial adoption is for White adults to adopt African American children.

This one-way phenomenon is less prevalent in foster care. Namely, even though African American adults serve as foster parents for White children, they are not allowed to adopt them. This phenomenon is evocative of the common practice during slavery where female slaves served as "wet nurses" and so-called "mammies" for their masters' children.

2. Racial Identity

The earliest adoptions attempted to mimic the biological family. Transracial adoptions make this attempt impossible and are not in the best interests of African American children. It is in the best interests of a child to preserve a child's racial, ethnic, and cultural heritage in adoption placement decisions. It is virtually impossible for White parents to raise African American children in a White environment and have the children retain their African American identity.

Identity is an individual's conception of the self. Racial matching is based on the concept that a child wants to be like his parents and that parents can more easily identify with a child who resembles them. Thus, racial matching provides an atmosphere that helps instill a sense of personal, social, and racial identity. Identity has been increasingly recognized as significant to a child's well-being. Studies show that while a sense of identity is important for all children, it is crucial for ethnic minority children adopted by White parents.

3. Cultural Genocide

According to the NABSW in the 1970s through the 1990s, transracial adoptions actually harm African American children. Taking African American children away from the African American community, it has been argued, is a form of "[cultural] genocide." The experience of African American children growing up in a predominantly White world makes it "impossible for them to ever take their rightful place among African American communities." Thus, "the ranks of the Black community are being depleted, but Blacks cannot truly [integrate] into the White community." It is further argued that transracial adoption deprives African American children of their identity, which essentially takes away their heritage. The concern is that African American children are both literally and figuratively annexed from the African American community.

4. African American Adoptive Parents

African American adoptive homes can be found for African American children. African American adoptive parents are in short supply because they encounter roadblocks in the adoption process, not because they are disinterested in adopting.

A 1991 study conducted by the North American Council on Adoptable Children (NACAC) found that "eighty-three percent of respondents said that they were aware of organizational and/or institutional barriers preventing or discouraging families of color seeking to adopt" (Barriers to Same Race Placements — April, 1991). The following problems were identified:

- Institutional/Systematic Racism — virtually all procedures and guidelines impacting standard agency adoption are developed from White, middle-class perspectives;
- Lack of People of Color in Managerial and Staff Positions;
- Fees — 75% of agencies surveyed said adoption fees are a barrier to minority families trying to adopt;
- "Adoption as a Business" Mentality/Reality;
- Communities of Color's Historical Tendencies toward "Informal" Adoption;
- Negative Perceptions of Agencies and Their Practices;
- Inflexible Standards — insistence upon young, two-parent, materially-endowed families eliminates many potentially viable minority homes; and

- General Lack of Recruitment Activity and Poor Recruitment Techniques— communities of color remain largely unaware of the need for their services.

Furthermore, transracial adoption will not relieve the number of African American children in foster care. Many Whites support race-matching, and White adoptive parents prefer White children over children of another race. The vast majority of prospective White parents, if interested in adopting African American children, are only interested in adopting healthy African American infants; yet there are more than enough prospective African American adoptive parents available for those infants.

5. Federal Legislation: MEPA and IEAA

By prohibiting race from being considered in placement decisions, the MEPA/IEAA lacks the power to allow the best interests of children to be considered. By eliminating racial considerations in adoption proceedings, these statutes completely ignore the racial attitudes of White prospective adoptive parents. This denial will permit racially insensitive White parents to adopt African American children (*DeWees v. Stevenson*, 779 F. Supp. 25 (E.D. Pa. 1991)). Therefore, not only are White adoptive parents generally unable to prepare African American children to cope with societal prejudices, some Whites are teaching, consciously or unconsciously, their adopted African American children to be prejudiced against African Americans.

One in six parents who adopted across racial lines identified that the problems they experienced were directly related to the transracial nature of the adoption. While Congress may pass legislation decreeing that racism is not a reality, fortunately, the courts appear willing to face this issue. For example, in the case *Adoption of Vito*, 712 N.E.2d 1188 (Mass. App. Ct. 1999), the judge considered the future difficulties that an African American child would face in an all-White community without contact with the African American community.

Due in large part to the fact that adoption is not a fundamental right, the constitutionality of using race as a factor has been upheld on Fourteenth Amendment grounds where the best interests of the child are considered. Empirical studies of transracially adopted African American children and adults have not conclusively proven that such adoptions are not psychologically harmful to these children.

B. Arguments in Support of Transracial Adoption

1. Statistics

Significant support for transracial adoption stems from the existence and effect of race-related statistics for foster care and domestic adoption. As of FY2013, DHHS reported that African American children comprised approximately 24% of the children in the foster care system (98,201 of 402,378 (Preliminary AFCARS Report 21 — July 2014)). Furthermore, approximately 24% of children who are available for adoption are African American (24,312 of 101,840). Meanwhile, over 70% of American adoptive parents are White (DHHS: NSAP Chartbook — Summer 2010).

Although many White families state their willingness to adopt transracially, domestic transracial adoptions comprise less than 1% of all completed adoptions. Further, the ratio of prospective adoptees to prospective adopters has been projected at approximately thirty-five to one.

While the number of African American children in foster care substantially outnumber the White children available for adoption (98,201 versus 42,344), African American children accounted for only 21% of the adoptions from foster care in FY2013. Accordingly, it can be concluded that African American children remained in foster care longer than the national mean of 21.8 months (Preliminary AFCARS Report 21 — July 2014).

Although African Americans adopt at the same rate as Whites, African Americans would have to adopt at a rate many times that of Whites to provide homes for all of the African American children available for adoption. Therefore, with the passage of MEPA/IEAA, Congress concluded that race matching was responsible, at least in part, for the length of time children spent in foster care. Furthermore, the older children grow, the less likely it becomes that they will ever find a permanent home.

Evidence demonstrates that children suffer irreparable harm from growing up without permanent parents. Almost 30% of children who grow up in unstable circumstances, including foster care, have reported instances of crime, alcoholism, or both. This startling figure is even more disturbing considering that the number of children in foster care is now double what it was during the 1970s, with infants and children under the age of four being the fastest growing population in adoption agencies.

2. Race Matching Harms Children

In passing the aforementioned Acts, Congress determined that racial matching and same-race placements were responsible, at least in part, for the length of time children spent in foster care. Furthermore, children are less likely to find permanent placements as they age. Race matching decreases the probability that children, particularly African American children, will be placed into permanent homes for adoption. Rather than same-race placement, it is more important that children receive love, receive attention, achieve permanency, and that they do not languish in foster care.

3. Success Rate of TRA

Adoptions are not all successful; however, the failure rate is unrelated to adoptions across racial lines. There is no evidence that transracial adoptions harm children; in fact, transracial adoptions have proven to be successful.

Pointedly, research data indicates that transracial adoptees fare well. Over 75% of transracial adoptions are considered successful—a number comparable to same-race adoptions. 68% of children who were adopted transracially do not feel any discomfort with their appearance compared to their adoptive parents or the community in which they were raised.

It can be concluded from these statistics that transracially adopted children are proud of their heritage. Finally, there is no evidence that adoptive parents form weaker emotional bonds with children who do not look like them as opposed to children who do look like them.

4. Self-Identity and White Privilege

While identity is admittedly a complex topic, social and cultural attitudes are learned, not inherited. Individuals are not born with a sense of self, but develop self-awareness through social interaction. Furthermore, an individual's self-concept is a combination of the aspects of one's self that the individual considers important—hence, self-concept is completely individualized.

Studies show that most transracial adoptees experience a positive sense of ethnic identity as well as a high comfort-level dealing with White people. Barbara Bennett Woodhouse summarizes this conflict:

> In an objective sense, it is impossible to say that a child has acquired a 'good' or 'bad' self-concept or acquired a 'healthy' or 'unhealthy' individual, racial, or cultural identity without also making tacit judgments regarding relative values of sameness and difference, individual and group, independence and interdependence.... White parents, by de-emphasizing race ... enable a Black child [to] cope better with racial attacks because the child may view the attacks less personally.

Barbara Bennett Woodhouse, *Are You My Mother?: Conceptualizing Children's Identity Rights in Transracial Adoptions*, 2 DUKE J. GENDER L. & POL'Y 107, 113–114 (1995).

Most White parents meet the identity needs of their adopted African American children. Many adoptive parents create a multi-racial environment for their children to offset potential identity problems and to provide same-race mentors. Furthermore, White adoptive parents are in a unique position to teach their Black children how to understand and operate within society as a whole.

5. Federal Legislation: MEPA and IEAA

Race-matching violates state and federal civil rights laws, as well as constitutional guarantees against racial discrimination. African American children are stigmatized as hard-to-place because same-race matching policies *make* them hard to place and jeopardize their opportunity for permanent placement.

The purpose of MEPA/IEAA is to facilitate adoption placements by making it illegal for government adoption workers to use race as a dominant factor to either delay or deny adoption placements. MEPA/IEAA does not promote numerical quotas, it does not prefer unqualified parents, and it does not foster reverse discrimination. On the contrary, MEPA/IEAA successfully breaks down the long-held belief that races and their families should remain separate and replaces it with the notion that adoption is about matching a parent to a child, not a parent or a child to a race.

IV. Studies of Transracial Adoptees and Their Families

Advocates of transracial adoption responded to the NABSW's criticisms by conducting numerous investigations on the effects of transracial adoption on African American children. Most of these studies consistently indicated that adolescent and younger African American children adjusted well in their adoptive homes.

The work of Lucille J. Grow and Deborah Shapiro annotates one of the earliest studies on the placement of African American children with White American parents. In 1974, Grow and Shapiro conducted a follow-up study of 125 adoptions of African American children by White parents. Children were classified as African American if one of the biological parents was African American.

The primary focus of this research was to assess the adjustment and wellbeing of pre-adolescent African American adoptees. Adjustment was calibrated by the child's responses to the California Test of Personality, which measures social and personal adjustment, and the Missouri Children's Behavior Check List Test. Researchers also evaluated interview data regarding the parents' assessment of the children's attitude toward race.

The study found that 77% of the children had adjusted successfully and that this percentage was similar to reports from previous studies. Grow and Shapiro also compared the responses of African American children adoptees with those of adopted White children and found that the scores from these two groups matched very closely. Grow and Shapiro concluded that the children were adjusting to their adoptive homes successfully.

In 1981, Arnold R. Silverman and William Feigelman reported their findings on the psychological adjustment of transracially adopted children. Their sample consisted of fifty-six White families who adopted African American children, and ninety-seven White families who adopted White American children. Each parent or couple was asked to make a judgment about their child's overall adjustment and the frequency of their child's emotional and growth problems.

The findings showed a positive correlation between age at adoption and maladjustment. Silverman and Feigelman interpreted this result as indicating that a child's age at adoption, not the transracial adoption itself, had the most significant impact on the child's development. Both researchers continue to support the position that transracial adoption is a viable option.

In 1983, Ruth G. McRoy and Louis A. Zurcher conducted the first study of transracial adoptees using a comparison group of interracial adoptees. They were also the first to examine the experiences of African American children from both the adoptive parents' and the adoptees' perspective. The sample consisted of sixty families, thirty White and thirty African American. Slightly more than half of the children available for adoption had two biological African American parents. Most of these children were placed with African American adoptive parents. Nearly all of the children with only one biological African American parent were placed with White parents. Face-to-face interviews were conducted with both the adoptive parents, and the children were evaluated on the Tennessee Self-Concept Scale. The results indicated that "transracial and intra-racial adoptive parents enjoyed their adopted children and considered their decision to adopt a good one."

The researchers also noted that the families were different in several aspects. The transracial adoptive parents were less likely than intra-racial adoptive parents to deliberately instruct their adoptees about African American heritage and pride. The transracial parents primarily emphasized that "all humans are alike." The intra-racial parents accentuated the positive qualities of being African American. The intra-racial adolescent adoptees tended to discuss racist experiences more openly and frequently with their parents than did the transracial adoptees. Nevertheless, McRoy and Zurcher concluded that although White adoptive parents did not behaviorally respond to the racial and cultural needs of African American children, they should still be considered as a resource for permanent placement for African Americans.

In order to determine the effects of transracial adoption over time, several scholars conducted longitudinal investigations. In 1986, John Shireman and Penny Johnson published their findings from a longitudinal study of adopted African American children reared in single parent, transracial, and African American homes. The children were studied at four, eight, twelve, sixteen and twenty years of age. The Clark Doll Test, a measure in which children attribute various qualities to either a White or an African American doll, was administered to adoptees at age four and at age eight.

The test indicated that the racial preferences and awareness of transracially adopted children remained constant, while that of a child in an intra-racial family continued to evolve over time. Shireman and Johnson concluded that although the racial development of transracial adoptees was "of concern," most of the children appeared to "grow well" in their adoptive homes.

Over a period of twenty years, Rita James Simon and Howard Altstein followed a group of families that adopted African American children. Their research began in 1972 and the original sample consisted of 204 families who had adopted transracially. Of the 366 adoptees, 120 were African American. Using projective measures such as the Clark Doll Test, pictures, and other instruments, Simon and Altstein found that "African American children perceived themselves as African American as accurately as White American children perceive themselves as White American."

They also found that the parents tended to believe that race did not and would not be a major issue for their children. A large majority, 77%, of the White parents lived in predominately White neighborhoods, and 63% of the adoptees reported that most of their friends were White. Simon and Altstein concluded that African American children reared by White parents fared no worse than other children raised by parents of the same race.

In 1997, Karen S. Vroegh reported the fifth phase of her longitudinal study of transracial adoption outcomes. The sample consisted of fifty-two late adolescent African American adoptees. Thirty-four of the adoptees were from transracial families and the remaining eighteen were from intra-racial families. Each of the participants was interviewed by an interracial team of researchers and were given the Rosenberg Self-Esteem Scale.

Findings revealed that 90% of the participants sampled were "doing ... well in life." The researchers also noted that 60% of the transracial adoptees wanted to change their weight and temper. Vroegh concluded that transracial adoptees had "developed identities," where 90% of the intra-racial adoptees, and 88% of the transracial adoptees, labeled themselves as either African American or of "mixed" race.

An extensive review of studies on transracial adoption conducted by Leslie Day Hollingsworth published in 1997 indicated that most of the data regarding the experiences of transracial adoptees was gathered only from the adoptive parents. This particular research method provided very little insight into the child's own perception of their adoptive experience.

Further, in 1996, M.G. Willis reported that when transracial adoptees were interviewed, many of the appraisal and evaluation procedures used by the researchers had numerous methodological limitations. For example, the Clark Doll Test, a projective measure used in several of the longitudinal studies, has been severely criticized as being invalid if used to evaluate anything more than a child's preference for a doll in a contrived, forced-choice situation.

Additionally, Rudolf Alexander and Carla Curtis charged in 1996 that when the research population involved African American and White adoptees, the behaviors and experiences of White children were held as the standard. Further, if White children were not part of the study, African American adoption experiences were compared to White children both indirectly and by assumption. Seminal studies such as the work of Grow and Shapiro and Simon and Altstein are prime examples of this tendency. In each of these two studies, researchers found that African American adoptees evidenced psychological outcomes similar to those found in White children. Based on these findings, the investigators concluded that transracial adoption was a logical option for African American children.

In 1996, Robert J. Taylor and Michael C. Thornton argued that of the studies that reported "the successful adjustment" of transracial adoptees, researchers omitted or minimized other important outcomes in their analyses—such as the presence of racial identity and awareness issues among transracial adoptees, and the large number of transracial adoptive families who resided in predominately White neighborhoods. Further, Taylor and Thornton asserted that, in general, White parents did not think that race would be a major issue for their transracially adopted children in the future.

A study was conducted by Colleen Butler-Sweet. She interviewed 32 African American middle class adoptees who were between the age of 18 and 30 years old. The adoptees were divided into three groups: monoracial families, biracial families, and transracial families. The study showed similarities between these groups of adoptees. Namely, the importance of academics, and the normal stresses of middle class families. Besides the similarities, there were differences. For monoracial families, espousing middle class habits and going to college were ways to deflect racism, while for biracial families going to college was just a normative activity. Interviewees from monoracial families focused on connections with other middle class African Americans, whereas biracial and transracial tended to see African American culture as urban and poor. Participants from monoracial families had more anxiety about "acting White" than did other participants. In conclusion, this study illuminated the fact that there might be a class component to how transracial adoptees assimilate and adjust to their new families.

V. Strategies to Facilitate a Transracial Adoption

As the aforementioned studies show, there are many factors that contribute to how well a transracial adoptee adjusts to the new environment. Nevertheless, there are some strategies to facilitate a positive experience. One is to become invested in parenting. Another is to not tolerate ethnic slurs. Surrounding oneself with supportive friends and family is important. Celebrating all cultures is key. Talking explicitly about race and culture is helpful. Exposing a child to a variety of experiences is important to developing self-esteem. Finally, taking the child to places where he will be exposed to people of his own race is important. (Transracial and Transcultural Adoption, www.childwelfare.gov/pubs/f_trans.cfm)

Checkpoints

- Race matching is placing an adoptee with adoptive parents of the same race. Transracial adoption is placing an adoptee with adoptive parents of a different race.

- Hospitals and churches performed the early foster-care placements; potential adoptive parents could return a child who was not the right fit.

- Cultural genocide began with Native American children being taken and placed into White families. Leaving very few children left to carry on traditions and family lines, the tribes were virtually decimated.

- MEPA was created to prohibit delay or discrimination due to race in child placement.

- IEAA was created to correct the loophole in MEPA: to end the practice of race matching, and to prohibit any reference to race in adoption proceedings. States that were found to be in violation of this would lose necessary funding.

- African American children outnumber White children in foster care. Over 70% of adoptive parents in the United States are White.

- Racial identity is an important factor in transracial adoptions. Studies show that children in transracial adoptions still maintain a self-identity of their own race, not their adoptive parent(s).

- There is no evidence showing transracial adoptions harm adoptees. In fact, studies show children left in foster care without placement are more detrimentally affected.

Chapter 7

Same Sex Adoption

Roadmap
- The history of same sex adoption in the United States
- The process same sex couples must go through for adoption
- Case law surrounding same sex adoptions and how it challenged prior precedent
- The pros and cons of same sex adoptions

I. History of Same Sex Adoption

Same sex adoption in the United States first emerged as a legal issue during the 1970s. Lesbians and gay males sought what any heterosexual individual or couple could have—a right to raise a family. However, homosexuals were consistently denied this right throughout the 1970s and 1980s. Conservative morals often played a role in the judicial opinions that described homosexuals as unfit to raise a child.

It was not until the 1990s that some states began to recognize that homosexuals should be given the right to adopt. The right to adopt usually hinges on the homosexual's relationship status. Most states permit a single homosexual to adopt. However, the majority of those states do not allow homosexual couples to adopt for fear of what would happen to that child raised in such a couple's household. Eight states continue to put up obstacles for homosexuals to adopt. These states are Utah, Nebraska, Wisconsin, Michigan, Ohio, Kentucky, Mississippi, and North Carolina (Parenting Law: Second Parent Adoption: http://hrc-assets.s3-website-us-east-1.amazonaws.com//files/assets/resources/second_parent_adoption_6-10-2014.pdf and Parenting Laws: Joint Adoption, http://hrc-assets.s3-website-us-east-1.amazonaws.com//files/assets/resources/joint_adoption_6-10-2014.pdf). Florida expressly bans all homosexuals from adopting (Fla. Stat. 63.042(3)). (For a discussion of Florida's stance on lesbi-gay adoption, see Part IX, *Florida—An Historically Anti-Gay Adoption State: A Case Study*, infra.) Though there are states that put up obstacles, twenty-two states allow second parent adoption as well as joint adoption. These states are California, Colorado, Connecticut, Delaware, District of Columbia, Hawaii, Illinois, Indiana, Iowa, Maine, Maryland, Massachusetts, Minnesota, Nevada, New Hampshire, New Jersey, New Mexico, New York, Oregon, Pennsylvania, Rhode Island, Vermont, and Washington. Arkansas allows joint adoption, and Idaho as well as Montana allow second parent adoption (Parenting Law: Second Parent Adoption, http://hrc-assets.s3-website-us-east-1.amazonaws.com //files/assets/resources/second_parent_adoption_6-10-2014.pdf and Parenting Laws: Joint Adoption, http://hrc-assets.s3-website-us-east-1.amazonaws.com// files/assets/resources/joint_adoption_6-10-2014.pdf).

II. Methods of Adoption for Same Sex Couples

As alluded to, there are different methods to adopt. The first involves states that allow homosexuals to marry or enter into civil unions. In those states, no formal proceeding is necessary for homosexuals to adopt the partner's child. If a child from such a marriage or civil union is not the biological child of one of the parents, the child is automatically treated as their child. The second method allows for homosexuals to adopt through a court proceeding. The third method allows same sex second parent adoptions.

Second parent adoption is comparable to that of a stepparent adoption. Prior to states allowing second parent adoptions, the only way for a same sex partner to adopt their partner's biological child was for the biological parent to terminate his or her parental rights. A second parent adoption refers to an adoption where the biological parent consents to his or her partner adopting the biological child. In such an adoption, the biological parent does not have to terminate their parental rights prior to the adoption and after the proceeding, both have equal parenting rights.

One of the first cases in the United States to recognize such an adoption was *Adoption of Tammy*, 416 Mass. 205 (1993), which was ultimately decided by the Massachusetts Supreme Judicial Court. In that case, a lesbian couple who had been together for ten years filed a joint petition to adopt Tammy, one of the women's biological daughter. The Court held that there was no law in Massachusetts that prohibited an unmarried couple living together from jointly petitioning to adopt a child. It went on to state that the adoption would be in the child's best interests because it would recognize the legal rights and responsibilities of the partner in case the couple separates or the biological mother dies. Furthermore, in deciding this case, the Court created an exception to the provision that called for the natural mother's rights to be terminated. The Court stated that it was not the legislature's intent to terminate the natural parent's legal relationship to the child "when the natural parent is a party to the adoption petition" and that provision only applied when a child is adopted by people who are not the natural parents. Following *Tammy*, other states with similar statutes have allowed second parent adoptions.

However, not all states have embraced second parent adoptions. Those states take a strict and literal reading of statutes that require a parent to terminate its rights in order for the child to be adopted by another. For example, in Nebraska, a biological mother and her partner jointly filed a petition to adopt the mother's child (*In re Adoption of Luke*, 263 Neb. 365, 366 (Neb. 2002)). The Court held that because the biological mother did not relinquish her parental rights when signing the petition, her partner could not adopt the child. The Court opined that the only exception to that provision was for a stepparent (rather than a second parent) adoption, which was also provided for in a statute.

III. The Court's Test for the Adoption of a Child — Best Interests of the Child

Courts use a "best interests of the child" standard to determine whether or not to grant an adoption. The majority of courts see homosexuality as a factor to be considered in determining the child's best interests and the courts have broad discretion as to how much weight to give that factor. There are three different versions of the best interests of the child standard when it comes to determining the significance of homosexuality: (a) the per se rule; (b) the middle ground approach; and (c) the nexus test.

The per se rule is a rare minority view. According to this test, there is an irrebuttable and irrefutable presumption that homosexuals are unfit parents. As a result, a homosexual's petition for adoption may be denied solely on the basis of that person's sexual orientation.

The middle ground approach allows the court to presume that having a homosexual parent adversely affects a child in some way. Courts using this approach are required to consider other factors besides the parent's sexuality in determining the best interests of the child. However, if the court finds that the child may be harmed due to the social stigma attached to the prospective parent's homosexuality, the parent may be found to be unfit. As such, there is a rather low threshold for finding a gay or lesbian person unfit to be a parent under this approach.

Finally, on the opposite end of the spectrum, the nexus test demands documented proof that a child is or would be adversely affected because of the parent's homosexuality. Under this test, the parent's sexual orientation is just one of many factors in deciding the best interests of the child and parental fitness.

IV. Arguments against Same Sex Adoption

Homosexual households are often viewed as improper and inappropriate. For example, in 1985, two children who lived with their homosexual foster parents in Massachusetts were removed because it was not deemed a proper, traditional household. These children were placed into a proper family—one that consisted of a single mom and her adult son who had a prior record of mental illness and sexual molestation.

There are four arguments regularly relied upon for denying an adoption petition brought by a single lesbi-gay individual or a lesbi-gay couple. First, children of homosexual parents will be unduly harassed—for instance, if the public sees the risk of HIV as a "gay man's disease." Second, raising a child in a lesbi-gay household will increase the likelihood that the child will accept the gay lifestyle for him or herself. Third, a child raised in a gay household will have lower morals than what is generally accepted by society—such a child is more prone to be promiscuous and display domestic violence. Fourth, children in gay households are more likely to be molested because homosexuals are prone to be pedophiles and/or have a sexual illness.

V. Arguments Supporting Same Sex Adoption

What was once deemed a proper, traditional household—namely, the nuclear family—is no longer the overwhelming stance. There are many types of families in today's society. Social views have changed and homosexuality is more accepted today than it ever was. As the Supreme Court of Vermont stated, "when social mores change, governing statutes must be interpreted to allow for those changes in a manner that does not frustrate the purposes behind their enactment. To deny the children of same-sex partners, as a class, the security of a legally recognized relationship with their second parent serves no legitimate state interest" (*Adoptions of B.L.V.B and E.L.V.B.*, 160 Vt. 368 (Vt. 1993)). As society evolves, so too, must its laws.

It is a fundamental right to have and raise children (*Lassiter v. Dep't of Soc. Servs. of Durham County, N.C.*, 452 U.S. 18, 38 (1981)). As such, supporters of same sex adoption argue that homosexuals cannot be denied this right.

Same sex adoption is supported by the Equal Protection Clause. Supporters of same sex adoption argue that a heightened standard must be applied when it comes to state statutes that prohibit homosexuals from adopting because it is not in the child's best interests. The standard should be heightened because homosexuals are a "suspect class." Since homosexuals are being excluded from adopting specifically because of their classification as homosexuals, a heightened scrutiny must be used. Even if a heightened standard is not used, any ban on same sex adoption fails to meet the rational basis test (*Fla. Dept. of Children and Families v. Adoption of X.X.G.*, 45 So.3d 79 (Fla. 3d DCA 2010)).

Supporters of same sex adoption argue that it is implicit in the Due Process Clause of the Constitution. Gays and lesbians need to be afforded the freedom to associate with whomever they please and form and preserve those relationships without undue interference by the state.

If the primary concern is for the child's best interests, it should not matter whether that child is raised in heterosexual home or not if that home is the best option for the child to have permanency. Homosexuals should not have to change or hide their sexual identity in order to adopt a child if they are loving parents that can provide for these children.

VI. The Use of the Full Faith and Credit Clause in Same Sex Adoption

The use of The Full Faith and Credit Clause in same sex adoption mirrors the societal changes occurring with same sex adoption, i.e., a transition to a more positive view of same sex couples and their ability to adopt. The Full Faith and Credit Clause (FFCC) of the Constitution (U.S. Const. Art. 4 §1) provides that judicial proceedings, acts, and records of one state shall be upheld in every other state. However, there is a public policy exemption to the FFCC that permits states to not recognize another state's judicial decisions if it violates that state's internal policies. Historically, the FFCC has been applied by states to reject acts of polygamy, incest, and miscegenation.

States have used the FFCC as a vehicle to not recognize out of state same sex adoptions. For further support of this position, states implement the Defense of Marriage Act of 1996 (DOMA), which holds that states are not required to recognize rights from same sex marriages or relationships. DOMA has been interpreted to mean that states are not required to recognize same sex adoptions.

Some states went so far as to enact statutes to prohibit the state from recognizing out of state same sex adoptions. One such state to prohibit this type of adoption was Oklahoma (Okla. Stat. § 7502-1.4(A)). This statute was later deemed unconstitutional (*Finstuen v. Crutcher*, 496 F.3d 1139 (10th Cir. 2007)).

Finstuen held that adoptions created in one state must be recognized nationwide under the FFCC. In that case, three homosexual couples and their adopted children challenged the Oklahoma statute. One out of state couple adopted an Oklahoma child. The homosexual couple requested that the state issue a new birth certificate with both of their names on it as the new parents. The couple's request was denied. The second lesbian couple adopted their child in California, but the family resided in Oklahoma. Oklahoma refused to issue a birth certificate with both mothers name on it. The third couple was permitted a second parent adoption in New Jersey. They subsequently moved to Oklahoma. The Court held that there is not public policy exception with respect to final judgments, and final adoption orders and decrees are judgments that must be recognized by all states under the FFCC.

VII. The Children of Gay/Lesbian Adoptive Parents

A. The Studies

Many studies have been conducted which compare children of homosexuals to children of heterosexuals. Those studies have found that children of homosexuals are no more likely to be homosexual than their counterparts. In one study, 92% of children of lesbians identified themselves as heterosexual and 90% of adult men who had gay fathers identified themselves as heterosexual. Additionally, similar studies have shown that the mental health, development, and/or general psychological stability of a child who was raised in a homosexual household is no different than a child raised in a heterosexual household.

B. Inheritance Issues

In *Tammy*, the Court delved into the reasons why a second parent adoption is permitted, one of which concerned inheritance issues. By allowing Tammy to be adopted by her biological mother's lesbian partner, Tammy gained the right to inherit from the partner's trusts and the rest of her family. Not only was she entitled to inherit from the partner and her family, but Tammy was also entitled to receive support, health insurance, and social security benefits from the partner.

VIII. Recognition of Same Sex Marriage

The current national jurisprudence reflects a trend towards supporting same sex marriage, which impinges upon same sex couples' ability to adopt. First is an examination of the national jurisprudence on same sex marriage and second, a discussion on how these same arguments are reflected in Florida's jurisprudence.

In *U.S. v. Windsor*, the Supreme Court of the United States declared DOMA's definition of marriage as between a man and a woman unconstitutional (*U.S. v. Windsor*, 133 S.Ct. 2675 (2013)). A citizen who was the survivor of a same sex partnership wanted to claim deductions on the federal estate tax when her partner died. The court affirmed the District Court of Appeals judgment in favor of the taxpayer saying that DOMA singled out a class of persons for special treatment, which was against the liberty interest protected by the Fifth Amendment.

The *Windsor* decision was foreshadowed by a First Circuit decision made in 2012 (*Massachusetts v. U.S. Dept. of Health and Human Services*, 682 F.3d 1 (2012)). This court heard the appeals of a group of cases questioning the validity of DOMA as applied to same sex couples in Massachusetts. Using a level of scrutiny between that of a rational basis and that of strict scrutiny, the court found that same sex couples were unduly penalized by DOMA and was therefore against the Equal Protection Clause. On Federalism grounds, the court found no precedence for a sweeping definition of marriage and felt that states were unduly burdened by having to accept the federal definition. The court also found a lack of evidence for the rationales for DOMA, such as that it would save money as well as that it would promote heterosexual marriage.

The Fourth Circuit court decision in *Bostic v. Schaefer* mirrored the decisions in *Windsor* and *Massachusetts* (*Bostic v. Schaefer*, 760 F.3d 352 (2014)). Using strict scrutiny, the court found Virginia statutes and constitutional provisions banning same sex marriages, as well as the recognition of same sex marriages performed elsewhere, violated the Due Process and Equal Protection Clauses of the Fourteenth Amendment. Virginia gave five arguments as to why same sex marriage should be prohibited, which were all found faulty by the court. *Id.* at 21. The court dismissed the federalism argument saying the community's will shouldn't be used as an excuse to deprive a group of a fundamental right. Tradition was dismissed because something that has been a certain way for a long time should not be immune to change. The argument for safeguarding marriage was challenged because marriage is not only about procreation. In addition, there is no reason to believe that same sex marriage will destabilize marriage more than no-fault divorce in traditional marriages. Prohibiting same sex marriage does not reduce out-of-wedlock births. Finally, children need stability to thrive and this is not necessarily guaranteed by the parents' sexual orientation.

There was a similar case in the Seventh Circuit (*Baskin v. Bogan*, 766 F.3d 648 (2014)). In *Baskin*, same sex couples challenged statutes and constitutional amendments in Indiana and Wisconsin banning same sex marriage. The court found Indiana's statute violated equal protection because it discriminates against a class of people and does not necessarily bring about the desired state interest of compelling fathers to parent unanticipated children. In addition, the court debunked Wisconsin's four arguments, which were the traditional definition of marriage; unforeseeable consequences of allowing same sex marriage; decisions should be left to the democratic process; and same sex marriages make marriage fragile. *Id.* at 666.

The Ninth Circuit has also ruled statutes and constitutional amendments banning same sex marriages as well as the non-recognition of same sex marriages performed elsewhere as unconstitutional (*Latta v. Otter*, 2014 WL 4977682 (2014)). In *Latta*, the defendants raise two main arguments: validating same sex marriages will lessen the attractiveness of heterosexual marriage, and that children need the complementarity of having a mother and a father. The court did not find any evidence supporting these contentions.

The Tenth Circuit has also ruled on same sex marriage. In *Kitchen v. Herbert*, the court ruled Utah statutes and a constitutional amendment that prohibited same sex marriage (and refused to recognize same sex marriages performed elsewhere) as unconstitutional because they denied this group their fundamental liberty right to marry (*Kitchen v. Herbert*, 755 F.3d 1193 (2014)). The court found that the four interests stated by the defendants were not furthered by the ban. These interests were the link between marriage and procreation; instability in heterosexual marriages; children need two different gender-styled parents; and the creation of religious strife. This circuit reiterated its ruling on same sex marriage in an additional case (*Bishop v. Barton*, 760 F.3d 1070 (2014)). In *Bishop*, the court said that the ban on same sex marriage burdens the fundamental right to marry, and that the state's interest in marriage is linked to procreation as well as being raised by their biological parents.

The lone Circuit to sustain the definition of marriage as between a man and a woman is a Sixth Circuit decision in 2014 (*DeBoer v. Snyder*, 772 F.3d 388 (2014)). In *DeBoer*, the Court overturned the District courts' decisions ruling statutory and constitutional definitions of marriage as between a man and a woman and the refusal to recognize out-of-state same sex marriages as unconstitutional. Based on originalism, up until 2003, all states defined marriage as between a man and a woman, so it must be allowed by the Fourteenth Amendment. It is not irrational for a state to provide incentives for a man and a woman to stay together to rear a child. The Supreme Court of the United States has rarely struck down a law based on animus. The right to marry can be fundamentally important without being a fundamental right. There is no precedent for heightened scrutiny based on sexual orientation. Decisions should be based on society's values, not judges', and the vast majority of states still define marriage as between a man and a woman.

As of January, 2015, 36 states had declared same sex marriage a constitutional right. In addition, this year presented a pivotal year for the United States Supreme Court. USSC agreed to decide on the issue of same sex marriage with respect to the states Kentucky, Ohio, Tennessee, and Michigan. These states are recent states that have held on to the same sex marriage ban, and ban marriages that were legally performed out-of-state. The cases were presented in April 2015, and an opinion was delivered in June 2015.

One of the cases involved a gay couple who were legally married in Maryland and moved to Ohio (*Obergefell v. Wymyslo*, 962 F.Supp. 2d 968 (S.D. Ohio 2013)). When one of the couple passed away, the state refused to honor their marriage certificate to the funeral home; the state did not recognize gay marriage or legal gay marriages performed out-of-state. *Id.* at 972. The District Court held the marriage recognition ban in Ohio is a violation of Due Process and the Equal Protection Clause. *Id.* at 968. Ohio's Supreme Court reversed this decision.

Also, valid same sex marriage licenses from other states had not been honored in Kentucky (*Bourke v. Beshear*, 996 F.Supp. 2d 542 (W.D. Kentucky 2014)). The Supreme Court of the United States agreed to decide this case, even though the appeal was earlier denied (*Bourke v. United States*, 133 S.Ct. 1794 (2013)). The Supreme Court had been silent on the issue of gay marriage, allowing individual states to decide first. With 36 states allowing gay marriage, the Court finally agreed to render a decision.

On June 26, 2015, the U.S. Supreme Court decided *Obergefell v. Hodges*, 576 U.S. ___ (2015). The 5–4 ruling held that there is a Constitutional right to same sex marriage. As a result, all states are required to issue marriage licenses to same sex couples and recognize as valid same sex marriages performed in other states.

The full effect of *Obergefell* on same sex adoption is yet to be decided.

IX. Florida—A Historically Anti-Gay Adoption State: A Case Study

Florida's goal for child adoption is to protect the child's well-being (Fla. Stat. § 63.022(2)–(3) (2002)). The best interest of the child standard governs all adoption proceedings and adoption placements. Specifically, to adopt a child, applicants must be "able to meet the physical, emotional, social, educational, and financial needs of a child" (Fla. Admin. Code Ann. r. 65C-16.005(2) (2005)). The court and state agencies determine an applicant's eligibility by evaluating factors such as: the child's ability to consent to the adoption; the applicant's child-rearing experience; the applicant's marital status; the applicant's residency status or future plans; the applicant's income, employment status and health, housing, and the neighborhood; whether the applicant has other children; and the applicant's moral character.

A. The Root of Florida's Discriminatory Intent

Florida's discriminatory treatment of lesbi-gay individuals and couples within the foster care and adoption system began in 1977 when Florida became the first state to statutorily prohibit lesbians and gays from adopting children.

The law specifies that "no person eligible to adopt under this statute may adopt if that person is a homosexual" (Fla. Stat. § 63.042(3) (2011)). Before passing the bill, the legislature did not order or consult any studies concerning the effects, if any, on children raised by lesbi-gay parents. Additionally, no evidence demonstrated that adoption by lesbian and gay individuals causes any problems.

Senator Don Chamberlin was the only state senator to speak out against the bill. He argued that the purpose of the bill was to discriminate against gays and lesbians. Chamberlin urged lawmakers to focus on the best interest of children rather than harm to homosexuals, stating that, "[t]he undeniable main concern of any adoption is the welfare of the child—all other concerns should yield to that" (Fla. Sen., Journal of the Fla. Senate, Reg. Sess. 370–371 (1977)). No one challenged Chamberlin's proposition that the bill's sole purpose was to discriminate against gays and lesbians. Relying on the bill sponsors, Democratic Senator Curtis Peterson of Lakeland, Florida, rhetoric and the support from Anita Bryant's "Save Our Children" Campaign, the legislature passed the statute with hardly any fact-finding or debate.

B. The Legal Challenges to Florida's Ban on Lesbi-Gay Adoption

1. Seebol v. Farie, *16 Fla. L. Weekly C52 (Fla. 16th Jud. Cir. Ct. 1991).*

In 1990, *Seebol v. Farie* was the first challenge to Florida's ban on lesbi-gay adoption. In this case, the Department of Health and Rehabilitation Services (HRS) denied plaintiff Edward Seebol's application to adopt a special-needs child because of Seebol's sexual orientation. Seebol was a long-time Key West resident who was actively involved in community projects, such as volunteering for Florida's guardian ad litem program and educating the public about AIDS. The Sixteenth Judicial Circuit for Monroe County concluded that the statute banning lesbi-gay adoption violated federal and state constitutional rights to privacy, equal protection, and due process of the law. The court also noted a lack of evidence showing that homosexual orientation in parents adversely affects children.

2. State v. Cox, *627 So. 2d 1210 (S. D. Fla. 1993).*

In 1993, *State v. Cox* presented the second challenge to Florida's adoption statute. James Cox and his partner Rodney Jackman signed up for an HRS pre-adoption parenting class in anticipation of adopting a child, and both disclosed their homosexual orientation. HRS refused to allow them to take the class and informed the couple that it would reject their adoption applications due to their sexual orientation. Cox and Jackman challenged the statute as a violation of their constitutional rights to privacy, equal protection, and substantive due process.

Relying on the reasoning in *Seebol v. Farie*, the trial court found the gay adoption ban unconstitutional. However, Florida's Second District Court of Appeal reversed, concluding that the legislature, not the courts, should decide whether lesbians and gays can adopt children. Florida's Supreme Court affirmed the Second District Court of Appeal's decision in 1995 (*Cox v. Florida Dept. of Health & Rehab. Serv.*, 656 So. 2d 902 (Fla. 1995)).

3. Matthews v. Weinberg, *645 So. 2d 487 (1994).*

Matthews v. Weinberg challenged HRS's policy banning "unmarried couples" from being foster parents and the policy prohibiting lesbians and gays from becoming licensed foster parents. Plaintiff Bonnie Lynn Matthews counseled emotionally disturbed children in foster care under HRS's supervision. She became a licensed foster parent specifically to care for a six-year-old patient whose then-foster mother wanted him removed from her home. The six-year-old boy lived with Matthews for over two months before HRS removed him after learning of Matthews's homosexuality.

The court held that the rules applied in this case were unofficial and thus invalid. Lesbi-gay individuals and couples were thereafter allowed to become foster parents.

4. Lofton v. Kearney, *157 F. Supp. 2d 1372 (S.D. Fla.2001).*

In *Lofton v. Kearney*, a group of plaintiffs challenged the adoption statute's ban on lesbi-gay adoption. The primary plaintiff, Steven Lofton, challenged the denial of his application to adopt his foster son, whom he cared for since infancy.

The state argued that the ban serves two functions: (1) to reflect the state's moral disapproval of a lesbi-gay lifestyle; and (2) to reflect the state's belief that it is in a child's best interest to reside in a two-parent marital home. The plaintiffs, on the other hand, argued that the law's true purpose was to discriminate against gays and lesbians. The U.S. District Court for the Southern District of Florida concluded that the true purpose behind the statute is immaterial. The court stated that, "[i]t is enough for the legislation to be supported by plausible or hypothesized reasons ... Whether this reasoning in fact underlay the legislative decision is irrelevant" (*Lofton*, 157 F. Supp. at 1383)).

Accordingly, the court upheld the statute and rejected the argument that the statute violates the Equal Protection clause. The U.S. Court of Appeals for the Eleventh Circuit affirmed, finding that the U.S. Constitution does not forbid Florida's policy judgment that it is not in a child's best interest for lesbians or gays to adopt them (*Lofton v. Kearney*, 358 F.3d 804, 827 (11th Cir. 2004)).

5. In re Adoption of John Doe, Minor, *2008 WL 4212559 (Fla. Cir. Ct. Aug. 29, 2008).*

At least one Florida Circuit Court Judge has confronted Florida's Ban of lesbi-gay adoption. On August 29, 2008, in *In re Adoption of John Doe, Minor*, Judge David J. Audlin held:

> [t]he Court concludes that as (a) an unconstitutional special law pertaining to the adoption of persons, (b) an unconstitutional bill of attainder, and (c) an unconstitutional violation of the separation of powers, section 63.042(3), in its categorical exclusion of all gays and lesbians from demonstrating their fitness to adopt, does not furnish

a legal basis for denying the relief sought by this petition. Accordingly, the relief sought by this Petitioner shall be and is GRANTED. (citations deleted).

At five years old, the minor male child came to petitioner and his partner's home in 2001 as a foster child. Petitioner and his partner were Florida-licensed foster parents at that time and had completed the state-mandated MAPP training. In 2007, the court held a hearing to determine whether petitioner and his partner should be granted permanent guardianship of the minor until he reaches eighteen years of age. In providing a definition of guardianship, Judge Audlin opined that:

> the Guardians, [Petitioner] and [his partner], or either of them acting individually, have all of the rights and duties of parents of the [minor], until he reaches the age of majority, including but not limited to, the right and duty to protect, train, and discipline the child and to provide the child with food, shelter, and education, and medical, dental, psychiatric and psychological care....

At the hearing on this petition for adoption, a psychologist, "Dr. F," qualified as an expert and testified that:

> [the minor] is very bonded to [Petitioner] and [his partner] and that if [the minor] is removed from the care of [Petitioner] and [his partner], removal could cause [the minor] to suffer attachment disorder and serious harm.... Petitioner is 52 years old, that his partner is 41 years old and that they have a very caring 15 year relationship and show obvious mutual respect for each other. [Petitioner's partner] is in agreement with [Petitioner's] decision to adopt.

The court, in its final Judgment, expressly agreed with and accepted this expert testimony.

The home study for adoption was entered into evidence and its author testified. The Opinion in *Doe* included the following:

> The home study's penultimate paragraph concludes by stating that '[I] would highly recommend the applicant, [Petitioner], for the adoption of one child, [the minor.]' The final paragraph states: 'However, this home study is not approvable due to [Petitioner]'s open disclosure of his sexual orientation, and therefore the adoption is disallowable by law.' (citation omitted).

At the hearing, Ms. D. testified that it is the duty of a social worker performing adoptive home studies to determine an applicant's eligibility to adopt under Florida law, which includes routinely inquiring of individuals whose heterosexuality is uncertain whether they are homosexual. (citation omitted).

The Petitioner entered into evidence abundant documentation regarding the legislative history of SB 354 (1977).

Judge Audlin heard extensive scientific-related testimony from Dr. David Brodzinski, Professor Emeritus of Developmental and Clinical Psychology at Rutgers University. The opinion states that Dr. Brodzinski has done extensive clinical work with adoptive parents who are gay or lesbian and that he was qualified as an expert to testify at the hearing. Judge Audlin found Dr. Brodzinski's testimony to be cogent, well-reasoned and persuasive.

Based on that testimony, the court found that:

> the depiction of existing research set forth in the 2004 Lofton panel opinion (358 F. 3d at 824–26) is, at minimum, not presently accurate. In view of Dr. Brodzinski's testimony that the categorical ban is irrational and scientifically inexplicable, the Court is unable to discern any coherent explanation for its enforcement in 2008, other than a willingness to passively leave intact the ban against this politically-disfavored group.

Finally, Judge Audlin determined that Florida's ban of lesbi-gay adoption was unconstitutional under the Florida State Constitution based on two rationales. First, as a "special law" rather than a "general law," the statute may not relate to certain persons as a class because such state action is limited to general laws. Second, section 63.042(3) is a Bill of Attainder, which is expressly prohibited under Section 10, Article I of the Florida Constitution.

As a circuit court opinion, *Doe* may have limited immediate application only in the 16th Circuit (Monroe County). With its breadth of justification and depth of analysis and supporting documentation, however, Doe signifies the onset of proper judicial activism in Florida.

6. In Re: Matter of the Adoption of X.X.G. and N.R.G., *45 So. 3d 79 (Fla. 3d DCA 2010).*

On December 11, 2004, two half-brothers, "John," born June 15, 2000, and "James," born August 2, 2004, were placed together with the petitioner, Martin Gill, who was a licensed foster caregiver. The children became available for adoption in July of 2006—after nearly two years in the petitioner's care. At the time of 2008 hearing, the two boys had been in foster care with the petitioner for four years. Thus, the boys, who had arrived at ages four years and four months at the time of "temporary" placement, were now eight and four years old in November of 2008.

Petitioner was in a committed relationship with his life partner, "John Roe." John Roe's biological son, who was 12 years old in 2008, also lived in the Doe-Roe household. Although these men co-parent John and James in their home, a strategic legal decision was made to have only one party seek adoption due to the lesbi-gay adoption ban.

The state and petitioner presented extensive expert testimony at the hearing (which is detailed in the Opinion). In addition, the Opinion outlines 56 stipulated facts, including "54. But for Section 64.042(3), Fla. Stats., DCF would have approved petitioner's application to adopt John and James."

As further proof of the trial court level "movement" to repeal Florida's 30-plus year ban of lesbi-gay adoption, Cindy Lederman, a Miami-Dade circuit court judge, ruled to allow an openly gay man in a committed homosexual relationship to adopt two minor foster children in his care. Specifically, Judge Lederman held that:

> Fla. Stat. § 63.042(3) violates the Petitioner's and the Children's equal protection rights guaranteed by Article I, § 2 of the Florida Constitution without satisfying a rational basis. Moreover, the statutory exclusion defeats a child's right to permanency as provided by federal and state law pursuant to [ASFA] of 1997.

The state appealed the decision to the Third District Court of Appeal in Miami, but allowed the children to remain in the petitioner's home and care until the appeals process was complete.

Under the same rational basis test used in *Lofton*, the appellate court found that because the state allows homosexuals to be foster parents or guardians of children, there is no rational basis to expressly prohibit them from adopting children. Further, the court cited that the statute specifically allows children to be adopted by an unmarried adult, which contradicts the state's policy argument that children have better role models in a married household. The court relied on expert testimony that showed children would not be more susceptible to domestic violence if placed in a gay household and homosexuals were not more susceptible to break up than an average heterosexual couple.

The state decided not to appeal the case to the Florida Supreme Court. The then-Governor Charlie Crist stated that the statutory ban on lesbi-gay adoption would no longer be enforced. Although the ban is lifted in practice, the 2011 issue of the Florida State Statutes still contain the anti-gay adoption language (Fla. Stat. 63.042(3) (2011)).

7. D.M.T. v. T.M.H., *129 So. 3d 320 (Fla. 2013).*

Current trends in same sex couples wanting to become parents involves technology. In *D.M.T v. T.M.H*, the parties were a lesbian couple who jointly decided to become parents. T.M.H. was the egg donor and D.M.T. carried the child. After the relationship ended, D.M.T. left with the child and T.M.H. wanted to claim her parental rights. The court concluded that Florida § 742.14 requiring donors to relinquish their parental rights was unconstitutional for several reasons. It denied people their constitutional right to parent. In addition, there is no rational basis for the statute. The court remanded the case to the trial court to determine time-sharing and child support.

8. A.A.B. v. B.O.C., *112 So. 3d 761 (Fla. App. 2 Dist. 2013).*

As with the previous case, this case deals with reproductive technology. In *A.A.B. v. B.O.C.*, there was a lesbian couple that were parenting a child. The child was conceived using the egg of A.A.B. and the sperm of B.O.C., the brother of A.A.B.'s partner, S.C..After three years, the relationship deteriorated with A.A.B. not wanting S.C. to have contact with the child. B.O.C. subsequently tried to establish paternity. The Court found that B.O.C. was a sperm donor that had relinquished his parental rights under FL § 742.14.

C. Constitutional Implications Support Lifting the Ban on Lesbi-Gay Adoption

1. Due Process and Privacy Rights

Florida's adoption law violates the substantive due-process clause because it seeks to enforce a particular view concerning the immorality of a lesbi-gay lifestyle on the state's citizens. The Supreme Court decision in *Lawrence v. Texas*, 539 U.S. 558 (2003), which recognized a fundamental right to private sexual intimacy, demonstrates the due-process implications against upholding this ban. Specifically, Florida favors the ban as a reflection of the state's moral disapproval of a lesbi-gay lifestyle. However, a state's traditional view of a particular practice as immoral is not a sufficient reason for upholding a law that prohibits that practice.

In *Lawrence*, the U.S. Supreme Court noted the traditional condemnation of the lesbi-gay lifestyle, but also mentioned the recognized constitutional protections for adults to make decisions in their private lives concerning sex. Accordingly, states should not use its power to enforce its views of the immorality of a lesbi-gay lifestyle on its residents.

Florida admits that the ban is meant to express its belief that a lesbi-gay lifestyle is immoral. The state justifies the ban by pointing out that the government may legitimately regulate public morality. However, *Lawrence* establishes that private sexual intimacy is not an area into which the government may intrude. In *Lawrence*, the Court reiterated that any law burdening a fundamental right must have a compelling governmental interest that is narrowly tailored to further that interest. In this instance, Florida's ban on lesbi-gay adoption burdens a fundamental right because gay individuals who wish to adopt children must either stop engaging in "current, voluntary gay activity" or not adopt a child. As shown in *Lawrence*, Florida's belief that a lesbi-gay lifestyle is immoral is an insufficient basis for determining the eligibility of potential adoptive parents.

a. Compelling Governmental Interest

ASFA provides and mandates a compelling state interest to place the children currently in the child welfare system into permanent homes in a timely manner.

b. Not Narrowly Tailored

Rationalizing its lesbi-gay adoption ban, Florida prefers a two-parent marital home because such homes are in the best interest of children. However, no evidence supports that placing children in a marital home with two parents is always in a child's best interest. Further, since the ban burdens gay applicants' right to private sexual intimacy, the state must show that the method by which it seeks to ensure that children are placed with a married mother and father is narrowly tailored to achieve its goals.

This law is not narrowly tailored because it does not further the state's goal of finding two-parent homes. Most notably, the adoption statute does not express a preference for married adoptive parents. Instead, it expressly allows "unmarried [adults]" to adopt. Furthermore, DCF administrative regulations, which are tied to Florida's adoption statutes, do not prefer married candidates over single candidates for adoption. The state's willingness to actively recruit single adoptive parents contradicts the purported justification of the ban based on the state's desire to place children in two-parent marital homes.

Even if the state preferred married couples over single persons when drafting the statute, prohibiting gay people from adopting children does not make it more likely that the state will find a married couple to adopt eligible children. The law is not narrowly tailored to find eligible children an adoptive home with a married mother and father. Furthermore, the law directly contradicts ASFA's goal of finding permanent homes for children.

2. Equal Protection

Even if homosexual relationships are not protected under the fundamental right to privacy, Florida's ban on lesbi-gay adoption may still be invalidated on equal protection grounds, further illuminating why repealing the ban is consistent with ASFA. The Equal Protection Clause proclaims that "no person shall be denied equal protection of the law" and mandates the same treatment of similarly situated people. A law that involves an identified class of people but "neither burdens a fundamental right nor targets a suspect class ... [will usually be upheld] so long as it bears a rational relation to some legitimate end" (*Romer v. Evans*, 517 U.S. 620, 631 (1996)). This "rational basis" analysis is usually a deferential standard and courts "insist on knowing the relation between the classification adopted and the object to be attained" (*Romer*, 517 U.S. at 632)). The means attained must have a legitimate state interest and not simply a "bare ... desire to harm a politically unpopular group." *Id.* As previously detailed, the state legislators' statements when the Florida legislation was introduced illustrated unvarnished homophobic sentiment.

In reviewing challenges to the adoption statute, courts have consistently framed the issue as whether banning lesbi-gay adoption serves the governmental purpose of finding a two-parent marital home for children. However, this characterization of the issue is flawed because the state's ultimate concern is centered on the best interests of the child. Therefore, courts should frame the issue as whether banning lesbi-gay adoption serves the legitimate governmental purpose of promoting the best interest of children whom need an adoptive home. An equal-protection analysis offers a resounding negative answer.

Florida's law categorically denies a group of citizens the opportunity to adopt children based on broad assumptions about their ability to adequately rear children. The law does not allow the state to evaluate any gay applicant's fitness for child-rearing; instead, the gay applicant is *per se* excluded from consideration based on sexual preference. Moreover, the law fails to address the state's true aim—to protect the best interests of children—by failing to exclude applicants who may actually pose a threat to the children's health and safety.

Even if the courts have justified a lesbi-gay adoption ban by solely finding children a home with a married mother and father, two facts undermine this argument: (1) the state does not exclude unmarried persons from adopting; and (2) banning gay persons from adopting will not assist the state in finding marital homes for children.

The law's purported justification of finding a two-parent marital home, without a "best interest of the child" analysis, is directly adverse to ASFA's mandate to evaluate permanency placements based on the child's best interest. In short, Florida's ban on lesbi-gay adoption is an example of legislation that reflects the desire to harm a politically unpopular group.

D. Repealing the Ban Is the Only Appropriate Remedy

Although the state's highest official (then-Governor Crist) stated in 2010 that the anti-gay ban would no longer be enforced, the statute still exists.

The Florida legislature should repeal the law banning lesbi-gay adoption because of the lack of stable and legally-protected alternatives to adoption for gay parents seeking to obtain custody of the children in their care. Alternative means for gay parents to care for unrelated children include guardianship; protective supervision; long-term custody; long-term licensed custody; lesbi-gay adoption of established foster children only; and/or denying their sexual orientation on the adoption application.

1. Guardianship

Florida has allowed some gay parents to become guardians of children in their care. Guardianship is a judicial process in which the state gives an adult the right to care for and make decisions for a ward of the state. In the case of foster children, when the court appoints a guardian, the child leaves the foster care system and state supervision terminates. Termination of the guardianship may occur if the guardian resigns, when the court, the ward, or any other interested person begins proceedings to remove the guardian, or when the ward reaches eighteen years of age. The flaw in the guardianship option is that it does not ensure a permanent relationship between the guardian and the ward because the guardianship relationship can terminate at any time.

2. Protective Supervision

When a child is under protective supervision, there is an assumption that the child will remain in this placement until he or she reaches the age of majority (Fla. Stat. § 39.521(1)(b)(3) (2006)). However, the custody arrangement remains subject to judicial supervision and the state can decide that the child should not continue to live with the caregiver. Further, an adult protective supervisor must expressly agree to the child's reunification with his or her biological parents if ordered. Protective supervision is an inadequate arrangement because it does not provide stability or the legal guarantees of adoption, where a parent would have recognized constitutional rights to the care, custody, and control of their children.

3. Planned Permanent Living Arrangement

A planned permanent living arrangement is an alternative to other court-mandated custody determinations (Fla. Stat. § 39.6241 (2006)). It is akin to the now-abolished long-term custody arrangement (Fla. Stat. § 39.622 (2004)). Planned permanent arrangements must be in the best interests of the child, stable and more secure than ordinary foster care, based upon compelling reasons, and subject to continued state supervision and court review every six months.

4. Lesbi-Gay Adoption of Established Foster Children Only

Advocates of lifting the lesbi-gay adoption ban have proposed legislation that attempts to balance the bright-line rule prohibiting gay individuals from adopting children with the need for adoptive homes for Florida's foster children.

In February 2006, the Florida legislature considered a bill that would have allowed lesbi-gay adoption of foster children within their care (Fla. Sen. Bill 172, 2006 Reg. Sess. (Sept. 8, 2005)). The bill had five requirements: (1) the child must be in foster care for at least two years; (2) the child must reside with the applicant; (3) the child must recognize the applicant as his or her parent; (4) permanency in the home must be more important to the child's development and psychological needs than temporary placement in foster care; and (5) the placement must be in the child's best interest. However, this law never made it past the Florida House of Representatives or the Senate committees; and thus failed to command a floor vote.

At a minimum, this proposed law would have allowed some lesbi-gay adoptions. Although this proposed law may have increased the likelihood of finding a permanent home for needy foster children, the proposal was not specific or detailed enough.

Gay individuals wishing to adopt would have had to undergo the application process to become foster parents, and then wait for their foster child to become eligible for adoption. As a foster parent, there is no guarantee that the child placed in their home would ever become eligible for adoption. Once the child became eligible for adoption, the foster parent would have to go through an additional screening and evaluation process to adopt. The proposed law also required lesbi-gay pre-adoptive parents to establish the eligibility criteria by clear and convincing evidence. Therefore, even after an extended application process, lesbi-gay foster parents still risk denial due to the higher evidentiary standards.

5. *Deny Sexual Orientation on Adoption Application*

Adoption applicants may choose not to reveal their sexual orientation on their applications for adoptions. However, this alternative is a poor choice because of the serious consequences that may result, such as the vacation or annulment of a prior adoption if the state discovers an applicant's untruthfulness (Fla. Stat. § 63.2325 (2002)). While in some circumstances it may be legal to omit information, it is illegal to intentionally give false information when asked explicit questions. Adoption applicants who knowingly fail to disclose their sexual orientation may be guilty of fraud and may have their adoption proceedings terminated or prior adoptions overturned.

On balance, the shortcomings of the various custody arrangements available to lesbi-gay individuals seeking to care for Florida's foster children shows that the ban on lesbi-gay adoption significantly disadvantages gay "parents" and their children. For their benefit, the best option is to repeal the ban on lesbi-gay adoption.

Checkpoints

- The first same sex adoption issues in the United States were in the 1970s.

- Courts have followed the "best interests of the child" standard, and although a very minor approach, some courts viewed homosexuals as unfit parents based on the relationship alone. Most courts follow the nexus approach demanding actual proof that the child would be harmed living with same sex parents.

- Presently, same sex adoption is protected under the Equal Protection Clause.

- Inheritance concerns are also a part of same sex adoptions as one partner may want to will their personal belongings to the biological child of the other partner.

- An early Florida statute specifically prohibits same sex couples from adopting a child, even though the standard is "the best interests of the child." Florida posts many cases showing the demand from same sex couples to adopt and have the statute amended. The Governor in 2010 declared the ban would not be followed, and it is lifted in practice. However, the ban has yet to be stricken.

- Many courts began to rule that denying same sex marriages is unconstitutional.

- In 2013, DOMA's definition of marriage between a man and a woman was declared unconstitutional. As social mores change and same sex marriage becomes a legally recognized union, it eases the pathway for future adoptions between same sex couples.

- As of June, 2015, 37 states allowed same sex marriage.

- On June 26, 2015, in a 5–4 decision, the U.S. Supreme Court decided *Oberge-fell v. Hodges*, 576 U.S. ___ (2015), which recognized a Constitutional right to same sex marriage. The full effect on same sex adoption is yet to be determined.

Chapter 8

The Indian Child Welfare Act of 1978 (ICWA) (25 U.S.C. §§ 1901–1963 (2014))

Roadmap

- The history of the ICWA
- How the ICWA shaped adoption procedures
- The importance of cultural identity in foster care and adoption proceedings

---

I. The History of ICWA: What Can Be Learned from It?

For nearly a century, Native American children were removed from their families by federal and state agencies and placed in non-Indian homes and institutions (25 U.S.C. § 1901(4)). The reasons for removal were often unwarranted and had deep roots in America's desire for Indians to be assimilated into white customs and traditions. Children were removed from reservations and placed in white adoptive homes far away from their Indian identities.

In 1958, the Indian Adoption Project was launched to further this desire of assimilation and rid Indian children of their Indian culture. The creators of the project justified their actions by citing the number of Indians who were alcoholics, illiterate, unemployed, and lived in unsuitable homes—often on U.S. government-created reservations. The creators saw the Native American custom of leaving their children with other Native Americans who were not in their nuclear family (but, rather members of their tribe) as neglect, socially irresponsible, and grounds for terminating their parental rights.

By 1969, 25–35% of Indian children were removed from their biological families. That was nearly nineteen times the rate of non-Indian children who were removed from their homes during the same time-period. When ICWA was passed, almost ten years later, over 90% of adopted Indian children were placed in non-Indian homes. At those astonishing rates, it was projected that Indian cultures were surely to be annihilated.

The 1978 House Report on the Indian Child Welfare Act (H.R. Rep. No. 1386 (1978), reprinted in 1978 U.S.C.C.A.N. 7530) stated that as many as one in four (some estimated up to 35%) of Native American children under the age of one had been adopted. Estimates showed that 85–90% of the removed children were placed with non-Native American families. The vast majority of the removals were based on vague grounds such as "neglect," "social deprivation," or unsupported allegations of "emotional damage" from living with their natural or biological parents.

Nationwide, at the time of H.R. Rep. No. 1386, more than 17% of school-age Native American children lived in Bureau of Indian Affairs institutional facilities or homes. The rate of outplacements for Native American children far outpaced that of the general population.

In its findings for the ICWA, Congress stated that "an alarmingly high percentage of Indian families are broken up by the removal, often unwarranted, of their children from them by nontribal public and private agencies and that an alarmingly high percentage of such children are placed in non-Indian foster and adoptive homes and institutions" (25 U.S.C. § 1901(4) (1978)). The effect of this trend was identified as a form of "cultural genocide."

II. ICWA — Provisions and Requirements

A. Child-Focused

At the Congressional hearings of ICWA, one tribal chief testified as to the importance of keeping Native American children within their tribes in order for the tribe to survive — so-called "cultural genocide." Without Native American children, the tribe's customs would not sustain and the tribe's ability to maintain as self-governing communities would be undermined. With the enactment of ICWA, Congress recognized Indian children were the primary means to preserve Indian culture and the integrity of Indian tribes (25 U.S.C. § 1901(3)).

Congress' stated purpose for the ICWA, as a reflection of United States policy, was "to protect the best interests of Indian children and to promote the stability and security of Indian tribes and families ..." (25 U.S.C. § 1902 (1978)). This goal was to be achieved "by making sure that Indian child welfare determinations are not based on 'a white, middle-class standard which, in many cases, forecloses placement with [an] Indian family'" (*Mississippi Band of Choctaw Indians v. Holyfield*, 490 U.S. 30, 37 (1989)). Congress found "that the States, exercising their recognized jurisdiction over Indian child custody proceedings through administrative and judicial bodies, have often failed to recognize the essential tribal relations of Indian people and the cultural and social standards prevailing in Indian communities and families" (25 U.S.C. § 1901(5) (1978)).

The Act applies to any "Indian" child involved in a child custody proceeding in state court. "'Indian child' means any unmarried person who is under age eighteen and is either (a) a member of an Indian tribe or (b) is eligible for membership in an Indian tribe and is the biological child of a member of an Indian tribe" (25 U.S.C. § 1903(4) (1978)). The Act establishes the "minimum Federal standards for the removal of Indian children from their families" and seeks to ensure "the placement of such children in foster and adoptive homes which will reflect the unique values of Indian culture ..." (25 U.S.C. § 1902 (1978)).

B. Indian Family Preference

The ICWA specifically and explicitly gives custody and adoption preference to members of the "Indian" child's extended "Indian" family, other "Indian" families, or members of the child's tribe (25 U.S.C. § 1915(a) (1978)). Unless there is a showing of good cause to the contrary, foster placements are to be made to either: (1) a member of the Indian child's extended family; (2) a foster home (either Indian or non-Indian) licensed by the Indian child's tribe; or (3) a tribe-approved children's institution (25 U.S.C. § 1915(b) (1978)).

The ICWA additionally requires that—prior to either foster care placement (even if temporary) or the termination of parental rights—remedial and rehabilitative programs be provided to prevent the breakup of an Indian family. Further, the state must prove beyond a reasonable doubt that it made active efforts to prevent the breakup of the family. Placing the child with a member of its extended tribal family is considered a remedial effort under the Act. Such a placement must be proven to have failed prior to any outplacement. Under the ICWA, the burden of proof for the termination of parental rights is proof beyond a reasonable doubt that serious emotional or physical harm to the child will occur if the custody situation continues.

Tribes must be notified of a proceeding and have the right to intervene in a state court child custody proceeding. Tribal courts have sole jurisdiction over cases involving Indian children who reside on the reservation and retain concurrent jurisdiction with state courts for Indian children not domiciled on the reservation. Moreover, all courts in the United States are required to give full faith and credit to the child custody determinations of tribal courts.

C. Procedural Issues in Accordance With ICWA

When an Indian child is the subject of an involuntary child custody proceeding in a state court, notice must be given to the Indian parent or custodian and the applicable Indian tribe (25 U.S.C. §1912(a)). That proceeding will not continue until at least ten days after the Indian parent or custodian and tribe received proper notification and they can request an additional twenty days to prepare for the proceeding (25 U.S.C. §1912(a)).

ICWA provides for representation of any indigent Indian that is a party to the proceeding (25 U.S.C. §1912(b)). It requires that each party have the right to examine reports and other documents that were filed with the court (25 U.S.C. §1912(c)). ICWA also ensures that remedial services and rehabilitative programs are available to the Indian family in order to prevent the breakup of such family prior to an Indian child's removal (25 U.S.C. §1912(d)).

At hearings on foster care placements, clear and convincing evidence that non-removal would "likely result in serious emotional or physical damage to the child" must be established in order to remove an Indian child while in termination of parental rights hearings, the determination must be supported by evidence beyond a reasonable doubt (25 U.S.C. §1912(e)(f)).

ICWA also provides for cases where an Indian parent or custodian voluntarily consents to foster care placement or to termination of parental rights (25 U.S.C. §1913). If any of the provisions of ICWA were violated, an Indian parent or custodian and the Indian child's tribe from which the Indian child was removed may petition for the court to invalidate the removal (25 U.S.C. §1914).

ICWA also sets out the preference of custody placements. In an adoptive placement, preference is given to a member of the Indian child's extended family, then to members if the child's tribe, and finally to other Indian families (25 U.S.C. §1915(a)). In foster care or pre-adoptive placements, preference is first given to a member of the child's extended family, then to a foster home that was licensed, approved, or specified by the child's tribe, then to an Indian foster home that was licensed or approved by a non-Indian licensing authority, and finally to a children's institution approved by a tribe or operated by a tribal organization (25 U.S.C. §1915(b)). In determining placement, the social and cultural standards of the child's Indian community are always taken into consideration (25 U.S.C. §1915(d)).

D. *Mississippi Band of Choctaw Indians v. Holyfield*, 490 U.S. 30 (1989).

The application of the ICWA is far-reaching. In *Mississippi Band of Choctaw Indians v. Holyfield*, 490 U.S. 30 (1989), the United States Supreme Court expressly held that ICWA does not permit Native American parents to circumvent the Act by going off the reservation to give birth when the parents are domiciled on the reservation. Thus, a parent cannot voluntarily consent to adoption by a non-Native American to avoid having the child raised in an Indian environment or to frustrate the purposes of the Act.

Mississippi Band of Choctaw Indians v. Holyfield, 490 U.S. 30 (1989), is one of the few United States Supreme Court decisions involving ICWA. Unfortunately, the court did not address the validity of the "existing family exception"—see below.

It did, however, provide several findings relevant to the exception. First, it stated the consequences of Indian children living in non-Indian environments, which included identity crises. Second, it found that tribes had their own compelling interest in where Indian children were placed. Indian children who were raised in non-Indian homes would not preserve their tribal ancestry, culture, and heritage, one of the main purposes for the enactment of ICWA. Lastly, the court dealt with the definition of "domicile" which was not defined in ICWA. *Holyfield* at 43. It held that Indian children could be domiciled on a reservation even though they themselves were never physically present on the reservation. *Id.* at 48–49. Thus, parents could not avoid ICWA by having a child outside of a reservation. *Holyfield* seemed to have raised new questions about the doctrine without explicitly referring to it.

Further, in the case of *In re Baby Girl Doe*, 865 P.2d 1090 (Mont. 1993), the Supreme Court of Montana held that a parent's desire for anonymity in the adoption process does not outweigh the purposes of the Act and therefore does not defeat its application.

E. Tribal Jurisdiction

ICWA specifically gives Indian tribes jurisdiction over Indian child custody proceedings (25 U.S.C. § 1911). It states that Indian tribes are to have exclusive jurisdiction over any child welfare proceeding that involves "an Indian child who resides or is domiciled within the reservation" of the tribe (25 U.S.C. § 1911(a)).

Additionally, unless a parent objects to or there is good cause to the contrary, any state court child custody proceeding that involves an Indian child who does not reside or is not domiciled on a reservation must be transferred to the tribal court (25 U.S.C. § 1911(b)). It also gives the child's Indian custodian and Indian tribe the right to intervene in any state court child custody proceeding that involves that Indian child at any point (25 U.S.C. § 1911(c)).

Importantly, the ultimate decisions of any tribal court in regards to an Indian child's custody proceeding is to be given full faith and credit by every state and territory of the United States (25 U.S.C. § 1911(d)).

A recent Florida case dealt with tribal jurisdiction (*Billie v. Stier*, 141 So. 3d 584 (Fla. App. 3rd Dist. 2014)). The mother started custody proceedings regarding a child in a tribal court. The mother was a Native American and the father was not. The parents had never been married. In this case, the father had never received notice of the reason for the hearings, had no opportunity to be heard and was not provided with an interpreter. The court removed jurisdiction from the tribal court to the circuit court because the tribal court hearing did not conform to the UCCJEA.

F. Parental Consent

The Act has rather onerous provisions for valid voluntary consent by Native American parents for either foster care placements or the termination of parental rights. Specifically, the act requires that (1) written consent be obtained; (2) the consent be recorded before a judge; (3) the judge certify that (a) the terms and consequences of the consent were explained and understood, and (b) either English or the parent's native language was used; and (4) the consent may be given within ten days after the "Indian" child's birth (25 U.S.C. § 1913(a) (1978)).

Consent to foster care placement may be withdrawn at any time and consent to parental rights termination may be withdrawn prior to the entry of a final adoption or termination decree (25 U.S.C. § 1913(b) (1978)).

III. Circumventing the Act — The History of the Existing Family Exception

A. *In re Adoption of Baby Boy L.*, 643 P.2d 168 (Kan. 1982).

A tactic utilized by both Native Americans and non-Native Americans alike to avoid the Act is the judicially-created "existing (Indian) family" exception — which was first devised in this case (*In re Adoption of Baby Boy L.*, 643 P.2d 168 (Kan. 1982)). Under the existing family exception, the ICWA has been held to apply only to family situations where the child is removed from an existing Native American family, home, or culture.

The *Baby Boy L* case involved a child who was conceived by an unmarried non-Indian woman and an Indian man. The same day the mother gave birth to Baby Boy L, she consented to his adoption by a non-Indian couple and they were granted temporary custody by a trial court. Notice was served on the Indian father, who was incarcerated at the time, and he filed an answer asking the court that the petition be denied, the court find him a fit father, his parental rights not be terminated, and that he be given custody of his son.

The father also notified the court that he was a member of an Indian tribe, which required notice to that tribe of the proceedings. The father then filed an amended answer asking that his son be placed with his extended family, others within the tribe, or with another Indian family as the requirements of ICWA laid out.

The tribe and paternal grandparents then petitioned to intervene in the matter. The trial court found that ICWA did not apply, denied the tribe's and grandparent's petitions to intervene, found the father unfit, and granted the petition for adoption.

On appeal, the Supreme Court of Kansas affirmed the rulings of the trial court, even though the court recognized the matter involved a child custody proceeding and Baby Boy L was an Indian child as defined by ICWA. In doing so, the court created the "existing family exception."

The Court reasoned that because Baby Boy L was never a member of an Indian home or culture from the time he was born to the present and therefore was not removed from an Indian family, ICWA does not apply. The Court believed that ICWA was only concerned with an Indian child that came from an existing Indian family unit. Since the *Baby Boy L* case, many courts have cited this exception and expounded upon it in order to circumvent the application of ICWA.

B. Effects of *Baby Boy L* Case

After *Baby Boy L*, primarily, this so-called exception tends to remove children of unwed non-Native American mothers from the purview and protection of the ICWA (*In re Adoption of Baby Boy D*, 742 P.2d 1059, 1063–64 (Okla. 1985)); however, the exception has been held to apply to unwed Native American mothers relinquishing custody (*In re Adoption of T.R.M.*, 525 N.E.2d 298, 302–03 (Ind. 1988)).

The ICWA has been held not to apply where the facts of the case show that (1) the child is in the custody of a non-Native American mother; (2) the child is not being removed from the custody of a Native American parent; and (3) the child is not being removed from a Native American cultural environment (*In re Adoption of D.M.J.*, 741 P.2d 1386, 1389 (Okla. 1985)).

Additionally, the ICWA has been held not to apply even where the child is removed from the custody of a Native American parent where that parent is found by the court to have no ties to the Native American community or culture (*In re Adoption of Crews*, 825 P.2d 305, 310 (Wash. 1992)). Finally, the New Jersey Supreme Court has held the definition of parent within the ICWA does not include an unwed, Native American father who has not taken affirmative steps to establish paternity as determined by state law (*In re Adoption of a Child of Indian Heritage*, 543 A.2d 925, 933–38 (N.J. 1988)).

Some courts, however, have not applied the judicially-created "existing family" exception and have followed the ICWA (*In re Adoption of T.N.F.*, 781 P.2d 973 (Alaska 1989); *In re Baby Boy Doe*, 849 P.2d 925 (Idaho 1993); *In re Adoption of S.S.*, 622 N.E.2d 832 (Ill. App. Ct. 1993)).

C. *In re Bridget R.*, 49 Cal. Rptr. 2d. 507, 536 (Ct. App. 1996).

ICWA has come under attack from the California Court of Appeals and from Congress. The California Court of Appeals held the "ICWA cannot be constitutionally applied [to invalidate a voluntary termination of parental rights] in the absence of evidence demonstrating that the biological parents had a significant social, cultural or political relationship with the Tribe" (*In re Bridget R.*, 49 Cal. Rptr. 2d. 507, 536 (Ct. App. 1996), *cert. denied*, 117 S. Ct. 693 (1997)). In *In Re Bridget R*, the California Court of Appeals stated that applying ICWA to non-tribal children

> runs afoul of the Constitution in three ways: (1) it impermissibly intrudes upon a power ordinarily reserved to the states; (2) it improperly interferes with Indian children's fundamental due process rights respecting family relationships; and (3) on the sole basis of race, it deprives them of equal opportunities to be adopted that are available to non-Indian children. . . .

The tribe argued unsuccessfully that the nuclear family should not be the focus. This opinion further clarified the "existing Indian family" exception and limited the reach of *Mississippi Band of Choctaw Indians v. Holyfield*, 490 U.S. 30 (1989).

Courts have extended the "existing family exception" to include that biological parents themselves had to have a sufficient relationship with the Indian community to be considered an existing family unit (*In re Bridget R*, 49 Cal.

Rptr.2d 507, 530 (Cal. 2d Dist. App. 1996)). This newly expounded upon exception precluded the parents from using cultural ties maintained by blood relatives. In order for ICWA to apply, the biological parents must have sufficient social, cultural, or political connections to an Indian tribe.

In the case of *In re Bridget R*, an appellate court reversed a trial court order that invalidated a voluntary termination of parental rights, removed a pair of twins from their adoptive placement of two years, and returned the twins to the biological father's extended family after the father withdrew his consent.

In reaching its decision, the California Court of Appeals looked to whether the biological parents "maintained any significant social, cultural or political relationship with the tribe" when the parents did not reside on the reservation. Relevant factors to consider include the distance from the reservation, participation in the tribal community, voting history in tribal elections, contributions to tribal charities, subscriptions to tribal newspapers, participation in tribal events, and the maintenance of social contacts within the tribe. The court went so far as to hold that exception is necessary in this case in order to preserve ICWA's constitutionality.

Bridget R. involved a biological father who purposely concealed his Native American heritage (he was 3/16th Native American) to help facilitate his twin-daughters' adoption (these twin daughters of a non-Native American mother were therefore 3/32nd Native American).

In direct response to the lower court's ruling in this case, companion bills were introduced in both the U.S. House and the U.S. Senate during the 104th Congress to limit the ability of tribes to reclaim children once they had been adopted—even where the tribe was not properly notified of the adoption proceeding (H.R. 1448, 104th Cong. (1995); S. 764, 104th Cong. (1995)).

Additionally, in response to the *Bridget R.* case, a controversial section of the Adoption Promotion and Stability Act of 1996 was introduced in an attempt to limit the application of the ICWA.

D. *In re Santos Y*, 112 Cal. Rptr. 2d 692, 699 (Cal. 2d Dist. App. 2001).

Similarly, in the case of *In re Santos Y*, the appellate court reversed the trial court's order that removed a child from his pre-adoptive placement of two and a half years and transferred him to a reservation. The court declined to apply ICWA since the child was not being removed from an existing Indian family. The court found that the Indian mother had no connection to the tribe prior to the tribe intervening in the case. Although she was an enrolled member of the tribe her entire life, the fact the mother did not live near the tribe nor had any other connection took precedent. In this case, the minor's interest in a stable placement outweighed the constitutionally protected interest of the Indian parent and tribe.

With this exception, state courts have the power to decide who is a Native American (referred to as Indian by ICWA) and who is not — despite the definition in ICWA. As a result, *Santos Y.* undermines the very purposes for which ICWA was enacted. It allows state courts to retain jurisdiction, ignore placement preferences, and deny Indian parents the right to revoke their consent to voluntary child custody placements.

IV. Current Applicability of ICWA

Not all courts have bought into the "existing family exception." In fact, the majority of states rejected the exception, primarily because of the plain language of ICWA. Other opponents of the exception argue that the exception frustrates the purpose of ICWA and allows non-Indians to determine whether an Indian parent meets its own view of Indian culture.

A. Proposed Amendments

Proposed amendments regarding the requirement for a "significant social, cultural, or political relationship with a tribe" to pre-exist for ICWA to apply have come and gone throughout the years. The most notable is Senate Bill 679, which was introduced by California State Senator Denise Moreno Ducheny in 2005. The bill protected an Indian child's membership and connection to a tribal community regardless of whether the child is in the physical custody of an Indian parent or custodian at the time of the proceeding, whether parental rights were terminated, and where the child has resided or been domiciled.

The bill also included the narrow instances where a court could deviate from the placement preferences as established in ICWA, and provided that a tribal decision on membership is conclusive. Most importantly, it made ICWA provisions mandatory by codifying them.

B. *In re A.J.S.*, 204 P.2d 543, 549 (Kan. 2009).

A recent and most notable decision on the "existing family doctrine" has come from the Kansas Supreme Court itself. In the case of *In re A.J.S.*, the Kansas Supreme Court abandoned the very exception it had created in *Baby Boy L.*

The facts of the *A.J.S.* case are eerily similar to *Baby Boy L.* In this case, the unwed non-Indian mother sought to terminate the Indian father's parental rights after she consented to the adoption of A.J.S. by members of her own non-Indian family. The Indian father objected and the tribe intervened. In *A.J.S.* (unlike in *Baby Boy L*), after close examination of the *Holyfield* case, the Supreme Court of Kansas recognized the importance of the Indian child's relationship to the tribe despite any parental relationship with the tribe. The court recognized that the majority of the states rejected the exception and the other states that once adopted the exception had now abandoned it.

The Supreme Court of Kansas set out four reasons for abandoning the "existing family doctrine." First, the court recognized that the exception was at odds with the plain meaning and language of ICWA, which made no exception for children like A.J.S. Second, it recognized that in *Holyfield* the exception does not meet the stated purpose of ICWA, which was to protect and promote the stability and security of Indian tribes and their interest in their Indian children. Third, it recognized its own flaw in one of its arguments in *Baby Boy L*—that either way the Indian child would not be raised in an Indian environment because the non-Indian mother would have revoked her consent to the adoption and raised the child herself if the adoptive placement did not work. A mother's desires will not overcome the list of placement preferences in ICWA if the act applies. Finally, the court was influenced by the overall criticism of the exception and declared that, in general, courts are right to not "essentialize" any ethnic or racial group.

C. Other Recent Cases

A recent Florida case interpreted when ICWA can be raised (*GL v. Dept. of Children and Families*, 80 So.3d 1065 (FL App. 5th Dist. 2012)). In this case, both parents of a child had their parental rights terminated due to drug use and criminal history. The mother was a Native American. ICWA was not raised at these hearings. The father fought the TPR. The court ruled that in involuntary TPR proceedings ICWA can be raised on appeal and that the trial court had reason to know that ICWA might apply and should have notified the tribe.

Nielson v. Ketchum, 640 F.3d 1117 (U.S. 10th Circuit 2011) interpreted who ICWA applies to with respect to the mother and grandmother. In this case, a biological mother contested the adoption of her child because she had consented to the adoption in less than ten days, which is the ICWA standard. She was not a member of the tribe, though her mother was. The court ruled that ICWA safeguards don't apply because the child was not a member of an Indian tribe.

The U.S. Supreme Court interpreted ICWA in its decision *Adoptive Couple v. Baby Girl*, 133 S.Ct. 2552 (2013). Here a biological dad who was 1.2% Native American contested the adoption of his daughter. Originally, the father had texted the mother that he wanted to relinquish his rights to the child and he made no meaningful attempt to assert those rights. Later he contested the adoption and was awarded custody when the child was 27 months old. The Supreme Court ruled that the adoption held. ICWA did not apply when the parent never had custody. There does not have to be a showing of remedial efforts to prevent the breakup if the parent never had custody. In addition, the couple should not be barred from adoption if there is no other couple that showed interest.

An Alaska Supreme Court case mirrored the decision in the 2013 U.S. Supreme Court case. In *Native Village of Tununak v. State of Alaska Dept. of Health Services*, 334 P.3d 165 (2014), a Native American mother's parental rights were terminated and the non-Native American foster parents sought to adopt the child. The court ruled for the foster parents. The court opined that it was bound by the U.S. Supreme Court decision in *Adoptive Couple v. Baby Girl*. Thus, the ICWA was inapplicable when no alternative party wanted to adopt the child in question. There was a biological grandmother who was Native American, and was considered as a possible placement. However, this placement was rejected because she did not move formally adopt the child, and she had an adult son who had a criminal background living with her.

V. Cultural Identity Is Worth Preserving

As of 2011, six states implemented the "existing family exception." Nineteen states had expressly rejected the doctrine, four of which previously adopted the exception only to reverse themselves. Three states barred their courts from adopting the exception, and in the remaining states, the exception was rejected by intermediate Appellate Courts. In sum, the trend prior to *Adoptive Couple* was to move away from the "existing family exception" whose purpose was to avoid the application of ICWA. Post-*Adoptive Couple*, the status of the existing family exception is unclear.

ICWA's creation came from the deplorable history of how Americans treated Indians throughout the centuries. It is a history that many Americans try to forget, but it is one that Indians carry with them. Cultural identity is important because it gives people a sense of belonging and tells them where they come from. It contributes to a person's well-being, which is why so many Indian children removed from their reservations did not thrive in non-Indian communities. For a child who does not look like the majority of children around him, it could be quite confusing and it is important for that child to know where he comes from. Without ICWA, Indian tribes and their customs could not sustain.

Two studies make recommendations for the implementation of ICWA. A national study was conducted (Findings from a National Needs Assessment of American Indian/Alaska Native Child Welfare Programs 91(3) Child Welfare 47–63 (2012)). The data collection involved a general survey of stakeholders, telephone interviews, and on-site assessments. Some of the recommendations from the study include: the development of a practice model; improved management information systems; increased training for foster care parents; increased coordination between state and tribal foster care systems; and updated tribal child welfare codes. Wisconsin is implementing a statewide state/tribal partnership (Best Outcomes for Indian Children (91(3) Child Welfare 135–156 (2012)). Some of the preliminary recommendations were communication must be flexible for rapid response; easy availability of technical assistance and clear explanation of data for practitioners; increased management of inter-agency suspicion; clearly articulating desired outcomes; prevention of burnout because change can take years; and patience and persistence.

On February 25, 2015, the BIA issued "Guidelines for State Courts and Agencies in Indian Child Custody Proceedings," 80 Federal Register 10146 (2015) (these new Guidelines supercede the 1979 ICWA Guidelines). The updated guidelines are meant to ensure that tribal children are not illegally removed from their communities and extended families; and that states comply with ICWA's mandates.

Checkpoints

- ICWA came about as protection for Native American tribes that were on the verge of extinction. So many Indian children were removed from their homes and placed in non-Indian adoptive families, creating a situation of "cultural genocide."

- ICWA specifically orders that a removed child be placed with a tribal relative or member. If there is none available, the child is to be placed in a home that respects and cultivates the tribe's practices and culture.

- Notice must be given to the Indian parent and to the tribe, and allowed a 10 day response period, before an involuntary removal of the child occurs. This procedural process can pose issues for DCF.

- Tribes are allowed access to all documents and records, and can reject the removal of a child in to foster care. This is to grant tribes the ability to determine the best interests of their children in preserving their culture.

- Preserving the Native American tribal communities is an important goal for the United States, and one that ICWA continues to follow.

Chapter 9

Step-Parent and
Second Parent Adoption

Roadmap

- The legal definition of a step-parent and its historical evolution
- The legal duties of the step-parent and the non-custodial biological parent
- Case law that shaped adoption procedures with step-parents
- How states differ in their regulations of step-parent adoptions

---

I. Step-Parent Adoption

A. Definition and History

A step-parent adoption refers to the legal relationship between a child and the child's biological parent's spouse. Historically, a step-parent had no legal duty of responsibility to a step-child. As a step-parent, the spouse does not have any biological ties to the child; however, as the legal spouse of the biological parent, the step-parent resides with the child and the biological custodial parent. In a step-parent adoption, the non-custodial parent's rights are terminated and the step-parent is granted full parental status while the custodial parent's rights remain intact. As such, the step-parent becomes a legally bound "substitute" for the non-custodial biological parent. At a rate of approximately 42% of all adoptions in the United States, step-parent adoption is the most common form of adoption.

Traditionally, adoption law only recognized biological and adoptive parents while excluding step-parents from any legal protections or obligations. The legal relationship between step-parents and their spouse's biological child became more relevant in recent decades as more biological parents divorced and remarried; and more unwed mothers married someone other than the child's biological father. According to the 2010 U.S. Census Report, there were an estimated 4,165,886 million step-children under of the age of eighteen living with a step-parent—experts have stated that this was a low estimate.

B. The Legal Issues of Step-Parenthood

As more step-families were created, the need for a uniform law regarding step-parents' legal rights became more apparent. Even though a minor child lived with a step-parent and maintained a parent-child relationship, the step-parent usually had no authority to make any medical or education decisions regarding the step-child. Step-parents demanded to be recognized as legal parents. Some of the relevant issues are: what legal authority (if any) a step-parent had over a minor step-child; whether they would have custody or visitation rights if they divorced the biological parent; whether they needed to support the child during the marriage and/or after a divorce; and whether the step-child could inherit from an intestate step-parent.

As a result, the states began enacting step-parent adoption statutes. Currently, forty-four states have enacted statutes regarding a step-parent's adoption rights. These statutes can be categorized as follows: eight states enacted statutes regarding a step-parent's custody rights; eleven states enacted statutes regarding a step-parent's visitation rights; fifteen states enacted statutes regarding a step-parent's child support obligations; and nineteen states enacted statutes regarding a child's inheritance rights to a step-parent who died intestate.

In addition, some states merely refer to the rights of "third parties" in general as opposed to directly referring to the rights of "step-parents" specifically. Those states' statutes can be categorized as follows: six states enacted statutes regarding a third party's adoption rights; twenty states enacted statutes regarding a third party's custody rights; thirteen states enacted statutes regarding a third party's visitation rights; and three states enacted statutes regarding a third party's child support obligation.

In sum, although some statutes have been enacted that relate to a step-parent's rights—either directly or indirectly—unfortunately, there is no consensus among the states of exactly what are the rights of step-parents.

Generally, without adoption, a step-parent's legal recognition as a custodian of a step-child is denied. Step-parents are typically denied legal recognition as a parent when a non-custodial parent is active in the child's life (to varying extents) and whose parental rights have not been terminated.

Even when the child primarily lives with a biological parent (who retains legal and physical custody) and the step-parent and the non-custodial parent has visitation rights only, the non-custodial parent still maintains their legal rights as a parent. The non-custodial parent has a right to be a part of the child's life, and owes a duty to support the child. However, varying from state-to-state, there are some limited exceptions to this rule.

C. Step-Parent Visitation Rights

Historically, since a step-parent had no legal rights vis-à-vis their step-child, if a step-parent divorced a custodial parent, the step-parent would not be able to obtain visitation rights to the child. However, in recent decades, some courts have allowed step-parents to petition the court for a visitation order. Other courts only allow step-parents to petition for visitation if they have shown a substantial relationship with the child, and not just merely because he or she was the step-parent of the child.

Some legal scholars argue that states must recognize the parental rights of both the non-custodial, biological parent and the step-parent. In doing such, a non-custodial parent would obtain court-ordered visitation even if its parental status was terminated.

D. Step-Parent Adoption — Requirements

Many states require that the custodial parent and the step-parent be married for at least one year before being eligible to proceed with a step-parent adoption.

Even more importantly, the non-custodial parent is required to consent to the step-parent adoption. However, states have recognized exceptions to the non-custodial parent's consent (or factors weighing in favor of termination of parental rights) in the following situations:

- Incarceration of the non-custodial parent.
- Non-custodial parent is deceased.
- Lack of communication with the child—essentially the child has been abandoned by the non-custodial parent. The non-payment of child support is often a factor in determining adequate communications with the child. States apply varied time-tables here.
- Non-custodial parent is "missing" and cannot be located. Again, states apply varied time-tables here.

E. Step-Parent Adoption — Procedure

A step-parent adoption begins with the step-parent filing an adoption petition with the court. The step-parent's spouse (i.e., the child's custodial parent) is usually required to consent to the adoption in writing. Depending on the child's age, his or her consent may be required. Proper notice must be given to the biological, non-custodial parent.

The non-custodial parent may either consent to the adoption or object to the adoption. If a non-custodial parent objects to the adoption, he or she is essentially trying to protect their rights as a parent to the child.

A non-custodial parent's consent to the adoption may be waived. Every state has enacted statutes that detail how a non-custodial parent's consent may be waived and how their rights are to be terminated. Consent is usually waived when the non-custodial parent has abandoned the child or when that parent is unfit to parent. A parent can be deemed unfit for a variety of reasons—including failure to maintain a relationship or contact with the child; failure to support the child; and/or failure to fulfill his or her duties as a parent over a period of time.

Generally, courts use the "best interests of the child" standard in determining whether adoption petitions will be granted or denied. In reaching its ruling, the court may consider the past conduct of the parent who objected to the petition. Other states allow courts to consider the child and how the child's current placement with the step-family affects the child.

Step-parent adoption is often a more streamlined process than with typical stranger adoption. As a result, some state statutes allow the homestudy requirement to be waived. As an example, the applicable statute in the state of Washington expressly exempts step-parent adoption from the homestudy requirement.

Despite gains in legal recognition for step-parents generally over the last several decades, it is important to note that—although nationwide step-parent adoption is the most common form of adoption—the majority of step-parents who are married to and reside with custodial parents (and their children) do not seek to adopt their step-children.

There are three recent state court cases that interpreted when step-parents can adopt their step-children. In *In re Adoption of JP*, 2011 Ark 535 (Supreme Court of Arkansas (2012)), the step-mother wanted to adopt her step-child whose biological mother had died. The court did not allow the adoption to proceed because they said it was not in the child's best interests, since the step-mother did not show an interest in furthering the child's relationship with the biological mother's family. In *In the Matter of Adoption of AMP*, 286 P.3d 746 (Supreme Court of Wyoming (2012)), the biological mother of the child had married again and the step-father wanted to adopt the child. The biological dad did not consent to the adoption. The court ruled that the adoption could be ordered without the biological father's consent because he willfully ignored his obligation to support the child. In *In re Adoption of TL*, 4 N.E. 3d 658 (S.C. Indiana 2014), again we have a step-father married to the biological mother of a child wanting to adopt a child and the biological father is contesting the adoption. The court upheld the adoption. The court found that the father's incarceration did not relieve him of his child support obligations; the father had the ability to pay some child support, and his choice not to subsequently terminated his parental rights.

F. Step-Parent Adoption — Inheritance Rights

A majority of states have held that intestacy laws do not grant a child rights of inheritance from a parent whose rights have been terminated and the child was subsequently adopted by a step-parent. As previously stated, step-parent adoption "substitutes" the step-parent for the non-custodial parent regarding all of the legal rights, duties, and privileges of parenthood — including inheritance rights.

1. Crumpton v. Mitchell, *303 N.C. 657 (1981)*.

George Crumpton fathered five children. Eventually two of these five children were adopted by their step-fathers. Subsequently, George's mother Ruth Crumpton died. Her will stated that her estate was to be distributed to her then-living issue *per stirpes* — namely to her blood relatives. Although Ruth's will was drafted prior to the adoption of the two grandchildren, Ruth did not die until after their adoption (and the will was not subsequently amended).

The court held that the two adopted children were no longer Ruth's legal blood relatives; and therefore, were not beneficiaries of her estate.

2. Sefcik v. Mouyos, *171 Ohio App. 3d 14 (2007)*.

In this case, Jonathon Sefcik was adopted by his step-father and his birth certificate was re-issued to reflect his new surname (Chastain). The step-father later divorced the biological mother. After the divorce, the child lived with his biological paternal grandmother — Ada Sefcik — and was raised by her. Eventually, Jonathan changed his surname back to Sefcik — and had a third birth certificate issued listing his biological father.

The Ohio court held that the step-father's divorce from the biological mother did not negate or effect the prior step-parent adoption. Thus, the court held that Jonathan was no longer *legally* related to his biological paternal grandmother despite his living with her, being raised by her, his subsequent name change, and third issuance of a birth certificate. Thus, any intestate inheritance was disallowed.

3. "Gifts" Allowed

Although children adopted by their step-parents are not able to inherit via intestacy from their biological relatives, the noncustodial, biological former parent may make a testamentary or *inter vivos* transfer or gift to the child.

II. Second Parent Adoption

A. Definition of Second Parent Adoption

Second parent adoption is similar to step-parent adoption. Second parent adoption generally involves the unmarried lesbi-gay partner of a custodial parent and the custodial parent's biological child. In a second parent adoption, the unmarried lesbi-gay partner seeks to adopt his or her partner's biological child. Prior to states allowing second parent adoptions, the only way for a lesbi-gay partner to adopt their partner's biological or adoptive child was for the biological/adoptive parent to terminate his or her parental rights.

A second parent adoption refers to an adoption where the biological parent consents to his or her lesbi-gay partner adopting the biological or adoptive parent's child. In such an adoption, the biological parent does not have to terminate their parental rights prior to the adoption; and following the adoption, both of the lesbi-gay partners have equal parenting rights.

In comparison to a step-parent adoption, it is more uncommon for an unmarried lesbi-gay partner be granted a petition to adopt the biological child of their partner than it is for a married step-parent to adopt—particularly since step-parent adoption is the most common form of adoption in the U.S., approximately 42%. Second parent adoption typically involves homosexual couples. However, in some states, second parent adoption is recognized for unmarried heterosexual couples—in New York, for example.

B. Where Is Second Parent Adoption Recognized?

Currently, thirty-two states have addressed the issue of second-parent adoption as an option for same-sex couples. Twenty-four states allow same sex couples to adopt. These states are: California, Colorado, Connecticut, Delaware, District of Columbia, Hawaii, Idaho, Illinois, Indiana, Iowa, Maine, Maryland, Massachusetts, Minnesota, Montana, Nevada, New Hampshire, New Jersey, New Mexico, New York, Oregon, Pennsylvania, Rhode Island, Vermont, and Washington. Eight states have obstacles to same-sex couples having access to second-parent adoption. These states are: Mississippi, Utah, Michigan, Kentucky, Nebraska, North Carolina, Ohio, and Wisconsin (Parenting Laws: Second Parent or Stepparent Adoption, http://hrc-assets.s3-web site-us-east-1.amazonaws.com//files/assets/resources/second_parent_adop tion_6-10-2014.pdf).

C. Cases

1. Adoption of Tammy, *416 Mass. 205 (1993)*.

One of the first cases to recognize second parent adoption was *Adoption of Tammy*, 416 Mass. 205 (1993). In that case, a lesbian couple of ten years filed a joint petition to adopt Tammy, one of the lesbian's biological daughter. The court held that there was no law in Massachusetts that prohibited an unmarried couple living together from jointly petitioning to adopt a child. The court further stated that the adoption would be in the child's best interests because it would recognize the legal rights and responsibilities of the partner in case the couple separates or the biological mother dies.

Furthermore, in deciding this case, the court created an exception to the provision that called for the natural mother's rights to be terminated. The court stated that it was not the legislature's intent to terminate the natural parent's legal relationship to the child "when the natural parent is a party to the adoption petition" and that provision only applied when a child is adopted by people who are not the natural parents.

It is important to note that the *Tammy* decision was decided long before the state of Massachusetts legally recognized homosexual marriage in *Goodridge v. Department of Public Health*, 798 N.E.2d 941 (2003). As such, the *Tammy* decision was based entirely on adoption statutes as opposed to the rights of homosexuals to marry.

Since *Tammy*, other states have followed and provided for second parent adoptions.

2. In re Jacob, *660 N.E.2d 937 (1995)*.

In 1995, New York recognized step-parent adoptions in *In re Jacob*, 660 N.E.2d 937 (1995). *In re Jacob* involved two cases — one involving an unmarried heterosexual couple and one involving a homosexual couple. In each case, both of the unmarried partners sought to adopt their partner's biological child.

The appellate court held that it was not the legislative intent for a biological parent to have to terminate their parental rights in order for their unmarried partner (heterosexual or homosexual) to adopt the child when the same biological parent consented to the adoption and when both parties wanted to raise the child. In reaching this decision, the court considered the best interests of the child.

The court reasoned that by allowing second parent adoptions, children are benefited by:

(1) gaining access to health insurance;
(2) social security benefits where applicable;
(3) life insurance benefits if either parent dies;
(4) gaining the right to inherit from the non-biological parent;
(5) the right to sue for wrongful death of the non-biological parent; and
(6) both parents would be under a legal duty to support the minor child financially.

3. In re Adoption of Luke, *263 Neb. 365, 366 (Neb. 2002)*.

However, not all states have embraced second parent adoptions. Those states take a strict and literal reading of statutes that require a parent to terminate its rights in order for the child to be adopted by another. In Nebraska, a biological mother and her lesbian partner jointly filed a petition to adopt the mother's child (*In re Adoption of Luke*, 263 Neb. 365, 366 (Neb. 2002)).

The court held that because the biological mother did not relinquish her parental rights when signing the adoption petition, her partner could not adopt the child. The court held that the only exception to that provision was for a step-parent adoption, which was also provided for in statute.

4. In re Adoption of T.K.J., *931 P.2d 488 (Colo. Ct. App. 1996)*.

A similar decision was reached in *In re Adoption of T.K.J.*, 931 P.2d 488 (Colo. Ct. App. 1996). In *T.K.J.*, a lesbian couple each had a biological child that the other sought to adopt while retaining their own parental rights over their own biological child. The court held that because neither woman wanted to terminate their parental rights, both of their children could not be up for adoption, and as a result, their adoption petitions were dismissed.

As in *Luke*, the court in *T.K.J.*, took a literal approach to reading the relevant adoption statute. The court also refused to expand the step-parent exception in regards to the termination of parental rights provision to include second parents.

5. Russell v. Bridgens, *647 N.W. 2d 56 (2002)*.

Shortly after *Luke*, the Nebraska Supreme Court addressed the full faith and credit issue in *Russell v. Bridgens*, 647 N.W. 2d 56 (2002). In *Russell*, while living in Pennsylvania, a lesbian partner adopted her partner's adopted child—through a so-called co-parent adoption.

The couple separated, and the partner and child moved to Nebraska where the partner filed for custody of and support for the minor child.

The Nebraska Supreme Court noted that the Pennsylvania Supreme Court was currently deciding on the validity of second parent adoptions. As such, the Nebraska Supreme Court advised the lower court that on remand the ultimate decision of the case depended upon the outcome of the Pennsylvania Supreme Court's decision regarding second parent adoptions, thus providing for full faith and credit to the decision of Pennsylvania.

6. Boseman v. Jarrell, *364 N.C. 537 (2010).*

Julia Boseman and Melissa Jarrell met in 1998. In 1999, they began living together in North Carolina. They decided that they wanted to raise a child together. In May of 2000, to make their dream a reality, they began the process of having a baby. They decided that Melissa would physically bear the child, but that Julia would be equally involved in every other aspect. Julia cared for Melissa during her pregnancy and was present at the birth. The couple chose their son's first name, and agreed that he should have a hyphenated last name composed of both of their surnames.

The parties shared "an equal role" in parenting. The child refers to Julia as "Mom" and to Melissa as "Mommy" and "shows lots of love and respect for both parties." Despite the couple's stated intentions, Julia was not legally the child's parent. To remedy this legal problem, in 2005, Julia sought and received a court order adopting the child without severing her partner's legally recognized parental rights. Melissa consented to the adoption.

Officially, by court order, their child now had two same-sex parents. However, since the Division of Social Services (DSS) would not index this type of adoption, the adoption court judge instructed the clerk "not ... to comply with" a statutory requirement that the clerk of court transmit a copy of the adoption decree to DSS, instead ordering that the clerk "securely maintain this file in the clerk's office."

In 2006, the couple separated. However, Julia continued to care for and support the minor child. Eventually, Melissa denied Julia custody of the child. Julia sued seeking custody of the minor child. In response, Melissa attacked the adoption decree, arguing that it was *void ab initio*, and contended that without the adoption decree, Julia could not seek custody of the minor child. The trial court ultimately awarded the parties joint legal custody of the minor child.

Melissa, the defendant, appealed. The Court of Appeals concluded that the adoption decree was valid and upheld trial court's custody determination.

The Supreme Court of North Carolina found the adoption decree *void ab initio* because the process did not meet the statutory requirements. In sum, the Court held that the statute allowing step-parent adoption does not apply to same-sex partners or second parent adoption.

Since the Supreme Court of North Carolina declared the adoption decree void *ab initio*, Julia/plaintiff could not legally be recognized as the minor child's parent. Thus, the Court was faced with a custody dispute between a parent and a third party.

As to the custody issue, the Court found that "defendant shared parental responsibilities with plaintiff and, when occurring in the family unit defendant created without any expectation of termination, acted inconsistently with her paramount parental status. The record contains clear and convincing evidence in support of that conclusion.... [B]ecause defendant has acted inconsistently with her paramount parental status, the trial court did not err by employing the 'best interest of the child' standard to reach its custody decision." Therefore, the lower court's determination of joint custody was upheld.

7. In the Matter of Adoption of Doe, *156 Idaho 345* (S.C. Idaho 2014).

In this case, a woman wanted to adopt her same-sex partner's child. The court ruled in her favor. The court found that the magistrate in the court below didn't fulfill her due process rights by dismissing her petition and that Idaho's adoption statute allows a second person to adopt a child, despite that person's marital status.

Checkpoints

- Step-parent adoption is the most common form of adoption.

- Non-custodial parent consent is required before step-parent adoption can proceed; the non-custodial parent can contest the request for adoption. There are certain circumstances where non-custodial parent consent is unattainable, and will be determined by the court if the adoption is allowed.

- Many states require that the step-parent and the parent be married for more than a year before petitioning for adoption. The spouse, or custodial parent, also must consent to the requested adoption.

- Generally, the "best interests of the child" standard is used by the courts when considering step-parent adoption requests.

- A successful step-parent adoption terminates, or replaces, the non-custodial parent's rights. This is especially important with reference to inheritance, as adopted out children will no longer have inheritance rights under the parent who terminated their parental rights.

- Second parent adoption is seen with lesbi-gay couples where the non-custodial parent's rights are not terminated; the lesbi-gay step parent consents to becoming a second parent with their partner.

- Until June of 2015, lesbi-gay adoptions have been difficult to classify because the parent union was not a legal marriage. The full effect of the USSC's decision in *Obergefell v. Hodges*, 576 U.S. ___ (2015) is yet to be determined.

Chapter 10

Kinship Care and Adoption

Roadmap
- The definition of kinship care and how it affects adoption
- How each state differs on defining kinship and awarding benefits
- Different statutes that have been enacted to better regulate kinship care

---

I. Kinship Care Defined

The term "kinship care" was originally coined in 1974 in research documenting the importance of kinship networks within the African American community in the United States (U.S. Dep't of Health and Hum. Servs., Administration for Children and Families, Children's Bureau, *Report to Congress on Kinship Foster Care V* 5, at http://aspe.hhs.gov/hsp/kinr2coo/index.htm (June 2000) ["2000 DHHS Kinship Report"]).

Kinship care has been defined by the Child Welfare League of America as "the full time nurturing and protection of children—who must be separated from their parents—by relatives, members of their tribes or clans, god-parents, step-parents, or other adults who have a kinship bond with a child." Kinship care is any form of residential caregiving provided to children by kin, whether full time or part-time, temporary or permanent, and whether initiated by private family agreement or under custodial supervision of a state child welfare agency.

Each State defines "relative" differently, including relatives by blood, marriage, or adoption ranging from the first to the fifth degree. Generally, preference is given to the child's grandparents, followed by aunts, uncles, adult siblings, and cousins. For Indian children, eight states allow members of the child's tribe to be considered "extended family members" for placement purposes. In 2007/2008, roughly 61% of kin caregivers were grandmothers; while 22% were aunts.

It should be noted, however, that there is nationwide confusion or discord over the definition of kinship care. To add to the confusion, by 2001, 20 states included non-relatives, such as neighbors, godparents, and other adults who have a close relationship with the child, within their definition of kin in reference to kinship care.

Seemingly following some states' lead, and signifying a modern, expanded view of kinship care, the 2000 DHHS Kinship Report noted that "[i]n its broadest sense, kinship care is any living arrangement in which a relative *or someone else emotionally close to the child* takes primary responsibility for rearing a child" (emphasis added). Further, a kinship parent has been statutorily defined, for example, in Maryland as "an individual who is related by blood or marriage within 5 degrees of consanguinity or affinity ... to a child who is in the care, custody, or guardianship of the local department [of child services] and with whom the child may be placed for temporary or long-term care *other than adoption*" (MD. CODE ANN. FAM. LAW § 5-534(a) (Supp. 1997) (emphasis added)).

As the Maryland statute implies, historically, there was an underlying premise within the child welfare system that kinship adoption was not as readily facilitated as "stranger" adoption. However, since the passage of the Fostering Connections to Success and Increasing Adoptions Act of 2008 (P.L 110-351) ("FCSIAA"), child welfare agencies are required to exercise due diligence in finding and notifying all adult relatives within 30 days after children are removed from their parents (*see generally* Chapter 14 — Reform Measures).

Historically, nation-wide, federal child welfare policy systematically overlooked the role of kinship caregivers — particularly informal kinship care givers — where child welfare agencies were not involved. Therefore, if states provided financial assistance to kin, the families received monies through income assistance programs rather than becoming a part of the child welfare system. A loophole existed where a child welfare agency helped to arrange the placement of a child with a relative, but did not seek court action for formal/legal custody of the child. Curiously, this "voluntary kinship care" placement or arrangement fell neither within the purview of informal, private kinship care nor formal, public kinship care. The numbers affected were considerable: in 1997 alone, across the nation, state agencies arranged for the so-called "voluntary" placement of approximately 283,000 children with kin. In 2000, more than 131,000 children were in the formal foster care system and placed with kin (so called formal kinship foster care).

In sum, kinship care arrangements can be generally divided into three categories:

(1) Informal Kinship Care—where neither the child welfare system nor the juvenile justice system are involved. Legal custody of the child remains with the parents. Thus, the child's parents can regain custody at any time. Further, the kin caregivers may have difficulty obtaining medical or financial benefits for the children or even enrolling them in school. Notably, only 15 states allow a non-legal caregiver to enroll a child in school (California, Connecticut, Delaware, Hawaii, Indiana, Louisiana, Maryland, New Jersey, North Carolina, Ohio, Oklahoma, Rhode Island, South Carolina, Utah, and Vermont).

(2) Voluntary Kinship Care—the child welfare system is involved, but the state does not take legal custody of the children. The court system may or may not be involved. The children are in the physical custody of kin, while the parents retain legal custody. The state may require the parents to sign a voluntary placement agreement with the child welfare agency; assign temporary legal custody to the kin caregiver; and/or assign temporary decision-making power to the kin caregiver.

(3) Formal Kinship Foster Care—by judicial determination, the child is placed in the legal custody of the State. In turn, the child welfare system then places the child with kin caregivers. Under the formal kinship foster care rubric, the State has legal custody of the child, while the kin caregiver has physical custody. Notably, these kin caregivers have rights and responsibilities similar to those of non-relative foster parents.

II. History and Background

The most obvious and key benefits of kinship care are family continuity and the reduced trauma of separation. However, a concern or challenge to kinship placement may be that similar issues or situations that caused the child's removal from his or her parents' home may be present in the kinship placement as well. Further, due to the familial relationship, the birth parent will more than likely have access to the child. Such access is particularly troubling where documented abuse and/or neglect were the reasons for the child's removal.

Despite the potential negative attributes, kinship placements allow children to live with family members that they know and trust, rather than subjecting children to the potential trauma of living with strangers. In addition, kinship placements usually facilitate the continuity of family identity and history and expanded concepts of ethnicity and culture.

Although the use of kinship foster care has risen dramatically due to the influx of children into the foster care system over the last twenty years, it still remains an "under-recognized component of the foster care system." Across the nation and across racial boundaries, the influx of children into foster care is undoubtedly due to increased incarceration rates, the drug epidemic, and the spread of HIV and AIDS.

Notably, as the number of kinship foster care homes rose, the number of non-kin foster care homes declined. In 1987, there were 147,000 non-kin foster care homes; in 1990, there were only 100,000. From 1986 to 1990, the number of children placed with kin rose from 18% to 31% of the total foster care placements, with the largest growth in urban areas. Between 1983 and 1985 and again between 1992 and 1993, the number of children in kinship care grew at a slightly faster rate than the number of children in the United States as a whole— 8.4% versus 6.6%. The number of children in kinship care decreased from an average of 2.16 million to 2.14 million between 1995–1997 and 1998–2000 and the average prevalence decreased from 3.05% to 2.98%.

Despite the early rise in kinship care, the 2001 DHHS Kinship report stated that "both the number and prevalence of kinship care children has decreased" since 1994. Obviously, these official DHHS statistics do not include informal, undocumented kinship care placements. For example, according to the 2000 United States Census, approximately 42% of the nation's grandparents lived in a familial constellation where they have responsibility for their grandchildren under the age of 18. It should be noted that 62% of these grandparent-headed households consist of a grandmother alone and 18% of these grandparent-headed households live in poverty.

From 1990 to 2000, the number of children living in households headed by grandparents rose by 30% to 4,500,000 (nearly 626,000 in California, over 448,000 in Texas, and over 297,000 in New York). In 2000, an estimated 2,350,477 grandparents were responsible for their own grandchildren under the age of eighteen. U.S. Census Bureau Statistics, as of April 1, 2000, http://factfinder.census.gov. In 2000, there were over 6,000,000 minor children living with kinship caregivers in the U.S. states, D.C. and Puerto Rico.

In addition, the 2001 DHHS Kinship report held that "[i]n 1998, approximately 2.13 million children in the United States, or just under 3%, were living in some type of kinship care arrangement. In 1997, approximately 200,000 children were in public kinship care, well below 1% of all U.S. children but 29% of all foster children."

In July 2010, the U.S. Census Bureau reported that approximately 6,400,000 grandparents had grandchildren living with them in 2008. Approximately 2,600,000 to 2,900,000 of these grandparents were responsible for most of the basic needs of the grandchildren who were living with them. The rise in the number of grandparents primarily caring for their grandchildren rose by 6% in a single year from 2007–2008. For White grandparents, the increase was 9% from 2007 to 2008; while African American grandparents had a 2% increase and Hispanic grandparents had no change. In 2008, caregiving grandparents were divided racially as follows: 53% White; 24% African American; 18% Hispanic; and 3% Asian.

Table 10.1 — Racial Make-Up of Grandparent Primary Caregivers
(2000–2008)
(Pew Research Center, 09/09/10)

Race	Total # 2008	Total % 2008	% Change 2007–08	% Change 2000–08
White	1,397,090	53%	↑9%	↑19%
African American	621,887	24%	↑2%	↓12%
Hispanic	483,182	18%	NC	↑14%
Asian	89,608	3%	↑3%	↑9%
Other	44,961	2%		
Total	2,636,728	100%	↑5%	↑8%

In 2009, the estimated number of grandchildren living with a grandparent was 7,000,000 — this accounted for 9% of all children in the United States (U.S. Census Bureau News, CB10-FF.16 (07/12/10)). However, the official 2010 U.S. Census indicated that 5,623,975 children in all 50 states plus Washington, D.C. and Puerto Rico were living with their grandparents. (U.S. Census Bureau, 2010 Census, http://factfinder2.census.gov).

On a macro level, the statistics are even greater. One 1996 study reported that 50% of New York City's 50,000 children in the foster care system had been placed with relative caregivers. A Census Bureau Report in 1993 reported that 4,300,000 children nationwide lived with relatives either other than or in addition to their parents. By 1998, although it is unclear how high the total figure for all children living with kin had risen, the Census Bureau reported that 4,000,000 children nationwide were living with one or more of their grandparents. A 1990 national study estimated that 31% of children placed by child welfare services were placed in kinship care.

DHHS data for the period of April 1996 through September 1996 indicated that 32% of children in foster care had been with a relative, 46% were in non-relative foster care, and 7% were in a group home where a number of children live in a dormitory-like setting rather than a family household. For FY 2010 (data reported as of June 2011), the AFCARS Report indicated that 26% of children in foster care had been with a relative, 48% were in non-relative foster care, and 6% were in a group home. More recently, the FY 2013 (data reported as of July 2014) AFCARS Report showed that 28% of children in foster care had been with a relative, 47% were in non-relative foster care, and 6% were in a group home.

The general goals of the child welfare system are to protect children from danger caused by their parents or other caregivers; to enhance family preservation and support; and to find permanence for the child. As illustrated below, kinship care and adoption achieve these goals.

III. Requirements to Become a Kinship Foster Caregiver

As of 2010, in most states, the placing agency must do an assessment to determine that the relative is "fit and willing" to provide a suitable placement for the child, able to ensure the child's safety, and able to meet the child's needs. Three states (Connecticut, Minnesota, and South Carolina) require the relative to complete requirements for licensure as a foster parent. Illinois and Wisconsin require the relative to be licensed before he or she can receive foster care assistance payments. Approximately 21 states and the District of Columbia require relatives to undergo a criminal background check that may include all adult members of the household.

Table 10.2 — Characteristics of Kinship Foster Parents vs. Non-Kin
(Future of Children, 2004)

% rates	Over age 60	Income ↓ poverty	No HS education	Single
Kin	18%	39%	32%	55%
Non-Kin	9%	13%	9%	29%

IV. The Statutory Framework and Case Law

The Adoption Assistance and Child Welfare Act of 1980, Pub. L. No. 96-272, 94 Stat. 500 ("AACWA"), has been touted as supportive of kinship care. However, although AACWA as originally passed by the United States House of Representatives included a provision giving preference to kinship foster care placements, the final act did not contain such provisions. Fortunately, in application, many state legislatures have interpreted the act to include such a preference based on Congress's originally-stated intent.

There are, however, what appear to be concerted efforts to undermine acknowledgement of and support for kinship care. For example, the final version of the Uniform Adoption Act ("UAA") changes course from previous drafts by reversing the order of placement priorities by placing kinship placements last. Kinship placement is fourth on a list of five categories, the fifth category being "any other individual selected by the agency" (UAA, §2-104, "Preferences for Placement When Agency Places Minor" (1994)).

Prior to 1997, individuals providing formal kinship foster care were eligible to receive federal maintenance payments from the Federal Aid to Families with Dependent Children Foster Care Program ("AFDC-FC"). This federal program provided federal matching funds to states that provided foster care to AFDC-eligible children. As part of welfare reform initiatives and pursuant to the Personal Responsibility and Work Opportunity Reconciliation Act of 1996 ("PRWORA"), Pub. L. No. 104-193, 110 Stat. 2105 (1996), in 1997, the AFDC program was replaced by the Temporary Assistance to Needy Families Program ("TANF") (*Aid to Families With Dependant Children and Temporary Assistance for Needy Families (Title IV-A), Ways and Means Committee*, GREEN BOOK 495 (U.S. Gov't Printing Office) (1998)). AFDC was a federally-designed program while TANF is designed and administered by individual states through federal block-grant funding.

The purposes of the TANF program are as follows: (1) provide assistance to needy families so that children may be cared for in their own homes or in the homes of relatives; (2) end the dependence of needy parents on government benefits by promoting job preparation, work, and marriage; (3) prevent and reduce the incidence of out-of-wedlock pregnancies and establish annual numerical goals for preventing and reducing the incidence of these pregnancies; and (4) encourage the formation and maintenance of two-parent families. TANF includes various work requirements necessary for benefits. Importantly, under federal welfare reform legislation, a five-year lifetime benefit cap has been placed on TANF benefits.

According to the DHHS—ACF, in FY 2008, of the 1,459,735 children in the United States receiving TANF benefits, 22.4% of these children were living with their grand-parents and another 9.2% were living with other relatives.

In general, states do not impose work requirements or time limits on voluntary kinship caregivers who receive child-only TANF grants, because these kinship caregivers are under no legal obligation to support the relative child. If kinship caregivers themselves receive TANF payments, federal work requirements and time limits do apply. States may exempt relative caregivers from state requirements and may support these caregivers in using state-only funds.

Historically, foster care benefits were generally larger than welfare payments. Although legally eligible to apply for these foster care payments, many kinship caregivers did not meet the objective qualifications for foster caregiver status, such as the number of bedrooms and square footage of the living areas, state or county licensing, and minimal training. Therefore, the majority of kinship caregivers relied on the lower TANF welfare payments for support.

During the mid-to-late 2000s, welfare reform tended to equalize the TANF/food stamps versus foster care payments. For example, a basic average guideline for the food stamp program will show that an average family of 4 can expect an amount up to $500 per month for food stamps. This figure will greatly vary based on the age of the family members and medical needs. A single person household will show an expected average of up to $200 per month in food stamps. These figures are averages and not state specific.

Cash allowance benefits for financial assistance is state regulated and allowances paid will also vary based on different criteria. However, an average expectation can be placed on a family of 4 receiving up to $900 for their TANF allowance. A single person household can expect an average of up to $300. In Indiana, the average welfare payment for a family of four is $346 a month. Combined with $668 in food stamps, about $1,014 a month is available as a welfare payment.

Alternatively, foster care payments vary by state and age of the child. Table 10.3 illustrates a sample of state-based payments on a monthly basis per foster child.

Table 10.3 — Basic Foster Care Payments (sample) (eff. 2004–08)

State	Age <1	Age 1–5	Age 6–11	Age 12–14	Age 15+
AR	$400	$400	$425	$450	$475
CA	$425	$425	$462/494	$546	$597
CN	$783	$783	$792	$859	$859
DC	$827	$827	$827	$899	$899
FL	$429	$429	$440	$440/515	$515
ID	$274	$274	$300	$300/431	$431
MA	$520	$520	$546	$546/565	$565
MI	$433	$433	$433	$433/535	$535
NH	$403	$403	$439	$439/518	$518
NJ	$454	$454	$489/510	$510/564	$564
TX	$652	$652	$652	$652	$652

Additionally, due to federal reimbursement guidelines that result in higher levels of state funding responsibility, some states refuse to award state foster care payments to eligible kinship foster care givers. In effect, these states are circumventing the long standing United States Supreme Court decision of *Miller v. Youakim*, 440 U.S. 125 (1979), which held that kinship foster care givers were eligible to receive state AFDC-FC funding on the same basis as non-kin foster caregivers.

Kinship caregivers are also shortchanging themselves on additional state and Federal benefits. In addition to TANF, kinship caregivers and relative children may be eligible for a wide range of federal and state programs. For example, almost all foster children and children cared for by kin who are outside the child welfare system and receive a TANF child-only payment are eligible for Medicaid. Kin are also eligible to receive Supplemental Security Income (SSI) for any related child who meets the disability guidelines of the program. Kin who are income-eligible for food stamps are eligible to receive additional food stamp benefits for related children. Depending upon the state, kin may also be eligible to receive housing assistance, subsidized child care, or emergency financial assistance.

However, historically, in spite of their eligibility, many kin caregivers do not receive this wide range of support. For example, in 2001 only 60% of kin caregivers who are income eligible receive food stamps and only 54% received Medicaid for their related child. In comparison, during the same time-frame, 78% of all food-stamp-eligible children participated in the program. Additionally, of all children eligible for both TANF and Medicaid, about 65% received Medicaid benefits.

Despite the opportunity for increased benefits as outlined above, some kinship caregivers, even if eligible, may balk at the prospect of further government involvement in and scrutiny of what they view as a private family matter. This may be particularly true in light of the fact that when a child becomes a ward of the state and a kinship caregiver receives government payments, the state is ultimately responsible for the child's care and placement under the rubric of formal kinship foster care. Thus, similar to the restrictions upon a non-kin foster caregiver, the kinship caregiver would have a secondary role in making important decisions.

As of 2010, 15 States and the District of Columbia had established kinship care or relative caregiver programs to provide relatives with benefits to help offset the cost of caring for a placed child (Alabama, Arizona, Connecticut, Delaware, Florida, Kentucky, Louisiana, Maryland, Mississippi, Nevada, Oklahoma, South Carolina, Tennessee, Texas, and Wisconsin). Also, 13 states had addressed foster care payments and financial support for kin caregivers (Alabama, Arizona, Connecticut, Florida, Illinois, Louisiana, Mississippi, Nevada, Oklahoma, Pennsylvania, South Carolina, Tennessee, and Wisconsin). In these states, if a relative meets the qualifications for being a foster parent, he or she may receive payments at the full foster care rate and any other benefits available to foster parents, whether in money or services.

More recently, the passage of the Preventing Sex Trafficking and Strengthening Safe Families Act of 2014 grants more benefits for kinship placement. The primary focus of the act is toward child permanency. After findings showing the best interest of the child is more often with a relative or a known caregiver, the act gives additional funding for kinship placement. This act is further defined in Chapter 14.

Studies of kinship foster care placements show that relative placements are more stable and the caregivers are more committed to caring for the children as long as necessary. This creates a double-edged sword because while the kinship foster caregiver is willing to care for the children indefinitely, reunification rates are statistically lower for kinship care than for non-kin foster care.

Despite data indicating that children are more likely to fare better when placed in kinship foster care than the home of a stranger, only since 1996 has federal legislation required that states give priority to placing children with relatives rather than non-kin providers as long as the kinship caregiver meets all relevant standards (Personal Responsibility and Work Opportunity Act of 1996 ("PRWOA"), *amending* Title IV-E, Social Security Act, 42 U.S.C.A. §671 (a)(19) (LexisNexis, 2010)).

Further, the Adoption and Safe Families Act of 1997 ("ASFA"), Pub. L. 105-89, called for more attention to kinship care as a unique type of foster care placement. However, this increased attention resulted in 18 states issuing stricter licensing for kin foster caregivers than prior to the passage of ASFA. However, kin can still be assessed differently from non-kin—20 states have a separate, less-stringent foster licensing process for kin versus non-kin caregivers.

As amended by the Fostering Connections to Success and Increasing Adoptions Act of 2008, Title IV-E further requires States to exercise due diligence to identify and provide notice to all grandparents and other adult relatives of the child (including any other adult relatives suggested by the parents) that the child has been or is being removed from the custody of his or her parents, explain the options the relative has to participate in the care and placement of the child, and describe the requirements to become a foster parent to the child (42 U.S.C. §671(a)(29) (LexisNexis 2010)).

As of July 2010, forty-one states and Puerto Rico statutorily give preference or priority to relative placements in their statutes. In nine states, the statutes specifically require state agencies to make reasonable efforts to identify and locate a child's relative when out-of-home placement is needed (namely, California, Illinois, Indiana, Iowa, Minnesota, Missouri, New Jersey, New York, and Oregon). As of that date, four states do not address the issue of the placement of children for foster care with relatives in their statutes (South Dakota, Vermont, West Virginia, and Wyoming). The remaining states use statutory language such as "may consider" placement with relatives.

Further, despite the fact that kinship caregivers have been found to be older, less financially stable single parents with less education and poorer health than non-kin caregivers, studies show that kinship caregivers on the whole receive less support, fewer services, and have less contact with state or federal agency workers than do non-kin foster caregivers.

The disparate treatment continued in 1992 when the Ninth Circuit affirmed an opinion upholding an Oregon statute that allowed state welfare agencies to spend more money per child if the child is not placed with relatives instead of paying less money per child and enabling more children to live with relatives (*Lipscomb v. Simmons*, 962 F.2d 1374, 1380, 1384 (9th Cir. 1992)).

In a perfect world perhaps every juvenile ward could have a custom-made child care plan funded by the state, giving both the benefits of care provided by loving relatives and medical services, counseling, and other professional services that would answer that child's particular needs at no cost to those relatives. The State of Oregon, finding itself in an imperfect budgetary environment, believed that it has allocated its limited resources in the best possible way in order to accomplish the goals of its foster care program.

At argument it was suggested that Oregon would be on firmer constitutional ground if it were to fashion a need-based schedule of payments to relatives providing foster care. The state is free to adopt any statutory scheme that meets minimal constitutional requirements. It is not the function of the judicial branch of the federal government, however, to fashion new and improved child-care plans for the states. Whether we would vote for the state's plan if it were placed before us as members of the legislative assembly is not the question we are to decide.

Id. at 1384.

This result essentially deprived some children of the option of living with relatives.

V. Current Trends in Kinship Care

The federal AFCARS Reports show that from federal Fiscal Year 2002 through FY 2010 (FFY = 10/01 through 09/30), the number of children in foster care in the 50 states plus Washington, DC, and Puerto Rico steadily declined from 523,000 to 408,425. In addition, the number of children in kinship foster care placements decreased from 125,955 to 103,943 from FY 2002 to FY 2010 (*see generally* Chapter 2 — Child Welfare System and Foster Care and *see* Table 10.4). While the net number of children in kinship foster care dropped, the annual number of kinship adoptions increased: From FY 2002 to FY 2010, the number of children in foster care adopted by kin went from 12,630 to 15,714 (*see* Table 10.4).

Table 10.4—Foster Care Kinship Placements (AFCAR Reports)

Fiscal Year	Total # in FC	# kinship care	% kinship care	% change
FY 2002	533,000	125,955	24%	NC
FY 2003	520,000	121,511	23%	↓1%
FY 2004	517,000	122,528	24%	↑1%
FY 2005	513,000	124,153	24%	NC
FY 2006	510,000	124,571	24%	NC
FY 2007	491,000	123,760	25%	↑1%
FY 2008	463,000	112,643	24%	↓1%
FY 2009	423,773	101,688	24%	NC
FY 2010	408,425	103,943	26%	↑2%
FY 2013	402,378	113,065	28%	↑2%

The federal AFCARS Reports show that in FY 2013 (FY 2009 through FY September 30, 2013) the number of children in foster care in the 50 states plus Washington, DC, and Puerto Rico oscillated a bit and ended up slightly declining from 418,672 to 402,378. In addition, the number of children in kinship foster care placements decreased from 125,955 to 113,065 from FY 2002 to FY 2013 (*see generally* Chapter 2—Child Welfare System and Foster Care and *see* Table 10.4). While the net number of children in kinship foster care dropped, the annual number of kinship adoptions almost remained the same: From FY 2010 to FY 2013, the number of children in foster care adopted by kin went from 15,714 to 15,524 (*see* Table 10.4).

The Fostering Connections to Success and Increasing Adoptions Act of 2008 ("FCSIAA") (Pub. L. 110-351) had the general purpose to amend Title IV-B & E of the Social Security Act to connect and support relative caregivers, improve outcomes for children in foster care, provide for tribal foster care and adoption access, improve incentives for adoption, and other purposes. Among its provisions, FCSIAA (1) created a new option for kinship guardian assistance payments (no greater than foster care maintenance payments) for eligible voluntary or formal kinship placements where legal guardianship of the child has been established (GAP does not apply to informal kinship placements); (2) extended Medicaid eligibility to include children receiving kinship guardian assistance payments; (3) designated kinship guardianship as a permanent placement under case plan provisions; (4) required that using due diligence—within 30 days of a child's removal—all adult relatives be identified and notified of their options to become a placement for the child; and (5) allowed a case-by-case waiver of non-safety foster care licensing standards for a relative foster family home.

VI. Interim and Alternative Programs

An interim step to adoption is subsidized kinship guardianship. There, the biological parents' rights are not terminated, but there is less government supervision and court intervention than with foster care. However, these subsidies are not reimbursed by the federal government, and therefore, only half of the states have implemented programs.

In light of the issues discussed above, some states have instituted alternative programs outside of both the child welfare and TANF systems to further facilitate kinship care.

The 2001 study by the Urban Institute, undertaken for DHHS, found 57 alternative programs: 34 were subsidized guardianship programs (10 of which were funded through TANF, 14 received state funds, and 1 received other federal funding); 23 were non-subsidized guardianship programs (4 of which were funded through TANF, 13 received state funds, 1 received other federal funding, 8 received local funding, and 10 received private financial support).

Fortunately, more attention is being paid to the needs of kinship caregivers as evidenced by the 2001 DHHS Kinship Care Report. The 2001 DHHS kinship care report listed the following so-called "lessons learned" about kinship care families:

- Kinship [care] families are diverse.
- Kinship care families have a wide range of needs.
- Kinship care families need more than money.
- Kinship care families benefit tremendously from support groups.
- Nearly all kinship care families need mental health services.
- Kinship care families need safe and accessible transportation.
- Kinship caregivers do not access available supports.
- Kinship caregivers want permanency, too.

VII. Kinship Adoption

Historically, kinship caregivers were less likely, and less willing, to adopt the children in their care. This was undoubtedly due to their reticence to sever a relative's parental rights, particularly where the caregiver is the child's grandparent. For example, in FY 1998, 64% of the children adopted from foster care were adopted by former foster parents, whereas only 14% were adopted by relatives (AFCARS Report). However, due to changes in federal and state laws (most recently FCSIAA of 2008 (Pub. L. 110-351)), which encouraged kinship care and kinship adoption, kinship adoption has risen from 24% of the total children adopted from foster care in FY2002 to 32% in FY2010. In the FY2013 report, of the 29,428 children who were adopted by a foster parent, 2,535 of those parents were a relative. Notably, 19,861 of the respondents did not identify whether the foster parent was a relative or a non-relative.

Table 10.5 — Children Adopted from Foster Care (AFCARS Reports)

Fiscal Year	Total # adopted from FC	# kinship adoptions	% kinship adoptions	% change
FY 2002	53,000	12,630	24%	NC
FY 2003	50,000	11,563	23%	↓1%
FY 2004	52,000	12,624	24%	↑1%
FY 2005	51,000	12,759	25%	↑1%
FY 2006	51,000	13,321	26%	↑1%
FY 2007	52,000	14,666	28%	↑2%
FY 2008	55,000	16,749	30%	↑2%
FY 2009	57,466	17,300	32%	↑2%
FY 2010	52,891	15,714	32%	NC

As of July 2010, in approximately seven states, state agencies must give preference to relatives when making adoptive placements for children in their custody (Arkansas, California, Illinois, Minnesota, Nebraska, Ohio, and Wisconsin). However, in four states, if the child has been placed in foster care with a non-relative and has been living with the same foster parent for significant period of time when he or she becomes available for adoption, the non-relative foster parent may be given first preference to adopt (California, Missouri, New York, and Tennessee).

Importantly, in approximately thirty-one states, when a parent makes a direct placement of the child with a relative, the state laws provide for a streamlined adoption process. Significantly, no pre-placement assessment or home study is required unless specifically ordered by the court. However, twelve states require that the child must have resided with the relative for a period of time or have established a significant relationship with the relative in some other way (Alabama, Alaska, California, Colorado, Delaware, Florida, Louisiana, Missouri, New Hampshire, New Mexico, North Dakota, and Virginia). Approximately twenty-one states require a criminal records check of the adopting relatives and other adult household members.

In conclusion, to get the country's foster system out of its current state, education programs must be implemented to disabuse kinship caregivers to the notion that it is in the child's best interest for parental bonds not to be broken. Stability and permanency are ultimately in the child's best interest. Kinship foster care and kinship adoption provide stability and permanency while keeping the child within its extended family.

Checkpoints

- A kinship relative can be defined as a blood relative, a neighbor, or someone who has provided care for the child. Kinship can be informal, voluntary, or formal in definition.

- Kinship placement can be helpful for the child because the child already has an established relationship with the caregiver. It can also be detrimental in situations where the child is taken from the parent for drug related offenses, and the caregiver and parent are in close contact.

- A goal of kinship care is to find permanency for the child. The number of grandparents as caregivers is on the rise.

- Many state legislatures have interpreted the AACWA as preferring kinship placement.

- Most states require a criminal background check and a home investigation before kinship placement.

- TANF was enacted to provide assistance for needy families, and to help with situations like kinship care placements.

- While the number of kinship foster placements has dropped, the number of kinship adoptions has increased.

- ASFA called for more attention to kinship placement as a unique alternative to foster care, but in turn caused many states to create stricter regulations on kinship care.

- A subsidized kinship guardianship is an interim step to adoption.

Chapter 11

Safe Haven Laws

Roadmap

- The definition of a safe haven law and its history in the United States
- The different safe haven laws among the states
- The effect of safe haven laws on communities
- The pros and cons of safe haven laws

I. History of Safe Haven Laws

The concept of safe havens for abandoned infants has existed for centuries. The Catholic Church created a system in which a turnstile type revolving door was placed outside of churches where mothers could place their unwanted newborns. After they rang an attached bell, the wheel rotated into the church where the baby was taken in and cared for.

This system caught on throughout Europe, but was widely abandoned during the 1800s. However, some European countries still use a similar mechanism or system, including Germany and Hungary.

Since the late 1990s, safe haven laws have been enacted in all fifty states of the U.S. The purpose of these laws is to save the lives of newborns that are at risk for being abandoned by their birth parents.

Originally, the exigent need for these types of laws stemmed from two highly publicized cases. In 1997, a high school student, while attending her prom, gave birth to her baby in a bathroom. She strangled the baby, left him in the bathroom's trash can, returned to the dance, and remained there for its duration.

A few months before the above mentioned case, after the woman gave birth, the parents (two college students) threw their newly born child into the trash can and left it there.

These cases brought about a national uproar. Texas was the first state to enact safe haven laws in 1999. Other states quickly followed suit. To date, all fifty states and Washington, DC, have adopted safe haven statutes.

II. The Purpose of Safe Haven Laws

The laws proclaimed to save lives by creating safe places for birth mothers to "drop off" their babies when they feel they cannot rise to the challenge of motherhood. These laws are also variously referred to as "state infant abandonment" laws, "safe surrender" laws, or "Baby Moses" laws.

The purpose of safe haven laws is to ensure that relinquished infants are left with persons who can provide the immediate care needed for their safety and well-being. To that end, approximately sixteen states and Puerto Rico require parents to relinquish their infants to a hospital or health-care facility. In seven states, emergency medical technicians, including personnel responding to 9-1-1 calls, may accept an infant. In addition, four states and Puerto Rico allow churches to act as safe havens, but the relinquishing parent must first determine that church personnel are present at the time the infant is left. In thirteen of the states that do not require hospital drop-off, the safe haven location must provide immediate medical attention and transfer the baby to a hospital as soon as possible.

In approximately thirteen states, infants who are 72 hours old or younger may be relinquished to a designated safe haven. Approximately nineteen states accept infants up to one month old. The remaining states specify varying age limits in their statutes.

Generally, the parents who relinquish their child in this manner have no intentions of getting the newborn back. As such, most safe haven laws allow the parents to relinquish their newborn anonymously. In the event that a birth parent changes their mind about relinquishing its newborn to the state, he or she may find they are without recourse. A few states, such as Alabama and Minnesota, have programs that allow for such an occurrence by providing the birth parent with an identity bracelet that identifies the newborn.

Twenty states have procedures in place for a parent to reclaim the infant, usually within a specified time period and before any petition to terminate parental rights has been granted. Five states also have provisions for a non-relinquishing father to petition for custody of the child. In seventeen states and Puerto Rico, the act of surrendering an infant to a safe haven is presumed to be a relinquishment of parental rights to the child, and no further parental consent is required for the child's adoption.

In most states, the parents are not required to provide any information about themselves or their family's medical history when relinquishing their newborn. Some require safe havens to try to get information from the birth parents, but if unsuccessful, the birth parent can still leave their newborn and are not compelled to provide the information. In twenty-five states, the provider is required to ask the parent for family and medical history information (although the information is not required to be given). In seventeen states, the provider is required to attempt to give the parent(s) information about the legal repercussions of leaving the infant and information about referral services. Georgia is one of the only states to require a mother to provide identification and permanent address.

Additionally, under safe haven statutes, parents are usually granted immunity from any criminal charges for child abandonment, or are at least granted the affirmative defense of complying with a safe haven law if subsequently charged with abandonment. In states that allow an affirmative defense, it is important to remember that the parent can still be convicted of abandonment if charges are brought against them and the jury does not believe the parent's defense.

While the specifics of each state statute may differ, they all designate certain locations where newborns can be dropped off, who can relinquish a newborn, and the age of the newborn. Designated locations tend to be a hospital, a police station, a fire station, or some other emergency medical service. Most states require that a birth parent relinquish the newborn under the safe haven laws, but some states allow an agent of a birth parent to do so.

III. Arguments for Safe Haven Laws

A. Safe Haven Laws Protect and Save Lives of Unwanted Newborns

Proponents of safe haven laws argue that even if only one child is saved under these laws, then the laws are effective. The option to drop off and relinquish their parental rights to newborns is argued to be more humane than those cases where birth parents have "thrown away" their unwanted infants. A study in 2002 showed that most infants killed within twenty-four hours of birth happen outside of a hospital. Therefore, a safe haven law gives the mother a chance to drop the baby off without having to resort to murdering the child.

However, the statistics on how many newborns are saved because of these laws are unclear. Individual cases of babies being abandoned often receive a lot of press, but the frequency of such acts is unknown.

Federal and state governments do not keep track of the number of babies abandoned in public places, but the Department of Health and Human Services did conduct such a study in 1998. It found 105 reports of newborns abandoned in public places. Of the 105 reports, 33 newborns were found dead.

B. Safe Haven Laws Prevent Crimes from Happening

Safe haven laws allow a birth parent to relinquish their newborn to a safe haven as opposed to leaving their newborn in a public place. By leaving a newborn in a public place, parents could face criminal charges of abandonment, and in the worst case, face homicide charges if their newborn dies.

In 2000, the Department of Justice found that 265 children one year of age or less had been murdered. The Center for Disease Control estimated that of the known probable infant homicides, 8% of the homicides occurred on the day of the infant's birth, also called neonaticide. Between 1983 and 1991, 139 infants were murdered on their first day of life. In another study released in June 2010, there are approximately 8 neonaticide deaths per 100,000 for children under the age of 1 year.

In a study conducted from 1976 to 2005 detailing the numbers of children murdered before the age of 5, it showed the younger the child, the greater the risk for infanticide. In those cases, a parent is most likely the murderer—31% were killed by fathers while 29% were killed by mothers.

In 2007, there was discussion in the court system of classifying neonaticide as a syndrome. However, a label of "neonaticide syndrome" would require the elements of the Frye test to be met, the most important being widely accepted in the field of science. The definition continued to be bounced around even in 2013. Because of the lack of strong parallels among victims, and therefore disagreement on a common definition, this has not yet been accepted by the court system.

C. Safe Haven Laws Create More Adoptable Infants

Proponents of safe haven laws argue that more infants are available for adoption as a result of safe haven laws. The rationale is that one less newborn who dies from an illegal abandonment is one more newborn who can be legally adopted.

IV. Arguments Against Safe Haven Laws

A. Safe Haven Laws Are Ineffective and Encourage Birth Parents to Abandon their Newborns

Opponents argue that safe haven laws are ineffective because newborns are still being abandoned in locations other than those designated by safe haven statutes.

Additionally, young birth mothers are often in denial about their pregnancy; do not receive counseling or medical care; and are unaware of the option of adoption. As a result, safe haven laws are an "easy out" for these young birth mothers.

Arguably, safe haven laws are ineffective because they fail to address the possibility of a birth mother's mental illness, specifically postpartum depression. When a birth mother suffers from a mental illness, she does not think about the consequences of her actions. In not recognizing this possibility, the safe haven laws treat all mothers who abandon their infants the same way—they terminate birth parent's rights the moment the newborn is left. Thus, the mentally ill birth mother cannot later return and reclaim her newborn after she realizes her mistake.

B. Safe Haven Babies Are Deprived of Their Right to Family Medical History

Safe haven laws deprive newborns of their right to a personal identity and knowledge of their family medical history. This is an important issue because many physical and mental illnesses can be tied to a person's genetics.

Further, the anonymity provision contradicts current research that shows the importance of collecting such information and the rise in open adoption. Those children adopted that do have access to their medical history are more likely to prevent, detect, pre-diagnose, and treat inherited diseases. Even in cases where birth parents remain anonymous in domestic adoptions, there is usually a court file that contains such information. That information usually can be opened by court order for compelling reasons. Due to the cloak of anonymity, there is no such file for safe haven adoptees.

Not only does the anonymity provision affect a safe haven adoptee's ability to obtain medical information, but it also prevents the safe haven adoptee from learning about their social history. A person's identity and a sense of where they came from is important to any child growing up. Without this knowledge, it could lead to a safe haven adoptee becoming an unstable and unproductive member of society.

C. What about the Birth Father?

In adoption proceedings, states must make diligent efforts to locate a birth father and provide them notice of a pending adoption proceeding before terminating that father's parental rights. Under safe haven laws, a birth mother could leave their newborn at a hospital and not inform the birth father of her actions. Because of the anonymous nature of the laws, it is nearly impossible for the state to search for birth fathers.

Further, if the birth mother uses a safe haven to drop off the child anonymously, a father would not be notified even if he is listed on the state's putative father registry. Also, in a case where the father uses the registry to search for a child, it would be useless because children are listed under the mother's name. In that case, the registry would not have the birth mother's name because she is able to remain anonymous under safe haven laws.

D. Safe Haven Laws Are Unnecessary

Opponents argue that safe haven laws are unnecessary because every state has laws that allow birth parents to voluntarily terminate their parental rights in a manner that usually imposes no criminal liability. These birth parents are able to retain their privacy while placing their child up for adoption.

In a similar situation where a birth parent leaves a newborn in a hospital after giving birth and clearly states her intention not to return, the state rarely prosecutes such birth parents. In that case, the state's goal is to place the newborn in a permanent adoptive home as soon as possible, not to punish the birth parent.

Further, the parents who do drop off their newborns at safe havens would be more likely to place their newborn up for adoption if the safe haven laws were not enacted. Because they took the initiative to protect their newborn by relinquishing them to a safe haven, they would probably do the same if the laws were not in place. In that scenario, at least a child may have the ability to get family medical history and the birth parents could have gotten counseling.

Contrarily, the parents who abandon their newborns at locations other than safe havens would continue to do so even if they were informed about safe havens.

E. Legal Implications — No Valid Consent

Some laws do not require the persons leaving the newborn to identify themselves. This raises serious issues if the newborn child was abducted from the birth parents prior to being placed at a safe haven. It also gives one birth parent the ability to abandon their newborn without the consent of the other birth parent.

Some of the laws do not require the person that drops off the newborn to sign any relinquishment document. One-third of the states do not address the termination of parental rights under safe haven laws. This could leave the newborn in the state system longer than anticipated if no formal consent to terminate parental rights was signed and filed if the state requires such a consent form. As such, newborns could be left in foster care until all legal requirements are met, which varies from state to state. For example, in New Mexico, abandoned children are ineligible for adoption due to the state's legal procedures.

Other states see abandonment as a waiver of parental rights. In states where adoptive families can adopt an abandoned newborn, the adoptive parents risk the possibility of members of the birth family seeking custody of the newborn.

The safe haven laws also have the ability to contradict a state's adoption law. States typically require a certain period of time to pass before a parent can voluntarily relinquish their parental rights. If this period is longer than that required by safe haven laws, it seems contradictory and unfair to the birth parents.

Professionals have long agreed that the waiting period after birth before a mother can voluntarily relinquish her parental rights is critical. Studies have shown that at least 50% of the birth mothers that considered adoption during their pregnancy ultimately decided to parent their newborns. Importantly, the ultimate decision to parent their child is often made days or even weeks after giving birth.

Therefore, if a birth mother can leave her child immediately after birth under safe haven laws, there is a possibility she could have changed her mind in the days or weeks following the relinquishment. Depending on state law, she may be past the point where she can change her mind about the safe haven relinquishment. Significantly, about half of the states do not statutorily address this issue at all.

Finally, while informing birth parents of all their rights (and counseling them about the emotional affects) is usually required in adoption law across the states, less than one-third of the states require safe havens to provide information about reunification or parental rights to birth parents abandoning their newborns.

Checkpoints

- The concept of safe haven laws began with churches accepting unwanted babies.

- Today, all fifty states have safe haven laws, although regulations differ from state to state.

- Most safe haven laws allow the parent to drop off the baby anonymously. Some states allow a drop off period for up to one month after the birth.

- The purpose of safe haven laws is to give unwanted babies a chance at life, and to save the parent from murdering the child. In addition, it opens a door for parents who want to adopt.

- Neonaticide, or infanticide, is when the child is murdered on the day of its birth.

- Arguments against safe haven laws are that statistics are unclear if the law really makes a difference. In addition, there isn't an opportunity to offer the mother psychiatric help, especially in the case of post-partum depression.

- Another negative drawback to safe haven laws is seen when the mother anonymously delivers the infant. The biological father cannot be found and given notice of the infant's birth, or a chance to terminate his parental rights.

- Some states offer a period where the mother can reclaim the unwanted infant; some view the drop off as a complete and voluntary surrender of all parental rights; and many states do not address this area at all.

Chapter 12

Snowflake Adoption

Roadmap

- The definition of in vitro fertilization (snowflake adoption)
- The process of a snowflake adoption from the biological and adoptive views
- The laws surrounding snowflake adoption
- Statistics of biological donors and resulting adoptions

I. What Is Embryo, a.k.a. "Snowflake," Adoption?

A. Process of in vitro Fertilization

An estimated 6.5 to 10 million couples in the United States cannot conceive a child through intercourse. The ability to conceive a child only through intercourse changed in 1978 when the first "test tube baby" was born through a process known as in vitro fertilization.

In vitro fertilization is the technique used to produce embryos in a lab environment. This technique involves fertilizing an egg and sperm in a Petri dish that is supplied with various nutrients. Prior to harvesting the eggs from the woman, she is injected with hormones in order for her to produce multiple egg follicles. The woman's eggs are removed from the woman through surgery known as laparoscopy. Outside of the uterus and in a laboratory environment, the eggs are fertilized with sperm and two to six fertilized embryos are surgically implanted in the woman's uterus.

Any remaining fertilized embryos are stored by a process called cryopreservation, in which the embryos are frozen and stored for future use by the couple. Once the genetic parents become pregnant and give birth, many of their embryos go unused. The genetic parents must then decide what to do with their remaining embryos.

B. Unutilized Embryos

As of September 2012, there were approximately 600,000 frozen embryos being stored in laboratories across the United States. There are several options available to genetic parents who no longer have a use for their embryos:

(1) The embryos can be kept in storage in case the parents ever decide to have another child, in which case the genetic parents continue to pay storage fees. Typically, the embryos can be stored for up to 5 years and remain "viable" for implantation.

(2) The embryos can be destroyed.

(3) The genetic couple could donate their embryos for scientific research. Most medical researchers believe that this research can lead to the ability to cure various diseases through stem cell research. However, opponents of donating embryos to research believe that this is a form of infanticide because they believe that life begins when an egg is fertilized with sperm. The majority of the medical community disagrees with that belief.

(4) The genetic couple could place their embryos for adoption — via a process called "snowflake adoption" because each embryo is unique.

C. Snowflake/Embryo Adoption

An embryo adoption consists of one family adopting the frozen embryos of another couple. The embryos are then implanted in the adoptive mother's uterus through a process known as in vitro fertilization.

As with a traditional adoption, an embryo adoption can be open or closed. In that sense, the genetic family can choose to have future contact with their genetic child or they can remain anonymous. Even if they choose to remain anonymous, typically, the genetic parents are required to release their medical and social history to the adoptive parents.

1. Nightlight Christian Adoptions

Embryo adoption is also known as a snowflake adoption. This term was coined by Nightlight Christian Adoptions. In 1997, Nightlight Christian Adoptions was the first agency to handle these types of adoptions. In a snowflake adoption, genetic parents control who receives their embryos. Because some courts treat embryos as property as opposed to a human being, contract law tends to govern snowflake adoptions.

However, Nightlight Christian Adoptions treats these adoptions just like traditional adoptions, including conducting a homestudy on the prospective adoptive parents.

As of December 2011, Nightlight Christian Adoptions had matched 480 genetic parents with 328 adoptive parents. These matches included approximately 3,075 embryos. A total of 293 children had been born as a result of the matching and adoption process.

2. The Process

In a snowflake adoption, genetic parents provide the agency with the characteristics the potential adoptive family are seeking—including age, income, career, religion, and race of the adoptive family. Genetic parents also have control over how much future contact they want with the adopted child.

If a potential adoptive family matches the criteria, their information is sent to the genetic parents. Genetic parents receive a biography of the family and photos—similar to the adoption notebook/binder required for typical private agency adoption placements. In addition, potential adoptive parents must provide a letter from a doctor ensuring the adoptive mother is able to carry and give birth to a child.

Once the genetic parents choose the adoptive family, the genetic parents' information is sent to the adoptive family for their consideration.

If both couples agree to the embryo adoption, a legal contract is drafted, signed, and sealed. Typically, the contract includes the terms of the adoption agreement and relinquishment forms. These forms specify that the genetic parents are relinquishing all rights to their embryos and future genetic children. The contract language matches a contract involving the transfer of property, although it also includes adoption language.

The adoption process takes approximately five to thirteen months before the embryos are shipped to the adoptive family's clinic—including the application, matching process, and the legal transfer of the embryos.

Once the proper forms are agreed to and fully executed, the embryos are shipped to a clinic chosen by the adoptive family.

Other than the storage fees for their embryos prior to making a match with the adoptive family, genetic parents do not pay for any costs in an embryo adoption. Sometimes blood work for the genetic family is required. However, the adoptive family reimburses or pays for those costs. The total cost to the adoptive parents is estimated at $12,000–$16,000.

If there are embryos remaining after the implantation process is complete, those embryos revert back to the genetic parents. At that point, the genetic parents would again begin to pay for the storage fees and the process of looking for another adoptive family, if they so desire.

Most embryo adoption agencies limit the number of embryos that are transferred to the adoptive parents to the ultimate number of children the adoptive family would be comfortable raising. This is especially important should more than one child be born as a result of the implantation process — i.e., twins, triplets, etc.

The Society for Assisted Reproductive Technology suggests that doctors only transfer two to three embryos at a time to try to reduce the rate of multiple pregnancies. Alternatively, other groups advocate for a single embryo transfer. In a clinical study in Seattle, WA, 76% of women who were implanted with a single embryo got pregnant compared to 78% of women who were implanted with two embryos.

3. Federal Regulations and Federal and State Funding

In an effort to make the process safe, the U.S. Food and Drug Administration (FDA) has regulated the transplantation of human tissue since 1993 (21 CFR 1270). The FDA regulates how embryos are to be recovered, processed, stored, labeled, packaged, and/or distributed. The FDA established a screening and testing process for donors to complete to ensure no diseases will be transmitted. As a result, donors are screened and tested for HIV, hepatitis B, hepatitis C, Creutzfeldt-Jakob disease, and syphilis.

While the testing and screening of sexually active donors are not required, the FDA recommends that the semen and egg donors be screened and tested before the transfer of embryos. Even anonymous donors are required to be screened.

The FDA has also established regulations and registration requirements for the agencies involved. Other than the federal regulations, it is discretionary whether the clinic requires further testing, screening, or implements further policies on releasing information and records.

In 2001, federal funding was permitted for the scientific research utilizing embryos. However, the research was limited to only those embryos that were created before the funding was given. Notably, Louisiana and Pennsylvania enacted statutes criminalizing the use of embryos in scientific research *in toto*. Additionally, North Dakota and Rhode Island enacted statutes that criminalized certain aspects of the use of embryos in scientific research.

Federal funding has been given to embryo adoption agencies in an effort to publicize frozen embryo adoption. In 2008, President George W. Bush established the Embryo Adoption Public Awareness Campaign, for which 3.9 million dollars were appropriated in that year alone.

In 2009, Georgia enacted the Option of Adoption Act. The Act established that embryo adoptions are to be governed by adoption law and recognized the adoptive parents as the legal parents of the resulting child. Under that Act, adoptive parents of embryos are eligible for the federal adoption tax credit.

D. Advantages of Snowflake Adoptions

For genetic parents, snowflake adoptions give them a sense of ease when transferring their embryos to an adoptive couple since they have the ability to choose the adoptive parents. The genetic parents can determine how open they want the adoption to be or if they want it to be a closed adoption. Home-studies are completed to ensure the safety of the future adopted child. In addition, education and counseling are offered to both families.

For adoptive parents, a snowflake adoption gives them something they are not able to do in traditional adoption — give birth to their adopted child. This is an attractive alternative for couples who are infertile. For infertile couples that cannot afford the costs of egg retrieval and fertilization, snowflake adoptions are a less expensive alternative.

Additionally, embryo adoptions also cost less than a traditional adoption. A typical embryo adoption costs anywhere from $7,000 to $10,000. Importantly, from a legal perspective, the adoptive parents are not buying the embryo, rather, they pay only for the expenses involved in the adoption. In vitro fertilization procedures and traditional private agency or independent adoptions can cost anywhere between $10,000 and $40,000+.

E. Disadvantages of Snowflake Adoptions

Snowflake adoptions may be more emotionally difficult than a traditional adoption because there is no guarantee of birthing a child. Studies show that there is only a 50% success rate in embryos surviving the thawing process and an additional 30% success rate in implantation. If embryos survive those processes, they are subject to any typical pregnancy risks.

Another risk for adoptive parents is the risk that they will conceive a child with a chromosome abnormality, including Down syndrome. Occasionally, when an egg or sperm cell is created, an extra chromosome is made or is missing, which leads to the child having Down syndrome. The risk of Down syndrome increases with age of the genetic donors.

Opponents of embryo adoption argue that it is a form of selecting "designer babies." As the argument goes, adoptive parents would only seek genetic parents with similar physical traits to their own — such as hair type, eye color, and race. As a result, opponents argue embryo adoption is unconstitutional as it is a form of discrimination. Proponents of embryo adoption counter that the same could be said of traditional adoption.

II. Legal Ramifications of Snowflake Adoptions

A. Early Cases

In the late 1980s, a legal question arose over who had control over embryos that were yet to be implanted in a woman. This issue arose in cases involving disputes between clinics and genetic couples as well as in disputes between genetic couples that were divorcing.

1. Disputes between Clinics and Genetic Couples — Misuse of Embryos

In 1989, a district court considered a dispute between a married couple and the fertility clinic where they underwent in vitro fertilization (*York v. Jones*, 717 F. Supp. 421 (E.D. Va. 1989)). The clinic refused to transfer the couple's frozen embryos to another clinic that the couple decided to utilize.

The Court concluded that the agreement between the couple and the clinic required the clinic to give the embryos back to the couple when the relationship between the clinic and couple ended. In that decision, the court defined the embryos as the couple's personal property and, as such, the clinic had to recognize the couple's property rights.

2. Genetic Couples Divorcing — What Happens to the Embryos

In 1992, the Tennessee Supreme Court took on the issue of who had control over cryopreserved embryos when a couple was divorcing (*Davis v. Davis*, 842 S.W.2d 588 (Tenn. 1992)).

The Court held that the parent who wished not to have a child superseded the other parent who wanted to bear the child unless a prior agreement was reached. Since *Davis*, the highest state courts in Iowa, Massachusetts, New Jersey, New York, and Washington have issued similar decisions. Those State Supreme Courts enforced prior agreements between the divorcing couple as to what could be done with the embryo(s) as long as it did not involve "forced procreation." "Forced procreation" is defined as one spouse using the embryo to get pregnant over the objection of the other.

B. Legal Status of Embryos

Currently there are some state laws that govern embryo adoption. Eight states enacted embryo donation statutes that mirror laws on sperm and egg donation. The Model Uniform Parentage Act proposed that any questions on parentage in the embryo donation context should be decided on the intent of the donation, not the genetics. State laws vary—as an example, New York has strict human tissue laws and does not allow any embryos to be shipped into the state.

A married couple in Tennessee is attempting to sell their unused, stored embryos on Facebook. They have enough children already through previous successful in vitro procedures, and consider their remaining embryos are human beings. Because of this, they wish to sell the embryos versus having them destroyed by the clinic. In Tennessee, there is statutory law that governs the transfer of embryos between the embryo custodian and the adoptive parents (Tenn. Code Ann. § 36-2-403 (West 2013)). A written contract between the parties is needed to have the embryo custodian relinquish all rights, and the embryo storage clinic could then transfer the embryos to the adoptive parents' clinic. The adoptive parents would then consider the embryo to be their legal child. At this point, there is no law governing the advertisement to sell one's embryos on avenues like social media (Facebook). Nor is there any restriction for this couple to choose their potential adoptive parents and relinquish their embryos to them. As long as both parties agree and there is a signed writing officiating this agreement, the transfer is legal.

In Arizona, there is a statute prohibiting an advertisement to sell human embryos (Ariz. Rev. Stat. Ann. § 36-2312 (2010)). The statue reads "a person shall not purchase or sell or offer to purchase or sell an in vitro human embryo and shall not advertise for the purchase or sale of an in vitro human embryo. This subsection does not prohibit payment to a physician by a patient." In this state, an offer by a parent to sell their embryos on Facebook would be disallowed.

It is obvious that states differ on their treatment of embryo classification and transfers. Due to this relatively new procedure, case law will shape the future of in vitro fertilization and snowflake adoptions.

1. As Human Beings

Some states have enacted statutes that declare an embryo as a human being or a "judicial person." As such, embryos are treated the same as newborn infants; in determining their future, a best interests of the child standard is applied. Louisiana has enacted such a statute. Under that statute and the like, an embryo cannot be owned and the embryo(s) cannot be destroyed by the genetic parents or clinic. Instead, both the genetic parents and clinic are temporary guardians of the embryo until it is implanted with the adoptive, married family. New Mexico is another state that protects the fetus and its future safety and well-being. In doing so, New Mexico's state law requires that all excess embryos must be implanted or they are to be frozen indefinitely.

Opponents of this viewpoint argue that embryos only carry a potential for life, and until they are implanted in a woman's uterus, they are not entitled to the same legal protections held by humans.

If an embryo can be adopted, it raises questions about:

(1) when the adoption occurs and when the genetic parents terminate and relinquish their rights to the embryo; especially since, in nearly all of the States, adoption can only occur after the birth of the child.

(2) the ability to destroy the embryos or donate them to research if they are considered people. If they are humans, they should not be able to be destroyed.

(3) implications that abortion and some fertility techniques should be criminalized. If criminalized, medical doctors would become the subject of wrongful death suits where embryos did not survive the thawing or implantation process.

2. As Property

In states that treat embryos as property, the genetic parents are granted the authority to determine how to dispose of their property because they are the property owners. Those who support this view argue that because an embryo cannot develop without being implanted into a women's uterus, an embryo resembles a property interest and not a human life

Even for those who view embryos as property, an issue remains when a couple decides to divorce—namely, what happens to the embryos upon divorce? Florida law, for example, requires a written agreement that contains the parties' wishes for disposal upon divorce prior to the IVF procedure. In Kansas, a couple may dispose of embryos only when it has been jointly agreed to by the parties.

3. As a Hybrid—More than a Property Interest, but Not a Human Being

Some states categorize embryos as something more than a property interest, but not as a human being. In such a categorization, embryos have some legal protection afforded to them. As a result, genetic parents maintain their property interest, but their property interest is not absolute in determining the future use of their embryos.

The *Davis* court ruled that an embryo was neither property nor a person, but was entitled to "special respect" because of its capacity to become a person

(*Davis v. Davis*, 842 S.W.2d 588 (Tenn. 1992)). Since that case, the highest state courts in Iowa, Massachusetts, New Jersey, New York, and Washington have all acknowledged that embryos are "unique and distinctive entities." Although a lot of state courts subscribe to this method of characterizing embryos, neither the state courts nor the state statutes define what protections embryos are entitled to.

Checkpoints

- Snowflake adoption, or embryo adoption, is where a human egg is fertilized with human sperm in a petri dish; the embryo is then cryogenically stored in a freezer until implantation.

- The term snowflake came about because each embryo is unique.

- These embryos can be stored for usually up to five years, can be implanted at a later time, can be used for scientific research, can be destroyed, or can be adopted out to different parents.

- Nightlight Christian Adoptions was one of the first companies to offer this type of service.

- In snowflake adoptions, genetic parents can choose their potential adoptive parents; adoptive parents can also choose desired characteristics of the genetic parents. The process is done through the health clinic and implantation carried out by licensed physicians.

- Clinics will limit the number of embryos delivered to an adoptive family. This is because many times, twins and triplets are born in the first implantation.

- The FDA regulates embryo transfers, requiring donators to be tested for diseases and potential genetic issues.

- Some states enacted statutes declaring their existing adoptions laws will govern the embryo adoptions; therefore, the adoptive parents carry the parental rights.

- Divorce presents an interesting legal issue for embryo adoption and storage because of who carries the parental rights.

- The question of defining the status of the embryo as human being or property is still being decided in state courts.

Chapter 13

Wrongful Adoption Tort

Roadmap

- The history surrounding the wrongful adoption tort
- The legal consequences for an agency's intentional misrepresentation
- The definitions of negligent failure to investigate, negative placement, and breach of contract
- The damages awarded in resulting lawsuits and the effect on the child and family

---

I. History

During the mid-twentieth century, it was widely recognized that adoption agencies and intermediaries were to provide as little information as possible about a child's health, medical history, and social background to potential adoptive parents. It was believed that the adoptive parents—and therefore the child—were better off in the long run without this information.

Information such as a pre-disposition to criminal behavior, mental illness, or any other physical or mental problem were usually concealed. Agencies often did not share this information for fear that they would not be able to find permanent homes for the affected children. In the alternative, the concern was that if they did share any derogatory information with the adoptive parents, the child would be (further) stigmatized. Additional concerns held by the adoption agencies regarding the release of such information included: the child would develop self-image problems; cause the child extreme anxiety; and adversely affect the privacy rights of the birth parents.

Prior to 1986, the only remedy available to adoptive parents whose adoption intermediaries (including public and private agencies and independent agents) failed to disclose essential information about the adopted child's health, education, and social background was to either annul or abrogate the adoption.

Courts disfavored annulments because they did not want the child to have to go through any more significant changes to his or her life. Additionally, most parents did not want to void the adoption of a child that they had already become emotionally attached to. As a result, parents began to bring suits against the adoption intermediaries in an effort to gain financial compensation for their child's medical expenses and any other expenses incurred due to the child's undisclosed issues.

The first court to ever hold such an intermediary liable for what became known as "wrongful adoption" was the Ohio Supreme Court in a 1986 case (*Burr v. Board of County Com'rs of Stark County*, 491 N.E.2d 1101 (Ohio 1986)).

In *Burr*, an adoption agency enticed the Burrs to adopt a baby boy who they said was healthy, born of a young unwed mother who could not care for the child and who voluntarily gave up the child. However, agency records revealed that the child was of low intelligence, at risk of having Huntington's disease, and the birth mother was a mental patient who was raped while hospitalized. The Burrs filed suit against the agency alleging fraud. Further, they testified that had they known the truth about the child they would have never adopted him.

The Court held that the agency must be held accountable for injuries that were a direct result from their "deceitful and material misrepresentations" that were relied upon by the adoptive parents. The Court affirmed the monetary damages awarded to the Burrs because the agency deliberately misinformed the couple about the child, and as a result, the couple was not able to make an informed decision whether to adopt the child.

Since the *Burr* decision, hundreds of lawsuits have been filed nationwide by adoptive parents against adoption intermediaries for their failure to disclose information about adoptive children's medical history and the children's educational and social background prior to adoption. Collectively, these suits were called "wrongful adoption" actions. As time went on, different legal theories emerged in addition to fraud and intentional misrepresentation, and were asserted for different types of conduct.

II. Causes of Action

A. Fraud: Intentional Misrepresentation

The *Burr* cause of action was based upon intentional misrepresentation. The Court found that every element of fraud—a tort—was proven. The elements of fraud are as follows:

(1) The agency knowingly made false representations to the adoptive parents about the child;

(2) The agency intended for the adoptive parents to rely on the false representations;

(3) The adoptive parents did rely on those false representations; and

(4) As a result, the adoptive parents incurred damages.

Since the *Burr* decision, no court has held that liability should not be imposed upon an adoption intermediary for its blatant misrepresentations.

In *Roe v. Catholic Charities*, 588 N.E.2d 354 (Ill. App. 1992), an Illinois appellate court held an adoption agency liable for its intentional misrepresentations to three different adoptive families. Arguably, the misrepresentations in *Roe* were far less elaborate than those found in *Burr*.

In *Roe*, the three families had agreed to adopt from Catholic Charities only if the child was physically and mentally "normal"; the agency provided everything it knew about the child's background; and the adoptive families would not incur any unusual or unexpected expenses. The agency told each family in turn that their child was as normal as children of a similar age and that they had no information about their background.

Despite their statements to the contrary, the agency knew that each of the three children had violent and abnormal tendencies. In addition, the agency knew that one child had seen several doctors and professionals concerning her violent and uncontrollable behavior and mental retardation. The agency knew that the second child involved also exhibited uncontrollable behavior, including smearing feces on the walls of previous foster homes. Finally, the agency was aware of the third child's violent behavior—in fact, he had stomped a foster family's dog to death. Since their adoptions, the children continued their violent behaviors and the adoptive parents incurred additional expenses to treat the children.

In reaching its conclusion to find the adoption agency liable for its intentional misrepresentations, the Court carefully considered whether its decision would likely hurt the adoption of handicapped children in general. The Court concluded that a policy of "truth and straightforward dealing" would help place handicapped children in appropriate adoptive homes. The parents would know up front what they were dealing with and whether they could afford to adopt the child or not. Further, the Court stated that if the parents knew of the child's problem at the outset of the adoption process, the child has a better chance of being "cured," or at the very least, effectively treated early on.

Agencies have also been held liable for their intentional misrepresentations about an adopted child's history of sexual abuse. In *Gibbs v. Ernst*, 647 A.2d 882 (Pa. 1994), the then prospective adoptive parents repeatedly asked the adoption agency whether the child had a history of sexual abuse. In response, the agency repeatedly denied any abuse of the child. Further, the agency assured the adoptive parents that if there was any evidence of sexual or physical abuse to the child, they would fully disclose that information. However, the agency did have access to information that the child was severely abused, both sexually and physically and did not disclose that information. The Court held an agency being deceitful about a child's past sexual and physical abuse established a cause of action based on intentional misrepresentation.

Since these cases, courts have continued to impose liability on adoption agencies when the agency knowingly and intentionally misrepresented information about a child's medical history and social background to adoptive parents.

B. Deliberate Concealment/Intentional Non-Disclosure

Other courts have imposed liability, not only for intentional misrepresentations, but also for intentionally withholding important information about a child's health or social background from the adoptive parents. The first court to publish an opinion on an intentional non-disclosure was in the Californian appellate court (*Michael J. v. Los Angeles County Dept. of Adoptions*, 247 Cal.Rptr. 504 (1988)). In *Michael J*, the adopted child had a port wine stain on his body. Medically, this "stain" indicated a nerve disorder which renders one prone to having epileptic seizures. The County knew that a physician examined the stain and that the doctor was unwilling to make a positive prognosis. Despite this information, the County concealed this fact from the adoptive parent when she asked about the stain.

The Court held that the county could be found liable for fraudulent concealment if the trier of fact found that the county intentionally failed to disclose a material fact. In this case, the material fact was the doctor's refusal to make a prognosis regarding the child's stain.

The Court concluded that there must be "good faith and full disclosure of material facts" when dealing with a child's present or past medical condition.

In addition to *Michael J*, the court in the above-mentioned case of *Roe v. Catholic Charities*, 588 N.E.2d 354 (Ill. App. 1992), also reasoned that agencies may be held liable for failing to disclose important medical and psychological information about a child to potential adoptive parents. In *Roe*, the court found that the agency had a duty to give a complete and honest answer to the parents' specific questions regarding the child's health and background. The agency breached its duty when it failed to give the parents the information when the agency possessed it.

The Supreme Judicial Court of Massachusetts reached the same conclusion in its decision of *Mohr v. Com.*, 653 N.E.2d 1104 (Mass. 1995). The SJC held that agencies can be held liable for both intentional and negligent misrepresentations, and in addition, agencies have an affirmative duty to disclose information about the child to prospective adoptive parents if that information will help the parents make an informed decision about whether they want to adopt that child.

The Court reasoned that not only does the information allow adoptive parents to make a completely informed decision, but it also allows parents to obtain appropriate medical care for the child in a timely fashion. Along with its predecessors, the Court also reasoned that full disclosure will encourage more adoptions and will instill more confidence in the adoption process. It also noted that any burden placed on the agencies because of this new full disclosure policy is—at most—only slight.

Further, the Court opined that its decision requiring full disclosure did not conflict with the biological parents' privacy interests because agencies can provide family history without releasing names or truly identifiable information. Finally, without the full disclosure policy, adoptive parents would have no remedy against the state for misrepresentations by a state adoption agency because these agencies are immune from intentional torts pursuant to state statute.

C. Negligent Misrepresentation

Negligent misrepresentation occurs when adoption agencies fail to use due care, usually resulting in the agency not providing the child's correct medical history and background to the potential adoptive parents. The Wisconsin Supreme Court was the first court to recognize liability for negligent misrepresentation (*Meracle v. Children's Services Society of Wisconsin*, 437 N.W.2d 532 (Wisc. 1989)). In *Meracle*, the adoptive parents met with the agency prior to the adoption and were informed that: the child's grandmother died of Huntington's Disease; the disease is transmitted genetically from generation to generation; the biological father tested negative for the disease; and therefore, the child's risk of developing the disease was no greater than any other child. The parents adopted the child and later found out the information the agency gave them about the disease was incorrect and misleading. At the time of the informational meeting, there existed no reliable test to determine whether one had inherited Huntington's Disease.

The child was later diagnosed with the disease and the adoptive parents filed suit against the agency alleging that the agency negligently misrepresented to them that the biological father did not have the disease.

The court held that because the agency voluntarily assumed the duty to inform the adoptive parents about the disease and the child's chances of protracting the disease, the agency was liable for negligently breaching that duty. Further, the Court opined that liability can be avoided by these agencies by not making affirmative misrepresentations about a child's health.

Another case that held an agency liable for negligent misrepresentation was *Mallette v. Children's Friend and Service*, 661 A.2d 67 (R.I. 1995). This case arose in Rhode Island, which is one of the few states without a statutory duty to disclose to adoptive parents the child's medical information. Despite this lack of a statutorily created duty, the Court still upheld a claim involving an adopted handicapped child.

Eight years after adopting a child, the parents discovered that the biological mother suffered from mental retardation and other disabilities. Prior to adopting the child, the agency told the parents that the biological mother's problems were the result of a trauma to the head, which was not supported in the records they later discovered.

The Court found the agency negligent in failing to provide correct information and records of the child's background and imposed a duty to use due care when agencies volunteer information to prospective adoptive parents. Once the agency began volunteering information, they assumed a duty not to make any negligent misrepresentations.

D. Negligent Non-Disclosure

Some courts also recognize negligent non-disclosure as a cause of action in wrongful adoption tort claims. In this type of action, the agency is accused of not disclosing a child's health and medical history when it actually had the records in its possession. It was not an intentional concealment of the records, but a negligent one. Liability for this action is sometimes sought under the theory of negligent misrepresentation.

In both the *Mohr* and *Roe* decisions discussed above, the Courts analyzed the claims under negligent misrepresentation, but also mentioned a separate duty to disclose information. However, in *Gibbs v. Ernst*, the court looked at this issue separate from the negligent and intentional misrepresentation claim. The *Gibbs* court recognized an affirmative duty on the part of the agency to provide adoptive parents with any relevant non-identifying information that the agency had in its possession. The court reasoned that the relationship between the agency and adoptive parents gives rise to such a duty. Massachusetts, Minnesota, Montana, and Washington have also recognized claims base on negligent non-disclosure.

Not all states recognize liability for negligent non-disclosure. California does not provide for this type of liability since it does not impose liability for any type of negligence. Rhode Island does not either. Although in *Mallette*, the court recognized a claim for negligent misrepresentation, it specifically stated that there would be no such common law duty to disclose. A close reading of *Burr* and *Meracle* also does not support a claim for negligent non-disclosure.

E. Other Causes of Action: Negligent Failure to Investigate, Negative Placement, and Breach of Contract

Some adoptive parents have cited a cause of action against agencies for their negligent failure to investigate a child's medical history or condition. No court has held an agency liable for such an action. In *Gibbs*, *Mallette*, and *Meracle*, claims of failure to investigate were at issue, but the courts refused to find that there was a duty to investigate. Instead, in *Gibbs*, the court found that there needs to be a good faith effort made by the agencies to obtain medical history yet there is no (absolute) duty placed on them to do so.

Another cause of action that emerged is for the negligent placement of a child with parents who are not able or not properly trained to meet that child's special needs. In *J.A. v. St. Joseph's Children's and Maternity Hospital* (2001 WL 34644556 (2001)), a Pennsylvania court recognized that parents could bring a wrongful adoption action on behalf of their special needs adopted child. Prior to the adoption, the prospective parents were required to give medical certifications to the agency. The mother's certification indicated that she had several illnesses that would decrease her life span. Aside from the certification, the agency took no other steps to measure the parents' fitness to care for a special needs child.

The court recognized a special relationship between the agency, the adoptive parents, and the child and a duty owed by the agency to the parents and child. The court concluded that the harm to the child because of the wrongful placement could be a foreseeable, reasonable injury. The trier of fact is able to determine whether the agency breached their duty.

On the other end of the spectrum, a Rhode Island trial court rejected an adopted child's claim of negligent placement (*Rowey v. Children's Friend and Service*, 2003 WL 23196347). Unlike *J.A.*, there was no evidence in *Rowey* that the adoptive parents could not care for the special needs child. In sum, there was no physical ailment that hindered the parents from parenting. Ultimately, the court concluded the child did not have standing to sue because the psychological injuries she complained of were not sufficient.

Another cause of action that adoptive parents have filed are breach of contract claims. In these cases, the parents sought damages based on the idea that the agency promised them a healthy child but failed to fulfill that promise. Several courts have denied this claim stating that a bargained exchange for a child's life is repugnant and that it is not reasonable for an agency to be held the guarantor of the child's health (*Allen v. Children's Services*, 567 N.E.2d 1346 (Ohio Ct. App. 1990)).

III. Constitutional Claims

Adoptive parents have also brought actions against agencies for failure to disclose medical information under Section 1983 of Title 42 of the United States Code. Title 42 allows those deprived of a Constitutional right to file suit against a person working under the power of state law. Plaintiffs have found it difficult to prevail on this claim (*Griffith v. Johnston*, 889 F.2d 1427 (5th Cir. 1990); *Young v. Francis*, 820 F. Supp. 940 (E.D. Pa. 1993); and *Collier v. Krane*, 763 F. Supp. 473 (D. Colo. 1991)).

IV. Damages

Adoptive parents incur great expenses as a result of either fraudulent or negligent misrepresentations made by agencies. Because most of these actions involve children with physical or mental health problems, adoptive parents incurred massive medical and out-of-pocket expenses. These expenses are the most sought after damages.

Courts are quick to award proven past medical expenses and future extraordinary medical expenses. Regarding future expenses, some courts limit awards to those expenses incurred until the child reaches twenty-one. A parent's lost wages have also been sought if the parent had to quit his or her job to take care of the child—however, courts are split on that outcome.

Adoptive parents often seek damages for emotional distress, the outcome of the case hinges upon the asserted theory of liability. Most studies and decisions indicate the courts are divided on this issue.

In the *Burr* decision, the Ohio Supreme Court allowed for damages that resulted from emotional distress. On the opposite end of the spectrum, courts in New York have explicitly ruled that in wrongful adoption cases, the adoptive parent's damages are limited to economic losses only (*Juman v. Louise Wise Services*, 678 N.Y.S. 2d 611 (App. Div. 1st 1998)).

In *Juman*, the court held that such an action is similar to that of a wrongful life action. In both cases, it is purely speculative and subjective as to whether a parent's emotional pain from raising a special needs child outweighs the emotional advantages of a parent-child relationship.

Punitive damages are usually limited to wrongful adoptions involving fraud. In both *Roe* and *Gibbs*, the courts granted punitive damages for intentional misrepresentation and non-disclosure. Additionally, when misrepresentation or non-disclosure contributed to the death of the child or a parent, plaintiffs have received damages under a wrongful death claim.

V. Defenses

A. Statute of Limitations

Many times adoptive parents do not file suit against agencies until years after the adoption has been finalized. Consequently, the statute of limitations may bar some adoptive parents from recovering.

In most states, for a wrongful adoption based on fraud, the statute begins to run when the fraud could reasonably have been discovered. However, in wrongful adoption claims based on negligence, the time begins to run when the plaintiffs knew or reasonably should have known that they were wrongfully injured by the defendant's conduct.

In cases where the child's condition became known before the defendant's fraudulent or negligent conduct was discovered, courts have held that it had not started to run until the defendant's misconduct was apparent. Some plaintiffs have been successful in extending or tolling the statute of limitations because of the defendant's fraudulent concealment. Courts are split on this interpretation.

B. Confidentiality Statutes

Some defendants argue that because of state statutes that require confidentiality in adoption or child protective services records, they were prohibited from disclosing a child's medical history.

The court in *Roe* explicitly rejected this defense and held there was no conflict between the disclosure statutes and the confidentiality statutes. Other courts have rejected this defense stating that agencies could have sought out a court order to release such confidential information in order to comply with its duty to disclose certain information.

Checkpoints

- The first case in the United States surrounding a wrongful adoption was in 1986 (*Burr*). This pivotal case resulted in the court determining the agency's failure to disclose the child's medical history as fraudulent misrepresentation.

- One of the drawbacks to full medical disclosure is a child never finding permanent placement. The alternate view is that with full disclosure, a handicapped child could be placed in a home that is ready and willing for these limitations.

- Agencies can be found liable for withholding medical information. Courts have found that full disclosure will put more faith in the adoption process.

- Once an agency volunteers medical history information about the child or the biological family, there is a duty to not provide false information. With the agency voluntarily sharing information, there also arises a duty to perform a "good faith" investigation of potential medical issues.

- The misrepresentation does not have to be intentional to be fraudulent, it can be an agency's negligence in disclosure of facts or reporting. There is a very high standard held to an agency when investigating a child's history and placing the child in a permanent home. Not all states recognize the tort of negligent misrepresentation in the adoptive proceedings.

- There is no complete duty to investigate on an agency. A "good faith" effort is sufficient.

- Most damages sought by adoptive parents surround the medical care, lost wages, and adoption costs put in to care for the child. Punitive damages are limited to those tort cases involving fraud.

- Statute of limitations can pose a problem for plaintiffs bringing a cause of action. States differ on their interpretations of when the injury occurred.

Chapter 14

Adoption Reforms

Roadmap

- The intent and regulations of the UAA
- The adoption of ASFA and its policies
- Understand the Foster Care Independence Act
- The relevance of the Preventing Sex Trafficking Act
- The continuing efforts of the government to improve adoption and foster care policies

---

I. Uniform Adoption Act of 1994

In 1994, the National Conference of Commissioners on Uniform State Laws completed a new Uniform Adoption Act (UAA). The Act provided the framework for States to facilitate and regulate adoptions, and at the same time, protect the best interests of the minor children being adopted. The American Bar Association and the American Academy of Adoption Attorneys both endorsed the Act. However, since its introduction, only Vermont has enacted the Act.

A. Direct Placement Adoptions

The UAA provides rules and regulations on direct and agency placement adoptions. It requires prospective adoptive parents to be evaluated by an independent professional before they are eligible to adopt a child. This regulation was implemented because many states did not require pre-placement evaluations in direct placement adoptions. As such, direct placement adoptions have largely been seen as a type of baby-selling, which is susceptible to price gouging.

The Act attempts to reduce this possibility by requiring pre-placement evaluations and by requiring full disclosure of all fees and costs the adoptive parents are expected to pay. The UAA specifically identifies the types of expenses adoptive parents are allowed to pay, such as fees for professional services and certain expenses to the birth parents. These fees and costs are scrutinized by the court during the adoption proceeding.

B. Consent

The UAA also requires birth parents to consent to the adoption in writing before an independent tribunal. The independent tribunal may be a judge, an attorney that does not represent either the birth parents or the adoptive parents, or a magistrate appointed by the court.

At this procedure, birth parents are informed of the full effects of the adoption and that they are entitled to get an independent attorney's advice. The consent to the adoption of an infant is not effective until the child is born, and a consent may be withdrawn for any reason within 192 hours after the child was born. For children that are not infants, the consent is effective as soon as the birth parents execute the consent form.

The consent form acknowledges that the birth parents understand the nature and effect of their consent. This requirement ensures that birth parents' rights are better protected. It also helps adoptive parents to show a court of law that the birth parents knew their rights, in case the birth parents want to reunify with their child after it has been placed in the adoptive home.

C. Birth Fathers' Rights

Birth mothers are encouraged to identify potential fathers if they are unknown at the time of the proceeding. By giving notice to birth fathers of the upcoming adoption, the potential for errors in the adoption process is reduced.

The UAA only requires consent from fathers that had a parenting relationship with the child to be adopted. Therefore, a father who has registered with a putative father registry (if any), but is not in the child's life, must file to establish paternity if he wishes to maintain his rights. The putative father has twenty days to file for paternity after he receives notice of the adoption proceeding.

If the putative father does not come forward within twenty days, or in the case of birth fathers that are not known at the time of the adoptive placement, the Act allows for the termination of their parental rights in favor of the adoptive parents (as long as it is not detrimental to the child).

If the father files for paternity within the allotted time frame, his rights may still be terminated if the court finds that the father either abandoned or neglected to show any responsibility for the child. Even if no fault can be found by the birth father, the court could still terminate his parental rights if not terminating them would be detrimental to the child. The right to appeal an adoption proceeding decision expires within 6 months after issuance. After that statutory limit, no unknown birth father can disturb the adoption, even when his rights were not terminated in the prior adoption proceeding.

D. Confidentiality and Birth Records

In most states, birth records are kept confidential and normally sealed by the court. Birth records include the adoptee's original birth certificate, any identifying information of the parties, and the record from the adoption proceedings. Under the Act, birth parents are required to provide a family health and genetic history that becomes a part of the adoption proceeding records.

Generally, the Act maintains the confidentiality of the birth records. However, it provides that the parties may volunteer their identities to the other side. As such, open adoptions are allowed under the UAA, as well as a waiver of confidentiality. The Act also allows a party to obtain non-identifying information from the birth records as well as the ability to obtain specific health information that was provided to the court. Upon a petition to the court, identifying information may be revealed after the court finds good cause to reveal such information; a compelling reason to do so; and that the benefit to the party requesting the information is greater than the harm to the party disclosing information.

II. Adoption and Safe Families Act of 1997 (Pub. L. 105-89)

The Adoption and Safe Families Act of 1997 (ASFA) was signed into law on November 19, 1997 by President Clinton. The stated purpose of ASFA was to promote the adoption of children in foster care. Prior to this Act, a major concern was that states focused on reunifying children with their parents despite the fact that they may be returning to unsafe homes and/or languishing in foster care.

One of the main focuses of ASFA was to find a permanent home for children in foster care as soon as possible. In order to meet this goal, ASFA required courts to expedite termination of parental rights proceedings and adoption proceedings when it found that a child could not be returned to the birth parents. ASFA also focused on how well the states performed in relation to ASFA's stated goals of safety, permanence, and well-being for children in foster care.

A. Permanent Placement

In an effort to expedite the process of placing children into permanent homes, ASFA requires that permanency planning hearings be held 12 months after a child enters foster care as opposed to the prior standard of 18 — the federal time requirement before ASFA's enactment.

ASFA also requires states to initiate proceedings that terminate a birth parent's rights if a child has been in foster care for at least 15 months of the last 22 months and for all abandoned newborns. ASFA allowed two exceptions to this requirement: if it was not in the child's best interests; or if a relative was providing a temporary home for the child.

Critics of ASFA argue that a filing of a termination of parental rights petition does not guarantee permanency. Others argue that some parent's rights are terminated unreasonably and without good cause.

B. "Reasonable Efforts"

Because of the growing concern over past emphasis on reunification, ASFA sought to limit the requirement of the state using "reasonable efforts" to reunify a child with his/her birth parents. ASFA provides that "reasonable efforts" are no longer required to reunify a child with his/her birth family if there are "aggravated circumstances." States vary on how they define "aggravated circumstances." In some states, such circumstances include: 1) parental substance abuse; 2) failure to comply with a reunification plan; 3) failure to locate a parent after a "diligent" search; 4) the mental illness or deficiency of a parent; 5) a child had previously been removed from the home twice before; 6) parental incarceration or institutionalization; and 7) parents declining services.

When there are no "aggravated circumstances" the state is limited to 15 months to try and reunify the child with its birth parents.

C. State Compliance with ASFA

In order to receive federal funds, states must comply with the requirements of ASFA. Under ASFA, states are required to look for placement of children nationwide as opposed to focusing on local placements. In an effort to monitor and improve state performance, states are also required to document and report every child's permanency plan.

ASFA also amended Title IV-B and IV-E of the Social Security Act, which governs federal funds to states for their child-protective efforts. Monetary incentives are given to states that increased the number of adoptions over the base year.

D. Prospective Foster or Adoptive Parents

Under ASFA, prospective foster or adoptive parents must undergo a criminal records check. This was necessary to ensure the safety of abused and neglected children. Prospective parents are disqualified as adoptive parents if previously convicted of a violent felony. Additionally, they may be disqualified if previously convicted of a discretionary crime.

III. Foster Care Independence Act of 1999

Approximately 20,000 youth in the United States age out of foster care each year. Annually, about 5,200 foster care youth run away from the system before they age out. The youth who age out and are run-aways are at a high risk to become homeless, incarcerated, and/or unemployed. States have tried to address these issues by creating foster care aging out programs.

In December of 1999, Congress enacted the Foster Care Independence Act (also called "FCIA" or the "Chafee Act") that amended Title IV-E of the Social Security Act. The purpose was to provide states with additional funding and more flexibility to implement programs that helped foster care children transition to independence and to be more self-sufficient.

The programs included independent living programs, which were designed to educate and train foster youths that were about to age out of the foster care system. In these programs, youth are trained how to obtain employment, and how to handle their financial accounts.

The Chaffee Act also provided funds to assist former foster youth, ages eighteen to twenty-one, in paying for their room and board. Further, the Act allowed states to extend Medicaid coverage to emancipated youth who, from age eighteen to twenty-one, remained in the foster care system. However, the Act stressed that states must continue to try and find permanent placements for the youths in independent living programs.

The Act funds $140 million each year to states, as opposed the previous $70 million award to states. States are given funds in proportion to the number of children they have in foster care. In order to receive these funds, states must match 20% of the funds. States are given great discretion in the types of services they implement for youth aging out the system. Due to this discretion, some youth are not serviced by their respective states. For example, Florida only gives Medicaid coverage to emancipated youth who meet certain academic requirements. Additionally, even if they meet those academic requirements, they are not guaranteed Medicaid coverage.

IV. Child Abuse Prevention and Enforcement Act of 2000

In order to reduce incidents of child abuse and neglect, Congress enacted the Child Abuse Prevention and Enforcement Act in 2000. The Act authorized states to use federal law enforcement funds in order to improve the criminal justice system. In doing so, state child welfare agencies are provided more timely and complete criminal records of prospective foster care and adoptive parents. This information ensures the safety and protection of children in foster care.

Under the Act, state law enforcement were able to use federal funds to enforce laws regarding child abuse and neglect; promote child abuse and neglect prevention programs; and establish programs between law enforcement and media outlets to provide useful information in order to apprehend suspects of child abuse and neglect.

V. Promoting Safe and Stable Families Amendments of 2001

The Promoting Safe and Stable Families Amendments were enacted in 2001. The Amendments extended the previous Promoting Safe and Stable Families program, which included community-based family support services, family preservation services, reunification services, and the promotion of adoptions. It amended Title IV-E of the Social Security Act to provide educational and training vouchers for foster care youth aging out of the system. It also provided authority to support programs designed to mentor children whose parents are incarcerated. In an effort to advertise safe haven laws, the Act included safe haven programs under the definition of family preservation services.

VI. Keeping Children and Families Safe Act of 2003

The Keeping Children and Families Safe Act was enacted to amend and improve various child welfare acts, including the Child Abuse Prevent and Treatment Act, the Adoption Opportunities Act, the Abandoned Infants Assistance Act, and the Family Violence Prevention and Services Act.

In order to receive a grant under CAPTA, states had to revise their policies and procedures regarding child protective services. Under the Act, a child protective services representative must advise the person of the complaints and allegations made against him at the initial meeting. To better protect the legal rights and safety of children and their families, child protective service representatives must also be trained in accordance with the provisions of the Act. The Act also requires states to disclose any confidential information if requested by a federal, state, or local government if they have a need for that information.

Further, the Act requires that states have medical professionals report to local child protective agencies any newborn who was exposed to drugs while in the birth mother's womb or is suffering from withdrawal at or after birth. This is proactive provision to protect at-risk newborns.

VII. Adoption Promotion Act of 2003

In December of 2003, Congress enacted the Adoption Promotion Act. Its main purpose was to reauthorize Title IV-E of the Social Security Act's adoption incentive payments program. The Act revised the requirements of the program — including payments for the adoption of young special needs children; and for the adoption of children nine years or older. The Act also authorized the DHHS Secretary to impose penalties against states that failed to provide data to the Adoption and Foster Care Analysis and Reporting System (AFCARS).

VIII. Fair Access Foster Care Act of 2005

The Fair Access Foster Care Act was enacted in November of 2005. The Act amended Title IV-E of the Social Security Act to allow nonprofits or for-profit child placement or child care agencies to make foster care maintenance payments on behalf of eligible children.

IX. Deficit Reduction Act of 2005

In February of 2006, Congress enacted the Deficit Reduction Act of 2005. The Act reauthorized the TANF program, Healthy Marriage and Family funds, Court Improvement Program, and Safe and Stable Families Program. The Act granted states funds for the promotion of healthy marriage and responsible fatherhood. It provides judges, attorneys, and legal personnel working on child welfare cases with training. It required courts and agencies to collaborate meaningfully with child welfare services programs. It allowed states to grant public access to certain child welfare proceedings.

X. Safe and Timely Interstate Placement of Foster Children Act of 2006

The Safe and Timely Interstate Placement of Foster Children Act was enacted in July of 2006. The Act sought to hold states accountable for the interstate placement of children in a timely and safe manner.

The Act required that states complete home studies within sixty days of a request by another state. States that completed these home studies within thirty days receive incentive payments. The requesting state must accept the studies within fourteen days unless the report was contrary to the best interests of the child. The Act also required caseworkers to visit children placed out of state more frequently. It required states to make sure foster parents, pre-adoptive parents, or caregivers of the child are promptly notified of proceedings regarding that child.

XI. Adam Walsh Child Protection and Safety Act of 2006

The Adam Walsh Child Protection and Safety Act was enacted in July of 2006. The Act required prospective foster or adoptive parents to be fingerprinted and have their prints checked in a national crime information database.

The Act also required child abuse and neglect registries to be checked to ensure that no one living in the prospective foster or adoptive home was listed in the registries within the past five years. States are mandated to comply with a request from another state to check a child abuse registry for a respective match. The Act also directed the Department of Health and Human Services to create a national registry for substantiated cases of child abuse or neglect, establish distribution standards for that information contained in the registry, and conduct a study on the information collected.

XII. Child and Family Services Improvement Act of 2006

In September of 2006, Congress enacted the Child and Families Services Improvement Act. The Act amended Title IV-B of the Social Security Act to reauthorize the Promoting Safe and Stable Families program. The Act required states to submit annual forms that reported on planned expenditures for child and family services during the upcoming fiscal year. Under the Act, states were also required to provide information on the number of families and children served by the state's child welfare agency. It also provided state funds to support caseworkers visiting children in foster care on a monthly basis. During their visits, caseworkers must focus on the issues involved in the child's case plan to ensure that child's well-being.

XIII. Tax Relief and Health Care Act of 2006

The Tax Relief and Health Care Act was enacted by Congress in December of 2006. The Act amended the Internal Revenue Code to extend certain provisions that were near expiration. It also amended the Social Security Act to exempt foster care children that were receiving assistance under Title IV-B and IV-E from the requirement to provide documentation of their citizenship or nationality under the Deficit Reduction Act of 2005. It required state plans to include procedures to verify a foster care child's citizenship or immigration status if that child receives assistance from Title IV-B and IV-E.

XIV. Fostering Connections to Success and Increasing Adoptions Act of 2008

In October of 2008, Congress enacted the Fostering Connections to Success and Increasing Adoptions Act (FCSIAA). Under this Act, states and Indian tribes were afforded a new option to provide kinship guardianship assistance payments on behalf of foster care children receiving assistance from Title IV-E. The Act allowed children that received kinship guardianship assistance payments to be eligible for Medicaid.

FCSIAA requires that relatives that are guardians of a foster care child and live with that child to be finger-printed for the purposes of conducting a criminal background check as well as a check for child abuse and neglect.

The Act also amended the Chafee Act to provide services for foster children who left the system and went into kinship care after the age of 16. For those same children, the Act permitted states to provide those children with education and training vouchers. Further, FCSIAA also provided grants to state, local, or tribal child welfare agencies to help at risk or foster care children reconnect with family members. The Act required Title IVE-E agencies to notify any adult relative of a child that was removed from his home within thirty days that they may be a placement option for the child. It also required states to place siblings in the same placement, if feasible.

XV. Protecting Incentives for the Adoption of Children with Special Needs Act of 2009

In May of 2009, Congress enacted the Protecting Incentives for the Adoption of Children with Special Needs Act. The purpose of the Act was to ensure, in accordance with the FCSIAA, that states receive adoption incentive payments for the fiscal year of 2008.

XVI. Child Abuse Prevention and Treatment Reauthorization Act of 2010

The Child Abuse Prevention and Treatment Reauthorization Act of 2010 was previously reauthorized in 2003 and first passed in 1974. Its purpose was to improve child protective services, training programs for case workers and mandatory reporters, and to enhance interagency communications.

XVII. Preventing Sex Trafficking and Strengthening Families Act of 2014

The Preventing Sex Trafficking and Strengthening Families Act of 2014 was passed by Congress and approved by President Obama on September 29, 2014. This act aids in the prevention of sex trafficking of children in foster care by identifying risks and using better documentation when sex trafficking has been reported. Improvements in documentation on children in foster care will help identify potential sex trafficking risks, like foster care runaways. The act orders individual states to develop procedures for the immediate locating of any foster care runaway, and to subsequently determine if the runaway was a result of sex trafficking. In addition, each state has to report statistics on runaways and the potential factors connected to the runaway. Another goal of the act is to support normalcy and permanency for foster care children, and to place foster care siblings in the same home.

The act also improves adoption incentives. The time period for caregivers to receive incentive payments has been increased. In addition, the incentive payments will be passed on to the kinship guardianship (a relative guardian), in the case of death or incapacity of the child's legal guardian.

Unfortunately, child sex trafficking is on the rise in the United States, leading to the passing of this act. With better documentation and awareness in the foster care system, child sex trafficking will hopefully be stopped.

XVIII. Proposed Bills

In March of 2011, the Welfare Reform Act of 2011 was introduced. Its purpose was to gather information on the total spending of welfare programs and to provide a spending limit on such programs. After not being enacted, this bill was reintroduced in May, 2014. Presently, this bill still has not been passed.

In April of 2011, the Dave Thomas Adoption Act of 2011 was introduced. Its purpose was to amend the Internal Revenue Code to allow prospective adoptive parents to withdraw from their individual retirement plans, penalty free, for the purpose of helping with adoption expenses. This bill was not passed. In April, 2013, this bill was reintroduced and failed to pass.

In May of 2011, the Every Child Deserves a Family Act was introduced. The purpose of this Act is to prohibit discrimination in foster care placements and adoptions. The Act proposed that a prospective foster care or adoptive parent's sexual orientation, gender identity, or marital status should not be an issue in determining the placement of a foster care child. In addition, the sexual orientation or gender identity of the foster care child or adoptee should not be an issue in determining a proper placement. This bill was not passed. In May, 2013, this bill was reintroduced and once again, failed to be enacted.

Checkpoints

- The UAA is an attempt to uniform adoption procedures to follow the best interests of the child standard. Only one state has adopted this act.

- ASFA was created to help facilitate safe placement of children through foster care.

- ASFA's goal is to achieve permanent placement for a foster child. Reunification with the parents is an initial goal. However, in many cases, termination of biological parental rights occurs.

- The Foster Care Independence Act helps foster children through the process of "aging out" of foster care.

- The Child Abuse Prevention Act helps fund states in their criminal investigation background checks of parents and potential adoptive parents.

- CAPTA was put in to place to further help child protection services.

- The Adoption Promotion and the Fair Access Foster Care Act both help social security benefits in adoptions and foster care.

- The Deficit Reduction Act helps provide state funding in promoting healthy families and responsible fatherhood.

- The Safe and Timely Interstate Placement of Foster Children Act helps facilitate timely home inspections for interstate child transfers. This is done by providing state funding when home inspections are completed within thirty days of a transfer.

- The Adam Walsh Child Protection and Safety Act provides fingerprinting for criminal background checks on those involved in the care or adoption of children.

- The Child and Family Services Improvement Act helps provide accurate statistics, promotes positive case plan construction, and focuses on improving the child's well-being.

- The Tax Relief and Health Care Act requires the IRS to grant foster children special exemptions.

- The FCSIAA provides funding for fingerprinting, for the guardians of foster care children, for foster children who were not placed, and for various other aspects of foster care placement.

- The Protecting Incentives for the Adoption of Children with Special Needs Act gives funding to states for staying in accordance with FCSIAA.

- The Child Abuse Prevention and Treatment Reauthorization Act helps improve child protection services.

- The Preventing Sex Trafficking and Strengthening Families Act of 2014 provides better protection for foster children from the rising crime of sex trafficking, and also improves adoption incentives.

- Many other acts continue to enter legislation as the government and agencies improve the adoption process and foster care system.

Chapter 15

2007 National Survey of Adoptive Parents (NSAP): Domestic Transracial Adoption

---

Roadmap

- The characteristics of the first national survey on adoptive parents
- The three different types of adoptions surveyed
- What the results from the survey project for the future of adoption

---

The following is a discussion of the 2007 National Survey of Adoptive Parents (NSAP).[1] Although this national survey was conducted in 2007 by the Federal Department of Health and Human Services ("DHHS"), the survey results were not fully released to the public until the summer of 2010. As such, the data remains timely and relevant today.

An analysis of the data was done by Professor Hawkins DeBose, a team of statisticians, and a professor of counseling from the University of Western Michigan (Kalamazoo, MI). Through this data, a number of research questions involving domestic transracial adoption were evaluated and answered. First, is an overview of the general NSAP results, and second is a discussion of one of the aforementioned team's individualized research questions.

---

1. This chapter is the text of a speech given by Professor Cynthia Hawkins DeBose at the International Society of Family Law ("ISOF") Conference in Nassau, Bahamas, in March 2011.

I. 2007: Background

DHHS conducted a national survey of adoptive parents. The purpose was to give an overview of adopted children throughout the United States. The findings from this study represent adopted children under the age of 18, and those children who are not living with either biological parent.

This was the first ever national survey that provided representative information about the characteristics, adoption experiences, and well-being of adopted children and their families in the United States. The purpose of the NSAP was to answer the question of how adopted children in the United States are faring; the comparisons were viewed through an entire host of indicators. The survey of adoptive parents was taken over a thirty minute telephonic survey. The findings represent a snapshot of adopted children under the age of eighteen and living with neither biological parent.

In the survey, the children represent three categories of adoptees: children adopted domestically from foster care; children adopted domestically through private adoption; and children adopted internationally by parents residing in the United States.

Adopted children comprise 2% of all United States children, and there are nearly 1.8 million adopted children in the United States today. The NSAP does not include: informal adoptions, or pre-adoption placement, children living with one biological parent and adopted by the step-parent, or adoptions that had already been dissolved or annulled. This study was primarily focused on analyzing true adoptions.

The NSAP was generated from the National Survey of Children's Health (NSCH). The NSCH is a nationally representative survey of randomly selected children under the age of eighteen and residing in the United States. A little background as to the sample of the study is as follows:

> In 2007, the NSCH included information on 91,642 children, which is a representative sample of the 73.8 million children residing in the United States. If the child in the 2007 NSCH sample was adopted, then the parents were asked to participate in the 2007 NSAP, an add-on survey to the NSCH. Of the 91,642 children sampled in the NSCH, 2,737 were adopted. A total of 2,089 adopted children are included in the 2007 NSAP report. Those 2,089 adopted children are a representative sample of the nearly 1.8 million adopted children in the US under age 18 in 2007.

As previously stated, the data from the 2007 NSAP study remains timely and relevant today. Statisticians and scholars across the United States are still reviewing and analyzing the data set, and will be for years to come.

A. Three Ways to Adopt in the United States

1. Foster Care Adoption

Children in the United States foster care system have been removed from their biological parents due to their inability or unwillingness to provide appropriate care for their children. The foster care system is administered by state-level government agencies, and is broadly funded by the Federal Government. This category represented approximately 37% (661,000) of U.S. adoptees.

2. Private Adoption

Children who were not involved in the foster care system and who were adopted privately within the United States fall under the category of private adoptions. These adoptions are either arranged independently or through an adoption agency. Private adoptions represented approximately 38% (677,000) of adoptees in the United States for this study.

3. International Adoption

Children who were born in a country other than the United States were considered under the category of International Adoptees. These children were specifically brought to the United States for adoption. International adoptees represented approximately 25% (444,000) of adoptees in the United States.

Although the NSAP included all three categories of adoption, the on-going data review concerned only the two forms of domestic adoption, namely foster care and private adoptions.

The racial distribution of adopted children is different from that of United States children in general. The breakdown in this study for all United States children was: 56% White, 14% Black, 20% Hispanic, 4% Asian, and 6% other. The statistics for adopted children was: 37% White, 23% Black, 15% Hispanic, 16% Asian, and 9% other.

B. Race of Adoptee by Adoption Type

There were significant differences between the race of the adoptee and the adoptive parents within the different adoption types. The adoptees in foster care were: 37%, White, 35% Black, 16% Hispanic. The adoptees in private adoptions were: 50% White, 25% Black, and 13% Hispanic. And the adoptees in international adoptions were: 59% Asian (33% from China and 11% from Korea), 19% White (from Russia), 3% Black, and 17% Hispanic (13% from Guatemala).

As far as the adoptive parents, the racial comparison with the adoptees proved to be interesting. In the United States, adoptee parents were: 73% White, 17% Black, and 5% Hispanic, 4% other, and 1% Asian. Most of the adoptive parents were White parents who were not always adopting children of the same race. Interestingly, with respect to international adoptions, White parents seemed to adopt a large number of Asian adoptees. The international adoptee definition is further detailed in the next section on transracial adoptions.

C. NSAP: Transracial Adoptions

It should be noted that the NSAP was the first major study to conflate domestic and international transracial adoption. In this project, domestic transracial adoptions and international transracial adoptions were separated out. The study found that 40% of all adoptions are "transracial, transethnic or transcultural." With respect to these three definitions of transracial, transethnic, or transcultural, 28% of adoptions are from foster care, 21% private, and 84% international. The study showed that many White United States adoptive parents who adopted internationally, adopted outside of their race.

D. 2007 NSAP: Gender

The study also defined gender placement in foster care, private adoptions, and international adoptions. First, the study showed that 50% of all adoptees are male. And the fairly even split was also reflected among the three types of adoptions: 57% are male in foster care, 51% in private, and 33% in international adoptions.

E. Household Composition

The study compiled data on how many other children reside in the adopted child's home. Many homes that adopted children already had other children living there. The study found that 38% of adopted children are the only child in the household, which is not a very high percentage. Most homes had more than one child. As far as those homes with other children, the study found that 29% of all adopted children have their birth sibling(s) living in the adoptive household with them. And further breaking down this study in to the three sections: 36% of children adopted from foster care were adopted with their birth siblings(s), 15% privately adopted children have their birth sibling(s) adopted with them, and 7% of international adopted children were adopted with their birth sibling(s). It could be concluded that there are situations of an adoptee who has a sibling to be adopted with the adoptee, and therefore the adoptive family opened their home to multiple children. This was most notably seen in foster care adoptions.

In other home composition statistics, 40% of foster care adoptees have other children in household — either adopted or adoptive parents' biological children. In private adoptions, 21% have other children in household. And 10% of international adoptions have other children living in the household.

Most adopted children end up living with two married parents. The study found that 69% of all adoptees live with their two married parents. In foster care, 70% of adoptees live with two married parents, 59% in private adoptions, and 82% in international adoptions.

F. 2007 NSAP: Birth Family Contact

A significant number of adopted children have contact with their biological parent(s). The study revealed: 39% of foster care adoptees have post-adoption, birth family contact, 68% of private adoptees do, and 6% of international adoptees have post-adoption, birth family contact.

G. 2007 NSAP: Demographics

The NSAP study focused on other specific areas of adoptees, like the child's age upon adoption. In general, adopted United States children are older than the general United States child population. For example, only 6% of the adopted population was under age 3, while 16% of the general population was under age 3; and 14% adopted children are under 5 years old, versus 27% of general population. These results raise interesting questions about present society and adoption: the time when a parent(s) decides to give a child up for adoption; the potential time delay surrounding the adoption process itself; a possible decline in the rate of newborn adoptions; and the probability of kinship adoptions taking the place of regular adoptions, which were not included in this study. Placement of the adoptee is viewed below.

Health was another statistic analyzed: 85% of adopted children were considered by their parents to be in excellent or very good health; and 88% of adoptees age 6 and up exhibited positive social behaviors.

As far as future adoptions, 87% adoptive parents today would definitely adopt child. And within the three categories: 81% of foster care adoptive parents would adopt, 93% of private, and 87% of international.

The study also looked at when the child achieved placement in the home. In private adoptions, 62% of adoptees were placed with their adoptive family at less than 1 month of age. As far as living with their birth families prior to adoption, 43% of adoptees lived with their birth families before going in to any adoption situation. In the category breakdown, the percentage of children who lived with their birth families prior to adoption was: 59% adopted from foster care, 39% from private adoption, and 25% of internationally adopted children.

H. 2007 NSAP: Health Status

The health status of the adopted child was analyzed in this study. The first part referenced statistics of all children in living in the United States: 19% of parents identified that their child had special health care needs, and 10% of parents identified that their child had moderate or severe health problems. As far as insurance, 85% of all children were insured during the last 12 months, with 76% of parents stating that their child had adequate health insurance. In addition, 10% of all children have been diagnosed with ADD or ADHD. Finally, 4% of all children over age 2 have been diagnosed as having a behavior conduct problem.

The adopted children gave different statistics: 39% of adopted children have special health care needs, and 26% of adopted children have moderate to severe health problems. As far as insurance, 91% of adopted children were insured within the last 12 months, and 78% had adequate health insurance. Finally, 26% of adopted children were diagnosed with ADD/ADHD, and 15% were diagnosed with behavior problems.

The health and behavior status of the adopted children was divided further into the three categories and specific types of behaviors. With respect to ADD/ADHD: 38% of foster care adoptions; 19% of private adoptions; and 17% of international adoptions reflected adoptees with either of these learning disabilities. Also, the study showed attachment disorder as occurring in 21% of foster care adoptees, 6% of private adoptees, and 8% of international adoptees. With respect to social problems, the adoptees that exhibited this type of behavior was found in 18% of foster care, 10% of private, and 11% of international adoptees. Finally, general behavior problems were reported to be exhibited by 25% of foster care adoptees, 11% of private, and 7% of international adoptees.

I. NSAP: School Performance

The study showed that parents were middle of the road in defining their adoptee's school performance: 50% of adoptive parents rated their child's school performance as either excellent or very good. This also means that 50% of adoptive parents rated their child's school performance as less than very good. The percentage of parents of school-aged children (ages 5–17) who were adopted from foster care, rated the child's reading as excellent or very good at 50%. These same parents rated the same foster care adoptee's Math performance at 41%. The percentage of parents of school-aged children adopted from private adoption, rated their child's reading skills as excellent was at 64%, and math at 58%. International adoptive parents rated reading skills as excellent at 63% and math at 65%.

J. NSAP: Parental Aggravation

This study also looked to parental aggravation; basically, the study measured how the adoptive parent felt in certain situations. Parental aggravation was measured by: how frequently during the prior month they felt their child was harder to care for than most children his/her age; how often the parent felt angry with the child; and whether the child did things that really bothered the parent a lot. In foster care, 84% of parents stated they were not aggravated (16% were). In private adoptions, 93% of parents replied that they were not aggravated (7% were). In international adoptions, 91% of parents stated they were not aggravated (9% were).

K. NSAP: Connection to Adoption

The prior connection to adoption was considered among the different categories of adoption. Within the three categories, 35% of the parent's friends had adopted, 31% of the parent's relative(s) was adopted, 24% of the parents had no prior connection to adoption, 6% either parent was adopted, and 4% the parent's brother/sister was adopted. Interestingly, most adoptive parents had relatively little contact with adoptions prior to adopting.

II. DeBose-Adkison Study: Overview

RESEARCH TEAM @ Stetson Law
- Professor Cynthia Hawkins DeBose, J.D.

RESEARCH TEAM @ Western Mich. Univ.
- Professor Carla Adkison-Bradley, Ph.D
- Assoc. Professor Jeffrey Terpstra, Ph.D
- Mr. Yusuf Bilgic, Statistical Consultant

As mentioned earlier, Professor DeBose worked with a professor of counseling psychology and several statisticians at Western Michigan University. They analyzed the NSAP through the lens of race and domestic transracial adoption.

A. DEB-ADK Study: Subjects

The focus was on analyzing the statistically significant differences between 3 sub-populations from NSAP. Generally, the analysis was over same race adoptions and transracial adoptions. Specifically speaking, the analysis compared White parents adopting White children (WW), Black parents adopting Black children (BB), and transracially adopting parents (TRA). Since 73% of the adoptive parents were White, and since Black parents rarely adopt White children, this group of parents will be overwhelmingly White parents adopting Black and Hispanic children.

Another factor considered was that only domestic adoptions were included, either privately or from foster care. In the study, both quantifiable and/or qualifiable (less-tangible) differences between the three groups were discussed.

B. DEB-ADK Study: Demographics

The total number of children in the study was 1386 (2089/NSAP), with 691 adopted through foster care and 695 adopted privately. The racial make-up of the children in the population was as follows: White—821 (59.2%), Black—304 (21.9%), Hispanic—126 (9.1%), Asian—9 (0.6%), and other—126 (9.1%). In the study, 51% were males and 49% were females. Finally, 45% children had other children living in their home, versus 55% where they were the only child.

C. DEB-ADK Study: Post-Adoptive Training

1. Research Question 1

Parents who were TRA adopters were less likely to have received post-adoption training and/or services than the other two sub-groups (WW & BB). Preliminary independent analysis of the sub-population found that parents who were TRA adopters were less likely to have received post-adoption training and/or services than the other two sub-groups (WW & BB).

This was particularly critical due to the societal issues and pressures associated with TRA. Understandably, under MEPA, potential adoptive parents cannot be queried about racial and cultural sensitivity, nor can adoption placements be based upon race. However, there were no restrictions on seeking associated training and services post-adoption.

D. DEB-ADK Study: Support Groups

1. Research Question 2

With respect to TRA children, very few participated in post adoption support groups. Out of the TRA parents, only a low percentage participated in post adoption support groups. Additionally, the team's analysis showed that very few TRA children participated in adoption support groups for children/youth; the analysis further revealed that TRA parents, although percentage-wise more participated in support groups, the actual percentage was low.

Checkpoints

- This study was conducted in 2007, with the results released in 2010. Today, this survey's results remain current.
- There were three types of adoption surveyed: foster care adoption, private adoption, and international adoption.
- Transracial adoptions were separated out in the survey.
- As far as race of the adopted child: White children were the most adopted from private adoptions and foster care adoptions; and Asian children were the most adopted out of international adoptions.
- 68% of private adoptees have post-adoption contact with the birth family, the highest of the three categories.
- Interestingly enough, most children adopted out from the three adoptions types live with two adoptive parents.
- School performance and health status of the adoptee was also surveyed.

Mastering Adoption Law and Policy Master Checklist

Chapter 1 • The History of Adoption
- ❏ The history of adoption
- ❏ The evolution of U.S. adoption
- ❏ Comparison of early adoption to modern adoption practices

Chapter 2 • The History of the U.S. Child Welfare System and Foster Care
- ❏ The development of the U.S. Child Welfare System
- ❏ How Child Protection Services shapes Foster Care
- ❏ Nongovernmental charities and Foster Care
- ❏ The history of the U.S. Foster Care System

Chapter 3 • Types of Adoption
- ❏ The three types of adoption—public agency, private agency, and non-agency
- ❏ The history and parameters of each of the types of adoption
- ❏ Fees associated with the three types
- ❏ Legal issues and regulations among the three types

Chapter 4 • Consent
- ❏ General issues of consent and adoption
- ❏ The effects of consent on biological and adoptive parents
- ❏ Putative father's rights
- ❏ Surrogacy and consent

Chapter 5 • Open Adoption
- ❏ The history and definition of open adoption
- ❏ Procedures for open adoption
- ❏ States and confidentiality
- ❏ The benefits and risks for birth parents, adoptive parents, and adoptees in open adoptions

Chapter 6 • Transracial Adoption
- ❏ The history of transracial adoption
- ❏ The effect of MEPA and IEAA on modern adoption
- ❏ Cultural genocide and its connection with adoption
- ❏ Pros and cons of transracial adoption
- ❏ Statistics

Chapter 7 • Same-Sex Adoption
- ❏ The history of U.S. same-sex adoption
- ❏ The process of same-sex adoption
- ❏ Case law
- ❏ The pros and cons of same-sex adoption
- ❏ Full effect of *Obergefell* case still unknown

Chapter 8 • The Indian Child Welfare Act of 1978 (ICWA)
- ❏ The history of ICWA
- ❏ How ICWA shaped adoption procedures
- ❏ The importance of cultural identity under ICWA

Chapter 9 • Step-Parent and Second Parent Adoption
- ❏ The legal definition and history of the term step-parent
- ❏ The legal duties of the step-parent and the non-custodial, biological parent
- ❏ Case law
- ❏ State regulation of step-parent adoptions

Chapter 10 • Kinship Care and Adoption
- ❏ The definition of kinship care and kinship adoption
- ❏ Varied state definitions and benefits
- ❏ Statutory regulation of kinship care

Chapter 11 • Safe Haven Laws
- ❏ The definition and history of U.S. safe haven laws
- ❏ Varied state statutes
- ❏ The effect of safe haven laws
- ❏ The pros and cons of safe haven laws

Chapter 12 • Snowflake Adoption
- ❏ The definition of "snowflake" adoption
- ❏ The process of a snowflake adoption
- ❏ Varied state laws
- ❏ Statistics

Chapter 13 • Wrongful Adoption Tort
❑ The history of wrongful adoption tort
❑ Intentional misrepresentation — legal consequences
❑ The definitions of negligent failure to investigate, negative placement, and breach of contract
❑ Damages

Chapter 14 • Adoption Reforms
❑ The intent and regulations of the UAA
❑ The adoption of ASFA and its policies
❑ Understand the Foster Care Independence Act
❑ The relevance of the Preventing Sex Trafficking Act
❑ Recent Congressional legislation

Chapter 15 • National Survey of Adoptive Parents (2007)(NSAP)
❑ The characteristics of the NSAP
❑ The types of adoptions surveyed
❑ What the results from the survey project for the future of adoption

Appendix A

50 State Comparison and National Survey
of State Laws

Family Law - Adoption: **Adoption** (July 2012)

50 STATE SURVEYS
STATUTES & REGULATIONS

OVERVIEW

FEDERAL

Adoption law is primarily subject to state laws and regulations. However, there are two federal laws protecting children and/or their biological parents during the adoption or termination of parental rights process.

The Adoption Assistance and Child Welfare Act, is federal legislation providing federal subsidies as well as requiring states to make adoption assistance payments to parents adopting children with special needs. 42 USCS § 670 through 42 USCS § 674. A determination is made of the adoptee child's eligibility prior to adoption, and the adopting parents and the state or other public agency agree to the amount of adoption assistance. 42 USCS § 673. The federal definition of a special needs child, which may vary at the state level, is a child:

(1) who cannot or should not be returned to the biological parents' home,
(2) for whom there is a special factor or condition, and
(3) an effort has been made to place the child with the appropriate adoptive parents without providing adoptive assistance. 42 USCS § 673.

Also protected by federal law are Indian children and their natural parents under the Indian Child Welfare Act. 25 U.S.C. § 1901 through 25 U.S.C. § 1963. Indian parents are given an extended period in which to revoke their consent to adopt or voluntarily terminate their parental rights. Additionally, Indian parents may revoke their consent after adoption or termination of parental rights and may withdraw consent at any time upon the grounds that consent was obtained through fraud or duress. 25 USCS § 1913. Although many of the states provide similar protections, most provide a much smaller time period in which withdrawal of consent may occur for non-Indian parents, if any. The Indian Children Welfare Act also provides preferences for adoption of Indian children by their relatives, others in their tribe and other Indian families. 25 USCS § 1915.

The Uniform Law Commissioners promulgated the Uniform Adoption Act (UAA) in 1994 in order to promote uniformity among state adoption laws. The UAA contains a procedure for pre-placement evaluation and qualification of

potential adoptive parents under administrative, not judicial proceedings. The UAA provides separate court proceedings for differing types of adoption including adoption of minors, adoption of adults, stepparent adoption and others. The UAA also addresses procedures for direct versus agency placement of children, the rights of birth parents, and the confidentiality of adoption records. Currently, the only state that has enacted the UAA is Vermont.

STATES

State adoption laws come from state statutes as well as case law; however, the scope of the following survey is limited to statutory provisions unaffected by case law. Most states require that the biological mother, parents, or other individual(s) or agency having legal custody or control of an adoptee consent, surrender, or relinquish the child before either an adoption proceeding or termination of parental rights proceeding may occur. Generally, the term "consent" is used in conjunction with adoptive proceedings, and the term "surrender" is used in conjunction with the action taken by birth parent(s) to voluntarily terminate their parental rights by making an adoption plan for their child. "Relinquishment" is the term generally used when a legal act is taken on the part of the birth parents to give up all legal rights to a child so that adoption proceedings may commence.

As the survey indicates, most states provide a list of persons and/or agencies required to consent to adoption before legal proceedings may commence. Some states provide a statutory waiting period referring to the time period which must lapse between birth and the time in which the consent to adoption may be legally be signed. In addition to a waiting period, many states also provide a specified period, within which, the birth parent(s) may revoke their written consent to adoption. Withdrawal or revocation of consent is usually barred after the petition for adoption is final or the court has entered a decree or order of adoption. Only a few states allow a consent to adopt to be signed or executed *before* birth, including, but not limited to Alabama and Colorado.

 LexisNexis®

50 State Surveys – Adoption

Like the UAA, most states provide laws for different types of adoption such as the adoption of minors, adults, mentally incompetent persons, step-parent adoptions, and others. Due to the scope of the varying types of adoption, the following survey focuses on independent, and/or the private adoption of minors.

Finally, most states address the issue of putative fathers, but who were not married to the child's mother before the child's birth and who have not acknowledged or established that they are the father in a judicial proceeding. Many states have created "Putative Father Registries" or other voluntary registries to provide putative fathers the opportunity to file a notice to claim paternity. Most putative father statutes outline the time period in which a putative father must file a claim, provide specific forms and administrative procedures to do so, and also guarantee notice of adoption or termination of parental rights proceedings once a claim of paternity has been properly filed in the state. In many states, a man who has not filed a notice of intent to claim paternity, or other similar filing, will not receive notice of any court proceedings relating to the child.

As indicated below, states that do not have a Putative Father Registry often provide alternative means for men to obtain a right to receive notice of proceedings or to determine judicially their paternity and parental rights. States without a Putative Father Registry may have provisions for voluntary acknowledgment of paternity.

ISSUE COVERAGE

Compiled July 2012, this survey adresses child adoption through private and public agencies, consent prior to or following birth, waiting periods, revocation of consent, and permissible payments to birth mothers. Highlighted issues include: (1) Adoption consent provisions, including: (a) Person(s) required to consent, (b) Waiting period, and/or (c) Relinquishment and/or withdrawal period; and (2) Putative father registries and other means of establishing paternity.

Please email your LexisNexis account representative and LNsurveys@lexisnexis.com to inquire about purchasing a custom survey created for you by a dedicated attorney researcher.

 LexisNexis®

50 State Surveys – Adoption

STATE	STATUTES & REGULATIONS	CONSENT TO ADOPT			PUTATIVE FATHER REGISTRY OR OTHER MEANS OF ESTABLISHING PATERNITY
		PERSON(S) REQUIRED TO CONSENT	WAITING PERIOD	RELINQUISHMENT AND/OR WITHDRAWAL PERIOD	
AL	Code of Ala. §§ 26-10-4.1 through 26-10C-2 Ala. Admin. Code r. 660-5-22-.01 through 660-5-22-.06	Adoptee if over 14 years old; Mother; Adoptee's presumed father if he and mother are/were married prior or within 300 days of birth, or attempted to marry before/after birth, or received child into home openly holding out as his own; Agency with custody; Putative father registered with State Code of Ala. § 26-10A-7		Revocation of consent by court within 14 days of birth or after consent signed, whichever comes last; Code of Ala. § 26-10A-13 Withdrawal of consent within 5 days of birth or consent, whichever comes last; Code of Ala. § 26-10A-14 Consent may be given either before or after birth; Code of Ala. § 26-10A-12	Putative Father Registry: Person must file with registry within 30 days of or before birth Code of Ala. § 26-10C-1
AK	Alaska Stat. § 25.20.050 Alaska Stat. §§ 25.23.005 through 25.23.240 7 Alaska Admin. Code 56.600 through 7 Alaska Admin. Code 56.670	Minor's Mother; Minor's father if married at time of conception, or father by adoption or other legitimacy; Persons lawfully entitled to custody; Court having custody; Minor if 10 years or older; Minor's spouse Alaska Stat. § 25.23.040		Relinquishment may be withdrawn within 10 days after birth or signing; Alaska Stat. § 25.23.180 Consent may be withdrawn after 10 day period upon court determination; Alaska Stat. § 25.23.070	Legitimation of Child: Child born out of wedlock legitimated when putative father marries mother; acknowledges paternity in writing; he/mother sign acknowledgment of paternity; or paternity determined by court Alaska Stat. § 25.20.050

3

50 State Surveys – Adoption

| STATE | STATUTES & REGULATIONS | CONSENT TO ADOPT | | | PUTATIVE FATHER REGISTRY OR OTHER MEANS OF ESTABLISHING PATERNITY |
		PERSON(S) REQUIRED TO CONSENT	WAITING PERIOD	RELINQUISHMENT AND/OR WITHDRAWAL PERIOD	
AZ	A.R.S. §§ 8-101 through 8-173 A.A.C. §§ R6-5-6601 through R6-5-7520	Birth/adoptive mother; Father, adoptive, or if married to mother at conception, or if paternity established; Child if 12 or older; Guardian with authority to consent; An agency with authority to consent; Guardian of any adult parent; Division with authority to consent/other legal proceedings A.R.S. § 8-106	Yes Consent given before 72 hours after birth invalid A.R.S. § 8-107	Consent to adopt is irrevocable, unless obtained by fraud, duress, or undue influence A.R.S. § 8-106	Putative Father's Registry: Must file intent to claim paternity before or within 30 days after birth to receive notice of adoption proceedings A.R.S. § 8-106.01
AR	A.C.A. §§ 9-9-101 through 9-9-702 A.C.A. §§ 20-18-701 through 20-18-705	Mother; Father, if married to mother at time of conception, or adoptive father, or has legal/physical custody of minor at time of petition, or proves significant custodial/financial relationship; Person(s) lawfully entitled to custody/empowered with consent; Court with jurisdiction/authority to consent; Minor if over 12 years old; Minor's spouse A.C.A. § 9-9-206		Relinquishment may be withdrawn within 10 days, or if waiver, 5 days after relinquishment signed or birth; A.C.A. 9-9-220 Consent may be withdrawn within 10 days, or if waiver, 5 days after birth or consent is signed, whichever is later; A.C.A. § 9-9-209	Putative Father Registry: Notice of paternity must be filed with registry before birth or adoption petition filed in order to receive notice of legal proceedings A.C.A. § 20-18-702

LexisNexis®

4

50 State Surveys – Adoption

STATE	STATUTES & REGULATIONS	CONSENT TO ADOPT			PUTATIVE FATHER REGISTRY OR OTHER MEANS OF ESTABLISHING PATERNITY
		PERSON(S) REQUIRED TO CONSENT	WAITING PERIOD	RELINQUISHMENT AND/OR WITHDRAWAL PERIOD	
CA	Cal Fam Code §§ 7520 through 7577 Cal Fam Code §§ 8500 through 109340 Cal Wel & Inst Code §§ 16100 through 16144.3 22 CCR 30850 through 22 CCR 35409	Birth parent(s) if living; Father if presumed by birth during marriage, legislative finding, or before mother's relinquishment/consent becomes irrevocable or her parental rights terminated Cal Fam Code § 8604		Revocation of consent is permitted within 30 days of signing consent Cal Fam Code § 8814.5	Establishment of Paternity by Voluntary Declaration: Voluntary declaration of paternity may be signed by natural mother and man identified as natural father, establishing paternity with same force/effect of court issued paternity Cal Fam Code § 7571
CO	C.R.S. 14-1-101 C.R.S. 19-4-105 through 19-4-113 C.R.S. 19-5-100.2 through 19-5-403 12 CCR 2509-4 through 12 CCR 2509-8	Order of the court; Guardian(s) of child where parents deceased; Parent in step-parent adoption where other parent deceased or rights terminated, or when parent shows other birth parent abandoned/failed without cause to provide reasonable support for child >1 year; Parent(s) in step-parent adoption where child conceived/born out of wedlock; Child if 12 years or older C.R.S. 19-5-203	Yes Petition may not be filed until 4 days after birth C.R.S. 19-5-103.5	Relinquishment may be revoked after entry of relinquishment within 90 days, if clear and convincing evidence of fraud or duress; C.R.S. 19-5-104 Consent may be given either before or after birth; C.R.S. 19-5-103.5	Determination of Father-Child Relationship: Child, his/her natural mother, presumed father, State, DHS may bring court action to declare existence or non-existence of child-father relationship; C.R.S. 19-4-107 Mother shall be informed when father acknowledges paternity in writing with Registrar of Vital Statistics; C.R.S. 19-4-105
CT	Conn. Gen. Stat. §§ 45a-706 through 45a-765	Statutory parent(s); Child over 12 years old;	Yes Consent shall	Adoption is irrevocable Conn. Gen. Stat. §	Claim for Paternity by Putative Father:

50 State Surveys – Adoption

STATE	STATUTES & REGULATIONS	CONSENT TO ADOPT		RELINQUISHMENT AND/OR WITHDRAWAL PERIOD	PUTATIVE FATHER REGISTRY OR OTHER MEANS OF ESTABLISHING PATERNITY
		PERSON(S) REQUIRED TO CONSENT	WAITING PERIOD		
	Conn. Gen. Stat. § 46b-172a Regs., Conn. State Agencies §§ 17a-116-6 through 17a-120-9 Regs., Conn. State Agencies §§ 17a-145-130 through 17a-145-160 Regs., Conn. State Agencies §§ 45a-728-1 through 45a-728-10	Parent(s) may agree in writing to adopt if they are the surviving parent, or mother of child born out of wedlock and putative father's rights terminated, or former single person who adopted and then married; Sole guardian if parental rights of non-parties terminated Conn. Gen. Stat. § 45a-724	not be executed within 48 hours after birth Conn. Gen. Stat. § 45a-715	45a-715	Any person claiming to be father can at any time file a claim for paternity with probate court where either mother or father resides; claim admissible in any action for paternity, prohibiting claimant from denying paternity Conn. Gen. Stat. § 46b-172a
DE	13 Del. C. § 8-401 through 13 Del. C. § 8-423 13 Del. C. § 901 through 13 Del. C. § 1115	Mother; Biological/presumed father provided consent not contain admission of paternity; If mother/father not living together as husband/wife openly and have not married since birth, court may dispense with father's consent requirement; Step-parent or blood relative adoption, and any person from whom consent required is deceased, then death certificate shall be filed in lieu of consent; Individual if under 18 years old 13 Del. C. § 908		Withdrawal of consent within 60 days from filing adoption petition 13 Del. C. § 909	Registry of Paternity: Man seeking notification of proceeding of adoption or termination of rights of child he may have fathered must register before birth or within 30 days after birth with paternity registry 13 Del. C. § 8-402
DC	D.C. Code §§ 4-301 through 4-346 D.C. Code §§ 16-301 through 16-316 D.C. Code §§ 16-909.01 through 16-	Adoptee 14 years and over; Both parents;			Establishment of Paternity: Voluntary acknowledgment of paternity creates a

50 State Surveys – Adoption

| STATE | STATUTES & REGULATIONS | CONSENT TO ADOPT | | | | PUTATIVE FATHER REGISTRY OR OTHER MEANS OF ESTABLISHING PATERNITY |
		PERSON(S) REQUIRED TO CONSENT	WAITING PERIOD	RELINQUISHMENT AND/OR WITHDRAWAL PERIOD		
	909.04 RULES GOVERNING ADOPTION PROCEEDINGS Rule 70	Living parent, if one dead; Court-appointed guardian; Child-placing agency or Mayor if parental rights of parent(s) terminated by a court and prospective adoptee has been lawfully placed under care/custody of agency or Mayor; Mayor in any situation not otherwise provided for D.C. Code § 16-304				conclusive presumption of paternity, admissible as evidence and recognized as basis for child support; paternity established by written statement of father and mother or through affidavit from laboratory of genetic testing affirming at least 99% probability of paternity D.C. Code § 16-909.01
FL	Fla. Stat. §§ 63.012 through 63.236 65C-15.036 through 65C-16.018, F.A.C.	Mother of minor; Father if, minor conceived/born while married to mother, by adoption, adjudicated by court, or upon filing affidavit of paternity; If unmarried biological father, if acknowledged in writing he is father; Minor if 12 years or old; Any person lawfully entitled to custody of minor if required by court; court having jurisdiction to determine custody if minor does not have authority to consent Fla. Stat. § 63.062	Yes Consent may be given by mother 48 hours after birth Fla. Stat. § 63.082	Consent may be revoked three business days after execution if child is over 6 months old Fla. Stat. § 63.082	Putative Father Registry: Unmarried biological father must file notarized claim of paternity form with registry at any time prior to birth, but not after petition for termination of parental rights; filing creates express consent to DNA testing requested by any party, registrant, or adoption entity Fla. Stat. § 63.054

7

50 State Surveys – Adoption

STATE	STATUTES & REGULATIONS	CONSENT TO ADOPT			PUTATIVE FATHER REGISTRY OR OTHER MEANS OF ESTABLISHING PATERNITY
		PERSON(S) REQUIRED TO CONSENT	WAITING PERIOD	RELINQUISHMENT AND/OR WITHDRAWAL PERIOD	
GA	O.C.G.A. §§ 19-8-1 through 19-8-43 O.C.G.A. § 19-11-9 Ga. Comp. R. & Regs. r. 290-9-2-.01 through 290-9-2-.15	Child over 14 years old; Each parent and/or guardian must voluntarily surrender rights to agency or consent to adoption, or have all rights terminated by court O.C.G.A. § 19-8-4		Withdrawal of surrender within 10 days after signing surrender; O.C.G.A. § 19-8-9, see also O.C.G.A. § 19-8-26 Pre-birth surrender permitted; O.C.G.A. § 19-8-4	Putative Father Registry: Two types of registration including persons acknowledging paternity before or after birth in signed writing, or persons registering to indicate possibility of paternity without acknowledgement O.C.G.A. § 19-11-9
GU	19 GCA § 4201 through 19 GCA § 4401 26 GAR § 1301 through 26 GAR § 1312	Each parent, or if no parent, guardian, where petition filed by child's blood relative within 2nd degree; Child's guardian, where filed by another person; Child if over 12 years old 19 GCA § 4206		Withdrawal of consent not permitted, unless best interest of child; Consent to adopt is irrevocable after order 19 GCA § 4208	
HI	HRS §§ 346-301 through 346-305 HRS §§ 578-1 through 578-17 HRS §§ 584-3.5 through 584-6 WCHR 17-805	Mother; Legal father as to whom child is legitimate; Biological, adjudicated by court, or presumed father; Concerned natural father with reasonable degree of interest, concern or responsibility for child's welfare during first 30 days after birth, prior to mother's consent, or time child is placed with adoptive parents; Any person/agency having legal custody;		Withdrawal of consent may not be withdrawn or repudiated after child has been placed for adoption, without express approval of court HRS § 578-2	Determination of Father-Child Relationship: An alleged father may bring an action declaring existence or nonexistence of the father and child relationship; HRS § 584-6 Expedited Paternity: Paternity may be expedited by voluntary

50 State Surveys – Adoption

STATE	STATUTES & REGULATIONS	CONSENT TO ADOPT			PUTATIVE FATHER REGISTRY OR OTHER MEANS OF ESTABLISHING PATERNITY
		PERSON(S) REQUIRED TO CONSENT	WAITING PERIOD	RELINQUISHMENT AND/OR WITHDRAWAL PERIOD	
		Court with custody if legal guardian/custodian not empowered to consent; Child if over 10 years old HRS § 578-2			acknowledgment HRS § 584-3.5
ID	Idaho Code §§ 16-1501 through 16-1515 IDAPA 16.06.01.700 through 16.06.01.923	Child if over 12 years old; Both parents if conceived/born within marriage; Mother if born outside marriage; Adjudicated biological parent(s) prior to mother's execution of consent; Unmarried biological father; Legally appointed custodian(s)/guardian(s); Appointed guardian/conservator of incapacitated adult; Adoptee's spouse; Unmarried biological father who has filed a voluntary acknowledgment of paternity; and Father of illegitimate child who has adopted child by acknowledgements Idaho Code § 16-1504		Adoption may not be overturned by court, except for fraud Idaho Code § 16-1512	Registration of Notice: Father, or person claiming to be father of child born out of wedlock may claim rights of paternity by commencing paternity proceedings and by filing with vital statistics unit notice of commencement of proceedings; notice of commencement of proceedings may be filed prior to birth, but must be filed prior to adoption placement Idaho Code § 16-1513
IL	45 ILCS 17/5-1 through 45 ILCS 17/5-99 750 ILCS 50/0.01 through 750 ILCS	Mother; Father if, married to mother at birth/within 300 days of birth (unless found not biological father by court),	Yes No surrender shall be	Consent to adopt is irrevocable 750 ILCS 50/9	Putative Father Registry: Putative father may register with Department of Children and Family services before,

50 State Surveys – Adoption

| STATE | STATUTES & REGULATIONS | CONSENT TO ADOPT | | | PUTATIVE FATHER REGISTRY OR OTHER MEANS OF ESTABLISHING PATERNITY |
		PERSON(S) REQUIRED TO CONSENT	WAITING PERIOD	RELINQUISHMENT AND/OR WITHDRAWAL PERIOD	
	55/1 720 ILCS 525/0.01 through 720 ILCS 525/5 89 Ill. Adm. Code 309.10 through 89 Ill. Adm. Code 309.190 89 Ill. Adm. Code 333.1 through 89 Ill. Adm. Code 333.6	or under adoption judgment, order of parentage, or acknowledgment of parentage/paternity, or openly lived with child, biological mother or held himself out as biological father up to 30 days after birth (if place in adoption within 6 months of birth); Legal guardian of child if no surviving parent; Agency if child surrendered for adoption; Any person/agency having legal custody by court order; Execution/verification of petition by any petitioner who is also a parent of child to be adopted shall be sufficient evidence of such parent's consent 750 ILCS 50/8; see also 750 ILCS 50/10	signed within 72 hours immediately following birth 750 ILCS 50/9		but no later than 30 days after birth; failure to register bars from thereafter bringing/maintaining any action to assert interest in child, unless proves impossibility of registering 750 ILCS 50/12.1
IN	Burns Ind. Code Ann. §§ 31-19-1-1 through 31-19-29-6 465 IAC 2-4-1 through 465 IAC 2-4-5	Living parent(s) if born in wedlock, including presumed biological father; Mother of child born out of wedlock, father with court established paternity; Each person, agency or county children/family office having lawful custody; Court, if legal guardian without power of consent; Child if over 14 years old; Spouse of child, if any Burns Ind. Code Ann. § 31-19-9-1		Consent may be withdrawn within 30 days after signed; Burns Ind. Code Ann. § 31-19-10-3 Consent may not be withdrawn after entry of adoption decree; Burns Ind. Code Ann. § 31-19-10-4	Putative Father Registry: If, on or before the date the mother executes consent to adoption, mother does not disclose paternity to an attorney/agency arranging the adoption, the father must register to be entitled to notice of adoption Burns Ind. Code Ann. § 31-19-5-5

LexisNexis®

50 State Surveys – Adoption

STATE	STATUTES & REGULATIONS	CONSENT TO ADOPT			PUTATIVE FATHER REGISTRY OR OTHER MEANS OF ESTABLISHING PATERNITY
		PERSON(S) REQUIRED TO CONSENT	WAITING PERIOD	RELINQUISHMENT AND/OR WITHDRAWAL PERIOD	
IA	Iowa Code § 144.12A Iowa Code §§ 600.1 through 600.25 441 IAC 107.1(600) through 441 IAC 108.10(238) 441 IAC 160.1(234) through 441 IAC 160.10(234) 441 IAC 200.1(600) through 441 IAC 201.11(600)	Guardian of adoptee; Spouse of petitioner who is a step-parent; Spouse of a petitioner who is separately petitioning to adopt; Adoptee if over 14 years old Iowa Code § 600.7		Consent may be withdrawn prior to adoption decree Iowa Code § 600.7	Paternity Registry: Paternity registry to record name, address, social security number, any other identifying information required of putative father wishing to register prior to birth no later than the date of petition to terminate parental rights filing Iowa Code § 144.12A
KS	K.S.A. § 23-2204 K.S.A. §§ 38-319 through 38-329 K.S.A. §§ 38-335 through 38-340 K.S.A. §§ 59-2111 through 59-2144 K.A.R. §§ 30-45-1 through 30-45-14	Living parent(s) of child; One parent, if other's consent found unnecessary; Legal guardian if both parents dead or their consent unnecessary; Court entering an order; Judge with jurisdiction, if parental rights not terminated; Child if over 14 years old K.S.A. § 59-2129	Yes Consent may not be given until 12 hours after birth K.S.A. § 59-2116		Acknowledgment of Paternity: Acknowledgment of paternity creates permanent father and child relationship, only ended by court order K.S.A. § 23-2204
KY	KRS §§ 199.470 through 199.5955 KRS § 406.021 922 KAR 1:010 through 922 KAR 1:540	Living parent of child, both if born in wedlock; Father of child born out of wedlock if paternity legally established;	Yes Consent may not be given before 72	Consent to adopt is irrevocable 20 days after later of placement of approval or	Determination of Paternity: Paternity may be determined upon complaint of mother, putative father,

LexisNexis®

50 State Surveys – Adoption

STATE	STATUTES & REGULATIONS	CONSENT TO ADOPT			PUTATIVE FATHER REGISTRY OR OTHER MEANS OF ESTABLISHING PATERNITY
		PERSON(S) REQUIRED TO CONSENT	WAITING PERIOD	RELINQUISHMENT AND/OR WITHDRAWAL PERIOD	
		Minor parent who is a party defendant when guardian ad litem appointed; Child if over 12 years old KRS § 199.500	hours after birth KRS § 199.500	execution of informed consent KRS § 199.500	child or agency; determined by either submitting affidavits or testimony of father's identity or if father admits paternity KRS § 406.021
LA	La. Ch.C. Art. 1001 through 1283.17 La. R.S. § 9:400 LAC 67:V.4501 through 67:V.5105	Mother; Father, regardless of actual paternity, if born of marriage, or presumed father, or alleged father who has established parental rights; Biological father whose paternity judged of filiation and has established parental rights; Custodial agency placing child for adoption, with exception for best interest of child La. Ch.C. Art. 1193		Consent may be given either before or after birth; La. Ch.C. Art. 1107.1 Consent is final and irrevocable; La. Ch.C. Art. 1123	State Voluntary Registry; Adoptees over 18 years old and parents may register; LAC 67:V.4505 Putative Father Registry: Record names/addresses of any person adjudicated to be father, who has filed acknowledgment by authentic act, or has filed with registry a judgment of filiation rendered by court recognizing father having acknowledged child born outside of marriage; La. R.S. 9:400
ME	18-A M.R.S. § 9-101 through 18-A M.R.S. § 9-404 22 M.R.S. § 4171 through 22 M.R.S. § 4176	Adoptee if over 14 years old; Both living parents; Person/agency having legal custody/guardianship of child or to whom child surrendered, with exceptions;	Yes Consent is not valid until 3 days after executed	Consent or surrender is final and irrevocable after duly executed; 18-A M.R.S. § 9-202 Except: Adoption may	Establishment of Paternity: Before consenting to an adoption mother must file an affidavit of paternity with court; judge determines how

50 State Surveys – Adoption

STATE	STATUTES & REGULATIONS	CONSENT TO ADOPT		WAITING PERIOD	RELINQUISHMENT AND/OR WITHDRAWAL PERIOD	PUTATIVE FATHER REGISTRY OR OTHER MEANS OF ESTABLISHING PATERNITY
		PERSON(S) REQUIRED TO CONSENT				
	CMR 10-148-013	Court appointed guardian, if child adoptee has no living parent, guardian or legal custodian who may consent 18-A M.R.S. § 9-302		18-A M.R.S. § 9-202	be annulled if obtained by fraud, duress, or undue influence; 18-A M.R.S. § 9-315	to give notice of proceedings to putative father; after notice, putative father has 20 days petition court to grant paternal rights 18-A M.R.S. § 9-201
MD	Md. FAMILY Code Ann. §§ 5-301 through 5-4C-07 Md. FAMILY Code Ann. § 5-1028 COMAR 07.02.12.01 through 07.02.13.09				Order for adoption may not be entered until 30 days after birth; Md. FAMILY LAW Code Ann. § 5-336 Revocation of consent within later of 30 days after parent signs adoption or adoption petition is filed; Md. FAMILY LAW Code Ann. § 5-339	Affidavit of Parentage: Unmarried father and mother shall have opportunity to execute affidavit of parentage; to be completed on standardized form, upon execution constitutes a legal finding of paternity; after 60 day period, may only be challenged in court on basis of fraud, duress or mistake of material fact Md. FAMILY LAW Code Ann. § 5-1028
MA	ALM GL ch. 209C, § 2 ALM GL ch. 210, § 1 through ch. 210, § 11A 102 CMR 5.01 through 102 CMR 5.14	Child to be adopted if over age of 12; Child's spouse, if any; Lawful parents, who may be previous adoptive parents, or surviving parent; Mother, only if child was born out of wedlock and not		Yes No sooner than 4th calendar day after birth	Consent to adopt is final and irrevocable from date of execution ALM GL ch. 210, § 2	Establishment of Paternity: Paternity may be established by filing acknowledgment of parentage executed by both parents with the court of Registrar of Vital Records or

LexisNexis®

13

50 State Surveys – Adoption

| State | Statutes & Regulations | Consent to Adopt | | Putative Father Registry or Other Means of Establishing Paternity |
| | | Person(s) Required to Consent | Waiting Period | Relinquishment and/or Withdrawal Period | |

State	Statutes & Regulations	Person(s) Required to Consent	Waiting Period	Relinquishment and/or Withdrawal Period	Putative Father Registry or Other Means of Establishing Paternity
	110 CMR 7.200 through 110 CMR 7.215	previously adopted ALM GL ch. 210, § 2	ALM GL ch. 210, § 2		pursuant to court order ALM GL ch. 209C, § 2
MI	MCLS §§ 710.21 through 710.70 MICH. ADMIN. CODE R 400.12601 through 400.12713	Each parent or surviving parent, with exceptions; Authorized representative of department or designee or of child-placement agency to whom child permanently committed by court; Court/ tribal court having permanent custody; Authorized representative of department or his/her designee or of a child-placement agency; Guardian, if appointed (under subsections 5, 6); Authorized representative of court/child-placement out of state agency with consent authority; Child if over 14 years old MCLS § 710.43			Notice of Intent to Claim Paternity: Before birth of child out of wedlock, person claiming to be father may file verified notice of intent to claim paternity; shall be presumed to be father unless mother denies; claimant entitled to notice of any hearing involving child to determine identity of father or determine or terminate parental rights MCLS § 710.33
MN	Minn. Stat. §§ 259.20 through 259.89 Minn. R. 9545.0835 Minn. R. 9560.0010 through 9560.0180	(effective August 2, 2012) Unmarried parent under 18 years old, then minor parent's parent(s)/guardian, if any; If either/both parents are disqualified, consent waived, and consent of guardian only shall be sufficient; If neither parent/guardian qualified to give consent, it may be given by commissioner; Agency overseeing adoption proceedings shall ensure	(eff. 8/02/12) Yes Consent may be given no sooner than 72 hours after birth and not later than 60 days	(effective August 2, 2012) Withdrawal of consent may be given for any reason within 10 working days of it being executed and acknowledged Minn. Stat. § 259.24	Father's Adoption Registry: Purpose of determining the identity and located of putative father interested in minor child; who is, expected to be, subject of adoption proceeding; in order to provide notice to putative father, otherwise not

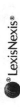

● LexisNexis®

14

50 State Surveys – Adoption

STATE	STATUTES & REGULATIONS	CONSENT TO ADOPT		RELINQUISHMENT AND/OR WITHDRAWAL PERIOD	PUTATIVE FATHER REGISTRY OR OTHER MEANS OF ESTABLISHING PATERNITY
		PERSON(S) REQUIRED TO CONSENT	WAITING PERIOD		
		minor parent offered opportunity to consult with attorney, clergy or physician before consenting. Minn. Stat. § 259.24	after placement. Minn. Stat. § 259.24		entitled to notice. Minn. Stat. § 259.52
MS	Miss. Code Ann. §§ 93-17-1 through 93-17-223. Miss. Code Ann. § 93-9-28	Parent(s); If both deceased, any 2 adult kin of child within 3rd degree, provided if one of such kin in possession of child, s/he shall join petition or be made party to suit; Guardian ad litem of abandoned child, upon petition showing parents' names unknown after inquiry; Persons with physical custody except foster parents; Any person to whom custody awarded by court; Agent of county Department of State of Mississippi that placed child for foster care by agreement or order. Miss. Code Ann. § 93-17-5	Yes. Consent may not be given before 72 hours after birth. Miss. Code Ann. § 93-17-5	Petition for determination of rights may be filed 30 days after birth. Miss. Code Ann. § 93-17-6	Voluntary Acknowledgment of Paternity: Voluntary acknowledgment of paternity form from the mother and father of any child born out of wedlock; clearly state that acknowledgment of paternity shall result in same legal effect as if father and mother married at time of birth. Miss. Code Ann. § 93-9-28
MO	§ 192.016 R.S.Mo. §§ 453.005 through 453.503 R.S.Mo. 13 CSR 40-38.010 through 13 CSR 40-38.020	Mother; Presumed father, or man who has filed action to establish paternity no later than 15 days after birth, or filed with putative father registry notice of intent to claim paternity prior to/within 15 days after birth; Child's current adoptive parents or legally recognized mother and father; Child if over 14 years old	Yes. Consent will be approved within 3 business days by court. § 453.030 R.S.Mo.	Waiver of consent may be made 2 days after birth; § 453.050 R.S.Mo. Revocation of consent may be made within 1 year for fraud or duress; § 453.160 R.S.Mo.	Putative Father Registry: Record names/addresses of father of child born out of wedlock; any person who filed notice of intent to claim paternity before or after birth of child born out of wedlock; any other adjudicated father; lack of knowledge of pregnancy

50 State Surveys – Adoption

STATE	STATUTES & REGULATIONS	CONSENT TO ADOPT			PUTATIVE FATHER REGISTRY OR OTHER MEANS OF ESTABLISHING PATERNITY
		PERSON(S) REQUIRED TO CONSENT	WAITING PERIOD	RELINQUISHMENT AND/OR WITHDRAWAL PERIOD	
		§ 453.030 R.S.Mo.			does not excuse failure to file claim of paternity in timely manner § 192.016 R.S.Mo.
MT	Mont. Code Anno., §§ 42-1-101 through 42-10-128 MONT. ADMIN. R. 37.8.310 through 37.8.311	Birth mother; Husband of birth mother if presumed father; Any person with court established parental rights; Any department/agency with custody/authority to place child for adoption; Legal guardian(s) if both parents dead or their rights have been judicially terminated; Child if 12 years of age or older unless incompetent Mont. Code Anno., § 42-2-301	Yes Not less than 72 hours after birth Mont. Code Anno., § 42-2-408	Relinquishment may not be revoked after order to terminate parental rights has been issued; Mont. Code Anno., § 42-2-410 Relinquishment and consent will be set aside for fraud or duress; Mont. Code Anno., § 42-2-417 Consent irrevocable after entry of adoption; Mont. Code Anno., § 42-4-210	Putative Father Registry: To receive notice of termination of parental rights proceeding, putative father's registry form must be filed not later than 72 hours of birth, regardless of knowledge of pregnancy Mont. Code Anno., § 42-2-206
NE	R.R.S. Neb. §§ 43-101 through 43-165 Nebraska Admin. Code Title 479, Ch. 8	Child if over 14 years old; Any district, county, separate juvenile court having custody of minor child by virtue of proceedings or Uniform Child Custody Jurisdiction and Enforcement Act; Both living parents if born in lawful wedlock, surviving	Yes Consent not valid unless signed at least 48	Biological father's relinquishment or consent or waiver of rights can only be challenged for fraud or duress up to 6 months after signing	Biological Father Registry: Putative fathers may file Request for Notification of Intended Adoption or a Notice of Objection to Adoption and Intent to

50 State Surveys – Adoption

| STATE | STATUTES & REGULATIONS | CONSENT TO ADOPT | | RELINQUISHMENT AND/OR WITHDRAWAL PERIOD | PUTATIVE FATHER REGISTRY OR OTHER MEANS OF ESTABLISHING PATERNITY |
		PERSON(S) REQUIRED TO CONSENT	WAITING PERIOD		
		parent if born in lawful wedlock, mother of child born out of wedlock, or mother and father of a child born out of wedlock R.R.S. Neb. § 43-104	hours after birth R.R.S. Neb. § 43-104	R.R.S. Neb. § 43-104.11	Obtain Custody R.R.S. Neb. § 43-104.01
NV	Nev. Rev. Stat. Ann. §§ 126.071 through 126.223 Nev. Rev. Stat. Ann. §§ 127.003 through 127.420 NAC 127.010 through 127.260	Both parents if both are living; one parent if other is dead; or Guardian of person appointed by court; Nev. Rev. Stat. Ann. § 127.040 Child if over 14 years old; Nev. Rev. Stat. Ann. § 127.020	Yes Consent invalid before or within 72 hours after birth Nev. Rev. Stat. Ann. § 127.020	Relinquishment cannot be revoked or nullified Nev. Rev. Stat. Ann. § 127.020	Evidence Relating to Paternity; Action may be brought by child, mother or man presumed to be father; evidence relating to paternity including medical or anthropological evidence relating to alleged father's paternity of child based on tests performed by experts Nev. Rev. Stat. Ann. § 126.131
NH	RSA 126-D:1 through 126-D:7 RSA 170-B:1 through 170-B:31 N.H. Admin. Rules, He-C 6438.01 through He-C 6438.18	Birth mother; Legal father; Birth father, provided entitled to notice and right to surrender his parental rights; Legal guardian, if both birth parents deceased, or parental rights of birth parent(s) have been surrendered or involuntarily terminated and guardian granted authority to surrender parenta rights;	Yes Surrender invalid within 72 hours after birth RSA 170-B:8	Withdrawal of surrender within 30 days RSA 170-B:12	Putative Father Registry: Notice to person claiming paternity; failure to register prior to birth of child bars alleged father from bringing an action to establish paternity and constitutes an abandonment of child and a waiver of any right to notice of hearing in any adoption

●LexisNexis®

17

50 State Surveys – Adoption

STATE	STATUTES & REGULATIONS	CONSENT TO ADOPT			PUTATIVE FATHER REGISTRY OR OTHER MEANS OF ESTABLISHING PATERNITY
		PERSON(S) REQUIRED TO CONSENT	WAITING PERIOD	RELINQUISHMENT AND/OR WITHDRAWAL PERIOD	
		Department/licensed child-placing agency given care, custody, and control including right to surrender RSA 170-B:5			proceeding RSA 170-B:6
NJ	N.J. Stat. §§ 9:3-37 through 9:3-56 N.J. Stat. § 9:17-41 N.J.A.C. 10:121-1.1 through 10:121C-6.3	Written consent of spouse, unless adoption jointly with spouse; N.J. Stat. § 9:3-43 Surrender must be approved by agency; N.J. Stat. § 9:3-41	Yes Surrender invalid if taken within 72 hours after birth N.J. Stat. § 9:3-41		Establishment of Parent-Child Relationship: Relationship between child and natural father may be established by proof that paternity adjudicated by law, giving full faith/credit to determination of paternity made by other state/jurisdiction, default judgment, or court order based on blood/genetic test N.J. Stat. § 9:17-41
NM	N.M. Stat. Ann. §§ 32A-5-1 through 32A-5-45 8.26.2.1 through 8.26.3.50 NMAC	Adoptee if 14 years or older; Adoptee's mother; Adoptee's proposed adoptive parent; Presumed or acknowledged father; Department/agency to whom adoptee has been relinquished or agency that has custody; Guardian of adoptee's parent when that guardian has	Yes Consent within 48 hours of birth is invalid N.M. Stat. Ann. § 32A-5-21	Consent or relinquishment may not be withdrawn before entry of decree, unless obtained by fraud N.M. Stat. Ann. § 32A-5-21	Putative Father Registry: for fathers who affirmatively assume responsibility for children they may have fathered and expedite adoptions of children whose biological fathers are unwilling to assume responsibility for their children by registering with putative father registry or

LexisNexis®

50 State Surveys – Adoption

STATE	STATUTES & REGULATIONS	CONSENT TO ADOPT		RELINQUISHMENT AND/OR WITHDRAWAL PERIOD	PUTATIVE FATHER REGISTRY OR OTHER MEANS OF ESTABLISHING PATERNITY
		PERSON(S) REQUIRED TO CONSENT	WAITING PERIOD		
		express authority to consent N.M. Stat. Ann. § 32A-5-17			otherwise acknowledging their children N.M. Stat. Ann. § 32A-5-20
NY	NY CLS Dom Rel §§ 109 through 117 NY CLS Soc Serv § 372-c 18 NYCRR § 420.1 through 18 NYCRR § 421.27	Adoptive child over 14 years old; Parent(s) surviving, of child conceived/born, in/out of wedlock; Mother, conceived/ born, in/out of wedlock; Father of child born out of wedlock and placed with adoptive parents > 6 months after birth, only if maintained substantial/continuous contact with child; Father of child born out of wedlock who openly lived with child for 6 months within 1 year period preceding adoption and held himself out as father; Father of child born out of wedlock < 6 months at time placed adoption if father lived with child's mother openly for continuous period of 6 months immediately preceding adoption, and held himself out as father, and paid fair/reasonable sum connected with pregnancy and birth; Any person or authorized agency having lawful custody NY CLS Dom Rel § 111		Revocation of consent no later than 45 days after execution NY CLS Dom Rel § 115-b	Putative Father Registry: Record names/addresses of any person adjudicated to be father of child born out of wedlock, before or after birth of child out of wedlock, notice of intent to claim paternity, any person adjudicated father by another state/jurisdiction, any person who has filed with registry and instrument acknowledging paternity NY CLS Soc Serv § 372-c
NC	N.C. Gen. Stat. §§ 7B-3700 through 7B-9999	Minor if 12 or more years old; Mother;		Consent to adoption of infant in utero or any minor may be revoked	Pre-birth Determination of Right to Consent:

LexisNexis®

19

50 State Surveys – Adoption

STATE	STATUTES & REGULATIONS	CONSENT TO ADOPT		RELINQUISHMENT AND/OR WITHDRAWAL PERIOD	PUTATIVE FATHER REGISTRY OR OTHER MEANS OF ESTABLISHING PATERNITY
		PERSON(S) REQUIRED TO CONSENT	WAITING PERIOD		
	N.C. Gen. Stat. §§ 48-1-100 through 48 Table 10A N.C.A.C. 43F.0801 through 10A N.C.A.C. 43F.0804	Any possible biological father who is/was married to mother at birth, or within 280 days after marriage terminated, or parties separated under written agreement; or attempted to marry mother before birth; Man, who has legally legitimate minor before filing; Man, who has acknowledged his paternity of minor, before earlier of filing or hearing; Man, who has received minor into home and openly held out minor as biological child; Adoptive father of minor; Guardian of minor; Agency that placed minor for adoption; Individuals who have not relinquished minor N.C. Gen. Stat. § 48-3-601		within 7 days of execution; N.C. Gen. Stat. § 48-3-608 Consent or relinquishment may be set aside for fraud or duress; N.C. Gen. Stat. § 48-2-406 Consent is otherwise final and irrevocable; N.C. Gen. Stat. § 48-3-607	Any time after 6 months from conception, birth mother, agency or adoptive parents may file special proceeding requesting court to determine whether consent of biological father required; biological father shall be served with notice of intent of biological mother to place child for adoption allowing father 15 days to assert a claim that his consent is required N.C. Gen. Stat. § 48-2-206
ND	N.D. Cent. Code. §§ 14-15-01 through 14-15.1-07 N.D. Cent. Code. §§ 14-20-11 through 14-20-12 N.D. Cent. Code. § 50-19-11 N.D. Admin. Code 33-04-08-01 through 33-04-08-05	Mother by birth or adoption; Father if by adoption or otherwise legitimate minor; Presumed biological father provided non-existence of father-child relationship not yet judicially determined; Lawful individual(s) entitled to custody or empowered to consent; Court with custody if legal guardian not empowered to		Consent cannot be withdrawn after decree of adoption N.D. Cent. Code. § 14-15-08	Acknowledgment of Paternity: Mother of man claiming to be father may sign acknowledgment of paternity with intent to establish man's paternity N.D. Cent. Code. § 14-20-11

LexisNexis®

20

50 State Surveys – Adoption

| STATE | STATUTES & REGULATIONS | CONSENT TO ADOPT | | | | PUTATIVE FATHER REGISTRY OR OTHER MEANS OF ESTABLISHING PATERNITY |
		PERSON(S) REQUIRED TO CONSENT	WAITING PERIOD	RELINQUISHMENT AND/OR WITHDRAWAL PERIOD		
		consent; Minor if over 10 years old; Spouse of minor to be adopted N.D. Cent. Code, § 14-15-05				
OH	ORC Ann. 3107.01 through 3107.99 OAC Ann. 5101:2-44-03 through 5101:2-44-13.1 OAC Ann. 5101:2-48-02 through 5101:2-49-25	Mother of minor; Father if conceived/ born while father married to mother, if child by adoption, or if established his child by court proceeding; Any person/agency having permanent custody or authorized by court order to consent; Juvenile court having jurisdiction to determine custody if legal guardian not authorized to consent; Minor if over 12 years old; Putative father if alleged to be father any time before placement, or has acknowledged child in notarized writing any time before placement; or has signed birth certificate; or has filed objection to adoption with agency/department having custody of minor within 30 days after petition to adopt filed, or placement in home of petitioner, whichever occurs first ORC Ann. 3107.06		Consent to adopt is irrevocable ORC Ann. 3107.084		Putative Father Registry: To register a father must complete registration form and submit it not later than 30 days after birth of child ORC Ann. 3107.062
OK	10 Okl. St. § 7501-1.1 through 10 Okl. St. § 7510-3.3 O.A.C. §§ 340:2-5-90 through 340:2-5-	Both parents of minor; One parent alone if other parent is dead; parental rights of other parent have been terminated, or		Extrajudicial consent revocable within 15 days of execution of		Paternity Registry: Father or putative father of child born out of wedlock

21

50 State Surveys – Adoption

STATE	STATUTES & REGULATIONS	CONSENT TO ADOPT		RELINQUISHMENT AND/OR WITHDRAWAL PERIOD	PUTATIVE FATHER REGISTRY OR OTHER MEANS OF ESTABLISHING PATERNITY
		PERSON(S) REQUIRED TO CONSENT	WAITING PERIOD		
	105 O.A.C. §§ 340:75-15-5 through 340:75-15-133	consent of other parent is otherwise not required; legal guardian or guardian ad litem if both parents dead or rights of parents terminated, or consent of both parents otherwise not required; Executive head of licensed agency; Any person with legal custody by court order 10 Okl. St. § 7503-2.1		consent 10 Okl. St. § 7503-2.6	may be filed for notice to receive notification of an adoption proceeding, notice of intent to claim paternity, an instrument acknowledging paternity of child, a waiver of interest; or other claim acknowledging or denying paternity 10 Okl. St. § 7506-1.1
OR	ORS § 109.070 ORS §§ 109.304 through 109.507 ORS §§ 417.090 through 417.105 ORS § 419B.460 Or. Admin. R. 413-010-0081 through 413-010-0086 Or. Admin. R. 413-030-0300 through 413-030-0320 Or. Admin. R. 413-040-0310 through 413-040-0320	Parents of child, or survivor of them; Guardian if child has no living parent; Next of kin in Oregon, if no living parent or guardian; Suitable person appointed by court to act in proceeding as next friend of child to give/withhold consent, if no living parent or guardian or next of kin qualified to consent ORS § 109.312		Consent for adoption may not be revoked, unless fraud or duress ORS § 109.312	Voluntary Adoption Registry; ORS § 109.450 Establishing Paternity: Paternity may be established by presumption, marriage of parents at birth of child, filing voluntary acknowledgment of paternity form in this/other state, filiation proceedings, or other legal proceedings ORS § 109.070
PA	23 Pa.C.S. § 2101 through 23 Pa.C.S. § 2910 23 Pa.C.S. § 5103 55 Pa. Code § 3130.36	Adoptee if over 12 years old; Spouse of adopting parent unless they join petition; Parents or surviving parent of adoptee under 18 years old;	Yes Consent not valid within 72 hours	Consent is irrevocable more than 30 days after execution 23 Pa.C.S. § 2711	Establishment of Registry; Medical records and other information; 23 Pa.C.S. § 2921 Acknowledgment and Claim

50 State Surveys – Adoption

State	Statutes & Regulations	Consent to Adopt			Putative Father Registry or Other Means of Establishing Paternity
		Person(s) Required to Consent	Waiting Period	Relinquishment and/or Withdrawal Period	
	55 Pa. Code § 3140.201 through 55 Pa. Code § 3140.210 55 Pa. Code § 3350.1 through 55 Pa. Code § 3350.108	Guardian of an incapacitated adoptee; Guardian of person of adoptee under 18 or of person(s) having custody, whenever adoptee has no parent whose consent is required 23 Pa.C.S. § 2711	after birth 23 Pa.C.S. § 2711		of Paternity: Name of father included on record of birth of child of unmarried parents only if: father and mother sign voluntary acknowledgment of paternity or court issued adjudication of paternity; 23 Pa.C.S. § 5103
PR	8 L.P.R.A. § 549 through 8 L.P.R.A. § 549g 31 L.P.R.A. § 531 through 31 L.P.R.A. § 539 32 L.P.R.A. § 2699 through 32 L.P.R.A. § 2699s	Adopter(s); Adoptee if over 10 years old; Father, mother or parents of adoptee who, at moment of adoption, possesses his/her patria potestas (power of father), as well as father or mother who do not possess patria potestas due to divorce; Father or mother who, on date petition filed has acknowledged minor to be adopted as his/her child; Secretary of Department of Family, when a non-emancipated minor to be adopted is under his/her guardianship/care and whose father, mother or parents have been deprived of patria potestas; Special/legal guardian designated for consenting to adoption; Minor parents over 18, married on filing adoption petition; Biological grandparents when biological parents are		Adoption by final decree shall extinguish any legal nexus between adoptee and his/her former biological or adoptive family 31 L.P.R.A. § 538	

● LexisNexis®

23

50 State Surveys – Adoption

STATE	STATUTES & REGULATIONS	CONSENT TO ADOPT			RELINQUISHMENT AND/OR WITHDRAWAL PERIOD	PUTATIVE FATHER REGISTRY OR OTHER MEANS OF ESTABLISHING PATERNITY
		PERSON(S) REQUIRED TO CONSENT	WAITING PERIOD			
RI	R.I. Gen. Laws §§ 15-7-2 through 15-7.2-15 R.I. Gen. Laws § 15-8-27 CRIR 03-240-811	non-emancipated minors 31 L.P.R.A. § 535 Parents of child or their survivor; Guardian of person of child, if neither parent living; Next of kin if no guardian; Court appointed suitable person as next friend if no next of kin; Child if over 14 years old; No consent by parents or others is required if child over 18 years old R.I. Gen. Laws § 15-7-5			Termination of rights or consent to adoption may be requested not sooner than 15 days after birth R.I. Gen. Laws § 15-7-6	Voluntary Acknowledgment: Man may acknowledge paternity in writing filed with clerk of family court; copy of acknowledgment shall be served upon mother and any presumed father R.I. Gen. Laws § 15-8-27
SC	S.C. Code Ann. §§ 63-9-10 through 63-9-2290 S.C. Code Regs. 114-4370 through 114-4380	Adoptee if over 14 years old; Surviving parent(s) of child conceived/born during marriage; Mother, if child born when not married; Father when child born when he was not married to mother, if child placed with prospective adoptive parents > 6 months after birth, only if father has maintained substantial/continuous/ repeated contact; Father lived with child/mother for continuous 6 month period before birth; Father paid fair/reasonable sum for pregnancy/birth			Withdrawal of consent or relinquishment not permitted except by court order if in best interest of child and if consent was given involuntarily given by coercion or duress S.C. Code Ann. § 63-9-350	Responsible Father Registry: to preserve right of notice of an adoption proceeding; may be filed with registry before or after birth of child; claim is null/void if filed on or after date petition for termination of parental rights or a petition for adoption is filed S.C. Code Ann. § 63-9-820

50 State Surveys – Adoption

STATE	STATUTES & REGULATIONS	CONSENT TO ADOPT		RELINQUISHMENT AND/OR WITHDRAWAL PERIOD	PUTATIVE FATHER REGISTRY OR OTHER MEANS OF ESTABLISHING PATERNITY
		PERSON(S) REQUIRED TO CONSENT	WAITING PERIOD		
		expenses; Legal guardian or legal custodian; Child placement agency facilitating adoption; Parent who is a child not subject to revocation by reason of minority S.C. Code Ann. § 63-9-310			
SD	S.D. Codified Laws § 25-4-54 S.D. Codified Laws §§ 25-6-1 through 25-6A-14 S.D. Codified Laws §§ 25-8-7 through 25-8-7.1 S.D. Codified Laws § 25-8-50 ARSD 67:14:11:01 through 67:14:32:31	Consent of child's parents required unless waived by court; S.D. Codified Laws § 25-6-4 Child if over 12 years old; S.D. Codified Laws § 25-6-5		Adoption is final and unconditional S.D. Codified Laws § 25-6-17	Affidavit of Paternity: Upon birth of child to unmarried woman, mother and alleged father shall have an opportunity to sign voluntary affidavit of paternity; S.D. Codified Laws § 25-8-50 Voluntary registration of adoptees, natural parents: consent to release of information about themselves; S.D. Codified Laws § 25-6-15.3
TN	Tenn. Code Ann. §§ 36-1-101 through 36-1-305 Tenn. Code Ann. § 36-2-318 Tenn. Comp. R. & Regs. R. 0250-7-11-.01 through 0250-7-13-.21	Child over 14 years old; Guardian ad litem for disabled child or adult; Child's parent for a step-parent or relative adoption; Agency with authority to surrender; or	Yes Surrender or consent not valid within 3	Revocation of surrender allowed within 10 days of	Putative Father Registry: Persons registered entitled to notice of pending adoption or termination proceedings; must file within 30 days of notice to

APPENDIX A

50 State Surveys – Adoption

STATE	STATUTES & REGULATIONS	CONSENT TO ADOPT			PUTATIVE FATHER REGISTRY OR OTHER MEANS OF ESTABLISHING PATERNITY
		PERSON(S) REQUIRED TO CONSENT	WAITING PERIOD	RELINQUISHMENT AND/OR WITHDRAWAL PERIOD	
		Other parental consent Tenn. Code Ann. § 36-1-102	days of birth Tenn. Code Ann. § 36-1-111	execution Tenn. Code Ann. § 36-1-112	establishing parentage claim or present a defense to termination or adoption case Tenn. Code Ann. § 36-2-318
TX	Tex. Fam. Code §§ 160.401 through 106.423; Tex. Fam. Code § 161.103; Tex. Fam. Code §§ 162.001 through 162.602; 40 TAC § 700.801 through 40 TAC § 700.894; 40 TAC § 749.191 through 40 TAC § 749.245	Managing conservator of adoption; Parent, if spouse of petitioner; Child if over 12 years old Tex. Fam. Code § 162.010	Yes Not before 48 hours after birth Tex. Fam. Code § 161.103	Consent may be revoked any time before granting adoption order Tex. Fam. Code § 162.011	Registry of Paternity: Man desiring notification of proceedings for adoption or termination of parental rights may register with Bureau of Vital Statistics Registry before the birth of child or not later than the 31st day after birth; Tex. Fam. Code § 160.402 Voluntary adoption registry: mutual consent; eligible registrants include 18 and over adoptees (Tex. Fam. Code § 162.406), parents, specified alleged fathers, and biological siblings; Tex. Fam. Code § 162.403
UT	Utah Code Ann. §§ 62A-4a-607 through 62A-4a-1010; Utah Code Ann. §§ 78B-6-101 through 78B-6-145	Adoptee if over 12 years old; Man, recognized by law as father, or father by previous legal adoption; Mother;	Yes May not consent until at least 24 hours after	Consent or relinquishment effective when signed, may not be revoked Utah Code Ann. § 78B-	Voluntary Adoption Registry: By mutual consent; adult adoptees and birth parents of adult adoptees, upon presentation of positive identification, may request

50 State Surveys – Adoption

STATE	STATUTES & REGULATIONS	CONSENT TO ADOPT			PUTATIVE FATHER REGISTRY OR OTHER MEANS OF ESTABLISHING PATERNITY
		PERSON(S) REQUIRED TO CONSENT	WAITING PERIOD	RELINQUISHMENT AND/OR WITHDRAWAL PERIOD	
	U.A.C. R495-879-8 through R495-880-1	Biological parent adjudicated to be child's biological father by court prior to mother's execution of consent; Biological parent who has executed/filed voluntary declaration of paternity; Unmarried biological father (Utah Code Ann. § 78B-6-121); Person/agency with authority to consent Utah Code Ann. § 78B-6-120	birth Utah Code Ann. § 78B-6-125	6-126	identifying information from the office Utah Code Ann. § 78B-6-144
VT	15A V.S.A. § 1-101 through 15A V.S.A. § 8-101	Birth mother; Biological father as identified by mother; Man is/was married when child born, or within 300 days after marriage terminated; or Man who has acknowledged paternity, or demonstrated commitment to parenthood responsibilities including personal, custodial, financial; Guardian if authorized by court to consent; Current adoptive/legally recognized mother and father 15A V.S.A. § 2-401	Yes May not consent sooner than 36 hours after birth 15A V.S.A. § 2-404	Consent or relinquishment may be revoked within 21 days of execution 15A V.S.A. § 2-408	Adoption Registry: Identifying information of adoptee's; 15A V.S.A. § 6-103 Petition to Terminate Parent and Child Relationship: Parent/alleged parent who has not consented to adoption or whose parental rights not terminated will be served a petition to terminate and notice of hearing; must file response within 20 days; 15A V.S.A. § 3-503
VA	Va. Code Ann. §§ 63.2-1200 through 63.2-1304; 22 VAC 40-130-290 through 22 VAC 40-	Birth mother; Any man who is acknowledged, adjudicated, or presumed father, or is registered with Putative Father		Consent revocable up to 7 days after execution if child over	Putative Father Registry: For notification of adoption/termination

27

50 State Surveys – Adoption

STATE	STATUTES & REGULATIONS	CONSENT TO ADOPT			PUTATIVE FATHER REGISTRY OR OTHER MEANS OF ESTABLISHING PATERNITY
		PERSON(S) REQUIRED TO CONSENT	WAITING PERIOD	RELINQUISHMENT AND/OR WITHDRAWAL PERIOD	
	130 Title Forms	Registry; Child placement agency with right to place for adoption; Child if over 14 years old; Va. Code Ann. § 63.2-1202		10 days old; Va. Code Ann. § 63.2-1234; Consent revocable prior to final order upon proof of fraud or duress, or upon written mutual consent of birth and adoptive parents after placement; Va. Code Ann. § 63.2-1204	proceedings for child that may have fathered; must register with Putative Father Registry before birth of child or within 10 days after birth; Va. Code Ann. § 63.2-1249
VI	16 V.I.C. § 141 through 16 V.I.C. § 147; 16 V.I.C. § 291 through 16 V.I.C. § 298; 34 V.I.C. § 351 through 34 V.I.C. § 359; CVIR 34-005-000, Sec. 104-101 through 34-005-000, Sec. 104-107; CVIR 34-011-000, Sec. 357-1 through 34-011-000, Sec. 357-13	Parents of child or survivor of them, or guardian ad litem; 16 V.I.C. § 142; Child if over 14 years old; 16 V.I.C. § 144			Voluntary Paternity Establishment: Paternity of child born out of wedlock may be voluntarily established by executing Acknowledgment of Paternity; considered legal finding of paternity if filed in compliance with rules, with same force and effect as court adjudication; 16 V.I.C. § 292
WA	Rev. Code Wash. (ARCW) § 26.26.101; Rev. Code Wash. (ARCW) §§ 26.33.010 through 26.34.080; WAC §§ 388-27-0005 through 388-27-	Adoptee if over 14 years old; Parents and any alleged father under 18 years old; Agency or department with custody; and Legal guardian of adoptee	Yes; Consent not valid sooner than 48 hours after	Consent revocable any time before adoption approved by court; Rev. Code Wash.	Establishment of Parent-Child Relationship: Un-rebutted presumption of paternity; signed acknowledgment of

50 State Surveys – Adoption

STATE	STATUTES & REGULATIONS	CONSENT TO ADOPT			PUTATIVE FATHER REGISTRY OR OTHER MEANS OF ESTABLISHING PATERNITY
		PERSON(S) REQUIRED TO CONSENT	WAITING PERIOD	RELINQUISHMENT AND/OR WITHDRAWAL PERIOD	
	0390	Rev. Code Wash. (ARCW) § 26.33.160	birth Rev. Code Wash. (ARCW) § 26.33.090	(ARCW) § 26.33.160	paternity; adjudication; adoption; or valid surrogate parentage contract Rev. Code Wash. (ARCW) § 26.26.101
WV	W. Va. Code §§ 48-22-101 through 48-23-801 W. Va. Code §§ 48-24-101 through 48-24-106 W. Va. CSR §§ 78-2-12 through 78-2-27	Parent(s) or surviving parent (adult/infant) of marital child; Outsider father of marital child adjudicated father or who has filed pending paternity action; Birth mother of non-marital chilc; Determined father W. Va. Code § 48-22-301; see also W. Va. Code § 48-22-109	Yes Consent may be executed 72 hours after birth W. Va. Code § 48-22-302	Revocation of consent allowed under certain circumstances W. Va. Code § 48-22-305	Paternity Proceedings: Civil action to establish paternity may be instituted in family court where child resides W. Va. Code § 48-24-101
WI	Wis. Stat. § 48.41 Wis. Stat. §§ 48.81 through 48.978 Wis. Stat. § 767.805 Wis. Stat. §§ 882.01 through 882.04 Wis. Adm. Code DCF 42.01 through DCF 42.05	Guardian of minor, written recommendation required Wis. Stat. § 48.841; see also Wis. Stat. § 48.85		Right to withdraw consent exists before termination of parental rights Wis. Stat. § 48.837	Voluntary Acknowledgment of Paternity: Statement acknowledging paternity filed with State Registrar is conclusive determination as judgment of paternity; may be requested by child, mother, presumed/alleged father, State, custodian or guardian Wis. Stat. § 767.805

● LexisNexis®

50 State Surveys – Adoption

| STATE | STATUTES & REGULATIONS | CONSENT TO ADOPT | | | PUTATIVE FATHER REGISTRY OR OTHER MEANS OF ESTABLISHING PATERNITY |
		PERSON(S) REQUIRED TO CONSENT	WAITING PERIOD	RELINQUISHMENT AND/OR WITHDRAWAL PERIOD	
WY	Wyo. Stat. §§ 1-22-101 through 1-22-203 WCWR 049-040-001 through 049-041-003	Consent to Adoption: Both parents if living, or survivor; Mother and putative father (if known); Mother alone, must sign affidavit providing notice if father is registered; Legal guardian if parental rights judicially terminated; Head of Agency with custody; Person with court ordered custody; Legally appointed guardian if parent(s) mentally incompetent Wyo. Stat. § 1-22-109			Putative Father Registry: Record name/addresses of any person adjudicated father of child born out of wedlock; must file notice of intent to claim paternity or acknowledgment of paternity Wyo. Stat. § 1-22-117

Appendix B

Synopsis of Major Federal Legislation (04/12)

Child Welfare Information Gateway

PROTECTING CHILDREN ■ STRENGTHENING FAMILIES

FACTSHEET

Current Through
April 2012

Major Federal Legislation Concerned With Child Protection, Child Welfare, and Adoption

The primary responsibility for child welfare services rests with the States, and each State has its own legal and administrative structures and programs that address the needs of children and families. However, States must comply with specific Federal requirements and guidelines in order to be eligible for Federal funding under certain programs.

Beginning with the passage of the Child Abuse Prevention and Treatment Act (CAPTA) in 1974, the U.S. Congress has implemented a number of laws that have had a significant impact on State

Electronic copies of this publication may be downloaded at http://www.childwelfare.gov/pubs/otherpubs/majorfedlegis.cfm

Order a copy of the PDF by calling 800.394.3366, or download it at http://www.childwelfare.gov/pubs/otherpubs/majorfedlegis.pdf

Use your smartphone to access this factsheet online.

Children's Bureau

Child Welfare Information Gateway
Children's Bureau/ACYF
1250 Maryland Avenue, SW
Eighth Floor
Washington, DC 20024
800.394.3366
Email: info@childwelfare.gov
http://www.childwelfare.gov

child protection and child welfare services.[1] Such legislation frequently requires Federal departments and agencies, such as the Children's Bureau within the U.S. Department of Health and Human Services, to issue or amend Federal policy and regulation.[2] New legislation also prompts responses at the State level, including enactment of State legislation, development or revision of State agency policy and regulations, and implementation of new programs.

The largest federally funded programs that support State and Tribal efforts for child welfare, foster care, and adoption activities are authorized under titles IV-B and IV-E of the Social Security Act (the Act). These programs are administered by the U.S. Department of Health and Human Services and include the title IV-B Child Welfare Services and Promoting Safe and Stable Families (formerly known as Family Preservation) programs, the title IV-E Foster Care Program, the title IV-E Adoption Assistance Program, and the title IV-E Chafee Foster Care Independence Program. The Social Services Block Grant (SSBG) is authorized under title XX of the Act and funds a wide range of programs that support various social policy goals.

To provide a framework for understanding the Federal legislation that has shaped the delivery of child welfare services, this publication presents a summary of Federal legislation since 1974 that has had a significant impact on the field. It provides an overview of each act and its major provisions. The full text of the acts included in this publication can be found on Information Gateway's Index of Federal Child Welfare Laws.

---

[1] The Federal Government started providing grants to States for preventive and protective services and foster care payments in 1935 with the Child Welfare Services Program, title IV-B of the Social Security Act. In 1961, legislation provided for foster care maintenance payments under the Aid to Dependent Children Program, title IV-A of the Social Security Act. Both of these programs were amended by the Adoption Assistance and Child Welfare Act of 1980.

[2] For information on the Children's Bureau policy, visit the website at http://www.acf.hhs. gov/programs/cb/laws_policies/index.htm

Major Federal Legislation Concerned With Child Protection, Child Welfare, and Adoption   **http://www.childwelfare.gov**

**Timeline of Major Federal Legislation Concerned With
Child Protection, Child Welfare, and Adoption**

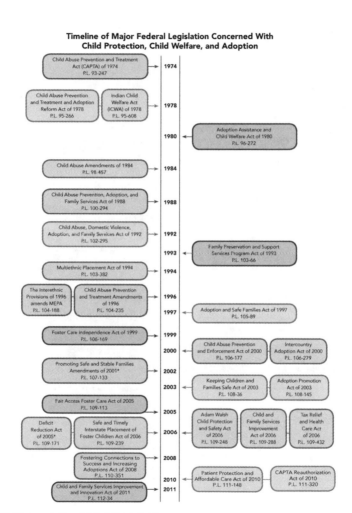

*Some acts were enacted the year following their introduction in Congress.

3

P.L. 112-34

Child and Family Services Improvement and Innovation Act

Overview

H.R. 2883

Enacted September 30, 2011

Purpose: To amend part B of title IV of the Social Security Act to extend the Child and Family Services Program through fiscal year (FY) 2016, and for other purposes.

Note: Children's Bureau offers guidance on this legislation in Information Memorandum ACYF-CB-IM-11-06, issued October 6, 2011, and Program Instruction ACYF-CB-PI-11-09, issued December 9, 2011.

Major Provisions of the Act

- Required each State plan for oversight and coordination of health care services for any child in foster care to include an outline of:
  » The monitoring and treatment of emotional trauma associated with a child's maltreatment and removal from home
  » Protocols for the appropriate use and monitoring of psychotropic medications
- Required each State plan for child welfare services to describe:
  » Activities to reduce the length of time children under age 5 are without a permanent family
  » Activities to address the developmental needs of such children who receive benefits or services
  » The sources used to compile information on child maltreatment deaths that the State agency is required by Federal law to report, as well as why the compilation does not include information on such deaths from specified State entities, if it does not, and how the State will include such information
- Revised provisions for monthly caseworkers visits to require that States take necessary steps to ensure that the total number of monthly caseworker visits to children in foster care during a fiscal year is at least 90% (raised to 95% for FY 2015 and thereafter) of the total number of such visits that would occur during the year if each child were visited once a month while in care.
- Required a State Safe and Stable Families Program plan to describe how the State identifies which populations are at the greatest risk of maltreatment and how services are targeted to them.
- Revised requirements for time-limited family reunification services provided to a child removed from the child's home and placed in out-of-home care, and to the child's parents or primary caregiver, in order to facilitate the child's safe, appropriate, and timely reunification with the parents or caregiver. Required services include:
  » Peer-to-peer mentoring and support groups for parents and primary caregivers
  » Services and activities designed to facilitate visitation of children by parents and siblings
- Extended through FY 2016 the specified reservations of funds for monthly caseworker visits and regional partnership grants; required monthly caseworker visit grants to be used to improve the quality of monthly caseworker visits, with an emphasis on improving caseworker decision making on the safety, permanency, and well-being of foster children
- Revised requirements for grants to assist children affected by a parent's or caretaker's methamphetamine or other substance abuse to remove the specification of methamphetamine and apply the grant program generally to children affected by a parent's or caretaker's substance abuse
- Revised the court improvement program to require grants to the highest State courts for increasing and improving engagement of the entire family in court processes relating to child welfare, family preservation, family reunification, and adoption
- Allowed a court to submit one application, rather than separate applications, for more than one grant
- Directed HHS, in order to improve data matching, to designate nonproprietary and interoperable standard data elements for any category of information required to be reported

- Required State title IV-B/IV-E agencies to meet the educational stability case plan requirement at the time of each placement change, not just at initial placement into foster care
- Amended the case review system definition to require that each child age 16 and older in foster care receives a free copy of any consumer credit report each year until discharged from foster care and be offered in interpreting the credit report and resolving any inconsistencies
- Renewed through FY 2014 the authority of HHS to authorize States to conduct child welfare program demonstration projects likely to promote the objectives of title IV-B or IV-E:
    » Repealed the requirement for State project applications to consider certain types of proposals; replaced the requirement with specified conditions for State eligibility to conduct a new demonstration project
    » Limits any child welfare demonstration project to 5 years unless HHS determines that it should be continued
    » Requires States authorized to conduct a demonstration project to obtain an evaluation of its effectiveness by an independent contractor
- Authorized a State to elect to establish a program to:
    » Permit part E foster care maintenance payments to a long-term therapeutic family treatment center on behalf of a child residing in the center
    » Identify and address domestic violence that endangers children and results in the placement of children in foster care
- Set forth child welfare improvement policies, at least two of which a State must have implemented or planned to implement within a certain period of time
- Treated as a State any Indian Tribe, Tribal organization, or Tribal consortium operating a title IV-E program

P.L. 111-320

CAPTA Reauthorization Act of 2010

Overview

S. 3817

Enacted December 20, 2010

Purpose: To amend the Child Abuse Prevention and Treatment Act, the Family Violence Prevention and Services Act, the Child Abuse Prevention and Treatment and Adoption Reform Act of 1978, and the Abandoned Infants Assistance Act of 1988, to reauthorize the Acts, and for other purposes.

Note: Children's Bureau offers guidance on the provisions of this legislation in Information Memorandum ACYF-CB-IM-11-02, issued February 15, 2011.

Major Provisions of the Act

- Amended the State plan eligibility provisions to require submission of a plan that will remain in effect for the duration of the State's participation in the program, with States required to:
    » Periodically review and revise the plan to reflect any changes in State programs
    » Provide notice to HHS of any substantive changes related to child abuse prevention that may affect the State's eligibility for the grant program
    » Provide notice to HHS of any significant changes in how the State is using grant funds
    » Prepare and submit to HHS an annual report describing how CAPTA funds were used
- Directed the Secretary of Health and Human Services (HHS) to complete studies and reports to Congress on:
    » Shaken baby syndrome
    » Efforts to coordinate the objectives and activities of agencies and organizations responsible for programs and activities related to child abuse and neglect
    » The effectiveness of citizen review panels in examining State and local child protection agencies and evaluating the extent to which they fulfill their child protection responsibilities

Major Provisions of the Act, Continued

- » How provisions for immunity from prosecution under State and local laws and regulations facilitate and inhibit individuals cooperating, consulting, or assisting in making good faith reports of child abuse or neglect
- Authorized grants to public or private agencies and organizations to develop or expand effective collaborations between child protective service (CPS) entities and domestic violence service entities to improve:
  - » Collaborative investigation and intervention procedures
  - » Provision for the safety of the nonabusing parent and children
  - » Provision of services to children exposed to domestic violence that also support the care-giving role of the nonabusing parent
- Amended the requirements for State plan assurances to include laws, policies, or programs for:
  - » Laws identifying categories of mandated reporters
  - » Including fetal alcohol spectrum disorders in procedures for referral and development of a plan of safe care for substance-exposed newborns
  - » Including differential response in screening and assessment procedures
  - » Requiring that guardians *ad litem* be trained in early childhood, child, and adolescent development
  - » Providing that reunification not be required where a parent has committed intrafamilial sexual abuse or must register with a sex offender registry
  - » Ensuring the provision of technology to track CPS reports from intake through final disposition
  - » Encouraging the appropriate involvement of families in decision-making
  - » Promoting and enhancing collaboration among child protective, substance abuse, and domestic violence agencies
  - » Requiring training and programs that address the needs of unaccompanied homeless youth
  - » Ensuring collaboration with community-based prevention programs and families affected by child abuse and neglect in the development of the State plan
  - » Ensuring that the State, to the maximum extent possible, has coordinated its CAPTA State plan with its title IV-B State plan
- Required additional data in the annual State data reports, including:
  - » The number of families that received differential response as a preventive service
  - » Caseload requirements and the average caseload for CPS workers
  - » The education, qualifications, and training requirements for CPS personnel
  - » The number of children referred to CPS under policies established to address the needs of infants born affected by illegal substance abuse or fetal alcohol spectrum disorder
  - » The number of children under age 3 involved in a substantiated case of child abuse or neglect who were eligible for referral to agencies providing early intervention services and the number of those children who were actually referred
- Reauthorized the Child Abuse Prevention and Treatment and Adoption Reform Act of 1978, including appropriations, through FY 2015. Amendments to the act required:
  - » Efforts to promote the adoption of older children, minority children, and children with special needs
  - » Recruitment of prospective adoptive families for children in foster care, including developing and using procedures to notify family and relatives when a child enters the child welfare system
- Authorized grants to States for improving efforts to increase the placement of foster care children legally free for adoption. Required that grant applications describe:
  - » How the State plans to improve the placement rate of children in permanent homes
  - » The methods the State, prior to submitting the application, has used to improve the placement of older children, minority children, and children with special needs, who are legally free for adoption
  - » The State's evaluation plan for determining the effectiveness of programs and methods of placement
  - » How the State plans to coordinate activities under this subsection with relevant activities under 42 U.S.C. 673

Major Federal Legislation Concerned With Child Protection, Child Welfare, and Adoption   **http://www.childwelfare.gov**

P.L. 111-148

Patient Protection and Affordable Care Act

Overview

H.R. 3590

Enacted March 23, 2010

Purpose: To amend the Public Health Service Act in order to provide better health-care coverage for all Americans, improve health-care services for underserved communities, and for other purposes.

Note: Children's Bureau offers guidance on the provisions of this legislation in Program Instruction ACYF-CB-PI-10-10, issued June 7, 2010.

Major Provisions of the Act

Provisions relevant to child welfare practice include:

- Extended Medicaid coverage to former foster care children younger than age 26
- Required a State Children's Health Insurance Program (CHIP) plan, beginning January 1, 2014, to use modified gross income and household income to determine CHIP eligibility
- Required a State to treat any child as a targeted low-income child eligible for CHIP who is determined to be ineligible for Medicaid as a result of the elimination of an income disregard based on expense or type of income
- Amended title V of the Social Security Act (Maternal and Child Health Services) to provide grants to eligible entities for early childhood home visitation programs
- Required the case review system for children aging out of foster care and independent living programs to include information about the importance of having a health-care power-of-attorney in transition planning
- Reauthorized appropriations for health centers to serve medically underserved populations
- Reauthorized appropriations for FY 2010-2014 for the expansion and improvement of emergency medical services for children who need treatment for trauma or critical care
- Authorized the award of grants and cooperative agreements for demonstration projects for the provision of coordinated and integrated services to special populations through the co-location of primary and specialty care services in community-based mental and behavioral health settings
- Established a Pregnancy Assistance Fund for grants to States to assist pregnant and parenting teens and women
- Increased from $10,000 to $13,170 the dollar limitation on the tax credit for adoption expenses and the tax exclusion for employer-provided adoption assistance, allowed an inflation adjustment to such limitation after 2010, and made the credit refundable

P.L. 110-351

Fostering Connections to Success and Increasing Adoptions Act of 2008

Overview

H.R. 6893

Enacted October 7, 2008

Purpose: To amend parts B and E of title IV of the Social Security Act to connect and support relative caregivers, improve outcomes for children in foster care, provide for tribal foster care and adoption access, improve incentives for adoption, and for other purposes.

Note: Children's Bureau offers guidance on the provisions of this legislation in Program Instruction ACYF-CB-PI-08-05, issued October 23, 2008.

Major Provisions of the Act

- Created a new plan option for States and Tribes to provide kinship guardianship assistance payments under title IV-E on behalf of children who have been in foster care of whom a relative is taking legal guardianship
- Extended eligibility for Medicaid to children receiving kinship guardianship assistance payments
- Required fingerprint-based criminal records checks of relative guardians, and child abuse and neglect registry checks of relative guardians and adults living in the guardian's home, before a relative guardian may receive title IV-E kinship guardianship assistance payments on behalf of a child
- Amended the Chafee Foster Care Independence Program to allow services to youth who leave foster care for kinship guardianship or adoption after age 16
- Amended the Education and Training Voucher Program to permit vouchers for youth who enter into kinship guardianship or are adopted from foster care after age 16
- Authorized grants to State, local, or Tribal child welfare agencies and private nonprofit organizations for the purpose of helping children who are in or at-risk of foster care reconnect with family members through:
  » Kinship navigator programs
  » Efforts to find biological family and reestablish relationships
  » Family group decision-making meetings
  » Residential family treatment programs
- Permitted States to extend title IV-E assistance to otherwise eligible youth remaining in foster care after reaching age 18 and to youth who at age 16 or older exited foster care to either a kinship guardianship or adoption, provided that they have not yet reached age 19, 20, or 21, as the State may elect, and are in school, employed, engaged in another activity designed to remove barriers to employment, or incapable of doing so due to a documented medical condition (effective October 1, 2010)
- Allowed States to claim Federal reimbursement for short-term training for relative guardians; private child welfare agency staff providing services to children receiving title IV-E assistance; child abuse and neglect court personnel; agency, child, or parent attorneys; guardians *ad litem*; and, court-appointed special advocates.
- Extended the Adoption Incentive Program through FY 2013 and doubled incentive payment amounts for special needs (to $4,000) and older child adoptions (to $8,000)
- Revised adoption assistance eligibility criteria to delink the adoption assistance program from the Aid to Families with Dependent Children requirements
- Phased-in, from FY 2010 to FY 2018, the revised adoption assistance eligibility criteria based on whether the child is defined as "an applicable child," primarily related to the age of the child in the year the agreement is entered into
- Allowed federally recognized Indian Tribes, Tribal organizations, and Tribal consortia to apply to receive title IV-E funds directly for foster care, adoption assistance, and kinship guardianship assistance (effective October 1, 2009)
- Required HHS to provide technical assistance and implementation services to Tribes seeking to operate title IV-B and IV-E programs
- Authorized one-time grants to Tribes that apply to assist in developing a title IV-E program
- Required title IV-E agencies to identify and notify all adult relatives of a child, within 30 days of the child's removal, of the relatives' options to become a placement resource for the child
- Required each child receiving a title IV-E foster care, adoption, or guardianship payment to be a full-time student unless he or she is incapable of attending school due to a documented medical condition
- Required title IV-E agencies to make reasonable efforts to place siblings removed from their home in the same foster care, adoption, or guardianship placement
- Permitted title IV-E agencies to waive on a case-by-case basis a nonsafety licensing standard for a relative foster family home
- Required States to ensure coordination of health care services, including mental health and dental services, for children in foster care

Major Provisions of the Act, Continued

- Required that, 90 days prior to a youth's emancipation, the caseworker develop a personalized transition plan as directed by the youth
- Required that a case plan include a plan for ensuring the educational stability of the child in foster care

P.L. 109-432

Tax Relief and Health Care Act of 2006

Overview

H.R.6111

Enacted December 20, 2006

Purpose: To amend the Internal Revenue Code of 1986 to extend expiring provisions, and for other purposes

Division B, section 405 of the Act amended the Social Security Act to exempt all foster children assisted under title IV-B or IV-E and children receiving title IV-E adoption assistance from the Medicaid citizenship documentation requirements of the Deficit Reduction Act of 2005.

Major Provisions of the Act

- Amended section 1903(x) of title XIX of the Social Security Act (the Act) (42 U.S.C. § 1386b) by including all foster children assisted by titles IV-B and IV-E of the Act and children receiving title IV-E adoption assistance in the groups exempt from the requirement to present documentary evidence of citizenship or nationality if they declare themselves to be citizens or nationals of the United States
- Added a new provision to title IV-E of the Act to require that State plans include procedures for verifying the citizenship or immigration status of children in foster care under State responsibility under titles IV-B or IV-E
- Amended section 1123A of the Act (42 U.S.C. 1320a-2a) to include review of State conformity with this requirement in the Child and Family Services Reviews (CSFRs)

P.L. 109-288

Child and Family Services Improvement Act of 2006

Overview

S. 3525

Enacted September 28, 2006

Purpose: To amend part B of title IV of the Social Security Act to reauthorize the Promoting Safe and Stable Families (PSSF) program, and for other purposes

Major Provisions of the Act

- Amended title IV-B, subpart 1 (Child Welfare Services Program) to:
  - » Change the program from a permanent authorization to a 5-year authorization, with $325 million for each of Federal FY 2007 through 2011
  - » Establish a new program purpose that allows a broader array of services and activities and promotes more flexibility for States to design their programs accordingly
- Amended title IV-B, subpart 2 with respect to the Promoting Safe and Stable Families (PSSF) program to:
  - » Reauthorize mandatory grants at $345 million for each of Federal FY 2007 through 2011
  - » Authorize discretionary grant appropriations of $200 million for each of Federal FY 2007 through 2011
  - » Appropriate $40 million for FY 2006 for States to spend through September 30, 2009, to support monthly caseworker visits with children in foster care under the responsibility of the State
  - » Set aside an additional $40 million for FY 2007 through FY 2011 to be divided between Regional Partnership/ Substance Abuse Grants and support of caseworker visits

Major Provisions of the Act, Continued

- Required each State to submit annually forms that:
  - » Report on planned child and family services expenditures for the immediately succeeding fiscal year
  - » Provide specified information about PSSF and certain other programs, including the numbers of families and of children, as well as the population, served by the State agency
- Reserved specified funds for States to support monthly caseworker visits with children in foster care under State responsibility, with a primary emphasis on activities designed to improve caseworker retention, recruitment, training, and ability to access the benefits of technology
- Required targeted grants to increase the well-being of, and to improve the permanency outcomes for, children affected by methamphetamine or other substance abuse
- Authorized competitive grants to regional partnerships to provide, through interagency collaboration and integration of programs and services, services and activities designed to increase the well-being of, improve permanency outcomes for, and enhance the safety of children who are in an out-of-home placement or are at risk of being placed in an out-of-home placement as a result of a parent's or caretaker's methamphetamine or other substance abuse
- Increased the set-asides for Indian Tribes from 2 to 3 percent of any discretionary funds appropriated and from 1 to 3 percent of the mandatory funds authorized and remaining after the separate reservation of funds for monthly caseworkers is made
- Required each State plan for child welfare services to describe standards for the content and frequency of caseworker visits for children in foster care that, at a minimum, ensure that:
  - » The children are visited on a monthly basis.
  - » The visits are well-planned and focused on issues pertinent to case planning and service delivery to ensure the children's safety, permanency, and well-being.
- Reauthorized and extended through FY 2011 the program for mentoring children of prisoners (MCOP)
- Required the Secretary to enter into a 3-year, renewable cooperative agreement with an eligible entity for a Service Delivery Demonstration Project to:
  - » Identify children of prisoners in need of mentoring services
  - » Provide their families with a voucher for mentoring services and a list of providers in their residential area
  - » Monitor and oversee the delivery of mentoring services by providers that accept the vouchers
- Reauthorized and extended through FY 2011 the basic Court Improvement Program
- Amended title IV-E to require certain foster care proceedings to include consultation in an age-appropriate manner with the child who is the subject of the proceeding

---

P.L. 109-248

Adam Walsh Child Protection and Safety Act of 2006

Overview

H.R. 4472

Enacted July 27, 2006

Purpose: To protect children from sexual exploitation and violent crime; to prevent child abuse and child pornography with an emphasis on comprehensive strategies across Federal/State/local communities to prevent sex offenders access to children; to promote Internet safety; and to honor the memory of Adam Walsh and other child crime victims

Major Federal Legislation Concerned With Child Protection, Child Welfare, and Adoption   http://www.childwelfare.gov

Major Provisions of the Act

- Required (1) fingerprint-based checks of the national crime information databases (NCID) for prospective foster or adoptive parents and (2) checks of State child abuse and neglect registries in which the prospective foster or adoptive parents and any other adults living in the home have resided in the preceding 5 years
- Permitted States that prior to September 30, 2005, had opted out of the criminal background checks until October 1, 2008, to comply with the fingerprint-based background check requirement; after October 1, 2008, no State is exempt from those requirements
- Required States to comply with any request for a child abuse registry check that is received from another State
- Required States to have in place safeguards to prevent the unauthorized disclosure of information in any child abuse and neglect registry maintained by the State and to prevent any such information from being used for a purpose other than the conducting of background checks in foster or adoptive placement cases
- Required the Attorney General, upon the request of a State, to conduct fingerprint-based checks of the national crime information databases to assist:
  - » Child welfare agencies in checking backgrounds of individuals under consideration as prospective foster or adoptive parents or in investigating child abuse or neglect incidents
  - » Private or public schools or educational agencies in checking backgrounds of prospective employees
- Directed the Secretary of Health and Human Services to:
  - » Create a national registry of substantiated cases of child abuse or neglect
  - » Establish standards for the dissemination of information in the registry
  - » Conduct a study on the feasibility of establishing data collection standards for the registry

---

P.L. 109-239

Safe and Timely Interstate Placement of Foster Children Act of 2006

Overview

H.R. 5403

Enacted July 3, 2006

Purpose: To improve protections for children and to hold States accountable for the safe and timely placement of children across State lines

Major Provisions of the Act

- Required each title IV-E State plan for foster care and adoption assistance to provide that the State shall:
  - » Have in effect procedures for orderly and timely interstate placement of children
  - » Complete home studies requested by another State within a specified period, which is 60 days in most cases but up to 75 days if specified circumstances warrant an extension
  - » Accept such studies received from another State within 14 days unless reliance on the report would be contrary to the child's welfare
- Authorized grants for timely interstate home study incentive payments to States that have approved plans and that have completed such studies within 30 days
- Increased the required frequency of State caseworker visits for children in out-of-State foster care placements without imposing restrictions on either State's ability to contract with a private agency to perform those visits
- Amended the definition of "case review system" to:
  - » Require a child's health and education record to be supplied to the foster parent or foster care provider at the time of placement and to provide it to the child at no cost when he/she leaves foster care by reason of having attained the age of majority
  - » Provide for a relative caregiver, foster parent, and preadoptive parent's right to be heard in certain proceedings respecting their foster child

Major Provisions of the Act, Continued
- Included among the purposes of grants to the highest State courts the assessment of the court's role in carrying out State laws requiring proceedings that determine the best strategy to use to expedite the interstate placement of children
- Required State courts to ensure that foster parents, preadoptive parents, and relative caregivers of a child in foster care are notified of certain proceedings held with respect to that child
- Provided for consideration of out-of-State placements in permanency hearings, case plans, and case reviews
- Required each plan for child welfare services to include the assurance that the State will eliminate legal barriers to facilitate timely adoptive or permanent placements for children

P.L. 109-171

Deficit Reduction Act of 2005

Overview

S. 1932

Enacted February 8, 2006

Purpose: Title VII of this act provides for reauthorization of the TANF program, Healthy Marriage and Family funds, Court Improvement Program, Safe and Stable Families Program, and other child welfare programs.

Major Provisions of the Act
- Prohibited access to Medicaid to an individual who declares he or she is a U.S. citizen unless one type of specified documentary evidence of U.S. citizenship or nationality is presented; certain classes were exempt from this requirement. *[Note: Foster children and children receiving title IV-E adoption assistance were later exempted from this requirement by P.L. 109-432.]*
- Replaced incentive bonuses to States for a decrease in the illegitimacy rate with healthy marriage promotion and responsible fatherhood grants, and limited the use of funds for:
  » Demonstration projects designed to test the effectiveness of Tribal governments or consortia in coordinating the provision of child welfare services to Tribal families at risk of child abuse or neglect
  » Activities promoting responsible fatherhood
- Prescribed the contents of applications for Court Improvement grants, including grants for improved data collection and training, and made appropriations for FY 2006-FY 2010 for grants to:
  » Ensure that the safety, permanence, and well-being needs of children are met in a timely and complete manner
  » Provide for the training of judges, attorneys, and other legal personnel in child welfare cases
- Required that courts and agencies demonstrate meaningful collaboration in child welfare services programs
- Permitted States to allow public access to certain State court child welfare proceedings
- Authorized appropriations for FY 2006 for Safe and Stable Families Programs
- Specified criteria under which States may receive Federal matching funds for allowable administrative expenses for children who are candidates for foster care, living in unallowable facilities, or placed with unlicensed relatives
- Clarified the home of removal for AFDC purposes when determining the eligibility of a child for title IV-E foster care maintenance payments and revised adoption assistance eligibility criteria to require AFDC at the time of the child's removal from the specified relative's home only

Major Federal Legislation Concerned With Child Protection, Child Welfare, and Adoption   **http://www.childwelfare.gov**

P.L. 109-113

Fair Access Foster Care Act of 2005

Overview

S. 1894

Enacted November 22, 2005

Purpose: To amend part E of title IV of the Social Security Act to allow foster care maintenance payments to be paid on behalf of eligible children through a nonprofit or for-profit child-placement or child care agency

Major Provisions of the Act

Amended section 472(b) of the Social Security Act (42 U.S.C. 672(b)) by striking the word "nonprofit" each place it appears

---

P.L. 108-145

Adoption Promotion Act of 2003

Overview

H.R. 3182

Enacted December 2, 2003

Purpose: To reauthorize the adoption incentive payments program under part E of title IV of the Social Security Act and for other purposes

Major Provisions of the Act

- Amended title IV-E to revise requirements with respect to States eligible to receive Adoption Incentives payments to provide payments for:
  - » Special needs adoptions that are not older child adoptions
  - » Adoptions of older children (age 9 and older)
- Modified requirements with respect to determination of numbers of special needs adoptions that are not older children as well as adoptions of older children
- Authorized the Secretary to impose specified penalties against a State for failure to provide necessary data to the Adoption and Foster Care Analysis and Reporting System (AFCARS)

P.L. 108-36

Keeping Children and Families Safe Act of 2003

Overview

S. 342

Enacted June 25, 2003

Purpose: To amend and improve the Child Abuse Prevention and Treatment Act (CAPTA), the Adoption Opportunities Act, the Abandoned Infants Assistance Act, and the Family Violence Prevention and Services Act

Major Provisions of the Act

- Reauthorized CAPTA through FY 2008
- Authorized an expanded continuing interdisciplinary and longitudinal research program; provided for an opportunity for public comment on research priorities
- Emphasized enhanced linkages between child protective service agencies and public health, mental health, and developmental disabilities agencies
- Mandated changes to State plan eligibility requirements for the CAPTA State grant, including:

Major Provisions of the Act, Continued

  » Policies and procedures to address the needs of infants born and identified as being affected by prenatal drug exposure
  » Provisions and procedures requiring that a CPS representative at the initial contact advise an individual of complaints and allegations made against him or her
  » Provisions addressing the training of CPS workers regarding their legal duties in order to protect the legal rights and safety of children and families
  » Provisions to require a State to disclose confidential information to any Federal, State, or local government entity with a need for such information
  » Provisions and procedures for referral of a child under age 3 who is involved in a substantiated case of child abuse or neglect to early intervention services funded under part C of the Individuals with Disabilities Education Act
- Directed the Secretary to provide for implementation of programs to increase the number of older foster children placed in adoptive families, including a grants program to eliminate barriers to placing children for adoption across jurisdictional boundaries
- Amended the Abandoned Infants Assistance grants program to prohibit grants unless the applicant agrees to give priority to infants and young children who:
  » Are infected with or exposed to the human immunodeficiency virus (HIV) or have a life-threatening illness
  » Have been perinatally exposed to a dangerous drug

P.L. 107-133

Promoting Safe and Stable Families Amendments of 2001

Overview

H.R. 2873

Enacted January 17, 2002

Purpose: To extend and amend the Promoting Safe and Stable Families program, provide new authority to support programs for mentoring children of incarcerated parents, and amend the Foster Care Independent Living program under title IV-E to provide for educational and training vouchers for youth aging out of foster care

Major Provisions of the Act

- Amended title IV-B, subpart 2 of the Social Security Act
- Added findings to illustrate the need for programs addressing families at risk for abuse and neglect and those adopting children from foster care
- Amended the definition of family preservation services to include infant safe haven programs
- Added strengthening parental relationships and promoting healthy marriages to the list of allowable activities
- Added new focus to the research, evaluation, and technical assistance activities
- Allowed reallocation of unused funds in title IV-B, subpart 2
- Created a matching grant program to support mentoring networks for children of prisoners
- Reauthorized funds for the Court Improvement Program
- Authorized a voucher program as part of the John H. Chafee Foster Care Independence Program to provide for education and training, including postsecondary training and education, to youth who have aged out of foster care

Major Federal Legislation Concerned With Child Protection, Child Welfare, and Adoption   **http://www.childwelfare.gov**

P.L. 106-279

Intercountry Adoption Act of 2000

Overview

H.R. 2909

Enacted October 6, 2000

Purpose: To provide for implementation by the United States of the Hague Convention on Protection of Children and Cooperation in Respect of Intercountry Adoption

Major Provisions of the Act

- Established the U.S. Central Authority within the Department of State with general responsibility for U.S. implementation of the Convention and annual reports to Congress
- Allowed the State Department to enter into agreements with one or more qualified accrediting entities to provide for the accreditation of agencies (nonprofit) and approval of persons (for-profit agencies and individuals) who seek to provide adoption services for adoptions covered by the Convention
- Permitted accrediting entities to:
  » Process applications for accreditation/approval
  » Be responsible for oversight, enforcement, and compliance by adoption service providers with the Convention, IAA, and implementing regulations
  » Perform information collection activities
- Authorized U.S. adoption service providers to provide services for Convention adoptions only if they have been Convention-accredited or -approved
- Mandated the Department of State and INS to establish a case registry for all intercountry adoptions incoming, outgoing, Hague Convention cases, and others
- Authorized the State Department to:
  » Monitor each accrediting entity's performance of its duties and their compliance with the Convention, the Intercountry Adoption Act (IAA), and applicable regulations
  » Issue certificates to cover Convention adoptions/placements for adoptions made in the U.S. necessary for their recognition so long as the department has received appropriate documentation to establish that the requirements of the Convention, IAA, and regulations have been met
- Established that Convention adoptions finalized in other countries party to the Convention to be recognized throughout the United States
- Provided procedures and requirements to be followed for the adoption of a child residing in the United States by persons resident in other countries party to the Convention
- Outlined certain case-specific duties to be performed by the accredited agency, the approved person, or the prospective adoptive parents acting on their own behalf if permitted by both countries involved
- Prohibited State courts from finalizing Convention adoptions or granting custody for a Convention adoption unless such a court has verified that the required determinations have been made by the country of origin and the receiving country
- Amended the Immigration and Nationality Act to provide for a new category of children adopted, or to be adopted, under the Hague Convention and meeting other requirements to qualify for immigrant visas
- Preserved Convention records on individual adoptions held by the State Department and INS without affecting Federal laws concerning access to identifying information
- Preempted State laws only to the extent that they are inconsistent with the IAA
- Had no effect on the Indian Child Welfare Act

Major Federal Legislation Concerned With Child Protection, Child Welfare, and Adoption   **http://www.childwelfare.gov**

P.L. 106-177

Child Abuse Prevention and Enforcement Act of 2000

Overview

H.R. 764

Enacted March 10, 2000

Purpose: To reduce the incidence of child abuse and neglect

Major Provisions of the Act

- Authorized the use of Federal law enforcement funds by States to improve the criminal justice system in order to provide timely, accurate, and complete criminal history record information to child welfare agencies, organizations, and programs that are engaged in the assessment of activities related to the protection of children, including protection against child sexual abuse, and placement of children in foster care
- Allowed the use of Federal grants by law enforcement:
  » To enforce child abuse and neglect laws, including laws protecting against child sexual abuse
  » To promote programs designed to prevent child abuse and neglect
  » To establish or support cooperative programs between law enforcement and media organizations to collect, record, retain, and disseminate information useful in the identification and apprehension of suspected criminal offenders
- Increased the amount of federally collected funds available to the States for implementation of State Children's Justice Act reforms

---

P.L. 106-169

Foster Care Independence Act of 1999

Overview

H.R. 3443

Enacted December 12, 1999

Purpose: To amend part E of title IV of the Social Security Act to provide States with more funding and greater flexibility in carrying out programs designed to help children make the transition from foster care to self-sufficiency

Major Provisions of the Act

- Revised the program of grants to States and expanded opportunities for independent living programs providing education, training, and employment services, and financial support for foster youth to prepare for living on their own
- Allowed funds to be used to pay for room and board for former foster youth age 18 to 21
- Required:
  » The Secretary to develop outcome measures to assess State performance in operating independent living programs
  » National data collection on services, individuals served, and outcomes
- Mandated that State plans for foster care and adoption assistance include certification that prospective parents will be adequately prepared to provide for the needs of the child and that such preparation will continue, as necessary, after placement of the child
- Provided States with the option to extend Medicaid coverage to 18- to 21-year-olds who have been emancipated from foster care
- Emphasized permanence by requiring that efforts to find a permanent placement continue concurrently with independent living activities
- Increased funding for adoption incentive payments

Major Federal Legislation Concerned With Child Protection, Child Welfare, and Adoption   **http://www.childwelfare.gov**

P.L. 105-89

Adoption and Safe Families Act of 1997

Overview

H.R. 897

Enacted November 19, 1997

Purpose: To promote the adoption of children in foster care

This act amended title IV-E of the Social Security Act.

Major Provisions of the Act

- Reauthorized the Family Preservation and Support Services Program:
  - » Renamed it the Safe and Stable Families Program
  - » Extended categories of services to include time-limited reunification services and adoption promotion and support services
- Ensured safety for abused and neglected children:
  - » Ensured health and safety concerns are addressed when a State determines placement for abused and neglected children
  - » Required HHS to report on the scope of substance abuse in the child welfare population, and the outcomes of services provided to that population
  - » Added "safety of the child" to every step of the case plan and review process
  - » Required criminal records checks for foster/adoptive parents who receive Federal funds on behalf of a child, unless a State opted out of this requirement
- Accelerated permanent placement:
  - » Required States to initiate court proceedings to free a child for adoption once that child had been waiting in foster care for at least 15 of the most recent 22 months, unless there was an exception
  - » Allowed children to be freed for adoption more quickly in extreme cases
- Promoted adoptions:
  - » Rewarded States that increased adoptions with incentive funds
  - » Required States to use reasonable efforts to move eligible foster care children towards permanent placements
  - » Promoted adoptions of all special needs children and ensured health coverage for adopted special needs children
  - » Prohibited States from delaying/denying placements of children based on the geographic location of the prospective adoptive families
  - » Required States to document and report child-specific adoption efforts
- Increased accountability:
  - » Required HHS to establish new outcome measures to monitor and improve State performance
  - » Required States to document child-specific efforts to move children into adoptive homes
- Clarified "reasonable efforts":
  - » Emphasized children's health and safety
  - » Required States to specify situations when services to prevent foster placement and reunification of families are not required
- Required shorter time limits for making decisions about permanent placements:
  - » Required permanency hearings to be held no later than 12 months after entering foster care
  - » Required States to initiate termination of parental rights proceedings after the child has been in foster care 15 of the previous 22 months, except if not in the best interest of the child, or if the child is in the care of a relative

P.L. 104-235

Child Abuse Prevention and Treatment Amendments of 1996

Overview

S. 919

Enacted October 3, 1996

Purpose: To modify and reauthorize the Child Abuse Prevention and Treatment Act (CAPTA)

Major Provisions of the Act

- Reauthorized CAPTA through FY 2001
- Abolished the National Center on Child Abuse and Neglect (NCCAN) and created the Office on Child Abuse and Neglect
- Added new requirements to address the problems of false reports of abuse and neglect, delays in termination of parental rights, and lack of public oversight of child protection
- Required States to institute an expedited termination of parental rights process for abandoned infants or when the parent is responsible for the death or serious bodily injury of a child
- Set the minimum definition of child abuse to include death, serious physical or emotional injury, sexual abuse, or imminent risk of harm
- Recognized the right of parental exercise of religious beliefs concerning medical care
- Continued the Community-Based Family Resource and Support Grants Program, the Adoption Opportunities Act, Abandoned Infants Assistance Act, Victims of Child Abuse Act, Children's Justice Act Grants, and the Missing Children's Assistance Act
- Provided for Federal grants for the establishment of not less than three citizen review panels in each State, such as child fatality panels or foster care review panels, for the purpose of examining the policies and procedures of State and local agencies and where appropriate, specific cases, to evaluate the extent to which the agencies are effectively discharging their child protection responsibilities, including:
  » A review of the extent to which the State child protective services system is coordinated with the foster care and adoption programs established under title IV-E
  » A review of child fatalities and near fatalities

P.L. 104-188

The Interethnic Provisions of 1996

Overview

H.R. 3448

Enacted August 20, 1996

Enacted as title I, subtitle H, section 1808, *Removal of Barriers to Interethnic Adoption*, of the Small Business Job Protection Act of 1996.

Major Provisions of the Act

- Established the title IV-E State Plan requirement that States and other entities that receive funds from the Federal Government and are involved in foster care or adoption placements may not deny any individual the opportunity to become a foster or adoptive parent based upon the race, color, or national origin of the parent or the child
- Established the title IV-E State Plan requirement that States and other entities that receive funds from the Federal Government and involved in foster care or adoption placements may not delay or deny a child's foster care or adoptive placement based upon the race, color, or national origin of the parent or the child
- Strengthened MEPA's diligent recruitment requirement by making it a title IV-B State Plan requirement

Major Provisions of the Act, Continued

- Established a system of graduated financial penalties for States that do not comply with the title IV-E State Plan requirement established under this law
- Repealed language in MEPA that allowed States and other entities to consider the cultural, ethnic, or racial background of a child, as well as the capacity of the prospective parent to meet the needs of such a child

---

P.L. 103-382

Multiethnic Placement Act of 1994

Overview

H.R. 6

Enacted October 20, 1994

These provisions were enacted as title V, part E, subpart 1, of the Improving America's Schools Act of 1994.

This title amended Title IV-E of the Social Security Act.

Major Provisions of the Act

- Prohibited State agencies and other entities that receive Federal funding and were involved in foster care or adoption placements from delaying, denying, or otherwise discriminating when making a foster care or adoption placement decision on the basis of the parent or child's race, color, or national origin
- Prohibited State agencies and other entities that received Federal funds and were involved in foster care or adoption placements from categorically denying any person the opportunity to become a foster or adoptive parent solely on the basis of race, color, or national origin of the parent or the child
- Required States to develop plans for the recruitment of foster and adoptive families that reflect the ethnic and racial diversity of children in the State for whom families are needed
- Allowed an agency or entity to consider the cultural, ethnic, or racial background of a child and the capacity of an adoptive or foster parent to meet the needs of a child with that background when making a placement
- Had no effect on the provisions of the Indian Child Welfare Act of 1978
- Made failure to comply with MEPA a violation of title VI of the Civil Rights Act

---

P.L. 103-66

Family Preservation and Support Services Program Act of 1993

Overview

H.R. 2264

Enacted August 10, 1993

Enacted as title XIII, chapter 2, subchapter C, part 1 of the Omnibus Budget Reconciliation Act of 1993

This title amended title IV-B of the Social Security Act.

Major Provisions of the Act

- Encouraged States to use funds to create a continuum of family-focused services for at-risk children and families
- Required States to engage in a comprehensive planning process to develop more responsive family support and preservation strategies
- Encouraged States to:
  » Use funds to integrate preventive services into treatment-oriented child welfare systems
  » Improve service coordination within and across State service agencies
  » Engage broad segments of the community in program planning at State and local levels

---

Major Provisions of the Act, Continued

- Broadened the definition of "family" to include people needing services regardless of family configuration: biological, adoptive, foster, extended, or self-defined
- Defined services to be provided by the States:
  - » Preservation services include activities designed to assist families in crisis, often where the child is at risk of being placed in out-of-home care because of abuse and/or neglect
  - » Support services include preventive activities, typically provided by community-based organizations, designed to improve nurturing of children and strengthen and enhance stability of families
- Provided grants to the highest court of each State to conduct assessments of the roles, responsibilities, and effectiveness of State courts in handling child welfare cases, and to implement changes deemed necessary as a result of the assessments [Court Improvement Program]

P.L. 102-295

Child Abuse, Domestic Violence, Adoption, and Family Services Act of 1992

Overview

S. 838

Enacted May 28, 1992

Purpose: To amend the Child Abuse Prevention and Treatment Act (CAPTA) to revise and extend programs under the Act

Major Provisions of the Act

- Revised provisions for research and assistance activities to include:
  - » Cultural distinctions relating to child abuse and neglect
  - » Culturally sensitive procedures with respect to child abuse cases
  - » The relationship of child abuse and neglect to cultural diversity
- Provided for assisting States in supporting child abuse and neglect prevention activities through community-based child abuse and neglect prevention grants
- Required HHS to provide information and service function related to adoption and foster care, including:
  - » Onsite technical assistance
  - » National public awareness efforts to unite children in need of adoption with appropriate adoptive parents
  - » Operation of a National Resource Center for Special Needs Adoption

P.L. 100-294

Child Abuse Prevention, Adoption, and Family Services Act of 1988

Overview

H.R. 1900

Enacted April 25, 1988

Purpose: To amend the Child Abuse Prevention and Treatment Act (CAPTA), the Child Abuse Prevention and Treatment and Adoption Reform Act, and the Family Violence Prevention and Services Act

Major Provisions of the Act

- Established the Inter-Agency Task Force on Child Abuse and Neglect, with responsibility for programs and activities related to child abuse and neglect
- Broadened the scope of research to include investigative and judicial procedures applicable to child abuse cases and the national incidence of child abuse and neglect

Major Provisions of the Act, Continued

- Established a national data collection system to include standardized data on false, unfounded, or unsubstantiated cases and the number of deaths due to child abuse and neglect
- Expanded the Adoption Opportunities program:
  » To increase the number of minority children placed in adoptive families, with an emphasis on recruitment of and placement with minority families
  » To provide for postlegal adoption services for families who have adopted special needs children
  » To increase the placement of foster care children legally free for adoption

---

P.L. 98-457

Child Abuse Amendments of 1984

Overview

H.R. 1904

Enacted October 9, 1984

Purpose: To extend and improve provisions of laws relating to child abuse and neglect and adoption

Major Provisions of the Act

- Required States to have in place procedures with State protective systems to respond to the reporting of medical neglect, including instances of withholding medically indicated treatment from disabled infants with life-threatening conditions
- Directed HHS to develop regulations and to provide training and technical assistance needed by care providers to carry out the provisions of the act
- Required State-level programs to facilitate adoption opportunities for disabled infants with life-threatening conditions
- Provided for the establishment and operation of a Federal adoption and foster care data-gathering and analysis system
- Provided for a national adoption exchange to match special needs children with prospective adoptive families

---

P.L. 96-272

Adoption Assistance and Child Welfare Act of 1980

Overview

H.R. 3434

Enacted June 17, 1980

Purpose: To establish a program of adoption assistance, strengthen the program of foster care assistance for needy and dependent children, and improve the child welfare, social services, and aid to families with dependent children programs

This act amended titles IV-B and XX of the Social Security Act.

Major Provisions of the Act

- Required States to make adoption assistance payments, which take into account the circumstances of the adopting parents and the child, to parents who adopt a child who is AFDC-eligible and is a child with special needs
- Defined a child with special needs as a child who:
  » Cannot be returned to the parent's home
  » Has a special condition such that the child cannot be placed without providing assistance
  » Has not been able to be placed without assistance

Major Provisions of the Act, Continued

- Required, as a condition of receiving Federal foster care matching funds, that States make "reasonable efforts" to prevent removal of the child from the home and return those who have been removed as soon as possible
- Required participating States to establish reunification and preventive programs for all in foster care
- Required the State to place a child in the least restrictive setting and, if the child will benefit, one that is close to the parent's home
- Required the court or agency to review the status of a child in any nonpermanent setting every 6 months to determine what is in the best interest of the child, with most emphasis placed on returning the child home as soon as possible
- Required the court or administrative body to determine the child's future status, whether it is a return to parents, adoption, or continued foster care, within 18 months after initial placement into foster care

---

P.L. 95-608

Indian Child Welfare Act (ICWA) of 1978

Overview

S. 1214

Enacted November 11, 1978

Purpose: To establish standards for the placement of Indian children in foster and adoptive homes and to prevent the breakup of Indian families

Major Provisions of the Act

- Established minimum Federal standards for the removal of Indian children from their families
- Required Indian children to be placed in foster or adoptive homes that reflect Indian culture
- Provided for assistance to Tribes in the operation of child and family service programs
- Created exclusive Tribal jurisdiction over all Indian child custody proceedings when requested by the Tribe, parent, or Indian "custodian"
- Granted preference to Indian family environments in adoptive or foster care placement
- Provided funds to Tribes or nonprofit off-reservation Indian organizations or multiservice centers for purpose of improving child welfare services to Indian children and families
- Required State and Federal courts to give full faith and credit to Tribal court decrees
- Set standard of proof for terminating Indian parents' parental rights that required the proof to be beyond a reasonable doubt

---

P.L. 95-266

Child Abuse Prevention and Treatment and Adoption Reform Act of 1978

Overview

H.R. 6693

Enacted April 24, 1978

Purpose: To promote the healthy development of children who would benefit from adoption by facilitating their placement in adoptive homes, and to extend and improve the provisions of the Child Abuse Prevention and Treatment Act (CAPTA)

Major Federal Legislation Concerned With Child Protection, Child Welfare, and Adoption   **http://www.childwelfare.gov**

Major Provisions of the Act
- Required the National Center on Child Abuse and Neglect (NCCAN) to:
    » Develop a comprehensive plan for facilitating the coordination of activities among agencies
    » Establish research priorities for making grants
    » Set aside funds to establish centers for the prevention, identification, and treatment of child sexual abuse
- Established the Adoption Opportunities Program to:
    » Facilitate placement of children with special needs in permanent adoptive homes
    » Promote quality standards for adoptive placement and the rights of adopted children
    » Provide for national adoption information exchange system
- Provided for annual summaries of research on child abuse and neglect

---

P.L. 93-247

Child Abuse Prevention and Treatment Act (CAPTA) of 1974

Overview

S. 1191

Enacted January 31, 1974

Purpose: To provide financial assistance for a demonstration program for the prevention, identification, and treatment of child abuse and neglect

Major Provisions of the Act
- Provided assistance to States to develop child abuse and neglect identification and prevention programs
- Authorized limited government research into child abuse prevention and treatment
- Created the National Center on Child Abuse and Neglect (NCCAN) within the Department of Health, Education, and Welfare to:
    » Administer grant programs
    » Identify issues and areas needing special focus for new research and demonstration project activities
    » Serve as the focal point for the collection of information, improvement of programs, dissemination of materials, and information on best practices to States and localities
- Created the National Clearinghouse on Child Abuse and Neglect Information
- Established Basic State Grants and Demonstration Grants for training personnel and to support innovative programs aimed at preventing and treating child maltreatment

U.S. Department of Health and Human Services
Administration for Children and Families
Administration on Children, Youth and Families
Children's Bureau

Appendix C

Uniform Adoption Act (1994)

UNIFORM ADOPTION ACT (1994)

Drafted by the

NATIONAL CONFERENCE OF COMMISSIONERS
ON UNIFORM STATE LAWS

and by it

APPROVED AND RECOMMENDED FOR ENACTMENT
IN ALL THE STATES

at its

ANNUAL CONFERENCE
MEETING IN ITS ONE-HUNDRED-AND-THIRD YEAR
IN CHICAGO, ILLINOIS
JULY 29 - AUGUST 5, 1994

Approved by the American Bar Association
Miami, Florida, February 14, 1995

UNIFORM ADOPTION ACT (1994)

Copies of this Act may be obtained from:

NATIONAL CONFERENCE OF COMMISSIONERS ON UNIFORM STATE LAWS
676 North St. Clair Street, Suite 1700
Chicago, Illinois 60611
312/915-0195

UNIFORM ADOPTION ACT (1994)

TABLE OF CONTENTS

3

8

UNIFORM ADOPTION ACT (1994)

PREFATORY NOTE

The guiding principle of the Uniform Adoption Act is a desire to promote the welfare of children and, particularly, to facilitate the placement of minor children who cannot be raised by their original parents with adoptive parents who can offer them stable and loving homes. The Act is premised on a belief that adoption offers significant legal, economic, social and psychological benefits not only for children who might otherwise be homeless, but also for parents who are unable to care for their children, for adults who want to nurture and support children, and for state governments ultimately responsible for the well-being of children.

The Act aims to be a comprehensive and uniform state adoption code that: (1) is consistent with relevant federal constitutional and statutory law; (2) delineates the legal requirements and consequences of different kinds of adoption; (3) promotes the integrity and finality of adoptions while discouraging "trafficking" in minors; (4) respects the choices made by the parties to an adoption about how much confidentiality or openness they prefer in their relations with each other, subject, however, to judicial protection of the adoptee's welfare; and (5) promotes the interest of minor children in being raised by individuals who are committed to, and capable of, caring for them.

The most striking characteristic of contemporary adoptions is the variety of contexts in which they occur. Of the 130,000 or more adoptions that are granted each year, over half are adoptions of minor children by stepparents or relatives. Perhaps another 15-20% or more are of older children, many of whom have previously been shunted back and forth between their birth families and foster care. Many of these children come to their adoptive parents with serious psychological or physical problems that will require years of treatment and loving parental attention. Approximately 7,000-10,000 adoptions of foreign born children occur annually despite the intricate web of domestic and foreign regulations that adoptive parents have to contend with in order to complete their families. In recent years, no more than 25-30% of all adoptions involve infants adopted by unrelated adults. For an analysis of the limited data available on different kinds of adoptions and an overview of contemporary adoption practice, see *Adoption* vol. 3 *Future of Children* (Packard Fdtn, 1993).

At present, the legal process of adoption is complicated not only by the different kinds of children who are adopted and the different kinds of people who seek to adopt, but also by an extraordinarily confusing system of state, federal, and international laws and regulations. Despite allegedly common goals, state adoption laws are not and never have been uniform, and there now appear to be more inconsistencies than ever from one state to another. There are no clear answers to such basic questions as who may place a child for adoption, whose consent is required and when is consent final, how much money can be paid to whom and for what, how much information can or should be shared between birth and adoptive families, what makes an individual suitable as an adoptive parent, and what efforts are needed to encourage the permanent placement of minority children and other children with special needs who languish in foster care. Hundreds of thousands of children in this country need permanent homes, and hundreds of thousands of adults have at least some interest in adoption but are often discouraged by the confusing laws and procedures as well as by high financial and emotional costs.

To reduce this confusion - which confounds consensual adoptions and not only the relatively small number that are contested - the National Conference of Commissioners on Uniform State Laws has approved a Uniform Adoption Act to enable the States to respond more flexibly and reasonably to the changing social, economic and constitutional character of contemporary adoption practice.

In examining virtually every aspect of adoption practice, the Drafting Committee was assisted by its Reporter, Law Professor Joan Heifetz Hollinger, the principal author and editor of *Adoption Law and Practice* 2 vol.(Matthew Bender Co., 1988, Supp. 1989-94), representatives from the Family Law Section of the American Bar Association, and dozens of advisers representing a wide array of professional and citizens organizations. After extensive discussion of the Act at five successive Annual Meetings, the Conference overwhelmingly approved it as a Uniform Act in August 1994.

The Act meets the changing psychosocial and economic aspects of contemporary adoptions by addressing the many different kinds of adoption that now occur and the different functions they serve. Adoptions may be characterized according to the kind of individuals being adopted - minors or adults, born in this country or foreign born, with or without special needs, with or without siblings. They may also be characterized according to the kind of individuals who are adopting - married couples, single individuals, stepparents, individuals previously related or unrelated to an adoptee. Another way to characterize adoptions is according to the type of placement - direct placement by a birth parent with an adoptive parent selected by the birth parent with or without the assistance of a lawyer or an agency, or placement by a public or private agency that has acquired custody of a minor from a birth parent through a voluntary relinquishment or an involuntary termination of parental rights. A fourth way to characterize adoptions is by the nature of the proceeding - contested or uncontested.

The Act goes beyond existing statutory laws to create a coherent framework for legitimizing and regulating both direct-placement and agency-supervised adoptions. The Act will facilitate the completion of consensual adoptions and expedite the resolution of contested adoptions. By promoting the integrity and finality of adoptions, the Act will serve the interests of children in establishing and maintaining legal ties to the individuals who are committed to, and capable of, parenting them. More specifically:

(1) The Act protects minor children against unnecessary separation from their birth parents, against placement with unsuitable adoptive parents, and against harmful delays in determination of their legal status.

(2) The Act protects birth parents from unwarranted termination of their parental rights. Minor children may not be adopted without parental consent or appropriate grounds for dispensing with parental consent. The Act attempts to ensure that a decision by a birth parent to relinquish a minor child and consent to the child's adoption is informed and voluntary. Once that decision is made, however, and expressed before a judge or another individual who is not implicated in any actual or potential conflict of interest with the birth parent, the decision is final and, with very few exceptions, irrevocable.

Involuntary as well as voluntary termination proceedings conform to constitutional standards of due process, but an individual's biological ties to a child are not alone sufficient to bestow full parental rights on that individual. The Act protects the parental status of biological parents who have actually functioned as a child's parents.

(3) The Act protects adoptive parents and adopted children by providing them with whatever information is reasonably available at the time of placement about the child's background, including health, genetic, and social history, and by providing access in later years to updated medical information.

(4) The Act discourages unlawful placement activities within and across state and national boundaries by keeping track of minor children once they have been placed for adoption, distinguishing between lawful

10

and unlawful adoption-related expenses and activities, insisting that agencies, lawyers, and other providers of professional services explain their adoption-related services and fees to people considering adoption, requiring judicial approval of adoption-related expenses, and imposing sanctions against unlawful activities.

(5) The Act encourages different kinds of people to adopt. No one may be categorically excluded from being considered as an adoptive parent. Nonetheless, preplacement (except in stepparent adoptions and when waived by a court for good cause) as well as post-placement evaluations of prospective adoptive parents are required, whether initiated by an agency or directly by a birth parent, in order to determine the suitability of particular individuals to be adoptive parents.

(6) Individuals who have served as a minor child's foster or de facto parents are given standing to seek to adopt the child, subject to the particular child's needs. Agencies receiving public funds are required actively to recruit prospective adoptive parents for children who are considered difficult to place because of their age, health, race, ethnicity, or other special needs. The Act prohibits the delay or denial of a child's adoptive placement solely on the basis of racial or ethnic factors. A child's guardian ad litem as well as other interested persons may seek equitable and other appropriate relief against discriminatory placement activities.

(7) The Act requires expedited hearings for contested adoptions and the appointment of a guardian ad litem for minor children whose well-being is threatened by protracted or contested proceedings. During a proceeding, courts are authorized and encouraged to make interim custody arrangements to protect minors against detrimental disruptions of stable custodial environments. Good faith efforts must be made to notify any parent or alleged parent whose rights have not previously been relinquished or terminated of the pendency of an adoption of the parent's child.

(8) The Act clarifies the relationship to adoption proceedings of the Uniform Child Custody Jurisdiction Act, the federal Parental Kidnapping Prevention Act, and the Interstate Compact on the Placement of Children. The Act supports the finality of adoption decrees by strictly limiting the time for appeals or other challenges and by presuming that a final order terminating parental rights or granting an adoption is valid. A final adoption may not be challenged by anyone for any reason more than six months after the order is entered. Even if a challenge is begun within that time, the adoption may not be set aside unless the challenger proves with clear and convincing evidence that the adoption is contrary to the child's best interests.

(9) The Act permits mutually agreed-upon communication between birth and adoptive families before and after an adoption is final. It also ensures that, except for consensual contacts, the privacy and autonomy of adoptive and birth families will be fully protected. The Act's mutual consent registry is a "user friendly" approach to the issue of whether and when to release identifying information among birth parents, adoptees, and other members of an adoptee's birth and adoptive families. This balanced and uniform procedure can be the basis of a national interstate network for the consensual disclosure of identifying information.

(10) The Act clarifies the legal and economic consequences of different types of adoption so that, within these formal structures, the emotional and psychological aspects of adoptive parent and child relationships can flourish.

UNIFORM ADOPTION ACT (1994)

[ARTICLE] 1. GENERAL PROVISIONS

SECTION 1-101. DEFINITIONS. In this [Act]:

(1) "Adoptee" means an individual who is adopted or is to be adopted.

(2) "Adult" means an individual who has attained 18 years of age.

(3) "Agency" means a public or private entity, including the department, that is authorized by the law of this State to place individuals for adoption.

(4) "Child" means a minor or adult son or daughter, by birth or adoption.

(5) "Court," with reference to a court of this State, means the [appropriate court].

(6) "Department" means the [department of social services, or health services, or children's services].

(7) "Guardian" means an individual, other than a parent, appointed by an appropriate court as general guardian or guardian of the person of a minor.

(8) "Legal custody" means the right and duty to exercise continuing general supervision of a minor as authorized by law. The term includes the right and duty to protect, educate, nurture, and discipline the minor and to provide the minor with food, clothing, shelter, medical care, and a supportive environment.

(9) "Minor" means an individual who has not attained 18 years of age.

(10) "Parent" means an individual who is legally recognized as a mother or father or whose consent to the adoption of a minor is required under Section 2-401(a)(1). The term does not include an individual whose parental relationship to a child has been terminated judicially or by operation of law.

(11) "Person" means an individual, corporation, limited liability company, business trust, estate, trust, partnership, association, agency, joint venture, government, governmental subdivision or instrumentality, public corporation, or any other legal or commercial entity.

(12) "Physical custody" means the physical care and supervision of a minor.

(13) "Place for adoption" means to select a prospective adoptive parent for a minor and transfer physical custody of the minor to the prospective adoptive parent.

(14) "Relative" means a grandparent, great grandparent, sibling, first cousin, aunt, uncle, great-aunt, great-uncle, niece, or nephew of an individual, whether related to the individual by the whole or the half blood, affinity, or adoption. The term does not include an individual's stepparent.

(15) "Relinquishment" means the voluntary surrender to an agency by a minor's parent or guardian, for purposes of the minor's adoption, of the rights of the parent or guardian with respect to the minor, including legal and physical custody of the minor.

(16) "State" means a State of the United States, the District of Columbia, the Commonwealth of Puerto Rico, or any territory or insular possession subject to the jurisdiction of the United States.

(17) "Stepparent" means an individual who is the spouse or surviving spouse of a parent of a child but who is not a parent of the child.

SECTION 1-102. WHO MAY ADOPT OR BE ADOPTED. Subject to this [Act], any individual may adopt or be adopted by another individual for the purpose of creating the relationship of parent and child between them.

SECTION 1-103. NAME OF ADOPTEE AFTER ADOPTION. The name of an adoptee designated in a decree of adoption takes effect as specified in the decree.

SECTION 1-104. LEGAL RELATIONSHIP BETWEEN ADOPTEE AND ADOPTIVE PARENT AFTER ADOPTION. After a decree of adoption becomes final, each adoptive parent and the adoptee have the legal relationship of parent and child and have all the rights and duties of that relationship.

SECTION 1-105. LEGAL RELATIONSHIP BETWEEN ADOPTEE AND FORMER PARENT AFTER ADOPTION. Except as otherwise provided in Section 4-103, when a decree of adoption becomes final:

(1) the legal relationship of parent and child between each of the adoptee's former parents and the adoptee terminates, except for a former parent's duty to pay arrearages for child support; and
(2) any previous court order for visitation or communication with an adoptee terminates.

SECTION 1-106. OTHER RIGHTS OF ADOPTEE. A decree of adoption does not affect any right or benefit vested in the adoptee before the decree becomes final.

SECTION 1-107. PROCEEDINGS SUBJECT TO INDIAN CHILD WELFARE ACT. A proceeding under this [Act] which pertains to an Indian child, as defined in the Indian Child Welfare Act, 25 U.S.C. Sections 1901 et seq., is subject to that Act.

SECTION 1-108. RECOGNITION OF ADOPTION IN ANOTHER JURISDICTION. A decree or order of adoption issued by a court of any other State which is entitled to full faith and credit in this State, or a decree or order of adoption entered by a court or administrative entity in another country acting pursuant to that country's law or to any convention or treaty on intercountry adoption which the United States has ratified, has the same effect as a decree or order of adoption issued by a court of this State. The rights and obligations of the parties as to matters within the jurisdiction of this State must be determined as though the decree or order were issued by a court of this State.

[ARTICLE] 2. ADOPTION OF MINORS

[PART] 1. PLACEMENT OF MINOR FOR ADOPTION

SECTION 2-101. WHO MAY PLACE MINOR FOR ADOPTION.

(a) The only persons who may place a minor for adoption are:

(1) a parent having legal and physical custody of the minor, as provided in subsections (b) and (c);

13

(2) a guardian expressly authorized by the court to place the minor for adoption;

(3) an agency to which the minor has been relinquished for purposes of adoption; or

(4) an agency expressly authorized to place the minor for adoption by a court order terminating the relationship between the minor and the minor's parent or guardian.

(b) Except as otherwise provided in subsection (c), a parent having legal and physical custody of a minor may place the minor for adoption, even if the other parent has not executed a consent or a relinquishment or the other parent's relationship to the minor has not been terminated.

(c) A parent having legal and physical custody of a minor may not place the minor for adoption if the other parent has legal custody or a right of visitation with the minor and that parent's whereabouts are known, unless that parent agrees in writing to the placement or, before the placement, the parent who intends to place the minor sends notice of the intended placement by certified mail to the other parent's last known address.

(d) An agency authorized under this [Act] to place a minor for adoption may place the minor for adoption, even if only one parent has executed a relinquishment or has had his or her parental relationship to the minor terminated.

SECTION 2-102. DIRECT PLACEMENT FOR ADOPTION BY PARENT OR GUARDIAN.

(a) A parent or guardian authorized to place a minor directly for adoption may place the minor only with a prospective adoptive parent for whom a favorable preplacement evaluation has been prepared pursuant to Sections 2-201 through 2-206 or for whom a preplacement evaluation is not required under Section 2-201(b) or (c).

(b) A parent or guardian shall personally select a prospective adoptive parent for the direct placement of a minor. Subject to [Article] 7, the parent or guardian may be assisted by another person, including a lawyer, health-care provider, or agency, in locating or transferring legal and physical custody of the minor to a prospective adoptive parent.

(c) A prospective adoptive parent shall furnish a copy of the preplacement evaluation to the parent or guardian and may provide additional information requested by the parent or guardian. The evaluation and any additional information must be edited to exclude identifying information, but information identifying a prospective adoptive parent need not be edited if the individual agrees to its disclosure. Subject to [Article] 7, a prospective adoptive parent may be assisted by another person in locating a minor who is available for adoption.

(d) If a consent to a minor's adoption is not executed at the time the minor is placed for adoption, the parent or guardian who places the minor shall furnish to the prospective adoptive parent a signed writing stating that the transfer of physical custody is for purposes of adoption and that the parent or guardian has been informed of the provisions of this [Act] relevant to placement for adoption, consent, relinquishment, and termination of parental rights. The writing must authorize the prospective adoptive parent to provide support and medical and other care for the minor pending execution of the consent within a time specified in the writing. The prospective adoptive parent shall acknowledge in a signed writing responsibility for the minor's support and medical and other care and for returning the minor to the custody of the parent or guardian if the consent is not executed within the time specified.

(e) A person who provides services with respect to direct placements for adoption shall furnish to an individual who inquires about the person's services a written statement of the person's services and a schedule of fees.

SECTION 2-103. PLACEMENT FOR ADOPTION BY AGENCY.

(a) An agency authorized to place a minor for adoption shall furnish to an individual who inquires about its services a written statement of its services, including the agency's procedure for selecting a prospective adoptive parent for a minor and a schedule of its fees.

(b) An agency that places a minor for adoption shall authorize in writing the prospective adoptive parent to provide support and medical and other care for the minor pending entry of a decree of adoption. The prospective adoptive parent shall acknowledge in writing responsibility for the minor's support and medical and other care.

(c) Upon request by a parent who has relinquished a minor child pursuant to [Part] 4, the agency shall promptly inform the parent as to whether the minor has been placed for adoption, whether a petition for adoption has been granted, denied, or withdrawn, and, if the petition was not granted, whether another placement has been made.

SECTION 2-104. PREFERENCES FOR PLACEMENT WHEN AGENCY PLACES MINOR.

(a) An agency may place a minor for adoption only with an individual for whom a favorable preplacement evaluation has been prepared pursuant to Sections 2-201 through 2-206. Placement must be made:

(1) if the agency has agreed to place the minor with a prospective adoptive parent selected by the parent or guardian, with the individual selected by the parent or guardian;

(2) if the agency has not so agreed, with an individual selected by the agency in accordance with the best interest of the minor.

(b) In determining the best interest of the minor under subsection (a)(2), the agency shall consider the following individuals in order of preference:

(1) an individual who has previously adopted a sibling of the minor and who makes a written request to adopt the minor;

(2) an individual with characteristics requested by a parent or guardian, if the agency agrees to comply with the request and locates the individual within a time agreed to by the parent or guardian and the agency;

(3) an individual who has had physical custody of the minor for six months or more within the preceding 24 months or for half of the minor's life, whichever is less, and makes a written request to adopt the minor;

(4) a relative with whom the minor has established a positive emotional relationship and who makes a written request to adopt the minor; and

(5) any other individual selected by the agency.

(c) Unless necessary to comply with a request under subsection (b)(2), an agency may not delay or deny a minor's placement for adoption solely on the basis of the minor's race, national origin, or ethnic background. A guardian ad litem of a minor or an individual with a favorable preplacement evaluation who makes a written request to an agency to adopt the minor may maintain an action or proceeding for equitable relief against an agency that violates this subsection.

(d) If practicable and in the best interest of minors who are siblings, an agency shall place siblings with the same prospective adoptive parent selected in accordance with subsections (a) through (c).

(e) If an agency places a minor pursuant to subsection (a)(2), an individual described in subsection (b)(3) may commence an action or proceeding within 30 days after the placement to challenge the agency's placement. If the individual proves by a preponderance of the evidence that the minor has substantial emotional ties to the individual and that an adoptive placement of the minor with the individual would be in the best interest of the minor, the court shall place the minor with the individual.

SECTION 2-105. RECRUITMENT OF ADOPTIVE PARENTS BY AGENCY. An agency receiving public funds pursuant to Title IV-E of the federal Adoption Assistance and Child Welfare Act, 42 U.S.C. Sections 670 et seq., or pursuant to [the State's adoption subsidy program], shall make a diligent search for and actively recruit prospective adoptive parents for minors in the agency's custody who are entitled to funding from those sources and who are difficult to place for adoption because of a special need as described in [the applicable law on minors with special needs]. The department shall prescribe the procedure for recruiting prospective adoptive parents pursuant to this section.

SECTION 2-106. DISCLOSURE OF INFORMATION ON BACKGROUND.

(a) As early as practicable before a prospective adoptive parent accepts physical custody of a minor, a person placing the minor for adoption shall furnish to the prospective adoptive parent a written report containing all of the following information reasonably available from any person who has had legal or physical custody of the minor or who has provided medical, psychological, educational, or similar services to the minor:

(1) a current medical and psychological history of the minor, including an account of the minor's prenatal care, medical condition at birth, any drug or medication taken by the minor's mother during pregnancy, any subsequent medical, psychological, or psychiatric examination and diagnosis, any physical, sexual, or emotional abuse suffered by the minor, and a record of any immunizations and health care received while in foster or other care;

(2) relevant information concerning the medical and psychological history of the minor's genetic parents and relatives, including any known disease or hereditary predisposition to disease, any addiction to drugs or alcohol, the health of the minor's mother during her pregnancy, and the health of each parent at the minor's birth; and

(3) relevant information concerning the social history of the minor and the minor's parents and relatives, including:

(i) the minor's enrollment and performance in school, results of educational testing, and any special educational needs;

(ii) the minor's racial, ethnic, and religious background, tribal affiliation, and a general description of the minor's parents;

(iii) an account of the minor's past and existing relationship with any individual with whom the minor has regularly lived or visited; and

(iv) the level of educational and vocational achievement of the minor's parents and relatives and any noteworthy accomplishments;

(4) information concerning a criminal conviction of a parent for a felony, a judicial order terminating the parental rights of a parent, and a proceeding in which the parent was alleged to have abused, neglected, abandoned, or otherwise mistreated the minor, a sibling of the minor, or the other parent;

(5) information concerning a criminal conviction or delinquency adjudication of the minor; and

(6) information necessary to determine the minor's eligibility for state or federal benefits, including subsidies for adoption and other financial, medical, or similar assistance.

(b) Before a hearing on a petition for adoption, the person who placed a minor for adoption shall furnish to the prospective adoptive parent a supplemental written report containing information required by subsection (a) which was unavailable before the minor was placed for adoption but becomes reasonably available to the person after the placement.

(c) The court may request that a respondent in a proceeding under [Article] 3, [Part] 5, supply the information required by this section.

(d) A report furnished under this section must indicate who prepared the report and, unless confidentiality has been waived, be edited to exclude the identity of any individual who furnished information or about whom information is reported.

(e) Information furnished under this section may not be used as evidence in any civil or criminal proceeding against an individual who is the subject of the information.

(f) The department shall prescribe forms designed to obtain the specific information sought under this section and shall furnish the forms to a person who is authorized to place a minor for adoption or who provides services with respect to placements for adoption.

SECTION 2-107. INTERSTATE PLACEMENT. An adoption in this State of a minor brought into this State from another State by a prospective adoptive parent, or by a person who places the minor for adoption in this State, is governed by the laws of this State, including this [Act] and the Interstate Compact on the Placement of Children.

SECTION 2-108. INTERCOUNTRY PLACEMENT. An adoption in this State of a minor brought into this State from another country by a prospective adoptive parent, or by a person who places the minor for adoption in this State, is governed by this [Act], subject to any convention or treaty on intercountry adoption which the United States has ratified and any relevant federal law.

[PART] 2. PREPLACEMENT EVALUATION

SECTION 2-201. PREPLACEMENT EVALUATION REQUIRED.

(a) Except as otherwise provided in subsections (b) and (c), only an individual for whom a current, favorable written preplacement evaluation has been prepared may accept custody of a minor for purposes of adoption. An evaluation is current if it is prepared or updated within the 18 months next preceding the placement of the minor with the individual for adoption. An evaluation is favorable if it contains a finding that the individual is suited to be an adoptive parent, either in general or for a particular minor.

(b) A court may excuse the absence of a preplacement evaluation for good cause shown, but the prospective adoptive parent so excused must be evaluated during the pendency of the proceeding for adoption.

(c) A preplacement evaluation is not required if a parent or guardian places a minor directly with a relative of the minor for purposes of adoption, but an evaluation of the relative is required during the pendency of a proceeding for adoption.

SECTION 2-202. PREPLACEMENT EVALUATOR.

(a) Only an individual qualified by [a state-approved licensing, certifying, or other procedure] to make a preplacement evaluation may do so.

(b) An agency from which an individual is seeking to adopt a minor may require the individual to be evaluated by its own qualified employee or independent contractor, even if the individual has received a favorable preplacement evaluation from another qualified evaluator.

SECTION 2-203. TIMING AND CONTENT OF PREPLACEMENT EVALUATION.

(a) An individual requesting a preplacement evaluation need not have located a prospective minor adoptee when the request is made, and the individual may request more than one evaluation.

(b) A preplacement evaluation must be completed within 45 days after it is requested. An evaluator shall expedite an evaluation for an individual who has located a prospective adoptee.

(c) A preplacement evaluation must be based upon a personal interview and visit at the residence of the individual being evaluated, personal interviews with others who know the individual and may have information relevant to the evaluation, and the information required by subsection (d).

(d) A preplacement evaluation must contain the following information about the individual being evaluated:

(1) age and date of birth, nationality, racial or ethnic background, and any religious affiliation;

(2) marital status and family history, including the age and location of any child of the individual and the identity of and relationship to anyone else living in the individual's household;

(3) physical and mental health, and any history of abuse of alcohol or drugs;

(4) educational and employment history and any special skills;

18

(5) property and income, including outstanding financial obligations as indicated in a current credit report or financial statement furnished by the individual;

(6) any previous request for an evaluation or involvement in an adoptive placement and the outcome of the evaluation or placement;

(7) whether the individual has been charged with having committed domestic violence or a violation of [the State's child protection statute], and the disposition of the charges, or whether the individual is subject to a court order restricting the individual's right to custody or visitation with a child;

(8) whether the individual has been convicted of a crime other than a minor traffic violation;

(9) whether the individual has located a parent interested in placing a minor with the individual for adoption and, if so, a brief description of the parent and the minor; and

(10) any other fact or circumstance that may be relevant in determining whether the individual is suited to be an adoptive parent, including the quality of the environment in the individual's home and the functioning of other children in the individual's household.

(e) An individual being evaluated must submit to fingerprinting and sign a release permitting the evaluator to obtain from an appropriate law enforcement agency any record indicating that the individual has been convicted of a crime other than a minor traffic violation.

(f) An individual being evaluated shall, at the request of the evaluator, sign any release necessary for the evaluator to obtain information required by subsection (d).

SECTION 2-204. DETERMINING SUITABILITY TO BE ADOPTIVE PARENT.

(a) An evaluator shall assess the information required by Section 2-203 to determine whether it raises a specific concern that placement of any minor, or a particular minor, in the home of the individual would pose a significant risk of harm to the physical or psychological well-being of the minor.

(b) If an evaluator determines that the information assessed does not raise a specific concern, the evaluator shall find that the individual is suited to be an adoptive parent. The evaluator may comment about any factor that in the evaluator's opinion makes the individual suited in general or for a particular minor.

(c) If an evaluator determines that the information assessed raises a specific concern, the evaluator, on the basis of the original or any further investigation, shall find that the individual is or is not suited to be an adoptive parent. The evaluator shall support the finding with a written explanation.

SECTION 2-205. FILING AND COPIES OF PREPLACEMENT EVALUATION.

(a) If a preplacement evaluation contains a finding that an individual is suited to be an adoptive parent, the evaluator shall give the individual a signed copy of the evaluation. At the individual's request, the evaluator shall furnish a copy of the evaluation to a person authorized under this [Act] to place a minor for adoption and, unless the individual requests otherwise, edit the copy to exclude identifying information.

(b) If a preplacement evaluation contains a finding that an individual is not suited to be an adoptive parent of any minor, or a particular minor, the evaluator shall immediately give a signed copy of the evaluation to the individual and to the department. The department shall retain for 10 years the copy and a copy of any court order concerning the evaluation issued pursuant to Section 2-206 or 2-207.

(c) An evaluator shall retain for two years the original of a completed or incomplete preplacement evaluation and a list of every source for each item of information in the evaluation.

(d) An evaluator who conducted an evaluation in good faith is not subject to civil liability for anything contained in the evaluation.

SECTION 2-206. REVIEW OF EVALUATION.

(a) Within 90 days after an individual receives a preplacement evaluation with a finding that he or she is not suited to be an adoptive parent, the individual may petition a court for review of the evaluation.

(b) If the court determines that the petitioner has failed to prove suitability by a preponderance of the evidence, it shall order that the petitioner not be permitted to adopt a minor and shall send a copy of the order to the department to be retained with the copy of the original evaluation. If, at the time of the court's determination, the petitioner has custody of a minor for purposes of adoption, the court shall make an appropriate order for the care and custody of the minor.

(c) If the court determines that the petitioner has proved suitability, the court shall find the petitioner suitable to be an adoptive parent and the petitioner may commence or continue a proceeding for adoption of a minor. The court shall send a copy of its order to the department to be retained with the copy of the original evaluation.

SECTION 2-207. ACTION BY DEPARTMENT. If, before a decree of adoption is issued, the department learns from an evaluator or another person that a minor has been placed for adoption with an individual who is the subject of a preplacement evaluation on file with the department containing a finding of unsuitability, the department shall immediately review the evaluation and investigate the circumstances of the placement and may request that the individual return the minor to the custody of the person who placed the minor or to the department. If the individual refuses to return the minor, the department shall immediately commence an action or proceeding to remove the minor from the home of the individual pursuant to [the State's child protection statute] and, pending a hearing, the court shall make an appropriate order for the care and custody of the minor.

[PART] 3. TRANSFER OF PHYSICAL CUSTODY OF MINOR BY HEALTH-CARE FACILITY FOR PURPOSES OF ADOPTION

SECTION 2-301. "HEALTH-CARE FACILITY" DEFINED. In this [part], "health-care facility" means a hospital, clinic, or other facility authorized by this State to provide services related to birth and neonatal care.

SECTION 2-302. AUTHORIZATION TO TRANSFER PHYSICAL CUSTODY.

(a) A health-care facility shall release a minor for the purpose of adoption to an individual or agency not otherwise legally entitled to the physical custody of the minor if, in the presence of an employee

20

authorized by the health-care facility, the woman who gave birth to the minor signs an authorization of the transfer of physical custody.

(b) An authorized employee in whose presence the authorization required under subsection (a) is signed shall attest the signing in writing.

SECTION 2-303. REPORTS TO DEPARTMENT.

(a) No later than 72 hours after a release pursuant to Section 2-302, a health-care facility that releases a minor for purposes of adoption shall transmit to the department a copy of the authorization required by Section 2-302 and shall report:

(1) the name, address, and telephone number of the person who authorized the release;

(2) the name, address, and telephone number of the person to whom physical custody was transferred; and

(3) the date of the transfer.

(b) No later than 30 days after a release pursuant to Section 2-302, the person to whom physical custody of a minor was transferred shall report to the department which, if any, of the following has occurred:

(1) the filing of a petition for adoption with the name and address of the petitioner;

(2) the acquisition of custody of the minor by an agency and the name and address of the agency;

(3) the return of the minor to a parent or other person having legal custody and the name and address of the parent or other person; or

(4) the transfer of physical custody of the minor to another individual and the name and address of the individual.

SECTION 2-304. ACTION BY DEPARTMENT.

(a) If the department receives a report required under Section 2-303(a) from a health-care facility, but does not receive the report required under Section 2-303(b) within 45 days after the transfer of a minor, the department shall immediately investigate to determine the whereabouts of the minor.

(b) If none of the dispositions listed in Section 2-303(b)(1) through (3) has occurred, or the minor has been transferred to an individual described in Section 2-303(b)(4) who has not filed a petition to adopt, the department shall immediately take appropriate action to remove the minor from the individual to whom the minor has been transferred.

(c) The department may also review and investigate compliance with Sections 2-101 through 2-106 and may maintain an action in the [appropriate] court to compel compliance.

[PART] 4. CONSENT TO AND RELINQUISHMENT FOR ADOPTION

SECTION 2-401. PERSONS WHOSE CONSENT REQUIRED.

(a) Unless consent is not required or is dispensed with by Section 2-402, in a direct placement of a minor for adoption by a parent or guardian authorized under this [Act] to place the minor, a petition to adopt the minor may be granted only if consent to the adoption has been executed by:

(1) the woman who gave birth to the minor and the man, if any, who:

(i) is or has been married to the woman if the minor was born during the marriage or within 300 days after the marriage was terminated or a court issued a decree of separation;

(ii) attempted to marry the woman before the minor's birth by a marriage solemnized in apparent compliance with law, although the attempted marriage is or could be declared invalid, if the minor was born during the attempted marriage or within 300 days after the attempted marriage was terminated;

(iii) has been judicially determined to be the father of the minor, or has signed a document that has the effect of establishing his parentage of the minor, and:

(A) has provided, in accordance with his financial means, reasonable and consistent payments for the support of the minor and has visited or communicated with the minor; or

(B) after the minor's birth, but before the minor's placement for adoption, has married the woman who gave birth to the minor or attempted to marry her by a marriage solemnized in apparent compliance with law, although the attempted marriage is or could be declared invalid; or

(iv) has received the minor into his home and openly held out the minor as his child;

(2) the minor's guardian if expressly authorized by a court to consent to the minor's adoption; or

(3) the current adoptive or other legally recognized mother and father of the minor.

(b) Unless consent is not required under Section 2-402, in a placement of a minor for adoption by an agency authorized under this [Act] to place the minor, a petition to adopt the minor may be granted only if consent to the adoption has been executed by:

(1) the agency that placed the minor for adoption; and

(2) any individuals described in subsection (a) who have not relinquished the minor.

(c) Unless the court dispenses with the minor's consent, a petition to adopt a minor who has attained 12 years of age may be granted only if, in addition to any consent required by subsections (a) and (b), the minor has executed an informed consent to the adoption.

SECTION 2-402. PERSONS WHOSE CONSENT NOT REQUIRED.

(a) Consent to an adoption of a minor is not required of:

(1) an individual who has relinquished the minor to an agency for purposes of adoption;

(2) an individual whose parental relationship to the minor has been judicially terminated or determined not to exist;

22

(3) a parent who has been judicially declared incompetent;

(4) a man who has not been married to the woman who gave birth to the minor and who, after the conception of the minor, executes a verified statement denying paternity or disclaiming any interest in the minor and acknowledging that his statement is irrevocable when executed;

(5) the personal representative of a deceased parent's estate; or

(6) a parent or other person who has not executed a consent or a relinquishment and who fails to file an answer or make an appearance in a proceeding for adoption or for termination of a parental relationship within the requisite time after service of notice of the proceeding.

(b) The court may dispense with the consent of:

(1) a guardian or an agency whose consent is otherwise required upon a finding that the consent is being withheld contrary to the best interest of a minor adoptee; or

(2) a minor adoptee who has attained 12 years of age upon a finding that it is not in the best interest of the minor to require the consent.

SECTION 2-403. INDIVIDUALS WHO MAY RELINQUISH MINOR.
A parent or guardian whose consent to the adoption of a minor is required by Section 2-401 may relinquish to an agency all rights with respect to the minor, including legal and physical custody and the right to consent to the minor's adoption.

SECTION 2-404. TIME AND PREREQUISITES FOR EXECUTION OF CONSENT OR RELINQUISHMENT.

(a) A parent whose consent to the adoption of a minor is required by Section 2-401 may execute a consent or a relinquishment only after the minor is born. A parent who executes a consent or relinquishment may revoke the consent or relinquishment within 192 hours after the birth of the minor.

(b) A guardian may execute a consent to the adoption of a minor or a relinquishment at any time after being authorized by a court to do so.

(c) An agency that places a minor for adoption may execute its consent at any time before or during the hearing on the petition for adoption.

(d) A minor adoptee whose consent is required may execute a consent at any time before or during the hearing on the petition for adoption.

(e) Before executing a consent or relinquishment, a parent must have been informed of the meaning and consequences of adoption, the availability of personal and legal counseling, the consequences of misidentifying the other parent, the procedure for releasing information about the health and other characteristics of the parent which may affect the physical or psychological well-being of the adoptee, and the procedure for the consensual release of the parent's identity to an adoptee, an adoptee's direct descendant, or an adoptive parent pursuant to [Article] 6. The parent must have had an opportunity to indicate in a signed document whether and under what circumstances the parent is or is not willing to release identifying information, and must have been informed of the procedure for changing the document at a later time.

SECTION 2-405. PROCEDURE FOR EXECUTION OF CONSENT OR RELINQUISHMENT.

(a) A consent or relinquishment executed by a parent or guardian must be signed or confirmed in the presence of:

(1) a judge of a court of record;

(2) an individual whom a judge of a court of record designates to take consents or relinquishments;

(3) an employee other than an employee of an agency to which a minor is relinquished whom an agency designates to take consents or relinquishments;

(4) a lawyer other than a lawyer who is representing an adoptive parent or the agency to which a minor is relinquished;

(5) a commissioned officer on active duty in the military service of the United States, if the individual executing the consent or relinquishment is in military service; or

(6) an officer of the foreign service or a consular officer of the United States in another country, if the individual executing the consent or relinquishment is in that country.

(b) A consent executed by a minor adoptee must be signed or confirmed in the presence of the court in the proceeding for adoption or in a manner the court directs.

(c) A parent who is a minor is competent to execute a consent or relinquishment if the parent has had access to counseling and has had the advice of a lawyer who is not representing an adoptive parent or the agency to which the parent's child is relinquished.

(d) An individual before whom a consent or relinquishment is signed or confirmed under subsection (a) shall certify in writing that he or she orally explained the contents and consequences of the consent or relinquishment, and to the best of his or her knowledge or belief, the individual executing the consent or relinquishment:

(1) read or was read the consent or relinquishment and understood it;

(2) signed the consent or relinquishment voluntarily and received or was offered a copy of it;

(3) was furnished the information and afforded an opportunity to sign the document described by Section 2-404(e);

(4) received or was offered counseling services and information about adoption; and

(5) if a parent who is a minor, was advised by a lawyer who is not representing an adoptive parent or the agency to which the parent's child is being relinquished, or, if an adult, was informed of the right to have a lawyer who is not representing an adoptive parent or an agency to which the parent's child is being relinquished.

24

(e) A prospective adoptive parent named or described in a consent to the adoption of a minor shall sign a statement indicating an intention to adopt the minor, acknowledging an obligation to return legal and physical custody of the minor to the minor's parent if the parent revokes the consent within the time specified in Section 2-404(a), and acknowledging responsibility for the minor's support and medical and other care if the consent is not revoked.

(f) If an agency accepts a relinquishment, an employee of the agency shall sign a statement accepting the relinquishment, acknowledging its obligation to return legal and physical custody of the child to the minor's parent if the parent revokes the relinquishment within the time indicated in Section 2-404(a), and acknowledging responsibility for the minor's support and medical and other care if the relinquishment is not revoked.

(g) An individual before whom a consent or a relinquishment is signed or confirmed shall certify having received the statements required by subsections (e) and (f).

(h) A consent by an agency to the adoption of a minor in the agency's legal custody must be executed by the head or an individual authorized by the agency and must be signed or confirmed under oath in the presence of an individual authorized to take acknowledgments.

(i) A consent or relinquishment executed and signed or confirmed in another State or country is valid if in accordance with this [Act] or with the law and procedure prevailing where executed.

SECTION 2-406. CONTENT OF CONSENT OR RELINQUISHMENT.

(a) A consent or relinquishment required from a parent or guardian must be in writing and contain, in plain English or, if the native language of the parent or guardian is a language other than English, in that language:

(1) the date, place, and time of the execution of the consent or relinquishment;

(2) the name, date of birth, and current mailing address of the individual executing the consent or relinquishment;

(3) the date of birth and the name or pseudonym of the minor adoptee;

(4) if a consent, the name, address, and telephone and telecopier numbers of the lawyer representing the prospective adoptive parent with whom the individual executing the consent has placed or intends to place the minor for adoption;

(5) if a relinquishment, the name, address, and telephone and telecopier numbers of the agency to which the minor is being relinquished; and

(6) specific instructions as to how to revoke the consent or relinquishment and how to commence an action to set it aside.

(b) A consent must state that the parent or guardian executing the document is voluntarily and unequivocally consenting to the transfer of legal and physical custody to, and the adoption of the minor by, a specific adoptive parent whom the parent or guardian has selected.

25

(c) A relinquishment must state that the individual executing the relinquishment voluntarily consents to the permanent transfer of legal and physical custody of the minor to the agency for the purposes of adoption.

(d) A consent or relinquishment must state:

(1) an understanding that after the consent or relinquishment is signed or confirmed in substantial compliance with Section 2-405, it is final and, except under a circumstance stated in Section 2-408 or 2-409, may not be revoked or set aside for any reason, including the failure of an adoptive parent to permit the individual executing the consent or relinquishment to visit or communicate with the minor adoptee;

(2) an understanding that the adoption will extinguish all parental rights and obligations the individual executing the consent or relinquishment has with respect to the minor adoptee, except for arrearages of child support, and will remain valid whether or not any agreement for visitation or communication with the minor adoptee is later performed;

(3) that the individual executing the consent or relinquishment has:

(i) received a copy of the consent or relinquishment;

(ii) received or been offered counseling services and information about adoption which explains the meaning and consequences of an adoption;

(iii) been advised, if a parent who is a minor, by a lawyer who is not representing an adoptive parent or the agency to which the minor adoptee is being relinquished, or, if an adult, has been informed of the right to have a lawyer who is not representing an adoptive parent or the agency;

(iv) been provided the information and afforded an opportunity to sign the document described in Section 2-404(e); and

(v) been advised of the obligation to provide the information required under Section 2-106;

(4) that the individual executing the consent or relinquishment has not received or been promised any money or anything of value for the consent or the relinquishment, except for payments authorized by [Article] 7;

(5) that the minor is not an Indian child as defined in the Indian Child Welfare Act, 25 U.S.C. Sections 1901 et seq.;

(6) that the individual believes the adoption of the minor is in the minor's best interest; and

(7) if a consent, that the individual who is consenting waives further notice unless the adoption is contested, appealed, or denied.

(e) A relinquishment may provide that the individual who is relinquishing waives notice of any proceeding for adoption, or waives notice unless the adoption is contested, appealed, or denied.

(f) A consent or relinquishment may provide for its revocation if:

26

(1) another consent or relinquishment is not executed within a specified period;

(2) a court decides not to terminate another individual's parental relationship to the minor; or

(3) in a direct placement for adoption, a petition for adoption by a prospective adoptive parent, named or described in the consent, is denied or withdrawn.

SECTION 2-407. CONSEQUENCES OF CONSENT OR RELINQUISHMENT.

(a) Except under a circumstance stated in Section 2-408, a consent to the adoption of a minor which is executed by a parent or guardian in substantial compliance with Sections 2-405 and 2-406 is final and irrevocable, and:

(1) unless a court orders otherwise to protect the welfare of the minor, entitles the prospective adoptive parent named or described in the consent to the legal and physical custody of the minor and imposes on that individual responsibility for the support and medical and other care of the minor;

(2) terminates any duty of a parent who executed the consent with respect to the minor, except for arrearages of child support; and

(3) terminates any right of a parent or guardian who executed the consent to object to the minor's adoption by the prospective adoptive parent and any right to notice of the proceeding for adoption unless the adoption is contested, appealed, or denied.

(b) Except under a circumstance stated in Section 2-409, a relinquishment of a minor to an agency which is executed by a parent or guardian in substantial compliance with Sections 2-405 and 2-406 is final and irrevocable and:

(1) unless a court orders otherwise to protect the welfare of the minor, entitles the agency to the legal custody of the minor until a decree of adoption becomes final;

(2) empowers the agency to place the minor for adoption, consent to the minor's adoption, and delegate to a prospective adoptive parent responsibility for the support and medical and other care of the minor;

(3) terminates any duty of the individual who executed the relinquishment with respect to the minor, except for arrearages of child support; and

(4) terminates any right of the individual who executed the relinquishment to object to the minor's adoption and, unless otherwise provided in the relinquishment, any right to notice of the proceeding for adoption.

SECTION 2-408. REVOCATION OF CONSENT.

(a) In a direct placement of a minor for adoption by a parent or guardian, a consent is revoked if:

(1) within 192 hours after the birth of the minor, a parent who executed the consent notifies in writing the prospective adoptive parent, or the adoptive parent's lawyer, that the parent revokes the consent, or the parent complies with any other instructions for revocation specified in the consent; or

(2) the individual who executed the consent and the prospective adoptive parent named or described in the consent agree to its revocation.

(b) In a direct placement of a minor for adoption by a parent or guardian, the court shall set aside the consent if the individual who executed the consent establishes:

(1) by clear and convincing evidence, before a decree of adoption is issued, that the consent was obtained by fraud or duress;

(2) by a preponderance of the evidence before a decree of adoption is issued that, without good cause shown, a petition to adopt was not filed within 60 days after the minor was placed for adoption; or

(3) by a preponderance of the evidence, that a condition permitting revocation has occurred, as expressly provided for in the consent pursuant to Section 2-406.

(c) If the consent of an individual who had legal and physical custody of a minor when the minor was placed for adoption or when the consent was executed is revoked, the prospective adoptive parent shall immediately return the minor to the individual's custody and move to dismiss a proceeding for adoption or termination of the individual's parental relationship to the minor. If the minor is not returned immediately, the individual may petition the court named in the consent for appropriate relief. The court shall hear the petition expeditiously.

(d) If the consent of an individual who had legal and physical custody of a minor when the minor was placed for adoption or the consent was executed is set aside under subsection (b)(1), the court shall order the return of the minor to the custody of the individual and dismiss a proceeding for adoption.

(e) If the consent of an individual who had legal and physical custody of a minor when the minor was placed for adoption or the consent was executed is set aside under subsection (b)(2) or (3) and no ground exists under [Article] 3, [Part] 5, for terminating the relationship of parent and child between the individual and the minor, the court shall dismiss a proceeding for adoption and order the return of the minor to the custody of the individual unless the court finds that return will be detrimental to the minor.

(f) If the consent of an individual who did not have physical custody of a minor when the minor was placed for adoption or when the consent was executed is revoked or set aside and no ground exists under [Article] 3, [Part] 5, for terminating the relationship of parent and child between the individual and the minor, the court shall dismiss a proceeding for adoption and issue an order providing for the care and custody of the minor according to the best interest of the minor.

SECTION 2-409. REVOCATION OF RELINQUISHMENT.

(a) A relinquishment is revoked if:

(1) within 192 hours after the birth of the minor, a parent who executed the relinquishment gives written notice to the agency that accepted it, that the parent revokes the relinquishment, or the parent complies with any other instructions for revocation specified in the relinquishment; or

(2) the individual who executed the relinquishment and the agency that accepted it agree to its revocation.

(b) The court shall set aside a relinquishment if the individual who executed the relinquishment establishes:

(1) by clear and convincing evidence, before a decree of adoption is issued, that the relinquishment was obtained by fraud or duress; or

(2) by a preponderance of the evidence, that a condition permitting revocation has occurred, as expressly provided for in the relinquishment pursuant to Section 2-406.

(c) If a relinquishment by an individual who had legal and physical custody of a minor when the relinquishment was executed is revoked, the agency shall immediately return the minor to the individual's custody and move to dismiss a proceeding for adoption. If the minor is not returned immediately, the individual may petition the court named in the relinquishment for appropriate relief. The court shall hear the petition expeditiously.

(d) If a relinquishment by an individual who had legal and physical custody of a minor when the relinquishment was executed is set aside under subsection (b)(1), the court shall dismiss a proceeding for adoption and order the return of the minor to the custody of the individual.

(e) If a relinquishment by an individual who had legal and physical custody of a minor when the relinquishment was executed is set aside under subsection (b)(2) and no ground exists under [Article] 3, [Part] 5, for terminating the relationship of parent and child between the individual and the minor, the court shall dismiss a proceeding for adoption and order the return of the minor to the custody of the individual unless the court finds that return will be detrimental to the minor.

(f) If a relinquishment by an individual who did not have physical custody of a minor when the relinquishment was executed is revoked or set aside and no ground exists under [Article] 3, [Part] 5, for terminating the relationship of parent and child between the individual and the minor, the court shall dismiss a proceeding for adoption and shall issue an order providing for the care and custody of the minor according to the best interest of the minor.

[ARTICLE] 3. GENERAL PROCEDURE FOR ADOPTION OF MINORS

[PART] 1. JURISDICTION AND VENUE

SECTION 3-101. JURISDICTION.

(a) Except as otherwise provided in subsections (b) and (c), a court of this State has jurisdiction over a proceeding for the adoption of a minor commenced under this [Act] if:

(1) immediately before commencement of the proceeding, the minor lived in this State with a parent, a guardian, a prospective adoptive parent, or another person acting as parent, for at least six consecutive months, excluding periods of temporary absence, or, in the case of a minor under six months of age, lived in this State from soon after birth with any of those individuals and there is available in this State substantial evidence concerning the minor's present or future care;

(2) immediately before commencement of the proceeding, the prospective adoptive parent lived in this State for at least six consecutive months, excluding periods of temporary absence, and there is available in this State substantial evidence concerning the minor's present or future care;

(3) the agency that placed the minor for adoption is located in this State and it is in the best interest of the minor that a court of this State assume jurisdiction because:

(i) the minor and the minor's parents, or the minor and the prospective adoptive parent, have a significant connection with this State; and

(ii) there is available in this State substantial evidence concerning the minor's present or future care;

(4) the minor and the prospective adoptive parent are physically present in this State and the minor has been abandoned or it is necessary in an emergency to protect the minor because the minor has been subjected to or threatened with mistreatment or abuse or is otherwise neglected; or

(5) it appears that no other State would have jurisdiction under prerequisites substantially in accordance with paragraphs (1) through (4), or another State has declined to exercise jurisdiction on the ground that this State is the more appropriate forum to hear a petition for adoption of the minor, and it is in the best interest of the minor that a court of this State assume jurisdiction.

(b) A court of this State may not exercise jurisdiction over a proceeding for adoption of a minor if at the time the petition for adoption is filed a proceeding concerning the custody or adoption of the minor is pending in a court of another State exercising jurisdiction substantially in conformity with [the Uniform Child Custody Jurisdiction Act] or this [Act] unless the proceeding is stayed by the court of the other State.

(c) If a court of another State has issued a decree or order concerning the custody of a minor who may be the subject of a proceeding for adoption in this State, a court of this State may not exercise jurisdiction over a proceeding for adoption of the minor unless:

(1) the court of this State finds that the court of the State which issued the decree or order:

(i) does not have continuing jurisdiction to modify the decree or order under jurisdictional prerequisites substantially in accordance with [the Uniform Child Custody Jurisdiction Act] or has declined to assume jurisdiction to modify the decree or order; or

(ii) does not have jurisdiction over a proceeding for adoption substantially in conformity with subsection (a)(1) through (4) or has declined to assume jurisdiction over a proceeding for adoption; and

(2) the court of this State has jurisdiction over the proceeding.

SECTION 3-102. VENUE. A petition for adoption of a minor may be filed in the court in the [county] in which a petitioner lives, the minor lives, or an office of the agency that placed the minor is located.

[PART] 2. GENERAL PROCEDURAL PROVISIONS

SECTION 3-201. APPOINTMENT OF LAWYER OR GUARDIAN AD LITEM.

(a) In a proceeding under this [Act] which may result in the termination of a relationship of parent and child, the court shall appoint a lawyer for any indigent, minor, or incompetent individual who appears in the proceeding and whose parental relationship to a child may be terminated, unless the court finds that the minor or incompetent individual has sufficient financial means to hire a lawyer, or the indigent individual declines to be represented by a lawyer.

(b) The court shall appoint a guardian ad litem for a minor adoptee in a contested proceeding under this [Act] and may appoint a guardian ad litem for a minor adoptee in an uncontested proceeding.

SECTION 3-203. CONFIDENTIALITY OF PROCEEDINGS. Except for a proceeding pursuant to [Article] 7, a civil proceeding under this [Act] must be heard in closed court.

SECTION 3-204. CUSTODY DURING PENDENCY OF PROCEEDING. In order to protect the welfare of the minor, the court shall make an interim order for custody of a minor adoptee according to the best interest of the minor in a contested proceeding under this [Act] for adoption or termination of a parental relationship and may make an interim order for custody in an uncontested proceeding.

SECTION 3-205. REMOVAL OF ADOPTEE FROM STATE. Before a decree of adoption is issued, a petitioner may not remove a minor adoptee for more than 30 consecutive days from the State in which the petitioner resides without the permission of the court, if the minor was placed directly for adoption, or, if an agency placed the minor for adoption, the permission of the agency.

[PART] 3. PETITION FOR ADOPTION OF MINOR

SECTION 3-301. STANDING TO PETITION TO ADOPT.

(a) Except as otherwise provided in subsection (c), the only individuals who have standing to petition to adopt a minor under this [article] are:

(1) an individual with whom a minor has been placed for adoption or who has been selected as a prospective adoptive parent by a person authorized under this [Act] to place the minor for adoption; or

(2) an individual with whom a minor has not been placed for adoption or who has not been selected or rejected as a prospective adoptive parent pursuant to [Article] 2, [Parts] 1 through 3, but who has had physical custody of the minor for at least six months immediately before seeking to file a petition for adoption and is allowed to file the petition by the court for good cause shown.

(b) The spouse of a petitioner must join in the petition unless legally separated from the petitioner or judicially declared incompetent.

(c) A petition for adoption of a minor stepchild by a stepparent may be filed under [Article] 4 and a petition for adoption of an emancipated minor may be filed under [Article] 5.

SECTION 3-302. TIME FOR FILING PETITION. Unless the court allows a later filing, a prospective adoptive parent with standing under Section 3-301(a)(1) shall file a petition for adoption no later than 30 days after a minor is placed for adoption with that individual.

SECTION 3-303. CAPTION OF PETITION. The caption of a petition for adoption of a minor must contain the name of or a pseudonym for the minor adoptee. The caption may not contain the name of the petitioner.

SECTION 3-304. CONTENT OF PETITION.

(a) A petition for adoption of a minor must be signed and verified by the petitioner and contain the following information or state why any of the information omitted is not contained in the petition:

(1) the full name, age, and place and duration of residence of the petitioner;

(2) the current marital status of the petitioner, including the date and place of any marriage, the date of any legal separation or divorce, and the date of any judicial determination that a petitioner's spouse is incompetent;

(3) that the petitioner has facilities and resources to provide for the care and support of the minor;

(4) that a preplacement evaluation containing a finding that the petitioner is suited to be an adoptive parent has been prepared or updated within the 18 months next preceding the placement, or that the absence of a preplacement evaluation has been excused by a court for good cause shown or is not required under Section 2-201;

(5) the first name, sex, and date, or approximate date, and place of birth of the minor adoptee and a statement that the minor is or is not an Indian child as defined in the Indian Child Welfare Act, 25 U.S.C. Sections 1901 et seq.;

(6) the circumstances under which the petitioner obtained physical custody of the minor, including the date of placement of the minor with the petitioner for adoption and the name of the agency or the name or relationship to the minor of the individual that placed the minor;

(7) the length of time the minor has been in the custody of the petitioner and, if the minor is not in the physical custody of the petitioner, the reason why the petitioner does not have custody and the date and manner in which the petitioner intends to obtain custody;

(8) a description and estimate of the value of any property of the minor;

(9) that any law governing interstate or intercountry placement was complied with;

(10) the name or relationship to the minor of any individual who has executed a consent or relinquishment to the adoption or a disclaimer of paternal interest, and the name or relationship to the minor of any individual whose consent or relinquishment may be required, but whose parental relationship has not been terminated, and any fact or circumstance that may excuse the lack of consent;

(11) that a previous petition by the petitioner to adopt has or has not been made in any court, and its disposition; and

(12) a description of any previous court order or pending proceeding known to the petitioner concerning custody of or visitation with the minor and any other fact known to the petitioner and needed to establish the jurisdiction of the court.

(b) The petitioner shall request in the petition:

(1) that the petitioner be permitted to adopt the minor as the petitioner's child;

(2) that the court approve the full name by which the minor is to be known if the petition is granted; and

(3) any other relief sought by the petitioner.

SECTION 3-305. REQUIRED DOCUMENTS.

(a) Before the hearing on a petition for adoption, the following must be filed:

(1) a certified copy of the birth certificate or other record of the date and place of birth of the minor adoptee;

(2) any consent, relinquishment, or disclaimer of paternal interest with respect to the minor that has been executed, and any written certifications required by Section 2-405(d) and (g) from the individual before whom a consent or relinquishment was executed;

(3) a certified copy of any court order terminating the rights and duties of the minor's parents or guardian;

(4) a certified copy of each parent's or former parent's marriage certificate, decree of divorce, annulment, or dissolution, or agreement or decree of legal separation, and a certified copy of any court order determining the parent's or former parent's incompetence;

(5) a certified copy of any existing court order or the petition in any pending proceeding concerning custody of or visitation with the minor;

(6) a copy of the preplacement evaluation and of the evaluation during the pendency of the proceeding for adoption;

(7) a copy of any report containing the information required by Section 2-106;

(8) a document signed pursuant to Section 2-404(e);

(9) a certified copy of the petitioner's marriage certificate, decree of divorce, annulment, or dissolution, or agreement or decree of legal separation, and a certified copy of any court order determining the incompetence of the petitioner's spouse;

(10) a copy of any agreement with a public agency to provide a subsidy for the benefit of a minor adoptee with a special need;

(11) if an agency placed the minor adoptee, a verified document from the agency stating:

(i) the circumstances under which it obtained custody of the minor for purposes of adoption;

(ii) that it complied with any provision of law governing an interstate or intercountry placement of the minor;

(iii) the name or relationship to the minor of any individual whose consent is required, but who has not executed a consent or a relinquishment or whose parental relationship has not been terminated, and any fact or circumstance that may excuse the lack of consent or relinquishment; and

(iv) whether it has executed its consent to the proposed adoption and whether it waives notice of the proceeding; and

(12) the name and address, if known, of any person who is entitled to receive notice of the proceeding for adoption.

(b) If an item required by subsection (a) is not available, the person responsible for furnishing the item shall file an affidavit explaining its absence.

[PART] 4. NOTICE OF PENDENCY OF PROCEEDING

SECTION 3-401. SERVICE OF NOTICE.

(a) Unless notice has been waived, notice of a proceeding for adoption of a minor must be served, within 20 days after a petition for adoption is filed, upon:

(1) an individual whose consent to the adoption is required under Section 2-401, but notice need not be served upon an individual whose parental relationship to the minor or whose status as a guardian has been terminated;

(2) an agency whose consent to the adoption is required under Section 2-401;

(3) an individual whom the petitioner knows is claiming to be or who is named as the father or possible father of the minor adoptee and whose paternity of the minor has not been judicially determined, but notice need not be served upon a man who has executed a verified statement, as described in Section 2-402(a)(4), denying paternity or disclaiming any interest in the minor;

(4) an individual other than the petitioner who has legal or physical custody of the minor adoptee or who has a right of visitation with the minor under an existing court order issued by a court in this or another State;

(5) the spouse of the petitioner if the spouse has not joined in the petition; and

(6) a grandparent of a minor adoptee if the grandparent's child is a deceased parent of the minor and, before death, the deceased parent had not executed a consent or relinquishment or the deceased parent's parental relationship to the minor had not been terminated.

(b) The court shall require notice of a proceeding for adoption of a minor to be served upon any person the court finds, at any time during the proceeding, is:

(1) a person described in subsection (a) who has not been given notice;

(2) an individual who has revoked a consent or relinquishment pursuant to Section 2-408(a) or 2-409(a) or is attempting to have a consent or relinquishment set aside pursuant to Section 2-408(b) or 2-409(b); or

(3) a person who, on the basis of a previous relationship with the minor adoptee, a parent, an alleged parent, or the petitioner, can provide information that is relevant to the proposed adoption and that the court in its discretion wants to hear.

SECTION 3-402. CONTENT OF NOTICE. A notice required by Section 3-401 must use a pseudonym for a petitioner or any individual named in the petition for adoption who has not waived confidentiality and must contain:

34

(1) the caption of the petition;

(2) the address and telephone number of the court where the petition is pending;

(3) a concise summary of the relief requested in the petition;

(4) the name, mailing address, and telephone number of the petitioner or petitioner's lawyer;

(5) a conspicuous statement of the method of responding to the notice of the proceeding for adoption and the consequences of failure to respond; and

(6) any statement required by [other applicable law or rule].

SECTION 3-403. MANNER AND EFFECT OF SERVICE.

(a) Personal service of the notice required by Section 3-401 must be made in a manner appropriate under [the rules of civil procedure for the service of process in a civil action in this State] unless the court otherwise directs.

(b) Except as otherwise provided in subsection (c), a person who fails to respond to the notice within 20 days after its service may not appear in or receive further notice of the proceeding for adoption.

(c) An individual who is a respondent in a petition to terminate the relationship of parent and child pursuant to [Part] 5 which is served upon the individual with the notice required by Section 3-401 may not appear in or receive further notice of the proceeding for adoption or for termination unless the individual responds to the notice as required by Section 3-504.

SECTION 3-404. INVESTIGATION AND NOTICE TO UNKNOWN FATHER.

(a) If, at any time in a proceeding for adoption or for termination of a relationship of parent and child under [Part] 5, the court finds that an unknown father of a minor adoptee may not have received notice, the court shall determine whether he can be identified. The determination must be based on evidence that includes inquiry of appropriate persons in an effort to identify an unknown father for the purpose of providing notice.

(b) The inquiry required by subsection (a) must include whether:

(1) the woman who gave birth to the minor adoptee was married at the probable time of conception of the minor, or at a later time;

(2) the woman was cohabiting with a man at the probable time of conception of the minor;

(3) the woman has received payments or promises of support, other than from a governmental agency, with respect to the minor or because of her pregnancy;

(4) the woman has named any individual as the father on the birth certificate of the minor or in connection with applying for or receiving public assistance; and

(5) any individual has formally or informally acknowledged or claimed paternity of the minor in a jurisdiction in which the woman resided during or since her pregnancy, or in which the minor has resided or resides, at the time of the inquiry.

(c) If inquiry pursuant to subsection (b) identifies as the father of the minor an individual who has not received notice of the proceeding, the court shall require notice to be served upon him pursuant to Section 3-403 unless service is not possible because his whereabouts are unknown.

(d) If, after inquiry pursuant to subsection (b), the court finds that personal service cannot be made upon the father of the minor because his identity or whereabouts is unknown, the court shall order publication or public posting of the notice only if, on the basis of all information available, the court determines that publication or posting is likely to lead to receipt of notice by the father. If the court determines that publication or posting is not likely to lead to receipt of notice, the court may dispense with the publication or posting of a notice.

(e) If, in an inquiry pursuant to this section, the woman who gave birth to the minor adoptee fails to disclose the identity of a possible father or reveal his whereabouts, she must be advised that the proceeding for adoption may be delayed or subject to challenge if a possible father is not given notice of the proceeding, that the lack of information about the father's medical and genetic history may be detrimental to the adoptee, and that she is subject to a civil penalty if she knowingly misidentified the father.

SECTION 3-405. WAIVER OF NOTICE.

(a) A person entitled to receive notice required under this [Act] may waive the notice before the court or in a consent, relinquishment, or other document signed by the person.

(b) Except for the purpose of moving to revoke a consent or relinquishment on the ground that it was obtained by fraud or duress, a person who has waived notice may not appear in the proceeding for adoption.

[PART] 5. PETITION TO TERMINATE RELATIONSHIP BETWEEN PARENT AND CHILD

SECTION 3-501. AUTHORIZATION. A petition to terminate the relationship between a parent or an alleged parent and a minor child may be filed in a proceeding for adoption under this [Act] by:

(1) a parent or a guardian who has selected a prospective adoptive parent for a minor and who intends to place, or has placed, the minor with that individual;

(2) a parent whose spouse has filed a petition under [Article] 4 to adopt the parent's minor child;

(3) a prospective adoptive parent of the minor who has filed a petition to adopt under this [article] or [Article] 4; or

(4) an agency that has selected a prospective adoptive parent for the minor and intends to place, or has placed, the minor with that individual.

SECTION 3-502. TIMING AND CONTENT OF PETITION.

(a) A petition under this [part] may be filed at any time after a petition for adoption has been filed under this [article] or [Article] 4 and before entry of a decree of adoption.

(b) A petition under this [part] must be signed and verified by the petitioner, be filed with the court, and state:

(1) the name or pseudonym of the petitioner;

(2) the name of the minor;

(3) the name and last known address of the parent or alleged parent whose parental relationship to the minor is to be terminated;

(4) the facts and circumstances forming the basis for the petition and the grounds on which termination of a parental relationship is sought;

(5) if the petitioner is a prospective adoptive parent, that the petitioner intends to proceed with the petition to adopt the minor if the petition to terminate is granted; and

(6) if the petitioner is a parent, a guardian, or an agency, that the petitioner has selected the prospective adoptive parent who is the petitioner in the proceeding for adoption.

SECTION 3-503. SERVICE OF PETITION AND NOTICE.

(a) A petition to terminate under this [part] and a notice of hearing on the petition must be served upon the respondent, with notice of the proceeding for adoption, in the manner prescribed in Sections 3-403 and 3-404.

(b) The notice of a hearing must inform the respondent of the method for responding and that:

(1) the respondent has a right to be represented by a lawyer and may be entitled to have a lawyer appointed by the court; and

(2) failure to respond within 20 days after service and, in the case of an alleged father, failure to file a claim of paternity within 20 days after service unless a claim of paternity is pending, will result in termination of the relationship of parent and child between the respondent and the minor unless the proceeding for adoption is dismissed.

SECTION 3-504. GROUNDS FOR TERMINATING RELATIONSHIP.

(a) If the respondent is served with a petition to terminate under this [part] and the accompanying notice and does not respond and, in the case of an alleged father, file a claim of paternity within 20 days after the service unless a claim of paternity is pending, the court shall order the termination of any relationship of parent and child between the respondent and the minor unless the proceeding for adoption is dismissed.

(b) If, under Section 3-404, the court dispenses with service of the petition upon the respondent, the court shall order the termination of any relationship of parent and child between the respondent and the minor unless the proceeding for adoption is dismissed.

(c) If the respondent responds and asserts parental rights, the court shall proceed with the hearing expeditiously. If the court finds, upon clear and convincing evidence, that one of the following grounds exists, and, by a preponderance of the evidence, that termination is in the best interest of the minor, the court shall terminate any relationship of parent and child between the respondent and the minor:

(1) in the case of a minor who has not attained six months of age at the time the petition for adoption is filed, unless the respondent proves by a preponderance of the evidence a compelling reason for not complying with this paragraph, the respondent has failed to:

(i) pay reasonable prenatal, natal, and postnatal expenses in accordance with the respondent's financial means;

(ii) make reasonable and consistent payments, in accordance with the respondent's financial means, for the support of the minor;

(iii) visit regularly with the minor; and

(iv) manifest an ability and willingness to assume legal and physical custody of the minor, if, during this time, the minor was not in the physical custody of the other parent;

(2) in the case of a minor who has attained six months of age at the time a petition for adoption is filed, unless the respondent proves by a preponderance of the evidence a compelling reason for not complying with this paragraph, the respondent, for a period of at least six consecutive months immediately preceding the filing of the petition, has failed to:

(i) make reasonable and consistent payments, in accordance with the respondent's means, for the support of the minor;

(ii) communicate or visit regularly with the minor; and

(iii) manifest an ability and willingness to assume legal and physical custody of the minor, if, during this time, the minor was not in the physical custody of the other parent;

(3) the respondent has been convicted of a crime of violence or of violating a restraining or protective order, and the facts of the crime or violation and the respondent's behavior indicate that the respondent is unfit to maintain a relationship of parent and child with the minor;

(4) the respondent is a man who was not married to the minor's mother when the minor was conceived or born and is not the genetic or adoptive father of the minor; or

(5) termination is justified on a ground specified in [the State's statute for involuntary termination of parental rights].

(d) If the respondent proves by a preponderance of the evidence that he or she had a compelling reason for not complying with subsection (c)(1) or (2) and termination is not justified on a ground stated in

38

subsection (c)(3) through (5), the court may terminate the relationship of parent and child between the respondent and a minor only if it finds, upon clear and convincing evidence, that one of the following grounds exists, and, by a preponderance of the evidence, that termination is in the best interest of the minor:

(1) if the minor is not in the legal and physical custody of the other parent, the respondent is not able or willing promptly to assume legal and physical custody of the minor, and to pay for the minor's support, in accordance with the respondent's financial means;

(2) if the minor is in the legal and physical custody of the other parent and a stepparent, and the stepparent is the prospective adoptive parent, the respondent is not able or willing promptly to establish and maintain contact with the minor and to pay for the minor's support, in accordance with the respondent's financial means;

(3) placing the minor in the respondent's legal and physical custody would pose a risk of substantial harm to the physical or psychological well-being of the minor because the circumstances of the minor's conception, the respondent's behavior during the mother's pregnancy or since the minor's birth, or the respondent's behavior with respect to other minors, indicates that the respondent is unfit to maintain a relationship of parent and child with the minor; or

(4) failure to terminate the relationship of parent and child would be detrimental to the minor.

(e) In making a determination under subsection (d)(4), the court shall consider any relevant factor, including the respondent's efforts to obtain or maintain legal and physical custody of the minor, the role of other persons in thwarting the respondent's efforts to assert parental rights, the respondent's ability to care for the minor, the age of the minor, the quality of any previous relationship between the respondent and the minor and between the respondent and any other minor children, the duration and suitability of the minor's present custodial environment, and the effect of a change of physical custody on the minor.

SECTION 3-505. EFFECT OF ORDER GRANTING PETITION. An order issued under this [part] granting the petition:

(1) terminates the relationship of parent and child between the respondent and the minor, except an obligation for arrearages of child support;

(2) extinguishes any right the respondent had to withhold consent to a proposed adoption of the minor or to further notice of a proceeding for adoption; and

(3) is a final order for purposes of appeal.

SECTION 3-506. EFFECT OF ORDER DENYING PETITION.

(a) If the court denies the petition to terminate a relationship of parent and child, the court shall dismiss the proceeding for adoption and shall determine the legal and physical custody of the minor according to the criteria stated in Section 3-704.

(b) An order issued under this [part] denying a petition to terminate a relationship of parent and child is a final order for purposes of appeal.

306APPENDIX C

[PART] 6. EVALUATION OF ADOPTEE AND PROSPECTIVE ADOPTIVE PARENT

SECTION 3-601. EVALUATION DURING PROCEEDING FOR ADOPTION.

(a) After a petition for adoption of a minor is filed, the court shall order that an evaluation be made by an individual qualified under Section 2-202.

(b) The court shall provide the evaluator with copies of the petition for adoption and of the items filed with the petition.

SECTION 3-602. CONTENT OF EVALUATION.

(a) An evaluation must be based on a personal interview with the petitioner in the petitioner's residence and observation of the relationship between the minor adoptee and the petitioner.

(b) An evaluation must be in writing and contain:

(1) an account of any change in the petitioner's marital status or family history, physical or mental health, home environment, property, income, or financial obligations since the filing of the preplacement evaluation;

(2) all reasonably available information concerning the physical, mental, and emotional condition of the minor adoptee which is not included in any report on the minor's health, genetic, and social history filed in the proceeding for adoption;

(3) copies of any court order, judgment, decree, or pending legal proceeding affecting the minor adoptee, the petitioner, or any child of the petitioner;

(4) a list of the expenses, fees, or other charges incurred, paid, or to be paid, and anything of value exchanged or to be exchanged, in connection with the adoption;

(5) any behavior or characteristics of the petitioner which raise a specific concern, as described in Section 2-204(a), about the petitioner or the petitioner's home; and

(6) a finding by the evaluator concerning the suitability of the petitioner and the petitioner's home for the minor adoptee and a recommendation concerning the granting of the petition for adoption.

SECTION 3-603. TIME AND FILING OF EVALUATION.

(a) The evaluator shall complete a written evaluation and file it with the court within 60 days after receipt of the court's order for an evaluation, unless the court for good cause allows a later filing.

(b) If an evaluation produces a specific concern, as described in Section 2-204(a), the evaluation must be filed immediately, and must explain why the concern poses a significant risk of harm to the physical or psychological well-being of the minor.

(c) An evaluator shall give the petitioner a copy of an evaluation when filed with the court and for two years shall retain a copy and a list of every source for each item of information in the evaluation.

40

[PART] 7. DISPOSITIONAL HEARING; DECREE OF ADOPTION

SECTION 3-701. TIME FOR HEARING ON PETITION. The court shall set a date and time for hearing the petition, which must be no sooner than 90 days and no later than 180 days after the petition for adoption has been filed, unless the court for good cause sets an earlier or later date and time.

SECTION 3-702. DISCLOSURE OF FEES AND CHARGES. At least 10 days before the hearing:

(1) the petitioner shall file with the court a signed and verified accounting of any payment or disbursement of money or anything of value made or agreed to be made by or on behalf of the petitioner in connection with the adoption, or pursuant to [Article] 7. The accounting must include the date and amount of each payment or disbursement made, the name and address of each recipient, and the purpose of each payment or disbursement;

(2) the lawyer for a petitioner shall file with the court an affidavit itemizing any fee, compensation, or other thing of value received by, or agreed to be paid to, the lawyer incidental to the placement and adoption of the minor;

(3) the lawyer for each parent of the minor or for the guardian of the minor shall file with the court an affidavit itemizing any fee, compensation, or other thing of value received by, or agreed to be paid to, the lawyer incidental to the placement and adoption of the minor;

(4) if an agency placed the minor for adoption, the agency shall file with the court an affidavit itemizing any fee, compensation, or other thing of value received by the agency for, or incidental to, the placement and adoption of the minor; and

(5) if a guardian placed the minor for adoption, the guardian shall file with the court an affidavit itemizing any fee, compensation, or other thing of value received by the guardian for, or incidental to, the placement and adoption of the minor.

SECTION 3-703. GRANTING PETITION FOR ADOPTION.

(a) The court shall grant a petition for adoption if it determines that the adoption will be in the best interest of the minor, and that:

(1) at least 90 days have elapsed since the filing of the petition for adoption unless the court for good cause shown waives this requirement;

(2) the adoptee has been in the physical custody of the petitioner for at least 90 days unless the court for good cause shown waives this requirement;

(3) notice of the proceeding for adoption has been served or dispensed with as to any person entitled to receive notice under [Part] 4;

(4) every necessary consent, relinquishment, waiver, disclaimer of paternal interest, or judicial order terminating parental rights, including an order issued under [Part] 5, has been obtained and filed with the court;

(5) any evaluation required by this [Act] has been filed with and considered by the court;

(6) the petitioner is a suitable adoptive parent for the minor;

(7) if applicable, any requirement of this [Act] governing an interstate or intercountry placement for adoption has been met;

(8) the Indian Child Welfare Act, 25 U.S.C. Sections 1901 et seq., is not applicable to the proceeding or, if applicable, its requirements have been met;

(9) an accounting and affidavit required by Section 3-702 have been reviewed by the court, and the court has denied, modified, or ordered reimbursement of any payment or disbursement that is not authorized by [Article] 7 or is unreasonable or unnecessary when compared with the expenses customarily incurred in connection with an adoption;

(10) the petitioner has received each report required by Section 2-106; and

(11) any document signed pursuant to Section 2-404(e) concerning the release of a former parent's identity to the adoptee after the adoptee attains 18 years of age has been filed with the court.

(b) Notwithstanding a finding by the court that an activity prohibited by this [Act] has occurred, if the court makes the determinations required by subsection (a), the court shall grant the petition for adoption and report the violation to the appropriate authorities.

(c) Except as otherwise provided in [Article] 4, the court shall inform the petitioner and any other individual affected by an existing order for visitation or communication with the minor adoptee that the decree of adoption terminates any existing order for visitation or communication.

SECTION 3-704. DENIAL OF PETITION FOR ADOPTION. If a court denies a petition for adoption, it shall dismiss the proceeding and issue an appropriate order for the legal and physical custody of the minor. If the reason for the denial is that a consent or relinquishment is revoked or set aside pursuant to Section 2-408 or 2-409, the court shall determine the minor's custody according to the criteria stated in those sections. If the petition for adoption is denied for any other reason, the court shall determine the minor's custody according to the best interest of the minor.

SECTION 3-705. DECREE OF ADOPTION.

(a) A decree of adoption must state or contain:

(1) the original name of the minor adoptee, if the adoption is by a stepparent or relative and, in all other adoptions, the original name or a pseudonym;

(2) the name of the petitioner for adoption;

(3) whether the petitioner is married or unmarried;

(4) whether the petitioner is a stepparent of the adoptee;

(5) the name by which the adoptee is to be known and when the name takes effect;

(6) information to be incorporated into a new birth certificate to be issued by the [State Registrar of Vital Records], unless the petitioner or an adoptee who has attained 12 years of age requests that a new certificate not be issued;

(7) the adoptee's date and place of birth, if known, or in the case of an adoptee born outside the United States, as determined pursuant to subsection (b);

(8) the effect of the decree of adoption as stated in Sections 1-104 through 1-106; and

(9) that the adoption is in the best interest of the adoptee.

(b) In determining the date and place of birth of an adoptee born outside the United States, the court shall:

(1) enter the date and place of birth as stated in the birth certificate from the country of origin, the United States Department of State's report of birth abroad, or the documents of the United States Immigration and Naturalization Service;

(2) if the exact place of birth is unknown, enter the information that is known and designate a place of birth according to the best information known with respect to the country of origin;

(3) if the exact date of birth is unknown, determine a date of birth based upon medical evidence as to the probable age of the adoptee and other evidence the court considers appropriate; and

(4) if documents described in paragraph (1) are not available, determine the date and place of birth based upon evidence the court finds appropriate to consider.

(c) Unless a petitioner requests otherwise and the former parent agrees, the decree of adoption may not name a former parent of the adoptee.

(d) Except for a decree of adoption of a minor by a stepparent which is issued pursuant to [Article] 4, a decree of adoption of a minor must contain a statement that the adoption terminates any order for visitation or communication with the minor that was in effect before the decree is issued.

(e) A decree that substantially complies with the requirements of this section is not subject to challenge solely because one or more items required by this section are not contained in the decree.

SECTION 3-706. FINALITY OF DECREE. A decree of adoption is a final order for purposes of appeal when it is issued and becomes final for other purposes upon the expiration of the time for filing an appeal, if no appeal is filed, or upon the denial or dismissal of any appeal filed within the requisite time.

SECTION 3-707. CHALLENGES TO DECREE.

(a) An appeal from a decree of adoption or other appealable order issued under this [Act] must be heard expeditiously.

(b) A decree or order issued under this [Act] may not be vacated or annulled upon application of a person who waived notice, or who was properly served with notice pursuant to this [Act] and failed to respond or appear, file an answer, or file a claim of paternity within the time allowed.

(c) The validity of a decree of adoption issued under this [Act] may not be challenged for failure to comply with an agreement for visitation or communication with an adoptee.

(d) A decree of adoption or other order issued under this [Act] is not subject to a challenge begun more than six months after the decree or order is issued. If a challenge is brought by an individual whose parental relationship to an adoptee is terminated by a decree or order under this [Act], the court shall deny the challenge, unless the court finds by clear and convincing evidence that the decree or order is not in the best interest of the adoptee.

[PART] 8. BIRTH CERTIFICATE

SECTION 3-801. REPORT OF ADOPTION.

(a) Within 30 days after a decree of adoption becomes final, the clerk of the court shall prepare a report of adoption on a form furnished by the [State Registrar of Vital Records] and certify and send the report to the [Registrar]. The report must include:

(1) information in the court's record of the proceeding for adoption which is necessary to locate and identify the adoptee's birth certificate or, in the case of an adoptee born outside the United States, evidence the court finds appropriate to consider as to the adoptee's date and place of birth;

(2) information in the court's record of the proceeding for adoption which is necessary to issue a new birth certificate for the adoptee and a request that a new certificate be issued, unless the court, the adoptive parent, or an adoptee who has attained 12 years of age requests that a new certificate not be issued; and

(3) the file number of the decree of adoption and the date on which the decree became final.

(b) Within 30 days after a decree of adoption is amended or vacated, the clerk of the court shall prepare a report of that action on a form furnished by the [Registrar] and shall certify and send the report to the [Registrar]. The report must include information necessary to identify the original report of adoption, and shall also include information necessary to amend or withdraw any new birth certificate that was issued pursuant to the original report of adoption.

SECTION 3-802. ISSUANCE OF NEW BIRTH CERTIFICATE.

(a) Except as otherwise provided in subsection (d), upon receipt of a report of adoption prepared pursuant to Section 3-801, a report of adoption prepared in accordance with the law of another State or country, a certified copy of a decree of adoption together with information necessary to identify the adoptee's original birth certificate and to issue a new certificate, or a report of an amended adoption, the [Registrar] shall:

(1) issue a new birth certificate for an adoptee born in this State and furnish a certified copy of the new certificate to the adoptive parent and to an adoptee who has attained 12 years of age;

(2) forward a certified copy of a report of adoption for an adoptee born in another State to the [Registrar] of the State of birth;

(3) issue a certificate of foreign birth for an adoptee adopted in this State and who was born outside the United States and was not a citizen of the United States at the time of birth, and furnish a certified copy of the certificate to the adoptive parent and to an adoptee who has attained 12 years of age;

(4) notify an adoptive parent of the procedure for obtaining a revised birth certificate through the United States Department of State for an adoptee born outside the United States who was a citizen of the United States at the time of birth; or

(5) in the case of an amended decree of adoption, issue an amended birth certificate according to the procedure in paragraph (1) or (3) or follow the procedure in paragraph (2) or (4).

(b) Unless otherwise specified by the court, a new birth certificate issued pursuant to subsection (a)(1) or (3) or an amended certificate issued pursuant to subsection (a)(5) must include the date and place of birth of the adoptee, substitute the name of the adoptive parent for the name of the individual listed as the adoptee's parent on the original birth certificate, and contain any other information prescribed by [the State's vital records law or regulations].

(c) The [Registrar] shall substitute the new or amended birth certificate for the original birth certificate in the [Registrar's] files. The original certificate and all copies of the certificate in the files of the [Registrar] or any other custodian of vital records in the State must be sealed and are not subject to inspection until 99 years after the adoptee's date of birth, but may be inspected as provided in this [Act].

(d) If the court, the adoptive parent, or an adoptee who has attained 12 years of age requests that a new or amended birth certificate not be issued, the [Registrar] may not issue a new or amended certificate for an adoptee pursuant to subsection (a), but shall forward a certified copy of the report of adoption or of an amended decree of adoption for an adoptee who was born in another State to the appropriate office in the adoptee's State of birth.

(e) Upon receipt of a report that an adoption has been vacated, the [Registrar] shall:

(1) restore the original birth certificate for an individual born in this State to its place in the files, seal any new or amended birth certificate issued pursuant to subsection (a), and not allow inspection of a sealed certificate except upon court order or as otherwise provided in this [Act];

(2) forward the report with respect to an individual born in another State to the appropriate office in the State of birth; or

(3) notify the individual who is granted legal custody of a former adoptee after an adoption is vacated of the procedure for obtaining an original birth certificate through the United States Department of State for a former adoptee born outside the United States who was a citizen of the United States at the time of birth.

(f) Upon request by an individual who was listed as a parent on a child's original birth certificate and who furnishes appropriate proof of the individual's identity, the [Registrar] shall give the individual a noncertified copy of the original birth certificate.

[ARTICLE] 4. ADOPTION OF MINOR STEPCHILD BY STEPPARENT

SECTION 4-101. OTHER PROVISIONS APPLICABLE TO ADOPTION OF STEPCHILD.

Except as otherwise provided by this [article], [Article] 3 applies to an adoption of a minor stepchild by a stepparent.

SECTION 4-102. STANDING TO ADOPT MINOR STEPCHILD.

(a) A stepparent has standing under this [article] to petition to adopt a minor stepchild who is the child of the stepparent's spouse if:

(1) the spouse has sole legal and physical custody of the child and the child has been in the physical custody of the spouse and the stepparent during the 60 days next preceding the filing of a petition for adoption;

(2) the spouse has joint legal custody of the child with the child's other parent and the child has resided primarily with the spouse and the stepparent during the 12 months next preceding the filing of the petition;

(3) the spouse is deceased or mentally incompetent, but before dying or being judicially declared mentally incompetent, had legal and physical custody of the child, and the child has resided primarily with the stepparent during the 12 months next preceding the filing of the petition; or

(4) an agency placed the child with the stepparent pursuant to Section 2-104.

(b) For good cause shown, a court may allow an individual who does not meet the requirements of subsection (a), but has the consent of the custodial parent of a minor to file a petition for adoption under this [article]. A petition allowed under this subsection must be treated as if the petitioner were a stepparent.

(c) A petition for adoption by a stepparent may be joined with a petition under [Article] 3, [Part] 5, to terminate the relationship of parent and child between a minor adoptee and the adoptee's parent who is not the stepparent's spouse.

SECTION 4-103. LEGAL CONSEQUENCES OF ADOPTION OF STEPCHILD.

(a) Except as otherwise provided in subsections (b) and (c), the legal consequences of an adoption of a stepchild by a stepparent are the same as under Sections 1-103 through 1-106.

(b) An adoption by a stepparent does not affect:

(1) the relationship between the adoptee and the adoptee's parent who is the adoptive stepparent's spouse or deceased spouse;

(2) an existing court order for visitation or communication with a minor adoptee by an individual related to the adoptee through the parent who is the adoptive stepparent's spouse or deceased spouse;

(3) the right of the adoptee or a descendant of the adoptee to inheritance or intestate succession through or from the adoptee's former parent; or

(4) A court order or agreement for visitation or communication with a minor adoptee which is approved by the court pursuant to Section 4-113.

(c) Failure to comply with an agreement or order is not a ground for challenging the validity of an adoption by a stepparent.

SECTION 4-104. CONSENT TO ADOPTION. Unless consent is not required under Section 2-402, a petition to adopt a minor stepchild may be granted only if consent to the adoption has been executed by a stepchild who has attained 12 years of age; and

(1) the minor's parents as described in Section 2-401(a);

(2) the minor's guardian if expressly authorized by a court to consent to the minor's adoption; or

(3) an agency that placed the minor for adoption by the stepparent.

SECTION 4-105. CONTENT OF CONSENT BY STEPPARENT'S SPOUSE.

(a) A consent executed by a parent who is the stepparent's spouse must be signed or confirmed in the presence of an individual specified in Section 2-405, or an individual authorized to take acknowledgements.

(b) A consent under subsection (a) must be in writing, must contain the required statements described in Section 2-406(a)(1) through (3) and (d)(3) through (6), may contain the optional statements described in Section 2-406(f), and must state that:

(1) the parent executing the consent has legal and physical custody of the parent's minor child and voluntarily and unequivocally consents to the adoption of the minor by the stepparent;

(2) the adoption will not terminate the parental relationship between the parent executing the consent and the minor child; and

(3) the parent executing the consent understands and agrees that the adoption will terminate the relationship of parent and child between the minor's other parent and the minor, and will terminate any existing court order for custody, visitation, or communication with the minor, but:

(i) the minor and any descendant of the minor will retain rights of inheritance from or through the minor's other parent;

(ii) a court order for visitation or communication with the minor by an individual related to the minor through the parent executing the consent, or an agreement or order concerning another individual which is approved by the court pursuant to Section 4-113 survives the decree of adoption, but failure to comply with the terms of the order or agreement is not a ground for revoking or setting aside the consent or the adoption; and

(iii) the other parent remains liable for arrearages of child support unless released from that obligation by the parent executing the consent and by a governmental entity providing public assistance to the minor.

(c) A consent may not waive further notice of the proceeding for adoption of the minor by the stepparent.

SECTION 4-106. CONTENT OF CONSENT BY MINOR'S OTHER PARENT.

(a) A consent executed by a minor's parent who is not the stepparent's spouse must be signed or confirmed in the presence of an individual specified in Section 2-405.

(b) A consent under subsection (a) must be in writing, must contain the required statements described in Section 2-406(a)(1) through (3) and (d)(3) through (6), may contain the optional statements described in Section 2-406(f), and must state that:

(1) the parent executing the consent voluntarily and unequivocally consents to the adoption of the minor by the stepparent and the transfer to the stepparent's spouse and the adoptive stepparent of any right the parent executing the consent has to legal or physical custody of the minor;

(2) the parent executing the consent understands and agrees that the adoption will terminate his or her parental relationship to the minor and will terminate any existing court order for custody, visitation, or communication with the minor, but:

(i) the minor and any descendant of the minor will retain rights of inheritance from or through the parent executing the consent;

(ii) a court order for visitation or communication with the minor by an individual related to the minor through the minor's other parent, or an agreement or order concerning another individual which is approved by the court pursuant to Section 4-113 survives the decree of adoption, but failure to comply with the terms of the order or agreement is not a ground for revoking or setting aside the consent or the adoption; and

(iii) the parent executing the consent remains liable for arrearages of child support unless released from that obligation by the other parent and any guardian ad litem of the minor and by a governmental entity providing public assistance to the minor; and

(3) the parent executing the consent has provided the adoptive stepparent with the information required by Section 2-106.

(c) A consent under subsection (a) may waive notice of the proceeding for adoption of the minor by the stepparent unless the adoption is contested, appealed, or denied.

SECTION 4-107. CONTENT OF CONSENT BY OTHER PERSONS.

(a) A consent executed by the guardian of a minor stepchild or by an agency must be in writing and signed or confirmed in the presence of the court, or in a manner the court directs, and:

(1) must state the circumstances under which the guardian or agency obtained the authority to consent to the adoption of the minor by a stepparent;

(2) must contain the statements required by Sections 4-104 and 4-105, except for any that can be made only by a parent of the minor; and

(3) may waive notice of the proceeding for adoption, unless the adoption is contested, appealed, or denied.

(b) A consent executed by a minor stepchild in a proceeding for adoption by a stepparent must be signed or confirmed in the presence of the court or in a manner the court directs.

SECTION 4-108. PETITION TO ADOPT.

(a) A petition by a stepparent to adopt a minor stepchild must be signed and verified by the petitioner and contain the following information or state why any of the information is not contained in the petition:

(1) the information required by Section 3-304(a) (1), (3), (5), and (8) through (12) and (b);

(2) the current marital status of the petitioner, including the date and place of marriage, the name and date and place of birth of the petitioner's spouse and, if the spouse is deceased, the date, place, and cause of death and, if the spouse is incompetent, the date on which a court declared the spouse incompetent;

(3) the length of time the minor has been residing with the petitioner and the petitioner's spouse and, if the minor is not in the physical custody of the petitioner and the petitioner's spouse, the reason why they do not have custody and when they intend to obtain custody; and

(4) the length of time the petitioner's spouse or the petitioner has had legal custody of the minor and the circumstances under which legal custody was obtained.

SECTION 4-109. REQUIRED DOCUMENTS.

(a) After a petition to adopt a minor stepchild is filed, the following must be filed in the proceeding:

(1) any item required by Section 3-305(a) which is relevant to an adoption by a stepparent; and

(2) a copy of any agreement to waive arrearages of child support.

(b) If any of the items required by subsection (a) is not available, the person responsible for furnishing the item shall file an affidavit explaining its absence.

SECTION 4-110. NOTICE OF PENDENCY OF PROCEEDING.

(a) Within 30 days after a petition to adopt a minor stepchild is filed, the petitioner shall serve notice of the proceeding upon:

(1) the petitioner's spouse;

(2) any other person whose consent to the adoption is required under this [article];

(3) any person described in Section 3-401(a)(3), (4), and (6) and (b); and

(4) the parents of the minor's parent whose parental relationship will be terminated by the adoption unless the identity or the whereabouts of those parents are unknown.

SECTION 4-111. EVALUATION OF STEPPARENT.

(a) After a petition for adoption of a minor stepchild is filed, the court may order that an evaluation be made by an individual qualified under Section 2-202 to assist the court in determining whether the proposed adoption is in the best interest of the minor.

(b) The court shall provide an evaluator with copies of the petition for adoption and of the items filed with the petition.

(c) Unless otherwise directed by the court, an evaluator shall base the evaluation on a personal interview with the petitioner and the petitioner's spouse in the petitioner's residence, observation of the relationship between the minor and the petitioner, personal interviews with others who know the petitioner and may have information relevant to the examination, and any information received pursuant to subsection (d).

(d) An evaluation under this section must be in writing and contain the following:

(1) the information required by Section 2-203(d) and (e);

(2) the information required by Section 3-602(b)(2) through (5); and

(3) the finding required by Section 3-602(b)(6).

(e) An evaluator shall complete an evaluation and file it with the court within 60 days after being asked for the evaluation under this section, unless the court allows a later filing.

(f) Section 3-603(b) and (c) apply to an evaluation under this section.

SECTION 4-112. DISPOSITIONAL HEARING; DECREE OF ADOPTION. Sections 3-701 through 3-707 apply to a proceeding for adoption of a minor stepchild by a stepparent, but the court may waive the requirements of Section 3-702.

SECTION 4-113. VISITATION AGREEMENT AND ORDER.

(a) Upon the request of the petitioner in a proceeding for adoption of a minor stepchild, the court shall review a written agreement that permits another individual to visit or communicate with the minor after the decree of adoption becomes final, which must be signed by the individual, the petitioner, the petitioner's spouse, the minor if 12 years of age or older, and, if an agency placed the minor for adoption, an authorized employee of the agency.

(b) The court may enter an order approving the agreement only upon determining that the agreement is in the best interest of the minor adoptee. In making this determination, the court shall consider:

(1) the preference of the minor, if the minor is mature enough to express a preference;

(2) any special needs of the minor and how they would be affected by performance of the agreement;

(3) the length and quality of any existing relationship between the minor and the individual who would be entitled to visit or communicate, and the likely effect on the minor of allowing this relationship to continue;

(4) the specific terms of the agreement and the likelihood that the parties to the agreement will cooperate in performing its terms;

(5) the recommendation of the minor's guardian ad litem, lawyer, social worker, or other counselor; and

(6) any other factor relevant to the best interest of the minor.

(c) In addition to any agreement approved pursuant to subsections (a) and (b), the court may approve the continuation of an existing order or issue a new order permitting the minor adoptee's former parent, grandparent, or sibling to visit or communicate with the minor if:

(1) the grandparent is the parent of a deceased parent of the minor or the parent of the adoptee's parent whose parental relationship to the minor is terminated by the decree of adoption;

(2) the former parent, grandparent, or sibling requests that an existing order be permitted to survive the decree of adoption or that a new order be issued; and

(3) the court determines that the requested visitation or communication is in the best interest of the minor.

(d) In making a determination under subsection (c)(3), the court shall consider the factors listed in subsection (b) and any objections to the requested order by the adoptive stepparent and the stepparent's spouse.

(e) An order issued under this section may be enforced in a civil action only if the court finds that enforcement is in the best interest of a minor adoptee.

(f) An order issued under this section may not be modified unless the court finds that modification is in the best interest of a minor adoptee and:

(1) the individuals subject to the order request the modification; or

(2) exceptional circumstances arising since the order was issued justify the modification.

(g) Failure to comply with the terms of an order approved under this section or with any other agreement for visitation or communication is not a ground for revoking, setting aside, or otherwise challenging the validity of a consent, relinquishment, or adoption pertaining to a minor stepchild, and the validity of the consent, relinquishment, and adoption is not affected by any later action to enforce, modify, or set aside the order or agreement.

[ARTICLE] 5. ADOPTION OF ADULTS AND EMANCIPATED MINORS

SECTION 5-101. WHO MAY ADOPT ADULT OR EMANCIPATED MINOR.

(a) An adult may adopt another adult or an emancipated minor pursuant to this [article], but:

(1) an adult may not adopt his or her spouse; and

(2) an incompetent individual of any age may be adopted only pursuant to [Articles] 2, 3, and 4.

(b) An individual who has adopted an adult or emancipated minor may not adopt another adult or emancipated minor within one year after the adoption unless the prospective adoptee is a sibling of the adoptee.

SECTION 5-102. LEGAL CONSEQUENCES OF ADOPTION. The legal consequences of an adoption of an adult or emancipated minor are the same as under Sections 1-103 through 1-106, but the legal consequences of adoption of an adult stepchild by an adult stepparent are the same as under Section 4-103.

SECTION 5-103. CONSENT TO ADOPTION.

(a) Consent to the adoption of an adult or emancipated minor is required only of:

(1) the adoptee;

(2) the prospective adoptive parent; and

(3) the spouse of the prospective adoptive parent, unless they are legally separated, or the court finds that the spouse is not capable of giving consent or is withholding consent contrary to the best interest of the adoptee and the prospective adoptive parent.

(b) The consent of the adoptee and the prospective adoptive parent must:

(1) be in writing and be signed or confirmed by each of them in the presence of the court or an individual authorized to take acknowledgments;

(2) state that they agree to assume toward each other the legal relationship of parent and child and to have all of the rights and be subject to all of the duties of that relationship; and

(3) state that they understand the consequences the adoption may have for any right of inheritance, property, or support each has.

(c) The consent of the spouse of the prospective adoptive parent:

(1) must be in writing and be signed or confirmed in the presence of the court or an individual authorized to take acknowledgments;

(2) must state that the spouse:

(i) consents to the proposed adoption; and

(ii) understands the consequences the adoption may have for any right of inheritance, property, or support the spouse has; and

(3) may contain a waiver of any proceeding for adoption.

SECTION 5-104. JURISDICTION AND VENUE.

(a) The court has jurisdiction over a proceeding for the adoption of an adult or emancipated minor under this [article] if a petitioner lived in this State for at least 90 days immediately preceding the filing of a petition for adoption.

(b) A petition for adoption may be filed in the court in the [county] in which a petitioner lives.

SECTION 5-105. PETITION FOR ADOPTION.

(a) A prospective adoptive parent and an adoptee under this [article] must jointly file a petition for adoption.

(b) The petition must be signed and verified by each petitioner and state:

(1) the full name, age, and place and duration of residence of each petitioner;

(2) the current marital status of each petitioner, including the date and place of marriage, if married;

(3) the full name by which the adoptee is to be known if the petition is granted;

(4) the duration and nature of the relationship between the prospective adoptive parent and the adoptee;

(5) that the prospective adoptive parent and the adoptee desire to assume the legal relationship of parent and child and to have all of the rights and be subject to all of the duties of that relationship;

(6) that the adoptee understands that a consequence of the adoption will be to terminate the adoptee's relationship as the child of an existing parent, but if the adoptive parent is the adoptee's stepparent, the adoption will not affect the adoptee's relationship with a parent who is the stepparent's spouse, but will terminate the adoptee's relationship to the adoptee's other parent, except for the right to inherit from or through that parent;

(7) the name and last known address of any other individual whose consent is required;

(8) the name, age, and last known address of any child of the prospective adoptive parent, including a child previously adopted by the prospective adoptive parent or his or her spouse, and the date and place of the adoption; and

(9) the name, age, and last known address of any living parent or child of the adoptee.

(c) The petitioners shall attach to the petition:

(1) a certified copy of the birth certificate or other evidence of the date and place of birth of the adoptee and the prospective adoptive parent, if available; and

(2) any required consent that has been executed.

SECTION 5-106. NOTICE AND TIME OF HEARING.

(a) Within 30 days after a petition for adoption is filed, the petitioners shall serve notice of hearing the petition upon any individual whose consent to the adoption is required under Section 5-103, and who has not waived notice, by sending a copy of the petition and notice of hearing to the individual at the address stated in the petition, or according to the manner of service provided in Section 3-403.

(b) The court shall set a date and time for hearing the petition, which must be at least 30 days after the notice is served.

SECTION 5-107. DISPOSITIONAL HEARING.

(a) Both petitioners shall appear in person at the hearing unless an appearance is excused for good cause shown. In the latter event an appearance may be made for either or both of them by a lawyer authorized in writing to make the appearance, or a hearing may be conducted by telephone or other electronic medium.

(b) The court shall examine the petitioners, or the lawyer for a petitioner not present in person, and shall grant the petition for adoption if it determines that:

(1) at least 30 days have elapsed since the service of notice of hearing the petition for adoption;

(2) notice has been served, or dispensed with, as to any person whose consent is required under Section 5-103;

(3) every necessary consent, waiver, document, or judicial order has been obtained and filed with the court;

(4) the adoption is for the purpose of creating the relationship of parent and child between the petitioners and the petitioners understand the consequences of the relationship; and

(5) there has been substantial compliance with this [Act].

SECTION 5-108. DECREE OF ADOPTION.

(a) A decree of adoption issued under this [article] must substantially conform to the relevant requirements of Section 3-705 and appeals from a decree, or challenges to it, are governed by Sections 3-706 and 3-707.

(b) The court shall send a copy of the decree to each individual named in the petition at the address stated in the petition.

(c) Within 30 days after a decree of adoption becomes final, the clerk of the court shall prepare a report of the adoption for the [State Registrar of Vital Records], and, if the petitioners have requested it, the report shall instruct the [Registrar] to issue a new birth certificate to the adoptee, as provided in [Article] 3, [Part] 8.

[ARTICLE] 6. RECORDS OF ADOPTION PROCEEDING: RETENTION, CONFIDENTIALITY, AND ACCESS

SECTION 6-101. RECORDS DEFINED. Unless the context requires otherwise, for purposes of this [article], "records" includes all documents, exhibits, and data pertaining to an adoption.

SECTION 6-102. RECORDS CONFIDENTIAL, COURT RECORDS SEALED.

(a) All records, whether on file with the court, or in the possession of an agency, the [Registrar of Vital Records or Statistics], a lawyer, or another provider of professional services in connection with an adoption, are confidential and may not be inspected except as provided in this [Act].

(b) During a proceeding for adoption, records are not open to inspection except as directed by the court.

54

(c) Within 30 days after a decree of adoption becomes final, the clerk of the court shall send to the [Registrar], in addition to the report of adoption required by Section 3-801, a certified copy of any document signed pursuant to Section 2-404(e) and filed in the proceeding for adoption.

(d) All records on file with the court must be retained permanently and sealed for 99 years after the date of the adoptee's birth. Sealed records and indices of the records are not open to inspection by any person except as provided in this [Act].

(e) Any additional information about an adoptee, the adoptee's former parents, and the adoptee's genetic history that is submitted to the court within the 99-year period, must be added to the sealed records of the court. Any additional information that is submitted to an agency, lawyer, or other professional provider of services within the 99-year period must be kept confidential.

SECTION 6-103. RELEASE OF NONIDENTIFYING INFORMATION.

(a) An adoptive parent or guardian of an adoptee, an adoptee who has attained 18 years of age, an emancipated adoptee, a deceased adoptee's direct descendant who has attained 18 years of age, or the parent or guardian of a direct descendant who has not attained 18 years of age may request the court that granted the adoption or the agency that placed the adoptee for adoption, to furnish the nonidentifying information about the adoptee, the adoptee's former parents, and the adoptee's genetic history that has been retained by the court or agency, including the information required by Section 2-106.

(b) The court or agency shall furnish the individual who makes the request with a detailed summary of any relevant report or information that is included in the sealed records of the court or the confidential records of the agency. The summary must exclude identifying information concerning an individual who has not filed a waiver of confidentiality with the court or agency. The department or the court shall prescribe forms and a procedure for summarizing any report or information released under this section.

(c) An individual who is denied access to nonidentifying information to which the individual is entitled under this [article] or Section 2-106 may petition the court for relief.

(d) If a court receives a certified statement from a physician which explains in detail how a health condition may seriously affect the health of the adoptee or a direct descendant of the adoptee, the court shall make a diligent effort to notify an adoptee who has attained 18 years of age, an adoptive parent or guardian of an adoptee who has not attained 18 years of age, or a direct descendant of a deceased adoptee that the nonidentifying information is available and may be requested from the court.

(e) If a court receives a certified statement from a physician which explains in detail why a serious health condition of the adoptee or a direct descendant of the adoptee should be communicated to the adoptee's genetic parent or sibling to enable them to make an informed reproductive decision, the court shall make a diligent effort to notify those individuals that the nonidentifying information is available and may be requested from the court.

(f) If the [Registrar] receives a request or any additional information from an individual pursuant to this section, the [Registrar] shall give the individual the name and address of the court or agency having the records, and if the court or agency is in another State, shall assist the individual in locating the court or agency. The [Registrar] shall prescribe a reasonable procedure for verifying the identity, age, or other relevant characteristics of an individual who requests or furnishes information under this section.

SECTION 6-104. DISCLOSURE OF IDENTIFYING INFORMATION.

(a) Except as otherwise provided in this [article], identifying information about an adoptee's former parent, an adoptee, or an adoptive parent which is contained in records, including original birth certificates, required by this [Act] to be confidential or sealed, may not be disclosed to any person.

(b) Identifying information about an adoptee's former parent must be disclosed by the [Registrar] to an adoptee who has attained 18 years of age, an adoptive parent or guardian of an adoptee who has not attained 18 years of age, a deceased adoptee's direct descendant who has attained 18 years of age, or the parent or guardian of a direct descendant who has not attained 18 years of age if one of these individuals requests the information and:

(1) the adoptee's former parent or, if the former parent is deceased or has been judicially declared incompetent, an adult descendant of the former parent authorizes the disclosure of his or her name, date of birth, or last known address, or other identifying information, either in a document signed pursuant to Section 2-404(e) and filed in the proceeding for adoption or in another signed document filed with the court, an agency, or the [Registrar]; or

(2) the adoptee's former parent authorizes the disclosure of the requested information only if the adoptee, adoptive parent, or direct descendant agrees to release similar identifying information about the adoptee, adoptive parent, or direct descendant and this individual authorizes the disclosure of the information in a signed document kept by the court, an agency, or the [Registrar].

(c) Identifying information about an adoptee or a deceased adoptee's direct descendant must be disclosed by the [Registrar] to an adoptee's former parent if that individual requests the information and:

(1) an adoptee who has attained 18 years of age, an adoptive parent or guardian of an adoptee who has not attained 18 years of age, a deceased adoptee's direct descendant who has attained 18 years of age, or the parent or guardian of a direct descendant who has not attained 18 years of age authorizes the disclosure of the requested information in a signed document kept by the court, an agency, or the [Registrar]; or

(2) one of the individuals listed in paragraph (1) authorizes the disclosure of the requested information only if the adoptee's former parent agrees to release similar information about himself or herself, and the former parent authorizes the disclosure of the information in a signed document kept by the court, an agency, or the [Registrar].

(d) Identifying information about an adult sibling of an adoptee who has attained 18 years of age must be disclosed by the [Registrar] to an adoptee if the sibling is also an adoptee and both the sibling and the adoptee authorize the disclosure.

(e) Subsection (d) does not permit disclosure of a former parent's identity unless that parent has authorized disclosure under this [Act].

SECTION 6-105. ACTION FOR DISCLOSURE OF INFORMATION.

(a) To obtain information not otherwise available under Section 6-103 or 6-104, an adoptee who has attained 18 years of age, an adoptee who has not attained 18 years of age and has the permission of an adoptive parent or guardian, an adoptive parent or guardian of an adoptee who has not attained 18 years of age, a deceased adoptee's direct descendant who has attained 18 years of age, the parent or guardian of a direct descendant who has not attained 18 years of age, or an adoptee's former parent may file a petition in the court to obtain information about another individual described in this section which is contained in records, including original birth certificates, required by this [Act] to be confidential or sealed.

(b) In determining whether to grant a petition under this section, the court shall review the sealed records of the relevant proceeding for adoption and shall make specific findings concerning:

(1) the reason the information is sought;

(2) whether the individual about whom information is sought has filed a signed document described in Section 2-404(e) or 6-104 requesting that his or her identity not be disclosed, or has not filed any document;

(3) whether the individual about whom information is sought is alive;

(4) whether it is possible to satisfy the petitioner's request without disclosing the identity of another individual;

(5) the likely effect of disclosure on the adoptee, the adoptive parents, the adoptee's former parents, and other members of the adoptee's original and adoptive families; and

(6) the age, maturity, and expressed needs of the adoptee.

(c) The court may order the disclosure of the requested information only upon a determination that good cause exists for the release based on the findings required by subsection (b) and a conclusion that:

(1) there is a compelling reason for disclosure of the information; and

(2) the benefit to the petitioner will be greater than the harm to any other individual of disclosing the information.

SECTION 6-106. STATEWIDE REGISTRY. The [Registrar] shall:

(1) establish a statewide confidential registry for receiving, filing, and retaining documents requesting, authorizing, or not authorizing, the release of identifying information;

(2) prescribe and distribute forms or documents on which an individual may request, authorize, or refuse to authorize the release of identifying information;

(3) devise a procedure for releasing identifying information in the [Registrar's] possession upon receipt of an appropriate request and authorization;

(4) cooperate with registries in other States to facilitate the matching of documents filed pursuant to this [article] by individuals in different States; and

(5) announce and publicize to the general public the existence of the registry and the procedure for the consensual release of identifying information.

SECTION 6-107. RELEASE OF ORIGINAL BIRTH CERTIFICATE.

(a) In addition to any copy of an adoptee's original birth certificate authorized for release by a court order issued pursuant to Section 6-105, the [Registrar] shall furnish a copy of the original birth certificate upon the request of an adoptee who has attained 18 years of age, the direct descendant of a deceased adoptee, or an adoptive parent or guardian of an adoptee who has not attained 18 years of age, if the individual who makes the request furnishes a consent to disclosure signed by each individual who was named as a parent on the adoptee's original birth certificate.

(b) When 99 years have elapsed after the date of birth of an adoptee whose original birth certificate is sealed under this [Act], the [Registrar] shall unseal the original certificate and file it with any new or amended certificate that has been issued. The unsealed certificates become public information in accordance with any statute or regulation applicable to the retention and disclosure of records by the [Registrar].

SECTION 6-108. CERTIFICATE OF ADOPTION. Upon the request of an adoptive parent or an adoptee who has attained 18 years of age, the clerk of the court that entered a decree of adoption shall issue a certificate of adoption which states the date and place of adoption, the date of birth of the adoptee, the name of each adoptive parent, and the name of the adoptee as provided in the decree.

SECTION 6-109. DISCLOSURE AUTHORIZED IN COURSE OF EMPLOYMENT. This [article] does not preclude an employee or agent of a court, agency, or the [Registrar] from:

(1) inspecting permanent, confidential, or sealed records for the purpose of discharging any obligation under this [Act];

(2) disclosing the name of the court where a proceeding for adoption occurred, or the name of an agency that placed an adoptee, to an individual described in Sections 6-103 through 6-105, who can verify his or her identity; or

(3) disclosing nonidentifying information contained in confidential or sealed records in accordance with any other applicable state or federal law.

SECTION 6-110. FEE FOR SERVICES. A court, an agency, or the [Registrar] may charge a reasonable fee for services, including copying services, it performs pursuant to this [article].

[ARTICLE] 7. PROHIBITED AND PERMISSIBLE ACTIVITIES IN CONNECTION WITH ADOPTION

SECTION 7-101. PROHIBITED ACTIVITIES IN PLACEMENT.

(a) Except as otherwise provided in [Article] 2, [Part] 1:

(1) a person, other than a parent, guardian, or agency, as specified in Sections 2-101 through 2-103, may not place a minor for adoption or advertise in any public medium that the person knows of a minor who is available for adoption;

(2) a person, other than an agency or an individual with a favorable preplacement evaluation, as required by Sections 2-201 through 2-207, may not advertise in any public medium that the person is willing to accept a minor for adoption;

(3) an individual, other than a relative or stepparent of a minor, who does not have a favorable preplacement evaluation or a court-ordered waiver of the evaluation, or who has an unfavorable evaluation, may not obtain legal or physical custody of a minor for purposes of adoption; and

(4) a person may not place or assist in placing a minor for adoption with an individual, other than a relative or stepparent, unless the person knows that the individual has a favorable preplacement evaluation or a waiver pursuant to Section 2-201.

(b) A person who violates subsection (a) is liable for a [civil penalty] not to exceed [$5,000] for the first violation, and not to exceed [$10,000] for each succeeding violation in an action brought by the [appropriate official]. The court may enjoin from further violations any person who violates subsection (a) and shall inform any appropriate licensing authority or other official of the violation.

SECTION 7-102. UNLAWFUL PAYMENTS RELATED TO ADOPTION.

(a) Except as otherwise provided in Sections 7-103 and 7-104, a person may not pay or give or offer to pay or give to any other person, or request, receive, or accept any money or anything of value, directly or indirectly, for:

(1) the placement of a minor for adoption;

(2) the consent of a parent, a guardian, or an agency to the adoption of a minor; or

(3) the relinquishment of a minor to an agency for the purpose of adoption.

(b) The following persons are liable for a [civil penalty] not to exceed [$5,000] for the first violation, and not to exceed [$10,000] for each succeeding violation in an action brought by the [appropriate official]:

(1) a person who knowingly violates subsection (a);

(2) a person who knowingly makes a false report to the court about a payment prohibited by this section or authorized by Section 7-103 or 7-104; and

(3) a parent or guardian who knowingly receives or accepts a payment authorized by Section 7-103 or 7-104 with the intent not to consent to an adoption or to relinquish a minor for adoption.

(c) The court may enjoin from further violations any person described in subsection (b) and shall inform any appropriate licensing authority or other official of the violation.

SECTION 7-103. LAWFUL PAYMENTS RELATED TO ADOPTION.

(a) Subject to the requirements of Sections 3-702 and 3-703 for an accounting and judicial approval of fees and charges related to an adoption, an adoptive parent, or a person acting on behalf of an adoptive parent, may pay for:

(1) the services of an agency in connection with an adoption;

(2) advertising and similar expenses incurred in locating a minor for adoption;

(3) medical, hospital, nursing, pharmaceutical, travel, or other similar expenses incurred by a mother or her minor child in connection with the birth or any illness of the minor;

(4) counseling services for a parent or a minor for a reasonable time before and after the minor's placement for adoption;

(5) living expenses of a mother for a reasonable time before the birth of her child and for no more than six weeks after the birth;

(6) expenses incurred in ascertaining the information required by Section 2-106;

(7) legal services, court costs, and travel or other administrative expenses connected with an adoption, including any legal services performed for a parent who consents to the adoption of a minor or relinquishes the minor to an agency;

(8) expenses incurred in obtaining a preplacement evaluation and an evaluation during the proceeding for adoption; and

(9) any other service the court finds is reasonably necessary.

(b) A parent or a guardian, a person acting on the parent's or guardian's behalf, or a provider of a service listed in subsection (a), may receive or accept a payment authorized by subsection (a). The payment may not be made contingent on the placement of a minor for adoption, relinquishment of the minor, or consent to the adoption. If the adoption is not completed, a person who is authorized to make a specific payment by subsection (a) is not liable for that payment unless the person has agreed in a signed writing with a provider of a service to make the payment regardless of the outcome of the proceeding for adoption.

SECTION 7-104. CHARGES BY AGENCY. Subject to the requirements of Sections 3-702 and 3-703 for an accounting and judicial approval of fees and charges related to an adoption, an agency may charge or accept a fee or other reasonable compensation from a prospective adoptive parent for:

(1) medical, hospital, nursing, pharmaceutical, travel, or other similar expenses incurred by a mother or her minor child in connection with the birth or any illness of the minor;

(2) a percentage of the annual cost the agency incurs in locating and providing counseling services for minor adoptees, parents, and prospective parents;

(3) living expenses of a mother for a reasonable time before the birth of a child and for no more than six weeks after the birth;

(4) expenses incurred in ascertaining the information required by Section 2-106;

(5) legal services, court costs, and travel or other administrative expenses connected with an adoption, including the legal services performed for a parent who relinquishes a minor child to the agency;

(6) preparation of a preplacement evaluation and an evaluation during the proceeding for adoption; and

(7) any other service the court finds is reasonably necessary.

SECTION 7-105. FAILURE TO DISCLOSE INFORMATION.

(a) A person, other than a parent, who has a duty to furnish the nonidentifying information required by Section 2-106, or authorized for release under [Article] 6, and who intentionally refuses to provide the information is subject to a [civil penalty] not to exceed [$5,000] for the first violation, and not to exceed [$10,000] for each succeeding violation in an action brought by the [appropriate official]. The court may enjoin the person from further violations of the duty to furnish nonidentifying information.

(b) An employee or agent of an agency, the court, or the [State Registrar of Vital Records] who intentionally destroys any information or report compiled pursuant to Section 2-106, or authorized for release under [Article] 6, is guilty of a [misdemeanor] [punishable upon conviction by a fine of not more than [$] or imprisonment for not more than [   ], or both].

(c) In addition to the penalties provided in subsections (a) and (b), an adoptive parent, an adoptee, or any person who is the subject of any information required by Section 2-106, or authorized for release under [Article] 6, may maintain an action for damages or equitable relief against a person, other than a parent who placed a minor for adoption, who fails to perform the duties required by Section 2-106 or [Article] 6.

(d) A prospective adoptive parent who knowingly fails to furnish information or knowingly furnishes false information to an evaluator preparing an evaluation pursuant to [Article] 2, [Part] 2 or [Article] 3, [Part] 6, with the intent to deceive the evaluator, is guilty of a [misdemeanor] [punishable upon conviction by a fine of not more than [$] or imprisonment for not more than [   ], or both].

(e) An evaluator who prepares an evaluation pursuant to [Article] 2, [Part] 2 or [Article] 3, [Part] 6 and who knowingly omits or misrepresents information about the individual being evaluated with the intent to deceive a person authorized under this [Act] to place a minor for adoption is guilty of a [misdemeanor] [punishable upon conviction by a fine of not more than [$] or imprisonment for not more than [   ], or both].

(f) A parent of a minor child who knowingly misidentifies the minor's other parent with an intent to deceive the other parent, an agency, or a prospective adoptive parent is subject to a [civil penalty] not to exceed [$5,000] in an action brought by the [appropriate official].

SECTION 7-106. UNAUTHORIZED DISCLOSURE OF INFORMATION.

(a) Except as authorized in this [Act], a person who furnishes or retains a report or records pursuant to this [Act] may not disclose any identifying or nonidentifying information contained in the report or records.

(b) A person who knowingly gives or offers to give or who accepts or agrees to accept anything of value for an unauthorized disclosure of identifying information made confidential by this [Act] is guilty of a [misdemeanor] [punishable upon conviction by a fine of not more than [$] or imprisonment for not more than [   ], or both,] for the first violation and of a [felony] [punishable upon conviction by a fine of not more than [$] or imprisonment for not more than [   ], or both,] for each succeeding violation.

(c) A person who knowingly gives or offers to give or who accepts or agrees to accept anything of value for an unauthorized disclosure of nonidentifying information made confidential by this [Act] is subject to a [civil penalty] not to exceed [$5,000] for the first violation, and not to exceed [$10,000] for each succeeding violation in an action brought by the [appropriate official].

(d) A person who makes a disclosure, that the person knows is unauthorized, of identifying or nonidentifying information from a report or record made confidential by this [Act] is subject to a [civil penalty] not to exceed [$2,500] for the first violation, and not to exceed [$5,000] for each succeeding violation in an action brought by the [appropriate official].

(e) The court may enjoin from further violations any person who makes or obtains an unauthorized disclosure and shall inform any appropriate licensing authority or other official of the violation.

(f) In addition to the penalties provided in subsections (b) through (e), an individual who is the subject of any of the information contained in a report or records made confidential by this [Act] may maintain an action for damages or equitable relief against any person who makes or obtains, or is likely to make or obtain, an unauthorized disclosure of the information.

(g) Identifying information contained in a report or records required by this [Act] to be kept confidential or sealed may not be disclosed under any other law of this State.

SECTION 7-107. ACTION BY DEPARTMENT. The department may review and investigate compliance with this [Act] and may maintain an action in the [appropriate court] to compel compliance.

[ARTICLE] 8. MISCELLANEOUS PROVISIONS

SECTION 8-101. UNIFORMITY OF APPLICATION AND CONSTRUCTION. This [Act] shall be applied and construed to effectuate its general purpose to make uniform the law with respect to the subject of this [Act] among the States enacting it.

SECTION 8-102. SHORT TITLE. This [Act] may be cited as the Uniform Adoption Act (1994).

SECTION 8-103. SEVERABILITY CLAUSE. If any provision of this [Act] or its application to any person or circumstance is held invalid, the invalidity does not affect other provisions or application of this [Act] which can be given effect without the invalid provision or application, and to this end the provisions of this [Act] are severable.

SECTION 8-104. EFFECTIVE DATE. This [Act] takes effect on ....

SECTION 8-105. REPEALS. The following acts and parts of acts are repealed:

(1) ....

(2) ....

(3) ....

SECTION 8-106. TRANSITIONAL PROVISIONS. A proceeding for adoption commenced before the effective date of this [Act] may be completed under the law in effect at the time the proceeding was commenced.

Uniform Law Commission
The National Conference of Commissioners on Uniform State Laws

Contact Us: **312.450.6600**

Legislative Fact Sheet - Adoption Act (1994)

Act	Adoption Act (1994)
Origin	Completed by the Uniform Law Commissioners in 1994.
Description	The Uniform Adoption Act is a comprehensive codification of adoption law, covering everything from birth parent consent to adoption records confidentiality.
Endorsements	American Bar Association, American Academy of Adoption Attorney
Enactments	Vermont
2011 Introductions	

Appendix D

Florida Adoption Statute (2014)

Select Year: [2014 ∨] [Go]

The 2014 Florida Statutes

<u>Title VI</u>   <u>Chapter 63</u>   <u>View Entire Chapter</u>
CIVIL PRACTICE AND PROCEDURE   ADOPTION

CHAPTER 63
ADOPTION

63.012   **Short title.**—This chapter shall be known as the "Florida Adoption Act."
History.—s. 1, ch. 73-159.

63.022   **Legislative intent.**—

(1)   The Legislature finds that:

(a)   The state has a compelling interest in providing stable and permanent homes for adoptive children in a prompt manner, in preventing the disruption of adoptive placements, and in holding parents accountable for meeting the needs of children.

(b)   An unmarried mother faced with the responsibility of making crucial decisions about the future of a newborn child is entitled to privacy, has the right to make timely and appropriate decisions regarding her future and the future of the child, and is entitled to assurance regarding an adoptive placement.

(c)   Adoptive children have the right to permanence and stability in adoptive placements.

(d)   Adoptive parents have a constitutional privacy interest in retaining custody of a legally adopted child.

(e)   An unmarried biological father has an inchoate interest that acquires constitutional protection only when he demonstrates a timely and full commitment to the responsibilities of parenthood, both during the pregnancy and after the child's birth. The state has a compelling interest in requiring an unmarried biological father to demonstrate that commitment by providing appropriate medical care and financial support and by establishing legal paternity rights in accordance with the requirements of this chapter.

(2) It is the intent of the Legislature that in every adoption, the best interest of the child should govern and be of foremost concern in the court's determination. The court shall make a specific finding as to the best interests of the child in accordance with the provisions of this chapter.

(3) It is the intent of the Legislature to protect and promote the well-being of persons being adopted and their birth and adoptive parents and to provide to all children who can benefit by it a permanent family life, and, whenever appropriate, to maintain sibling groups.

(4) The basic safeguards intended to be provided by this chapter are that:

(a) The minor is legally free for adoption and that all adoptions are handled in accordance with the requirements of law.

(b) The required persons consent to the adoption or the parent-child relationship is terminated by judgment of the court.

(c) The required social studies are completed and the court considers the reports of these studies prior to judgment on adoption petitions.

(d) A sufficient period of time elapses during which the minor has lived within the proposed adoptive home under the guidance of an adoption entity, except stepparent adoptions or adoptions of a relative.

(e) All expenditures by adoption entities or adoptive parents relative to the adoption of a minor are reported to the court and become a permanent record in the file of the adoption proceedings, including, but not limited to, all legal fees and costs, all payments to or on behalf of a birth parent, and all payments to or on behalf of the minor.

(f) Social and medical information concerning the minor and the parents is furnished by the parent when available and filed with the court before a final hearing on a petition to terminate parental rights pending adoption, unless the petitioner is a stepparent or a relative.

(g) A new birth certificate is issued after entry of the adoption judgment.

(h) At the time of the hearing, the court may order temporary substitute care when it determines that the minor is in an unsuitable home.

(i) The records of all proceedings concerning custody and adoption of a minor are confidential and exempt from s. 119.07(1), except as provided in s. 63.162.

(j) The birth parent, the prospective adoptive parent, and the minor receive, at a minimum, the safeguards, guidance, counseling, and supervision required in this chapter.

(k) In all matters coming before the court under this chapter, the court shall enter such orders as it deems necessary and suitable to promote and protect the best interests of the person to be adopted.

(l) In dependency cases initiated by the department, where termination of parental rights occurs, and siblings are separated despite diligent efforts of the department, continuing postadoption communication or contact among the siblings may be ordered by the court if found to be in the best interests of the children.

(5) It is the intent of the Legislature to provide for cooperation between private adoption entities and the Department of Children and Families in matters relating to permanent placement options for children in the care of the department whose birth parents wish to participate in a private adoption plan with a qualified family.

History.—s. 2, ch. 73-159; s. 2, ch. 75-226; s. 13, ch. 77-147; s. 1, ch. 78-190; s. 1, ch. 80-296; s. 1, ch. 82-166; s. 1, ch. 87-16; s. 2, ch. 87-397; s. 18, ch. 90-360; s. 1, ch. 91-99; s. 2, ch. 92-96; s. 22, ch. 96-406; s. 172, ch. 97-101; s. 2, ch. 98-50; s. 6, ch. 2001-3; s. 1, ch. 2003-58; s. 2, ch. 2012-81; s. 25, ch. 2014-19.

63.032 Definitions.—As used in this chapter, the term:

(1) "Abandoned" means a situation in which the parent or person having legal custody of a child, while being able, makes little or no provision for the child's support or makes little or no effort to communicate with the child, which situation is sufficient to evince an intent to reject parental responsibilities. If, in the opinion of the court, the efforts of such parent or person having legal custody of the child to support and communicate with the child are only marginal efforts that do not evince a settled purpose to assume all parental duties, the court may declare the child to be abandoned. In making this decision, the court may consider the conduct of a father towards the child's mother during her pregnancy.

(2) "Adoption" means the act of creating the legal relationship between parent and child where it did not exist, thereby declaring the child to be legally the child of the adoptive parents and their heir at law and entitled to all the rights and privileges and subject to all the obligations of a child born to such adoptive parents in lawful wedlock.

(3) "Adoption entity" means the department, a child-caring agency registered under s. 409.176, an intermediary, a Florida child-placing agency licensed under s. 63.202, or a child-placing agency licensed in another state which is licensed by the department to place children in the State of Florida.

(4) "Adoption plan" means an arrangement made by a birth parent or other individual having a legal right to custody of a minor, born or to be born, with an adoption entity in furtherance of placing the minor for adoption.

(5) "Adult" means a person who is not a minor.

(6) "Agency" means any child-placing agency licensed by the department pursuant to s. 63.202 to place minors for adoption.

(7) "Child" means any unmarried person under the age of 18 years who has not been emancipated by court order.

(8) "Court" means a circuit court of this state and, if the context requires, the court of any state that is empowered to grant petitions for adoption.

(9) "Department" means the Department of Children and Families.

(10) "Intermediary" means an attorney who is licensed or authorized to practice in this state and who is placing or intends to place a child for adoption, including placing children born in another state with citizens of this state or country or placing children born in this state with citizens of another state or country.

(11) "Legal custody" has the meaning ascribed in s. 39.01.

(12) "Parent" means a woman who gives birth to a child and who is not a gestational surrogate as defined in s. 742.13 or a man whose consent to the adoption of the child would be required under s. 63.062(1). If a child has been legally adopted, the term "parent" means the adoptive mother or father of the child. The term does not include an individual whose parental relationship to the child has been legally terminated or an alleged or prospective parent.

(13) "Person" includes a natural person, corporation, government or governmental subdivision or agency, business trust, estate, trust, partnership, or association, and any other legal entity.

(14) "Placement" means the process of a parent or legal guardian surrendering a child for adoption and the prospective adoptive parents receiving and adopting the child and all actions by any adoption entity participating in placing the child.

(15) "Primarily lives and works outside Florida" means that a person lives and works outside this state at least 6 months and 1 day per year, is a member of the military who designates a state other than Florida as his or her place of residence in accordance with the Servicemembers Civil Relief Act,

Pub. L. No. 108-189, or is a citizen of the United States living in a foreign country who designates a state other than Florida as his or her place of residence.

(16)   "Relative" means a person related by blood to the person being adopted within the third degree of consanguinity.

(17)   "Suitability of the intended placement" means the fitness of the intended placement, with primary consideration being given to the best interests of the child.

(18)   "To place" means the process whereby a parent or legal guardian surrenders a child for adoption and the prospective adoptive parents receive and adopt the child, and includes all actions by any person or adoption entity participating in the process.

(19)   "Unmarried biological father" means the child's biological father who is not married to the child's mother at the time of conception or on the date of the birth of the child and who, before the filing of a petition to terminate parental rights, has not been adjudicated by a court of competent jurisdiction to be the legal father of the child or has not filed an affidavit pursuant to s. 382.013(2)(c).

History.—s. 3, ch. 73-159; s. 3, ch. 75-226; s. 14, ch. 77-147; s. 2, ch. 80-296; s. 2, ch. 82-166; s. 1, ch. 84-101; s. 3, ch. 87-397; s. 1, ch. 88-109; ss. 3, 25, ch. 92-96; s. 11, ch. 97-101; s. 7, ch. 2001-3; s. 2, ch. 2003-58; s. 6, ch. 2007-5; s. 3, ch. 2008-151; s. 3, ch. 2012-81; s. 26, ch. 2014-19.

63.037   Proceedings applicable to cases resulting from a termination of parental rights under chapter 39.—A case in which a minor becomes available for adoption after the parental rights of each parent have been terminated by a judgment entered pursuant to chapter 39 shall be governed by s. 39.812 and this chapter. Adoption proceedings initiated under chapter 39 are exempt from the following provisions of this chapter: requirement for search of the Florida Putative Father Registry provided in s. 63.054(7), if a search was previously completed and documentation of the search is contained in the case file; disclosure requirements for the adoption entity provided in s. 63.085(1); general provisions governing termination of parental rights pending adoption provided in s. 63.087; notice and service provisions governing termination of parental rights pending adoption provided in s. 63.088; and procedures for terminating parental rights pending adoption provided in s. 63.089.

History.—s. 8, ch. 2001-3; s. 4, ch. 2008-151; s. 4, ch. 2012-81.

63.039   Duty of adoption entity to prospective adoptive parents; sanctions.—

(1)   An adoption entity placing a minor for adoption has an affirmative duty to follow the requirements of this chapter and specifically the following provisions, which protect and promote the well-being of persons being adopted and their parents and prospective adoptive parents by promoting certainty, finality, and permanency for such persons. The adoption entity must:

(a)   Provide written initial disclosure to the prospective adoptive parent at the time and in the manner required under s. 63.085.

(b)   Provide written disclosure to the parent at the time and in the manner required under s. 63.085.

(c)   When a written consent for adoption is obtained, obtain the consent at the time and in the manner required under s. 63.082.

(d)   When a written consent or affidavit of nonpaternity for adoption is obtained, obtain a consent to adoption or affidavit of nonpaternity that contains the language required under s. 63.062 or s. 63.082.

(e)   Include in the petition to terminate parental rights pending adoption all information required under s. 63.087.

(f)   Obtain and file the affidavit of inquiry pursuant to s. 63.088(4), if the required inquiry is not conducted orally in the presence of the court.

(g)   When the identity of a person whose consent to adoption is necessary under this chapter is known but the location of such a person is unknown, conduct the diligent search and file the affidavit required under s. 63.088(5).

(h)   Serve a petition and notice of hearing to terminate parental rights pending adoption at the time and in the manner prescribed by law.

(i)   Obtain the written waiver of venue required under s. 63.062, if applicable.

(j)   Provide an adoption disclosure statement, as required under s. 63.085(1), to all persons whose consent is required under s. 63.062(1).

(2)   With the exception of an adoption by a relative or stepparent, all adoptions of minor children require the use of an adoption entity that will assume the responsibilities provided in this section.

(3)   If a court finds that a consent to adoption or an affidavit of nonpaternity taken under this chapter was obtained by fraud or duress attributable to the adoption entity, the court may award all sums paid by the prospective adoptive parents or on their behalf in anticipation of or in connection with the adoption. The court may also award reasonable attorney's fees and costs incurred by the prospective adoptive parents in connection with the adoption and any litigation related to placement or adoption of a minor. The court may award reasonable attorney's fees and costs, if any, incurred by the person whose consent or affidavit was obtained by fraud or duress. Any award under this subsection to the prospective adoptive parents or to the person whose consent or affidavit was obtained by fraud or duress must be paid directly to them by the adoption entity or by any applicable insurance carrier on behalf of the adoption entity if the court determines, after an evidentiary hearing held subsequent to the entry of a final order in the underlying termination of parental rights or adoption action, that the actions or failures of the adoption entity directly contributed to the finding of fraud or duress.

(4)   The prevailing party in an action to set aside a judgment terminating parental rights pending adoption or a judgment of adoption may be awarded reasonable attorney's fees and costs pursuant to Rule 1.540(b)(3), Florida Rules of Civil Procedure. An award under this subsection must be paid by the adoption entity or by the applicable insurance carrier on behalf of the adoption entity if the court finds that the acts or omissions of the entity were the basis for the court's order granting relief to the prevailing party.

(5)   Within 30 days after the entry of an order of the court finding sanctionable conduct on the part of an adoption entity, the clerk of the court must forward to:

(a)   The Florida Bar any order that imposes sanctions under this section against an attorney acting as an adoption entity.

(b)   The Department of Children and Families any order that imposes sanctions under this section against a licensed child-placing agency or a child-placing agency licensed in another state that is qualified by the department.

(c)   The entity under s. 409.176 that certifies child-caring agencies any order that imposes sanctions under this section against a child-caring agency registered under s. 409.176.

(d)   The Office of Attorney General any order that imposes sanctions under this section against the department.

History.—s. 9, ch. 2001-3; s. 3, ch. 2003-58; s. 5, ch. 2008-151; s. 5, ch. 2012-81; s. 27, ch. 2014-19.

63.042   Who may be adopted; who may adopt.—

(1)   Any person, a minor or an adult, may be adopted.

(2)   The following persons may adopt:

(a)   A husband and wife jointly;

(b)   An unmarried adult; or

(c)   A married person without the other spouse joining as a petitioner, if the person to be adopted is not his or her spouse, and if:

1.   The other spouse is a parent of the person to be adopted and consents to the adoption; or

2.   The failure of the other spouse to join in the petition or to consent to the adoption is excused by the court for good cause shown or in the best interest of the child.

(3)   No person eligible to adopt under this statute may adopt if that person is a homosexual.

(4)   No person eligible under this section shall be prohibited from adopting solely because such person possesses a physical disability or handicap, unless it is determined by the court or adoption entity that such disability or handicap renders such person incapable of serving as an effective parent.

History.—s. 4, ch. 73-159; s. 1, ch. 77-140; s. 1, ch. 80-194; s. 4, ch. 92-96; s. 336, ch. 95-147; s. 4, ch. 2003-58.

63.0422   Prohibited conditions on adoptions; firearms and ammunition.—An adoption agency or entity, whether public or private, may not:

(1)   Make a determination that a person is unsuitable to adopt based on the lawful possession, storage, or use of a firearm or ammunition by any member of the adoptive home.

(2)   Require an adoptive parent or prospective adoptive parent to disclose information relating to a person's lawful possession, storage, or use of a firearm or ammunition as a condition to adopt.

(3)   Restrict the lawful possession, storage, or use of a firearm or ammunition as a condition for a person to adopt.

History.—s. 1, ch. 2010-6.

63.0423   Procedures with respect to surrendered infants.—

(1)   Upon entry of final judgment terminating parental rights, a licensed child-placing agency that takes physical custody of an infant surrendered at a hospital, emergency medical services station, or fire station pursuant to s. 383.50 assumes responsibility for the medical and other costs associated with the emergency services and care of the surrendered infant from the time the licensed child-placing agency takes physical custody of the surrendered infant.

(2)   The licensed child-placing agency shall immediately seek an order from the circuit court for emergency custody of the surrendered infant. The emergency custody order shall remain in effect until the court orders preliminary approval of placement of the surrendered infant in the prospective home, at which time the prospective adoptive parents become guardians pending termination of parental rights and finalization of adoption or until the court orders otherwise. The guardianship of the prospective adoptive parents shall remain subject to the right of the licensed child-placing agency to remove the surrendered infant from the placement during the pendency of the proceedings if such removal is deemed by the licensed child-placing agency to be in the best interests of the child. The licensed child-placing agency may immediately seek to place the surrendered infant in a prospective adoptive home.

(3)   The licensed child-placing agency that takes physical custody of the surrendered infant shall, within 24 hours thereafter, request assistance from law enforcement officials to investigate and determine, through the Missing Children Information Clearinghouse, the National Center for Missing and Exploited Children, and any other national and state resources, whether the surrendered infant is a missing child.

(4)   The parent who surrenders the infant in accordance with s. 383.50 is presumed to have consented to termination of parental rights, and express consent is not required. Except when there is actual or suspected child abuse or neglect, the licensed child-placing agency shall not attempt to pursue, search for, or notify that parent as provided in s. 63.088 and chapter 49. For purposes of s. 383.50 and this section, an infant who tests positive for illegal drugs, narcotic prescription drugs,

alcohol, or other substances, but shows no other signs of child abuse or neglect, shall be placed in the custody of a licensed child-placing agency. Such a placement does not eliminate the reporting requirement under s. 383.50(7). When the department is contacted regarding an infant properly surrendered under this section and s. 383.50, the department shall provide instruction to contact a licensed child-placing agency and may not take custody of the infant unless reasonable efforts to contact a licensed child-placing agency to accept the infant have not been successful.

(5)   A petition for termination of parental rights under this section may not be filed until 30 days after the date the infant was surrendered in accordance with s. 383.50. A petition for termination of parental rights may not be granted until a parent has failed to reclaim or claim the surrendered infant within the time period specified in s. 383.50.

(6)   A claim of parental rights of the surrendered infant must be made to the entity having legal custody of the surrendered infant or to the circuit court before which proceedings involving the surrendered infant are pending. A claim of parental rights of the surrendered infant may not be made after the judgment to terminate parental rights is entered, except as otherwise provided by subsection (9).

(7)   If a claim of parental rights of a surrendered infant is made before the judgment to terminate parental rights is entered, the circuit court may hold the action for termination of parental rights in abeyance for a period of time not to exceed 60 days.

(a)   The court may order scientific testing to determine maternity or paternity at the expense of the parent claiming parental rights.

(b)   The court shall appoint a guardian ad litem for the surrendered infant and order whatever investigation, home evaluation, and psychological evaluation are necessary to determine what is in the best interests of the surrendered infant.

(c)   The court may not terminate parental rights solely on the basis that the parent left the infant at a hospital, emergency medical services station, or fire station in accordance with s. 383.50.

(d)   The court shall enter a judgment with written findings of fact and conclusions of law.

(8)   Within 7 business days after recording the judgment, the clerk of the court shall mail a copy of the judgment to the department, the petitioner, and any person whose consent was required, if known. The clerk shall execute a certificate of each mailing.

(9)(a)   A judgment terminating parental rights pending adoption is voidable, and any later judgment of adoption of that minor is voidable, if, upon the motion of a parent, the court finds that a person knowingly gave false information that prevented the parent from timely making known his or her desire to assume parental responsibilities toward the minor or from exercising his or her parental rights. A motion under this subsection must be filed with the court originally entering the judgment. The motion must be filed within a reasonable time but not later than 1 year after the entry of the judgment terminating parental rights.

(b)   No later than 30 days after the filing of a motion under this subsection, the court shall conduct a preliminary hearing to determine what contact, if any, will be permitted between a parent and the child pending resolution of the motion. Such contact may be allowed only if it is requested by a parent who has appeared at the hearing and the court determines that it is in the best interests of the child. If the court orders contact between a parent and the child, the order must be issued in writing as expeditiously as possible and must state with specificity any provisions regarding contact with persons other than those with whom the child resides.

(c)   The court may not order scientific testing to determine the paternity or maternity of the minor until such time as the court determines that a previously entered judgment terminating the parental rights of that parent is voidable pursuant to paragraph (a), unless all parties agree that such testing is in the best interests of the child. Upon the filing of test results establishing that person's maternity or paternity of the surrendered infant, the court may order visitation only if it appears to be in the best interests of the child.

(d) Within 45 days after the preliminary hearing, the court shall conduct a final hearing on the motion to set aside the judgment and shall enter its written order as expeditiously as possible thereafter.

(10)   Except to the extent expressly provided in this section, proceedings initiated by a licensed child-placing agency for the termination of parental rights and subsequent adoption of a newborn left at a hospital, emergency medical services station, or fire station in accordance with s. 383.50 shall be conducted pursuant to this chapter.

History.—s. 5, ch. 2000-188; s. 2, ch. 2001-53; s. 5, ch. 2003-58; s. 3, ch. 2008-90; s. 6, ch. 2012-81.

63.0425   Grandparent's right to notice.—

(1)   If a child has lived with a grandparent for at least 6 months within the 24-month period immediately preceding the filing of a petition for termination of parental rights pending adoption, the adoption entity shall provide notice to that grandparent of the hearing on the petition.

(2)   This section does not apply if the placement for adoption is the result of the death of the child's parent and a different preference is stated in the parent's will.

(3)   This section does not apply in stepparent adoptions.

(4)   This section does not contravene the provisions of s. 63.142(4).

History.—s. 1, ch. 87-397; s. 10, ch. 2001-3; s. 6, ch. 2003-58; s. 6, ch. 2008-151.

63.0427   Agreements for continued communication or contact between adopted child and siblings, parents, and other relatives.—

(1)   A child whose parents have had their parental rights terminated and whose custody has been awarded to the department pursuant to s. 39.811, and who is the subject of a petition for adoption under this chapter, shall have the right to have the court consider the appropriateness of postadoption communication or contact, including, but not limited to, visits, written correspondence, or telephone calls, with his or her siblings or, upon agreement of the adoptive parents, with the parents who have had their parental rights terminated or other specified biological relatives. The court shall consider the following in making such determination:

(a)   Any orders of the court pursuant to s. 39.811(7).

(b)   Recommendations of the department, the foster parents if other than the adoptive parents, and the guardian ad litem.

(c)   Statements of the prospective adoptive parents.

(d)   Any other information deemed relevant and material by the court.

If the court determines that the child's best interests will be served by postadoption communication or contact, the court shall so order, stating the nature and frequency of the communication or contact. This order shall be made a part of the final adoption order, but the continuing validity of the adoption may not be contingent upon such postadoption communication or contact and the ability of the adoptive parents and child to change residence within or outside the State of Florida may not be impaired by such communication or contact.

(2)   Notwithstanding s. 63.162, the adoptive parent may, at any time, petition for review of a communication or contact order entered pursuant to subsection (1), if the adoptive parent believes that

the best interests of the adopted child are being compromised, and the court may order the communication or contact to be terminated or modified, as the court deems to be in the best interests of the adopted child; however, the court may not increase contact between the adopted child and siblings, birth parents, or other relatives without the consent of the adoptive parent or parents. As part of the review process, the court may order the parties to engage in mediation. The department shall not be required to be a party to such review.

History.—s. 3, ch. 98-50; s. 24, ch. 99-2; s. 52, ch. 99-193; s. 11, ch. 2001-3; s. 7, ch. 2003-58; s. 7, ch. 2012-81.

63.043   Mandatory screening or testing for sickle-cell trait prohibited.—No person, firm, corporation, unincorporated association, state agency, unit of local government, or any public or private entity shall require screening or testing for the sickle-cell trait as a condition for becoming eligible for adoption if otherwise eligible for adoption under the laws of this state.

History.—s. 4, ch. 78-35; s. 8, ch. 2003-58.

63.052   Guardians designated; proof of commitment.—

(1)   For minors who have been placed for adoption with an adoption entity, other than an intermediary, such adoption entity shall be the guardian of the person of the minor and has the responsibility and authority to provide for the needs and welfare of the minor.

(2)   For minors who have been voluntarily surrendered to an intermediary through an execution of a consent to adoption, the intermediary shall be responsible for the minor until the time a court orders preliminary approval of placement of the minor in the prospective adoptive home, after which time the prospective adoptive parents shall become guardians pending finalization of adoption, subject to the intermediary's right and responsibility to remove the child from the prospective adoptive home if the removal is deemed by the intermediary to be in the best interests of the child. The intermediary may not remove the child without a court order unless the child is in danger of imminent harm. The intermediary does not become responsible for the minor child's medical bills that were incurred before taking physical custody of the child after the execution of adoption consents. Prior to the court's entry of an order granting preliminary approval of the placement, the intermediary shall have the responsibility and authority to provide for the needs and welfare of the minor. A minor may not be placed in a prospective adoptive home until that home has received a favorable preliminary home study, as provided in s. 63.092, completed and approved within 1 year before such placement in the prospective home. The provisions of s. 627.6578 shall remain in effect notwithstanding the guardianship provisions in this section.

(3)   If a minor is surrendered to an adoption entity for subsequent adoption and a suitable prospective adoptive home is not available pursuant to s. 63.092 at the time the minor is surrendered to the adoption entity, the minor must be placed in a licensed foster care home, with a person or family that has received a favorable preliminary home study pursuant to subsection (2), or with a relative until a suitable prospective adoptive home is available.

(4)   If a minor is voluntarily surrendered to an adoption entity for subsequent adoption and the adoption does not become final within 180 days after termination of parental rights, the adoption entity must report to the court on the status of the minor and the court may at that time proceed under s. 39.701 or take action reasonably necessary to protect the best interest of the minor.

(5)   The recital in a written consent, answer, or recommendation filed by an adoption entity that the minor has been permanently committed to the adoption entity or that the adoption entity is duly licensed shall be prima facie proof of such commitment. A consent for adoption signed by an adoption entity need not comply with s. 63.082.

(6)   Unless otherwise authorized by law or ordered by the court, the department is not responsible for expenses incurred by other adoption entities participating in a placement of a minor.

(7)   The court retains jurisdiction of a minor who has been placed for adoption until the adoption is final. After a minor is placed with an adoption entity or prospective adoptive parent, the court may review the status of the minor and the progress toward permanent adoptive placement.

History.—s. 5, ch. 73-159; s. 15, ch. 77-147; s. 3, ch. 80-296; s. 5, ch. 92-96; s. 125, ch. 98-403; s. 12, ch. 2001-3; s. 9, ch. 2003-58; s. 8, ch. 2012-81.

63.053   Rights and responsibilities of an unmarried biological father; legislative findings.—

(1)   In enacting the provisions contained in this chapter, the Legislature prescribes the conditions for determining whether an unmarried biological father's actions are sufficiently prompt and substantial so as to require protection of a constitutional right. If an unmarried biological father fails to take the actions that are available to him to establish a relationship with his child, his parental interest may be lost entirely, or greatly diminished, by his failure to timely comply with the available legal steps to substantiate a parental interest.

(2)   The Legislature finds that the interests of the state, the mother, the child, and the adoptive parents described in this chapter outweigh the interest of an unmarried biological father who does not take action in a timely manner to establish and demonstrate a relationship with his child in accordance with the requirements of this chapter. An unmarried biological father has the primary responsibility to protect his rights and is presumed to know that his child may be adopted without his consent unless he strictly complies with this chapter and demonstrates a prompt and full commitment to his parental responsibilities.

(3)   The Legislature finds that a birth mother and a birth father have a right of privacy.

History.—s. 10, ch. 2003-58; s. 9, ch. 2012-81.

63.054   Actions required by an unmarried biological father to establish parental rights; Florida Putative Father Registry.—

(1)   In order to preserve the right to notice and consent to an adoption under this chapter, an unmarried biological father must, as the "registrant," file a notarized claim of paternity form with the Florida Putative Father Registry maintained by the Office of Vital Statistics of the Department of Health which includes confirmation of his willingness and intent to support the child for whom paternity is claimed in accordance with state law. The claim of paternity may be filed at any time before the child's birth, but may not be filed after the date a petition is filed for termination of parental rights. In each proceeding for termination of parental rights, the petitioner must submit to the Office of Vital Statistics a copy of the petition for termination of parental rights or a document executed by the clerk of the court showing the style of the case, the names of the persons whose rights are sought to be terminated, and the date and time of the filing of the petition. The Office of Vital Statistics may not record a claim of paternity after the date a petition for termination of parental rights is filed. The failure of an unmarried biological father to file a claim of paternity with the registry before the date a petition for termination of parental rights is filed also bars him from filing a paternity claim under chapter 742.

(a)   An unmarried biological father is excepted from the time limitations for filing a claim of paternity with the registry or for filing a paternity claim under chapter 742, if:

1.   The mother identifies him to the adoption entity as a potential biological father by the date she executes a consent for adoption; and

2. He is served with a notice of intended adoption plan pursuant to s. 63.062(3) and the 30-day mandatory response date is later than the date the petition for termination of parental rights is filed with the court.

(b) If an unmarried biological father falls within the exception provided by paragraph (a), the petitioner shall also submit to the Office of Vital Statistics a copy of the notice of intended adoption plan and proof of service of the notice on the potential biological father.

(c) An unmarried biological father who falls within the exception provided by paragraph (a) may not file a claim of paternity with the registry or a paternity claim under chapter 742 after the 30-day mandatory response date to the notice of intended adoption plan has expired. The Office of Vital Statistics may not record a claim of paternity 30 days after service of the notice of intended adoption plan.

(2) By filing a claim of paternity form with the Office of Vital Statistics, the registrant expressly consents to submit to and pay for DNA testing upon the request of any party, the registrant, or the adoption entity with respect to the child referenced in the claim of paternity.

(3) The Office of Vital Statistics of the Department of Health shall adopt by rule the appropriate claim of paternity form in English, Spanish, and Creole in order to facilitate the registration of an unmarried biological father with the Florida Putative Father Registry and shall, within existing resources, make these forms available through local offices of the Department of Health and the Department of Children and Families, the Internet websites of those agencies, and the offices of the clerks of the circuit court. The claim of paternity form shall be signed by the unmarried biological father and must include his name, address, date of birth, and physical description. In addition, the registrant shall provide, if known, the name, address, date of birth, and physical description of the mother; the date, place, and location of conception of the child; and the name, date, and place of birth of the child or estimated date of birth of the expected minor child, if known. The claim of paternity form shall be signed under oath by the registrant.

(4) Upon initial registration, or at any time thereafter, the registrant may designate a physical address other than his residential address for sending any communication regarding his registration. Similarly, upon initial registration, or at any time thereafter, the registrant may designate, in writing, an agent or representative to receive any communication on his behalf and receive service of process. The agent or representative must file an acceptance of the designation, in writing, in order to receive notice or service of process. The failure of the designated representative or agent of the registrant to deliver or otherwise notify the registrant of receipt of correspondence from the Florida Putative Father Registry is at the registrant's own risk and may not serve as a valid defense based upon lack of notice.

(5) The registrant may, at any time prior to the birth of the child for whom paternity is claimed, execute a notarized written revocation of the claim of paternity previously filed with the Florida Putative Father Registry, and upon receipt of such revocation, the claim of paternity shall be deemed null and void. If a court determines that a registrant is not the father of the minor or has no parental rights, the court shall order the Department of Health to remove the registrant's name from the registry.

(6) It is the obligation of the registrant or, if designated under subsection (4), his designated agent or representative to notify and update the Office of Vital Statistics of any change of address or change in the designation of an agent or representative. The failure of a registrant, or designated agent or representative, to report any such change is at the registrant's own risk and may not serve as a defense based upon lack of notice, and the adoption entity or petitioner has no further obligation to search for

the registrant unless the person petitioning for termination of parental rights or adoption has actual notice of the registrant's address and whereabouts from another source.

(7)   In each proceeding for termination of parental rights or each adoption proceeding in which parental rights are being terminated simultaneously with entry of the final judgment of adoption, as in a stepparent and relative adoption filed under this chapter, the petitioner must contact the Office of Vital Statistics by submitting an application for a search of the Florida Putative Father Registry. The petitioner must provide the same information, if known, on the search application form that the registrant furnished under subsection (3). Thereafter, the Office of Vital Statistics shall issue a certificate signed by the State Registrar certifying:

(a)   The identity and contact information, if any, for each registered unmarried biological father whose information matches the search request sufficiently so that such person may be considered a possible father of the subject child; or

(b)   That a diligent search has been made of the registrants who may be the unmarried biological father of the subject child and that no matching registration has been located in the registry.

The certificate must be filed with the court in the proceeding to terminate parental rights or the adoption proceeding. If a termination of parental rights and an adoption proceeding are being adjudicated separately, the Florida Putative Father Registry need only be searched for the termination of parental rights proceeding.

(8)   If an unmarried biological father does not know the county in which the birth mother resides, gave birth, or intends to give birth, he may initiate an action in any county in the state, subject to the birth mother's right to change venue to the county where she resides.

(9)   The Department of Health shall establish and maintain a Florida Putative Father Registry through its Office of Vital Statistics, in accordance with the requirements of this section. The Department of Health may charge a nominal fee to cover the costs of filing and indexing the Florida Putative Father Registry and the costs of searching the registry.

(10)   The Department of Health shall, within existing resources, prepare and adopt by rule application forms for initiating a search of the Florida Putative Father Registry and shall make those forms available through the local offices of the Department of Health and the Department of Children and Families and the offices of the clerks of the circuit court.

(11)   The Department of Health shall produce and distribute, within existing resources, a pamphlet or publication informing the public about the Florida Putative Father Registry and which is printed in English, Spanish, and Creole. The pamphlet shall indicate the procedures for voluntary acknowledgment of paternity, the consequences of acknowledgment of paternity, the consequences of failure to acknowledge paternity, and the address of the Florida Putative Father Registry. Such pamphlets or publications shall be made available for distribution at all offices of the Department of Health and the Department of Children and Families and shall be included in health class curricula taught in public and charter schools in this state. The Department of Health shall also provide such pamphlets or publications to hospitals, adoption entities, libraries, medical clinics, schools, universities, and providers of child-related services, upon request. In cooperation with the Department of Highway Safety and Motor Vehicles, each person applying for a Florida driver license, or renewal thereof, and each person applying for a Florida identification card shall be offered the pamphlet or publication informing the public about the Florida Putative Father Registry.

(12)   The Department of Health shall, within existing resources, provide additional information about the Florida Putative Father Registry and its services to the public in English, Spanish, and Creole using public service announcements, Internet websites, and such other means as it deems appropriate.

(13)   The filing of a claim of paternity with the Florida Putative Father Registry does not excuse or waive the obligation of a petitioner to comply with the requirements of s. 63.088(4) for conducting a diligent search and required inquiry with respect to the identity of an unmarried biological father or legal father which are set forth in this chapter.

(14)   The Office of Vital Statistics of the Department of Health is authorized to adopt rules to implement this section.

History.—s. 11, ch. 2003-58; s. 2, ch. 2006-265; s. 7, ch. 2008-151; s. 10, ch. 2012-81; s. 28, ch. 2014-19.

63.0541   Public records exemption for the Florida Putative Father Registry.—

(1)   All information contained in the Florida Putative Father Registry is confidential and exempt from s. 119.07(1) and s. 24(a), Art. I of the State Constitution.

(2)   Information made confidential and exempt by this section shall be disclosed to:

(a)   An adoption entity, upon the filing of a request for a diligent search of the Florida Putative Father Registry in connection with the planned adoption of a child.

(b)   The registrant unmarried biological father, upon receipt of a notarized request for a copy of his registry entry only.

(c)   The birth mother, upon receipt of a notarized request for a copy of any registry entry in which she is identified as the birth mother.

(d)   The court, upon issuance of a court order concerning a petitioner acting pro se in an action under this chapter.

(3)   The database comprising the Florida Putative Father Registry shall remain separate from all other databases.

History.—ss. 1, 2, ch. 2003-56; ss. 1, 2, ch. 2008-168.

63.062   Persons required to consent to adoption; affidavit of nonpaternity; waiver of venue.—

(1)   Unless supported by one or more of the grounds enumerated under s. 63.089(3), a petition to terminate parental rights pending adoption may be granted only if written consent has been executed as provided in s. 63.082 after the birth of the minor or notice has been served under s. 63.088 to:

(a)   The mother of the minor.

(b)   The father of the minor, if:

1.   The minor was conceived or born while the father was married to the mother;

2.   The minor is his child by adoption;

3.   The minor has been adjudicated by the court to be his child before the date a petition for termination of parental rights is filed;

4.   He has filed an affidavit of paternity pursuant to s. 382.013(2)(c) or he is listed on the child's birth certificate before the date a petition for termination of parental rights is filed; or

5.   In the case of an unmarried biological father, he has acknowledged in writing, signed in the presence of a competent witness, that he is the father of the minor, has filed such acknowledgment with the Office of Vital Statistics of the Department of Health within the required timeframes, and has complied with the requirements of subsection (2).

The status of the father shall be determined at the time of the filing of the petition to terminate parental rights and may not be modified, except as otherwise provided in s. 63.0423(9)(a), for purposes of his obligations and rights under this chapter by acts occurring after the filing of the petition to terminate parental rights.

(c)   The minor, if 12 years of age or older, unless the court in the best interest of the minor dispenses with the minor's consent.

(d)   Any person lawfully entitled to custody of the minor if required by the court.

(e)   The court having jurisdiction to determine custody of the minor, if the person having physical custody of the minor does not have authority to consent to the adoption.

(2)   In accordance with subsection (1), the consent of an unmarried biological father shall be necessary only if the unmarried biological father has complied with the requirements of this subsection.

(a)1.   With regard to a child who is placed with adoptive parents more than 6 months after the child's birth, an unmarried biological father must have developed a substantial relationship with the child, taken some measure of responsibility for the child and the child's future, and demonstrated a full commitment to the responsibilities of parenthood by providing reasonable and regular financial support to the child in accordance with the unmarried biological father's ability, if not prevented from doing so by the person or authorized agency having lawful custody of the child, and either:

a.   Regularly visited the child at least monthly, when physically and financially able to do so and when not prevented from doing so by the birth mother or the person or authorized agency having lawful custody of the child; or

b.   Maintained regular communication with the child or with the person or agency having the care or custody of the child, when physically or financially unable to visit the child or when not prevented from doing so by the birth mother or person or authorized agency having lawful custody of the child.

2.   An unmarried biological father who openly lived with the child for at least 6 months within the 1-year period following the birth of the child and immediately preceding placement of the child with adoptive parents and who openly held himself out to be the father of the child during that period shall be deemed to have developed a substantial relationship with the child and to have otherwise met the requirements of this paragraph.

(b)   With regard to a child who is 6 months of age or younger at the time the child is placed with the adoptive parents, an unmarried biological father must have demonstrated a full commitment to his parental responsibility by having performed all of the following acts prior to the time the mother executes her consent for adoption:

1.   Filed a notarized claim of paternity form with the Florida Putative Father Registry within the Office of Vital Statistics of the Department of Health, which form shall be maintained in the confidential registry established for that purpose and shall be considered filed when the notice is entered in the registry of notices from unmarried biological fathers.

2.   Upon service of a notice of an intended adoption plan or a petition for termination of parental rights pending adoption, executed and filed an affidavit in that proceeding stating that he is personally fully able and willing to take responsibility for the child, setting forth his plans for care of the child, and agreeing to a court order of child support and a contribution to the payment of living and medical expenses incurred for the mother's pregnancy and the child's birth in accordance with his ability to pay.

3.   If he had knowledge of the pregnancy, paid a fair and reasonable amount of the living and medical expenses incurred in connection with the mother's pregnancy and the child's birth, in accordance with his financial ability and when not prevented from doing so by the birth mother or person or authorized agency having lawful custody of the child. The responsibility of the unmarried biological father to provide financial assistance to the birth mother during her pregnancy and to the child after birth is not abated because support is being provided to the birth mother or child by the

adoption entity, a prospective adoptive parent, or a third party, nor does it serve as a basis to excuse the birth father's failure to provide support.

(c)   The mere fact that a father expresses a desire to fulfill his responsibilities towards his child which is unsupported by acts evidencing this intent does not meet the requirements of this section.

(d)   The petitioner shall file with the court a certificate from the Office of Vital Statistics stating that a diligent search has been made of the Florida Putative Father Registry of notices from unmarried biological fathers described in subparagraph (b)1. and that no filing has been found pertaining to the father of the child in question or, if a filing is found, stating the name of the putative father and the time and date of filing. That certificate shall be filed with the court prior to the entry of a final judgment of termination of parental rights.

(e)   An unmarried biological father who does not comply with each of the conditions provided in this subsection is deemed to have waived and surrendered any rights in relation to the child, including the right to notice of any judicial proceeding in connection with the adoption of the child, and his consent to the adoption of the child is not required.

(3)   Pursuant to chapter 48, an adoption entity shall serve a notice of intended adoption plan upon any known and locatable unmarried biological father who is identified to the adoption entity by the mother by the date she signs her consent for adoption if the child is 6 months of age or less at the time the consent is executed. Service of the notice of intended adoption plan is not required when the unmarried biological father signs a consent for adoption or an affidavit of nonpaternity or when the child is more than 6 months of age at the time of the execution of the consent by the mother. The notice may be served at any time before the child's birth or before placing the child in the adoptive home. The recipient of the notice may waive service of process by executing a waiver and acknowledging receipt of the plan. The notice of intended adoption plan must specifically state that if the unmarried biological father desires to contest the adoption plan he must, within 30 days after service, file with the court a verified response that contains a pledge of commitment to the child in substantial compliance with subparagraph (2)(b)2. and a claim of paternity form with the Office of Vital Statistics, and must provide the adoption entity with a copy of the verified response filed with the court and the claim of paternity form filed with the Office of Vital Statistics. The notice must also include instructions for submitting a claim of paternity form to the Office of Vital Statistics and the address to which the claim must be sent. If the party served with the notice of intended adoption plan is an entity whose consent is required, the notice must specifically state that the entity must file, within 30 days after service, a verified response setting forth a legal basis for contesting the intended adoption plan, specifically addressing the best interests of the child.

(a)   If the unmarried biological father or entity whose consent is required fails to timely and properly file a verified response with the court and, in the case of an unmarried biological father, a claim of paternity form with the Office of Vital Statistics, the court shall enter a default judgment against the unmarried biological father or entity and the consent of that unmarried biological father or entity shall no longer be required under this chapter and shall be deemed to have waived any claim of rights to the child. To avoid an entry of a default judgment, within 30 days after receipt of service of the notice of intended adoption plan:

1.   The unmarried biological father must:

a.   File a claim of paternity with the Florida Putative Father Registry maintained by the Office of Vital Statistics;

b.   File a verified response with the court which contains a pledge of commitment to the child in substantial compliance with subparagraph (2)(b)2.; and

c.   Provide support for the birth mother and the child.

2.   The entity whose consent is required must file a verified response setting forth a legal basis for contesting the intended adoption plan, specifically addressing the best interests of the child.

(b)   If the mother identifies a potential unmarried biological father within the timeframes required by the statute, whose location is unknown, the adoption entity shall conduct a diligent search pursuant to s. 63.088. If, upon completion of a diligent search, the potential unmarried biological father's location remains unknown and a search of the Florida Putative Father Registry fails to reveal a match, the adoption entity shall request in the petition for termination of parental rights pending adoption that the court declare the diligent search to be in compliance with s. 63.088, that the adoption entity has no further obligation to provide notice to the potential unmarried biological father, and that the potential unmarried biological father's consent to the adoption is not required.

(4)   Any person whose consent is required under paragraph (1)(b), or any other man, may execute an irrevocable affidavit of nonpaternity in lieu of a consent under this section and by doing so waives notice to all court proceedings after the date of execution. An affidavit of nonpaternity must be executed as provided in s. 63.082. The affidavit of nonpaternity may be executed prior to the birth of the child. The person executing the affidavit must receive disclosure under s. 63.085 prior to signing the affidavit. For purposes of this chapter, an affidavit of nonpaternity is sufficient if it contains a specific denial of parental obligations and does not need to deny the existence of a biological relationship.

(5)   A person who signs a consent to adoption or an affidavit of nonpaternity must be given reasonable notice of his or her right to select a person who does not have an employment, professional, or personal relationship with the adoption entity or the prospective adoptive parents to be present when the consent to adoption or affidavit of nonpaternity is executed and to sign the consent or affidavit as a witness.

(6)   The petitioner must make good faith and diligent efforts as provided under s. 63.088 to notify, and obtain written consent from, the persons required to consent to adoption under this section.

(7)   If parental rights to the minor have previously been terminated, the adoption entity with which the minor has been placed for subsequent adoption may provide consent to the adoption. In such case, no other consent is required. The consent of the department shall be waived upon a determination by the court that such consent is being unreasonably withheld and if the petitioner has filed with the court a favorable preliminary adoptive home study as required under s. 63.092.

(8)   A petition to adopt an adult may be granted if:

(a)   Written consent to adoption has been executed by the adult and the adult's spouse, if any, unless the spouse's consent is waived by the court for good cause.

(b)   Written notice of the final hearing on the adoption has been provided to the parents, if any, or proof of service of process has been filed, showing notice has been served on the parents as provided in this chapter.

(9)   A petition for termination of parental rights must be filed in the appropriate county as determined under s. 63.087(2). If a parent whose consent is required objects to venue in the county where the action was filed, the court may transfer venue to a proper venue consistent with this chapter and chapter 47 unless the objecting parent has previously executed a waiver of venue.

(10)   The waiver of venue must be a separate document containing no consents, disclosures, or other information unrelated to venue.

History.—s. 6, ch. 73-159; s. 4, ch. 75-226; s. 16, ch. 77-147; s. 1, ch. 77-446; s. 6, ch. 92-96; s. 11, ch. 95-280; s. 84, ch. 97-237; s. 13, ch. 2001-3; s. 12, ch. 2003-58; s. 2, ch. 2004-389; s. 3, ch. 2006-265; s. 8, ch. 2008-151; s. 11, ch. 2012-81.

63.063   Responsibility of parents for actions; fraud or misrepresentation; contesting termination of parental rights and adoption.—

(1)   Each parent of a child conceived or born outside of marriage is responsible for his or her actions and is not excused from strict compliance with this chapter based upon any action, statement, or omission of the other parent or a third party, except as provided in s. 63.062(2)(a).

(2)   Any person injured by a fraudulent representation or action in connection with an adoption may pursue civil or criminal penalties as provided by law. A fraudulent representation is not a defense to compliance with the requirements of this chapter and is not a basis for dismissing a petition for termination of parental rights or a petition for adoption, for vacating an adoption decree, or for granting custody to the offended party. Custody and adoption determinations must be based on the best interests of the child in accordance with s. 61.13.

(3)   The Legislature finds no way to remove all risk of fraud or misrepresentation in adoption proceedings and has provided a method for absolute protection of an unmarried biological father's rights through compliance with this chapter. In balancing the rights and interests of the state and of all parties affected by fraud, including the child, the adoptive parents, and the unmarried biological father, the Legislature has determined that the unmarried biological father is in the best position to prevent or ameliorate the effects of fraud and, therefore, has the burden of preventing fraud.

(4)   The Legislature finds that an unmarried biological father who resides in another state may not, in every circumstance, be reasonably presumed to know and comply with the requirements of this chapter. Therefore, if all of the following requirements have been met, an unmarried biological father may contest a termination of parental rights or subsequent adoption and, before entry of the final judgment of adoption, assert his interest in the child. Following such assertion, the court may proceed with an evidentiary hearing if:

(a)   The unmarried biological father resides and has resided in another state where the unmarried mother was also located or resided.

(b)   The unmarried mother left that state without notifying or informing the unmarried biological father that she could be located in this state.

(c)   The unmarried biological father has, through every reasonable means, attempted to locate the mother but does not know or have reason to know that the mother is residing in this state.

(d)   The unmarried biological father has substantially complied with the requirements of the state where the mother previously resided or was located in order to protect and preserve his parental interest and rights with regard to the child.

History.—s. 13, ch. 2003-58; s. 9, ch. 2008-151; s. 12, ch. 2012-81.

63.064   Persons whose consent to an adoption may be waived.—The court may waive the consent of the following individuals to an adoption:

(1)   A parent who has deserted a child without means of identification or who has abandoned a child.

(2)   A parent whose parental rights have been terminated by order of a court of competent jurisdiction.

(3)   A parent who has been judicially declared incompetent and for whom restoration of competency is medically improbable.

(4)   A legal guardian or lawful custodian of the person to be adopted, other than a parent, who has failed to respond in writing to a request for consent for a period of 60 days or who, after examination of his or her written reasons for withholding consent, is found by the court to be withholding his or her consent unreasonably.

(5)   The spouse of the person to be adopted, if the failure of the spouse to consent to the adoption is excused by reason of prolonged and unexplained absence, unavailability, incapacity, or circumstances that are found by the court to constitute unreasonable withholding of consent.

History.—s. 14, ch. 2003-58.

63.082   Execution of consent to adoption or affidavit of nonpaternity; family social and medical history; revocation of consent.—

(1)(a)   Consent to an adoption or an affidavit of nonpaternity shall be executed as follows:

1.   If by the person to be adopted, by oral or written statement in the presence of the court or by being acknowledged before a notary public and in the presence of two witnesses.

2.   If by an agency, by affidavit from its authorized representative.

3.   If by any other person, in the presence of the court or by affidavit acknowledged before a notary public and in the presence of two witnesses.

4.   If by a court, by an appropriate order or certificate of the court.

(b)   A minor parent has the power to consent to the adoption of his or her child and has the power to relinquish his or her control or custody of the child to an adoption entity. Such consent or relinquishment is valid and has the same force and effect as a consent or relinquishment executed by an adult parent. A minor parent, having executed a consent or relinquishment, may not revoke that consent upon reaching the age of majority or otherwise becoming emancipated.

(c)   A consent or an affidavit of nonpaternity executed by a minor parent who is 14 years of age or younger must be witnessed by a parent, legal guardian, or court-appointed guardian ad litem.

(d)   The notice and consent provisions of this chapter as they relate to the father of a child do not apply in cases in which the child is conceived as a result of a violation of the criminal laws of this or another state or country, including, but not limited to, sexual battery, unlawful sexual activity with certain minors under s. 794.05, lewd acts perpetrated upon a minor, or incest.

(2)   A consent that does not name or otherwise identify the adopting parent is valid if the consent contains a statement by the person consenting that the consent was voluntarily executed and that identification of the adopting parent is not required for granting the consent.

(3)(a)   The department must provide a family social and medical history form to an adoption entity that intends to place a child for adoption. Forms containing, at a minimum, the same information as the forms promulgated by the department must be attached to the petition to terminate parental rights pending adoption and must contain biological and sociological information or information as to the family medical history regarding the minor and the parents. This form is not required for adoptions of relatives, adult adoptions, or adoptions of stepchildren, unless parental rights are being or were terminated pursuant to chapter 39. The information must be filed with the court in the termination of parental rights proceeding.

(b)   A good faith and diligent effort must be made to have each parent whose identity is known and whose consent is required interviewed by a representative of the adoption entity before the consent is executed. A summary of each interview, or a statement that the parent is unidentified, unlocated, or unwilling or unavailable to be interviewed, must be filed with the petition to terminate parental rights pending adoption. The interview may be excused by the court for good cause. This interview is not required for adoptions of relatives, adult adoptions, or adoptions of stepchildren, unless parental rights are being or were terminated pursuant to chapter 39.

(c)   If any person who is required to consent is unavailable because the person cannot be located, an affidavit of diligent search required under s. 63.088 shall be filed.

(d)   If any person who is required to consent is unavailable because the person is deceased, the petition to terminate parental rights pending adoption must be accompanied by a certified copy of the death certificate. In an adoption of a stepchild or a relative, the certified copy of the death certificate of the person whose consent is required may be attached to the petition for adoption if a separate petition for termination of parental rights is not being filed.

(4)(a)   An affidavit of nonpaternity may be executed before the birth of the minor; however, the consent to an adoption may not be executed before the birth of the minor except in a preplanned adoption pursuant to s. 63.213.

(b)   A consent to the adoption of a minor who is to be placed for adoption may be executed by the birth mother 48 hours after the minor's birth or the day the birth mother is notified in writing, either on her patient chart or in release paperwork, that she is fit to be released from the licensed hospital or birth center, whichever is earlier. A consent by any man may be executed at any time after the birth of the child. The consent is valid upon execution and may be withdrawn only if the court finds that it was obtained by fraud or duress.

(c)   If the minor to be adopted is older than 6 months of age at the time of the execution of the consent, the consent to adoption is valid upon execution; however, it is subject to a revocation period of 3 business days.

(d)   The consent to adoption or the affidavit of nonpaternity must be signed in the presence of two witnesses and be acknowledged before a notary public who is not signing as one of the witnesses. The notary public must legibly note on the consent or the affidavit the date and time of execution. The witnesses' names must be typed or printed underneath their signatures. The witnesses' home or business addresses must be included. The person who signs the consent or the affidavit has the right to have at least one of the witnesses be an individual who does not have an employment, professional, or personal relationship with the adoption entity or the prospective adoptive parents. The adoption entity must give reasonable advance notice to the person signing the consent or affidavit of the right to select a witness of his or her own choosing. The person who signs the consent or affidavit must acknowledge in writing on the consent or affidavit that such notice was given and indicate the witness, if any, who was selected by the person signing the consent or affidavit. The adoption entity must include its name, address, and telephone number on the consent to adoption or affidavit of nonpaternity.

(e)   A consent to adoption being executed by the birth parent must be in at least 12-point boldfaced type and shall contain the following recitation of rights:

CONSENT TO ADOPTION

YOU HAVE THE RIGHT TO SELECT AT LEAST ONE PERSON WHO DOES NOT HAVE AN EMPLOYMENT, PROFESSIONAL, OR PERSONAL RELATIONSHIP WITH THE ADOPTION ENTITY OR THE PROSPECTIVE ADOPTIVE PARENTS TO BE PRESENT WHEN THIS AFFIDAVIT IS EXECUTED AND TO SIGN IT AS A WITNESS. YOU MUST ACKNOWLEDGE ON THIS FORM THAT YOU WERE NOTIFIED OF THIS RIGHT AND YOU MUST INDICATE THE WITNESS OR WITNESSES YOU SELECTED, IF ANY.

YOU DO NOT HAVE TO SIGN THIS CONSENT FORM. YOU MAY DO ANY OF THE FOLLOWING INSTEAD OF SIGNING THIS CONSENT OR BEFORE SIGNING THIS CONSENT:

1.   CONSULT WITH AN ATTORNEY;

2.   HOLD, CARE FOR, AND FEED THE CHILD UNLESS OTHERWISE LEGALLY PROHIBITED;

3. PLACE THE CHILD IN FOSTER CARE OR WITH ANY FRIEND OR FAMILY MEMBER YOU CHOOSE WHO IS WILLING TO CARE FOR THE CHILD;

4. TAKE THE CHILD HOME UNLESS OTHERWISE LEGALLY PROHIBITED; AND

5. FIND OUT ABOUT THE COMMUNITY RESOURCES THAT ARE AVAILABLE TO YOU IF YOU DO NOT GO THROUGH WITH THE ADOPTION.

IF YOU DO SIGN THIS CONSENT, YOU ARE GIVING UP ALL RIGHTS TO YOUR CHILD. YOUR CONSENT IS VALID, BINDING, AND IRREVOCABLE EXCEPT UNDER SPECIFIC LEGAL CIRCUMSTANCES. IF YOU ARE GIVING UP YOUR RIGHTS TO A NEWBORN CHILD WHO IS TO BE IMMEDIATELY PLACED FOR ADOPTION UPON THE CHILD'S RELEASE FROM A LICENSED HOSPITAL OR BIRTH CENTER FOLLOWING BIRTH, A WAITING PERIOD WILL BE IMPOSED UPON THE BIRTH MOTHER BEFORE SHE MAY SIGN THE CONSENT FOR ADOPTION. A BIRTH MOTHER MUST WAIT 48 HOURS FROM THE TIME OF BIRTH, OR UNTIL THE DAY THE BIRTH MOTHER HAS BEEN NOTIFIED IN WRITING, EITHER ON HER PATIENT CHART OR IN RELEASE PAPERS, THAT SHE IS FIT TO BE RELEASED FROM A LICENSED HOSPITAL OR BIRTH CENTER, WHICHEVER IS SOONER, BEFORE THE CONSENT FOR ADOPTION MAY BE EXECUTED. ANY MAN MAY EXECUTE A CONSENT AT ANY TIME AFTER THE BIRTH OF THE CHILD. ONCE YOU HAVE SIGNED THE CONSENT, IT IS VALID, BINDING, AND IRREVOCABLE AND CANNOT BE INVALIDATED UNLESS A COURT FINDS THAT IT WAS OBTAINED BY FRAUD OR DURESS.

IF YOU BELIEVE THAT YOUR CONSENT WAS OBTAINED BY FRAUD OR DURESS AND YOU WISH TO INVALIDATE THAT CONSENT, YOU MUST:

1. NOTIFY THE ADOPTION ENTITY, BY WRITING A LETTER, THAT YOU WISH TO WITHDRAW YOUR CONSENT; AND

2. PROVE IN COURT THAT THE CONSENT WAS OBTAINED BY FRAUD OR DURESS.

This statement of rights is not required for the adoption of a relative, an adult, a stepchild, or a child older than 6 months of age. A consent form for the adoption of a child older than 6 months of age at the time of the execution of consent must contain a statement outlining the revocation rights provided in paragraph (c).

(5) A copy or duplicate original of each consent signed in an action for termination of parental rights pending adoption must be provided to the person who executed the consent to adoption. The copy must be hand delivered, with a written acknowledgment of receipt signed by the person whose consent is required at the time of execution. If a copy of a consent cannot be provided as required in this subsection, the adoption entity must execute an affidavit stating why the copy of the consent was not delivered. The original consent and acknowledgment of receipt, or an affidavit stating why the copy of the consent was not delivered, must be filed with the petition for termination of parental rights pending adoption.

(6)(a) If a parent executes a consent for placement of a minor with an adoption entity or qualified prospective adoptive parents and the minor child is in the custody of the department, but parental rights have not yet been terminated, the adoption consent is valid, binding, and enforceable by the court.

(b) Upon execution of the consent of the parent, the adoption entity shall be permitted to intervene in the dependency case as a party in interest and must provide the court that acquired jurisdiction over the minor, pursuant to the shelter or dependency petition filed by the department, a copy of the preliminary home study of the prospective adoptive parents and any other evidence of the suitability of the placement. The preliminary home study must be maintained with strictest confidentiality within the dependency court file and the department's file. A preliminary home study must be provided to the court in all cases in which an adoption entity has intervened pursuant to this section. Unless the court has concerns regarding the qualifications of the home study provider, or concerns that the home study may not be adequate to determine the best interests of the child, the home study provided by the adoption entity shall be deemed to be sufficient and no additional home study needs to be performed by the department.

(c)　If an adoption entity files a motion to intervene in the dependency case in accordance with this chapter, the dependency court shall promptly grant a hearing to determine whether the adoption entity has filed the required documents to be permitted to intervene and whether a change of placement of the child is appropriate.

(d)　Upon a determination by the court that the prospective adoptive parents are properly qualified to adopt the minor child and that the adoption appears to be in the best interests of the minor child, the court shall immediately order the transfer of custody of the minor child to the prospective adoptive parents, under the supervision of the adoption entity. The adoption entity shall thereafter provide monthly supervision reports to the department until finalization of the adoption. If the child has been determined to be dependent by the court, the department shall provide information to the prospective adoptive parents at the time they receive placement of the dependent child regarding approved parent training classes available within the community. The department shall file with the court an acknowledgment of the parent's receipt of the information regarding approved parent training classes available within the community.

(e)　In determining whether the best interests of the child are served by transferring the custody of the minor child to the prospective adoptive parent selected by the parent, the court shall consider the rights of the parent to determine an appropriate placement for the child, the permanency offered, the child's bonding with any potential adoptive home that the child has been residing in, and the importance of maintaining sibling relationships, if possible.

(f)　The adoption entity shall be responsible for keeping the dependency court informed of the status of the adoption proceedings at least every 90 days from the date of the order changing placement of the child until the date of finalization of the adoption.

(g)　In all dependency proceedings, after it is determined that reunification is not a viable alternative and prior to the filing of a petition for termination of parental rights, the court shall advise the biological parent who is a party to the case of the right to participate in a private adoption plan.

(7)　If a person is seeking to revoke consent for a child older than 6 months of age:

(a)　The person seeking to revoke consent must, in accordance with paragraph (4)(c), notify the adoption entity in writing by certified mail, return receipt requested, within 3 business days after execution of the consent. As used in this subsection, the term "business day" means any day on which the United States Postal Service accepts certified mail for delivery.

(b)　Upon receiving timely written notice from a person whose consent to adoption is required of that person's desire to revoke consent, the adoption entity must contact the prospective adoptive parent to arrange a time certain for the adoption entity to regain physical custody of the minor, unless, upon a motion for emergency hearing by the adoption entity, the court determines in written findings that placement of the minor with the person who had legal or physical custody of the child immediately before the child was placed for adoption may endanger the minor or that the person who desires to revoke consent is not required to consent to the adoption, has been determined to have abandoned the child, or is otherwise subject to a determination that the person's consent is waived under this chapter.

(c)   If the court finds that the placement may endanger the minor, the court shall enter an order continuing the placement of the minor with the prospective adoptive parents pending further proceedings if they desire continued placement. If the prospective adoptive parents do not desire continued placement, the order must include, but need not be limited to, a determination of whether temporary placement in foster care, with the person who had legal or physical custody of the child immediately before placing the child for adoption, or with a relative is in the best interests of the child and whether an investigation by the department is recommended.

(d)   If the person revoking consent claims to be the father of the minor but has not been established to be the father by marriage, court order, or scientific testing, the court may order scientific paternity testing and reserve ruling on removal of the minor until the results of such testing have been filed with the court.

(e)   The adoption entity must return the minor within 3 business days after timely and proper notification of the revocation of consent or after the court determines that revocation is timely and in accordance with the requirements of this chapter upon consideration of an emergency motion, as filed pursuant to paragraph (b), to the physical custody of the person revoking consent or the person directed by the court. If the person seeking to revoke consent claims to be the father of the minor but has not been established to be the father by marriage, court order, or scientific testing, the adoption entity may return the minor to the care and custody of the mother, if she desires such placement and she is not otherwise prohibited by law from having custody of the child.

(f)   Following the revocation period described in paragraph (a), consent may be set aside only when the court finds that the consent was obtained by fraud or duress.

(g)   An affidavit of nonpaternity may be set aside only if the court finds that the affidavit was obtained by fraud or duress.

(h)   If the consent of one parent is set aside or revoked in accordance with this chapter, any other consents executed by the other parent or a third party whose consent is required for the adoption of the child may not be used by the parent whose consent was revoked or set aside to terminate or diminish the rights of the other parent or third party whose consent was required for the adoption of the child.

History.—s. 8, ch. 73-159; s. 17, ch. 77-147; s. 2, ch. 78-190; s. 2, ch. 91-99; s. 7, ch. 92-96; s. 14, ch. 2001-3; s. 15, ch. 2003-58; s. 10, ch. 2008-151; s. 13, ch. 2012-81; s. 9, ch. 2013-15.

63.085   Disclosure by adoption entity.—

(1)   DISCLOSURE REQUIRED TO PARENTS AND PROSPECTIVE ADOPTIVE PARENTS.—Within 14 days after a person seeking to adopt a minor or a person seeking to place a minor for adoption contacts an adoption entity in person or provides the adoption entity with a mailing address, the entity must provide a written disclosure statement to that person if the entity agrees or continues to work with the person. The adoption entity shall also provide the written disclosure to the parent who did not initiate contact with the adoption entity within 14 days after that parent is identified and located. For purposes of providing the written disclosure, a person is considered to be seeking to place a minor for adoption if that person has sought information or advice from the adoption entity regarding the option of adoptive placement. The written disclosure statement must be in substantially the following form:

ADOPTION DISCLOSURE

THE STATE OF FLORIDA REQUIRES THAT THIS FORM BE PROVIDED TO ALL PERSONS CONSIDERING ADOPTING A MINOR OR SEEKING TO PLACE A MINOR FOR ADOPTION, TO ADVISE THEM OF THE FOLLOWING FACTS REGARDING ADOPTION UNDER FLORIDA LAW:

1.   The name, address, and telephone number of the adoption entity providing this disclosure is:
Name:
Address:
Telephone Number:

2.   The adoption entity does not provide legal representation or advice to parents or anyone signing a consent for adoption or affidavit of nonpaternity, and parents have the right to consult with an attorney of their own choosing to advise them.

3.   With the exception of an adoption by a stepparent or relative, a child cannot be placed into a prospective adoptive home unless the prospective adoptive parents have received a favorable preliminary home study, including criminal and child abuse clearances.

4.   A valid consent for adoption may not be signed by the birth mother until 48 hours after the birth of the child, or the day the birth mother is notified, in writing, that she is fit for discharge from the licensed hospital or birth center. Any man may sign a valid consent for adoption at any time after the birth of the child.

5.   A consent for adoption signed before the child attains the age of 6 months is binding and irrevocable from the moment it is signed unless it can be proven in court that the consent was obtained by fraud or duress. A consent for adoption signed after the child attains the age of 6 months is valid from the moment it is signed; however, it may be revoked up to 3 business days after it was signed.

6.   A consent for adoption is not valid if the signature of the person who signed the consent was obtained by fraud or duress.

7.   An unmarried biological father must act immediately in order to protect his parental rights. Section 63.062, Florida Statutes, prescribes that any father seeking to establish his right to consent to the adoption of his child must file a claim of paternity with the Florida Putative Father Registry maintained by the Office of Vital Statistics of the Department of Health by the date a petition to terminate parental rights is filed with the court, or within 30 days after receiving service of a Notice of Intended Adoption Plan. If he receives a Notice of Intended Adoption Plan, he must file a claim of paternity with the Florida Putative Father Registry, file a parenting plan with the court, and provide financial support to the mother or child within 30 days following service. An unmarried biological father's failure to timely respond to a Notice of Intended Adoption Plan constitutes an irrevocable legal waiver of any and all rights that the father may have to the child. A claim of paternity registration form for the Florida Putative Father Registry may be obtained from any local office of the Department of Health, Office of Vital Statistics, the Department of Children and Families, the Internet websites for these agencies, and the offices of the clerks of the Florida circuit courts. The claim of paternity form must be submitted to the Office of Vital Statistics, Attention: Adoption Unit, P.O. Box 210, Jacksonville, FL 32231.

8.   There are alternatives to adoption, including foster care, relative care, and parenting the child. There may be services and sources of financial assistance in the community available to parents if they choose to parent the child.

9.   A parent has the right to have a witness of his or her choice, who is unconnected with the adoption entity or the adoptive parents, to be present and witness the signing of the consent or affidavit of nonpaternity.

10.   A parent 14 years of age or younger must have a parent, legal guardian, or court-appointed guardian ad litem to assist and advise the parent as to the adoption plan and to witness consent.

11.   A parent has a right to receive supportive counseling from a counselor, social worker, physician, clergy, or attorney.

12.   The payment of living or medical expenses by the prospective adoptive parents before the birth of the child does not, in any way, obligate the parent to sign the consent for adoption.

(2)   DISCLOSURE TO ADOPTIVE PARENTS.—

(a)   At the time that an adoption entity is responsible for selecting prospective adoptive parents for a born or unborn child whose parents are seeking to place the child for adoption or whose rights were terminated pursuant to chapter 39, the adoption entity must provide the prospective adoptive parents with information concerning the background of the child to the extent such information is disclosed to the adoption entity by the parents, legal custodian, or the department. This subsection applies only if the adoption entity identifies the prospective adoptive parents and supervises the placement of the child in the prospective adoptive parents' home. If any information cannot be disclosed because the records custodian failed or refused to produce the background information, the adoption entity has a duty to provide the information if it becomes available. An individual or entity contacted by an adoption entity to obtain the background information must release the requested information to the adoption entity without the necessity of a subpoena or a court order. In all cases, the prospective adoptive parents must receive all available information by the date of the final hearing on the petition for adoption. The information to be disclosed includes:

1.   A family social and medical history form completed pursuant to s. 63.162(6).

2.   The biological mother's medical records documenting her prenatal care and the birth and delivery of the child.

3.   A complete set of the child's medical records documenting all medical treatment and care since the child's birth and before placement.

4.   All mental health, psychological, and psychiatric records, reports, and evaluations concerning the child before placement.

5.   The child's educational records, including all records concerning any special education needs of the child before placement.

6.   Records documenting all incidents that required the department to provide services to the child, including all orders of adjudication of dependency or termination of parental rights issued pursuant to chapter 39, any case plans drafted to address the child's needs, all protective services investigations identifying the child as a victim, and all guardian ad litem reports filed with the court concerning the child.

7.   Written information concerning the availability of adoption subsidies for the child, if applicable.

(b)   When disclosing information pursuant to this subsection, the adoption entity must redact any confidential identifying information concerning the child's parents, foster parents and their families, siblings, relatives, and perpetrators of crimes against the child or involving the child.

(c)   If the prospective adoptive parents waive the receipt of any of the records described in paragraph (a), a copy of the written notification of the waiver to the adoption entity shall be filed with the court.

(3)   ACKNOWLEDGMENT OF DISCLOSURE.—The adoption entity must obtain a written statement acknowledging receipt of the disclosures required under this section and signed by the persons receiving the disclosure or, if it is not possible to obtain such an acknowledgment, the adoption entity must execute an affidavit stating why an acknowledgment could not be obtained. If the disclosure was delivered by certified mail, return receipt requested, a return receipt signed by the person from whom

acknowledgment is required is sufficient to meet the requirements of this subsection. A copy of the acknowledgment of receipt of the disclosure must be provided to the person signing it. A copy of the acknowledgment or affidavit executed by the adoption entity in lieu of the acknowledgment must be maintained in the file of the adoption entity. The original acknowledgment or affidavit must be filed with the court.

(4) REVOCATION OF CONSENT.—Failure to meet the requirements of this section does not constitute grounds for revocation of a consent to adoption or withdrawal of an affidavit of nonpaternity unless the extent and circumstances of such a failure result in a material failure of fundamental fairness in the administration of due process, or the failure constitutes or contributes materially to fraud or duress in obtaining a consent to adoption or affidavit of nonpaternity.

History.—s. 1, ch. 84-28; s. 2, ch. 88-109; s. 8, ch. 92-96; s. 338, ch. 95-147; s. 15, ch. 2001-3; s. 16, ch. 2003-58; s. 11, ch. 2008-151; s. 14, ch. 2012-81.

63.087   Proceeding to terminate parental rights pending adoption; general provisions.—

(1) JURISDICTION.—A court of this state which is competent to decide child welfare or custody matters has jurisdiction to hear all matters arising from a proceeding to terminate parental rights pending adoption.

(2) VENUE.—

(a) A petition to terminate parental rights pending adoption must be filed:

1. In the county where the child resides; or

2. In the county where the adoption entity is located.

(b) If a petition for termination of parental rights has been filed and a parent whose consent is required objects to venue, there must be a hearing in which the court shall determine whether that parent intends to assert legally recognized grounds to contest a termination of parental rights and, if so, the court may transfer venue to a proper venue under this subsection. For purposes of selecting venue, the court shall consider the ease of access to the court for the parent and the factors set forth in s. 47.122.

(c) If there is a transfer of venue, the court may determine which party shall bear the cost of venue transfer.

For purposes of the hearing under this subsection, witnesses located in another jurisdiction may testify by deposition or testify by telephone, audiovisual means, or other electronic means before a designated court or at another location. Documentary evidence transmitted from another location by technological means that do not produce an original writing may not be excluded from evidence on an objection based on the means of transmission. The court on its own motion may otherwise prescribe the manner and terms upon which the testimony is taken.

(3) PREREQUISITE FOR ADOPTION.—A petition for adoption may not be filed until after the date the court enters the judgment terminating parental rights pending adoption. Adoptions of relatives, adult adoptions, or adoptions of stepchildren are not required to file a separate termination of parental rights proceeding pending adoption. In such cases, the petitioner may file a joint petition for termination of parental rights and adoption, attaching all required consents, affidavits, notices, and acknowledgments. Unless otherwise provided by law, this chapter applies to joint petitions.

(4) PETITION.—

(a) A proceeding seeking to terminate parental rights pending adoption pursuant to this chapter must be initiated by the filing of an original petition after the birth of the minor.

(b)   The petition may be filed by a parent or person having physical custody of the minor. The petition may be filed by an adoption entity only if a parent or person having physical or legal custody who has executed a consent to adoption pursuant to s. 63.082 also consents in writing to the adoption entity filing the petition. The original of such consent must be filed with the petition.

(c)   The petition must be entitled: "In the Matter of the Termination of Parental Rights for the Proposed Adoption of a Minor Child."

(d)   The petition to terminate parental rights pending adoption must be in writing and signed by the petitioner under oath stating the petitioner's good faith in filing the petition. A written consent to adoption, affidavit of nonpaternity, or affidavit of diligent search under s. 63.088, for each person whose consent to adoption is required under s. 63.062, must be executed and attached.

(e)   The petition must include:

1.   The minor's name, gender, date of birth, and place of birth. The petition must contain all names by which the minor is or has been known, excluding the minor's prospective adoptive name but including the minor's legal name at the time of the filing of the petition. In the case of an infant child whose adoptive name appears on the original birth certificate, the adoptive name shall not be included in the petition, nor shall it be included elsewhere in the termination of parental rights proceeding.

2.   All information required by the Uniform Child Custody Jurisdiction and Enforcement Act and the Indian Child Welfare Act.

3.   A statement of the grounds under s. 63.089 upon which the petition is based.

4.   The name, address, and telephone number of any adoption entity seeking to place the minor for adoption.

5.   The name, address, and telephone number of the division of the circuit court in which the petition is to be filed.

6.   A certification of compliance with the requirements of s. 63.0425 regarding notice to grandparents of an impending adoption.

(5)   SUMMONS TO BE ISSUED.—The petitioner shall cause a summons to be issued substantially in the form provided in Form 1.902, Florida Rules of Civil Procedure. Petition and summons shall be served upon any person whose consent has been provided but who has not waived service of the pleadings and notice of the hearing thereon and also upon any person whose consent is required but who has not provided that consent.

(6)   ANSWER AND APPEARANCE REQUIRED.—An answer to the petition or any pleading requiring an answer must be filed in accordance with the Florida Family Law Rules of Procedure. Failure to file a written response to the petition constitutes grounds upon which the court may terminate parental rights. Failure to personally appear at the hearing constitutes grounds upon which the court may terminate parental rights. Any person present at the hearing to terminate parental rights pending adoption whose consent to adoption is required under s. 63.062 must:

(a)   Be advised by the court that he or she has a right to ask that the hearing be reset for a later date so that the person may consult with an attorney; and

(b)   Be given an opportunity to admit or deny the allegations in the petition.

History.—s. 16, ch. 2001-3; s. 17, ch. 2003-58; s. 8, ch. 2005-2; s. 12, ch. 2008-151; s. 15, ch. 2012-81.

63.088   Proceeding to terminate parental rights pending adoption; notice and service; diligent search.—

(1)   NOTICE REQUIRED.—An unmarried biological father, by virtue of the fact that he has engaged in a sexual relationship with a woman, is deemed to be on notice that a pregnancy and an adoption proceeding regarding that child may occur and that he has a duty to protect his own rights and interest.

He is, therefore, entitled to notice of a birth or adoption proceeding with regard to that child only as provided in this chapter. If a mother fails to identify an unmarried biological father to the adoption entity by the date she signs her consent for adoption, the unmarried biological father's claim that he did not receive actual notice of the adoption proceeding is not a defense to the termination of his parental rights.

(2)   INITIATE LOCATION PROCEDURES.—When the location of a person whose consent to an adoption is required but is not known, the adoption entity must begin the inquiry and diligent search process required by this section within a reasonable time period after the date on which the person seeking to place a minor for adoption has evidenced in writing to the adoption entity a desire to place the minor for adoption with that entity, or not later than 30 days after the date any money is provided as permitted under this chapter by the adoption entity for the benefit of the person seeking to place a minor for adoption.

(3)   LOCATION AND IDENTITY KNOWN.—Before the court may determine that a minor is available for adoption, each person whose consent is required under s. 63.062, who has not executed a consent for adoption or an affidavit of nonpaternity, and whose location and identity have been determined by compliance with the procedures in this section must be personally served, pursuant to chapter 48, at least 20 days before the hearing with a copy of the petition to terminate parental rights pending adoption and with notice in substantially the following form:

NOTICE OF PETITION AND HEARING
TO TERMINATE PARENTAL RIGHTS
PENDING ADOPTION

A petition to terminate parental rights pending adoption has been filed. A copy of the petition is being served with this notice. There will be a hearing on the petition to terminate parental rights pending adoption on _(date)_ at _(time)_ before _(judge)_ at _(location, including complete name and street address of the courthouse)_ . The court has set aside _(amount of time)_ for this hearing.

UNDER SECTION 63.089, FLORIDA STATUTES, FAILURE TO TIMELY FILE A WRITTEN RESPONSE TO THIS NOTICE AND THE PETITION WITH THE COURT AND TO APPEAR AT THIS HEARING CONSTITUTES GROUNDS UPON WHICH THE COURT SHALL END ANY PARENTAL RIGHTS YOU MAY HAVE OR ASSERT REGARDING THE MINOR CHILD.

(4)   REQUIRED INQUIRY.—In proceedings initiated under s. 63.087, the court shall conduct an inquiry of the person who is placing the minor for adoption and of any relative or person having legal custody of the minor who is present at the hearing and likely to have the following information regarding the identity of:

(a)   Any man to whom the mother of the minor was married at any time when conception of the minor may have occurred or at the time of the birth of the minor;

(b)   Any man who has filed an affidavit of paternity pursuant to s. 382.013(2)(c) before the date that a petition for termination of parental rights is filed with the court;

(c)   Any man who has adopted the minor;

(d)   Any man who has been adjudicated by a court as the father of the minor child before the date a petition for termination of parental rights is filed with the court; and

(e)   Any man whom the mother identified to the adoption entity as a potential biological father before the date she signed the consent for adoption.

The information sought under this subsection may be provided to the court in the form of a sworn affidavit by a person having personal knowledge of the facts, addressing each inquiry enumerated in this subsection, except that, if the inquiry identifies a father under paragraph (a), paragraph (b), paragraph (c), or paragraph (d), the inquiry may not continue further. The inquiry required under this subsection may be conducted before the birth of the minor.

(5)   LOCATION UNKNOWN; IDENTITY KNOWN.—If the inquiry by the court under subsection (4) identifies any person who has not executed a consent to adoption or an affidavit of nonpaternity, and the location of the person is unknown, the adoption entity must conduct a diligent search for that person which must include inquiries concerning:

(a)   The person's current address, or any previous address, through an inquiry of the United States Postal Service through the Freedom of Information Act;

(b)   The last known employment of the person, including the name and address of the person's employer;

(c)   Names and addresses of relatives to the extent they can be reasonably obtained from the petitioner or other sources, contacts with those relatives, and inquiry as to the person's last known address. The petitioner must pursue any leads to any addresses where the person may have moved;

(d)   Information as to whether or not the person may have died and, if so, the date and location;

(e)   Telephone listings in the area where the person last resided;

(f)   Inquiries of law enforcement agencies in the area where the person last resided;

(g)   Highway patrol records in the state where the person last resided;

(h)   Department of Corrections records in the state where the person last resided;

(i)   Hospitals in the area where the person last resided;

(j)   Records of utility companies, including water, sewer, cable television, and electric companies, in the area where the person last resided;

(k)   Records of the Armed Forces of the United States as to whether there is any information as to the person;

(l)   Records of the tax assessor and tax collector in the area where the person last resided; and

(m)   Search of one Internet databank locator service.

A person contacted by a petitioner or adoption entity requesting records under this subsection must release the requested records to the petitioner or adoption entity without the necessity of a subpoena or a court order, except when prohibited by law. An affidavit of diligent search conducted in accordance with this section must be filed with the court. The diligent search may be conducted before the birth of the minor. A judgment terminating parental rights and approving a diligent search that fails to locate a person is valid and is not subject to direct or collateral attack because the mother failed or refused to provide the adoption entity with sufficient information to locate the person.

(6)   CONSTRUCTIVE SERVICE.—This subsection only applies if, as to any person whose consent is required under s. 63.062 and who has not executed a consent to adoption or an affidavit of nonpaternity, the location of the person is unknown and the inquiry under subsection (4) fails to locate the person. The unlocated person must be served notice under subsection (3) by constructive service in the manner provided in chapter 49. The notice shall be published in the county where the person was last known to have resided. The notice, in addition to all information required under chapter 49, must include a physical description, including, but not limited to, age, race, hair and eye color, and approximate height and weight of the person, the minor's date of birth, and the place of birth of the

minor. Constructive service by publication shall not be required to provide notice to an identified birth father whose consent is not required pursuant to ss. 63.062 and 63.064.

History.—s. 17, ch. 2001-3; s. 18, ch. 2003-58; s. 13, ch. 2008-151; s. 16, ch. 2012-81.

63.089   Proceeding to terminate parental rights pending adoption; hearing; grounds; dismissal of petition; judgment.—

(1)   HEARING.—The court may terminate parental rights pending adoption only after a hearing.

(2)   HEARING PREREQUISITES.—The court may hold the hearing only when:

(a)   For each person whose consent to adoption is required under s. 63.062:

1.   A consent under s. 63.082 has been executed and filed with the court;

2.   An affidavit of nonpaternity under s. 63.082 has been executed and filed with the court;

3.   Notice has been provided under ss. 63.087 and 63.088; or

4.   The certificate from the Office of Vital Statistics has been provided to the court stating that a diligent search has been made of the Florida Putative Father Registry created in s. 63.054 and that no filing has been found pertaining to the father of the child in question or, if a filing is found, stating the name of the putative father and the time and date of the filing.

(b)   For each notice and petition that must be served under ss. 63.087 and 63.088:

1.   At least 20 days have elapsed since the date of personal service and an affidavit of service has been filed with the court;

2.   At least 30 days have elapsed since the first date of publication of constructive service and an affidavit of service has been filed with the court; or

3.   An affidavit of nonpaternity, consent for adoption, or other document that affirmatively waives service has been executed and filed with the court.

(c)   The minor named in the petition has been born.

(d)   The petition contains all information required under s. 63.087 and all affidavits of inquiry, diligent search, and service required under s. 63.088 have been obtained and filed with the court.

(3)   GROUNDS FOR TERMINATING PARENTAL RIGHTS PENDING ADOPTION.—The court may enter a judgment terminating parental rights pending adoption if the court determines by clear and convincing evidence, supported by written findings of fact, that each person whose consent to adoption is required under s. 63.062:

(a)   Has executed a valid consent under s. 63.082 and the consent was obtained according to the requirements of this chapter;

(b)   Has executed an affidavit of nonpaternity and the affidavit was obtained according to the requirements of this chapter;

(c)   Has been served with a notice of the intended adoption plan in accordance with the provisions of s. 63.062(3) and has failed to respond within the designated time period;

(d)   Has been properly served notice of the proceeding in accordance with the requirements of this chapter and has failed to file a written answer or personally appear at the evidentiary hearing resulting in the judgment terminating parental rights pending adoption;

(e)   Has been properly served notice of the proceeding in accordance with the requirements of this chapter and has been determined under subsection (4) to have abandoned the minor;

(f)   Is a parent of the person to be adopted, which parent has been judicially declared incapacitated with restoration of competency found to be medically improbable;

(g)   Is a person who has legal custody of the person to be adopted, other than a parent, who has failed to respond in writing to a request for consent for a period of 60 days or, after examination of his or her written reasons for withholding consent, is found by the court to be withholding his or her consent unreasonably;

(h)   Has been properly served notice of the proceeding in accordance with the requirements of this chapter, but has been found by the court, after examining written reasons for the withholding of consent, to be unreasonably withholding his or her consent; or

(i)   Is the spouse of the person to be adopted who has failed to consent, and the failure of the spouse to consent to the adoption is excused by reason of prolonged and unexplained absence, unavailability, incapacity, or circumstances that are found by the court to constitute unreasonable withholding of consent.

(4)   FINDING OF ABANDONMENT.—A finding of abandonment resulting in a termination of parental rights must be based upon clear and convincing evidence that a parent or person having legal custody has abandoned the child in accordance with the definition contained in s. 63.032. A finding of abandonment may also be based upon emotional abuse or a refusal to provide reasonable financial support, when able, to a birth mother during her pregnancy or on whether the person alleged to have abandoned the child, while being able, failed to establish contact with the child or accept responsibility for the child's welfare.

(a)   In making a determination of abandonment at a hearing for termination of parental rights under this chapter, the court shall consider, among other relevant factors not inconsistent with this section:

1.   Whether the actions alleged to constitute abandonment demonstrate a willful disregard for the safety or welfare of the child or the unborn child;

2.   Whether the person alleged to have abandoned the child, while being able, failed to provide financial support;

3.   Whether the person alleged to have abandoned the child, while being able, failed to pay for medical treatment; and

4.   Whether the amount of support provided or medical expenses paid was appropriate, taking into consideration the needs of the child and relative means and resources available to the person alleged to have abandoned the child.

(b)   The child has been abandoned when the parent of a child is incarcerated on or after October 1, 2001, in a federal, state, or county correctional institution and:

1.   The period of time for which the parent has been or is expected to be incarcerated will constitute a significant portion of the child's minority. In determining whether the period of time is significant, the court shall consider the child's age and the child's need for a permanent and stable home. The period of time begins on the date that the parent enters into incarceration;

2.   The incarcerated parent has been determined by a court of competent jurisdiction to be a violent career criminal as defined in s. 775.084, a habitual violent felony offender as defined in s. 775.084, convicted of child abuse as defined in s. 827.03, or a sexual predator as defined in s. 775.21; has been convicted of first degree or second degree murder in violation of s. 782.04 or a sexual battery that constitutes a capital, life, or first degree felony violation of s. 794.011; or has been convicted of a substantially similar offense in another jurisdiction. As used in this section, the term "substantially similar offense" means any offense that is substantially similar in elements and penalties to one of those listed in this subparagraph, and that is in violation of a law of any other jurisdiction, whether that of another state, the District of Columbia, the United States or any possession or territory thereof, or any foreign jurisdiction; or

3. The court determines by clear and convincing evidence that continuing the parental relationship with the incarcerated parent would be harmful to the child and, for this reason, termination of the parental rights of the incarcerated parent is in the best interests of the child.

(5) DISMISSAL OF PETITION.—If the court does not find by clear and convincing evidence that parental rights of a parent should be terminated pending adoption, the court must dismiss the petition and that parent's parental rights that were the subject of such petition shall remain in full force under the law. The order must include written findings in support of the dismissal, including findings as to the criteria in subsection (4) if rejecting a claim of abandonment.

(a) Parental rights may not be terminated based upon a consent that the court finds has been timely revoked under s. 63.082 or a consent to adoption or affidavit of nonpaternity that the court finds was obtained by fraud or duress.

(b) The court must enter an order based upon written findings providing for the placement of the minor, but the court may not proceed to determine custody between competing eligible parties. The placement of the child should revert to the parent or guardian who had physical custody of the child at the time of the placement for adoption unless the court determines upon clear and convincing evidence that this placement is not in the best interests of the child or is not an available option for the child. The court may not change the placement of a child who has established a bonded relationship with the current caregiver without providing for a reasonable transition plan consistent with the best interests of the child. The court may direct the parties to participate in a reunification or unification plan with a qualified professional to assist the child in the transition. The court may order scientific testing to determine the paternity of the minor only if the court has determined that the consent of the alleged father would be required, unless all parties agree that such testing is in the best interests of the child. The court may not order scientific testing to determine paternity of an unmarried biological father if the child has a father as described in s. 63.088(4)(a)-(d) whose rights have not been previously terminated. Further proceedings, if any, regarding the minor must be brought in a separate custody action under chapter 61, a dependency action under chapter 39, or a paternity action under chapter 742.

(6) JUDGMENT TERMINATING PARENTAL RIGHTS PENDING ADOPTION.—

(a) The judgment terminating parental rights pending adoption must be in writing and contain findings of fact as to the grounds for terminating parental rights.

(b) Within 7 days after filing, the court shall mail a copy of the judgment to the department. The clerk shall execute a certificate of the mailing.

(c) The judgment terminating parental rights pending adoption legally frees the child for subsequent adoption, adjudicates the child's status, and may not be challenged by a person claiming parental status who did not establish parental rights before the filing of the petition for termination, except as specifically provided in this chapter.

(7) RELIEF FROM JUDGMENT TERMINATING PARENTAL RIGHTS.—

(a) A motion for relief from a judgment terminating parental rights must be filed with the court originally entering the judgment. The motion must be filed within a reasonable time, but not later than 1 year after the entry of the judgment. An unmarried biological father does not have standing to seek relief from a judgment terminating parental rights if the mother did not identify him to the adoption entity before the date she signed a consent for adoption or if he was not located because the mother failed or refused to provide sufficient information to locate him.

(b) No later than 30 days after the filing of a motion under this subsection, the court must conduct a preliminary hearing to determine what contact, if any, shall be permitted between a parent and the child pending resolution of the motion. Such contact shall be considered only if it is requested by a parent who has appeared at the hearing and may not be awarded unless the parent previously established a bonded relationship with the child and the parent has pled a legitimate legal basis and established a prima facia case for setting aside the judgment terminating parental rights. If the court orders contact between a parent and child, the order must be issued in writing as expeditiously as possible and must state with specificity any provisions regarding contact with persons other than those with whom the child resides.

(c)   At the preliminary hearing, the court, upon the motion of any party or upon its own motion, may order scientific testing to determine the paternity of the minor if the person seeking to set aside the judgment is alleging to be the child's father and that fact has not previously been determined by legitimacy or scientific testing. The court may order visitation with a person for whom scientific testing for paternity has been ordered and who has previously established a bonded relationship with the child.

(d)   Unless otherwise agreed between the parties or for good cause shown, the court shall conduct a final hearing on the motion for relief from judgment within 45 days after the filing and enter its written order as expeditiously as possible thereafter.

(e)   If the court grants relief from the judgment terminating parental rights and no new pleading is filed to terminate parental rights, the placement of the child should revert to the parent or guardian who had physical custody of the child at the time of the original placement for adoption unless the court determines upon clear and convincing evidence that this placement is not in the best interests of the child or is not an available option for the child. The court may not change the placement of a child who has established a bonded relationship with the current caregiver without providing for a reasonable transition plan consistent with the best interests of the child. The court may direct the parties to participate in a reunification or unification plan with a qualified professional to assist the child in the transition. The court may not direct the placement of a child with a person other than the adoptive parents without first obtaining a favorable home study of that person and any other persons residing in the proposed home and shall take whatever additional steps are necessary and appropriate for the physical and emotional protection of the child.

(8)   RECORDS; CONFIDENTIAL INFORMATION.—All papers and records pertaining to a petition to terminate parental rights pending adoption are related to the subsequent adoption of the minor and are subject to s. 63.162. An unmarried biological father does not have standing to seek the court case number or access the court file if the mother did not identify him to the adoption entity before the date she signed the consent for adoption. The confidentiality provisions of this chapter do not apply to the extent information regarding persons or proceedings is made available as specified under s. 63.088.

History.—s. 18, ch. 2001-3; s. 19, ch. 2003-58; s. 13, ch. 2004-371; s. 14, ch. 2008-151; s. 17, ch. 2012-81.

63.092   Report to the court of intended placement by an adoption entity; at-risk placement; preliminary study.—

(1)   REPORT TO THE COURT.—The adoption entity must report any intended placement of a minor for adoption with any person who is not a relative or a stepparent if the adoption entity participates in the intended placement. The report must be made to the court before the minor is placed in the home or within 2 business days thereafter.

(2)   AT-RISK PLACEMENT.—If the minor is placed in the prospective adoptive home before the parental rights of the minor's parents are terminated under s. 63.089, the placement is an at-risk placement. If the placement is an at-risk placement, the prospective adoptive parents must acknowledge in writing before the minor may be placed in the prospective adoptive home that the placement is at risk. The prospective adoptive parents shall be advised by the adoption entity, in

writing, that the minor is subject to removal from the prospective adoptive home by the adoption entity or by court order at any time prior to the finalization of the adoption.

(3) PRELIMINARY HOME STUDY.—Before placing the minor in the intended adoptive home, a preliminary home study must be performed by a licensed child-placing agency, a child-caring agency registered under s. 409.176, a licensed professional, or an agency described in s. 61.20(2), unless the adoptee is an adult or the petitioner is a stepparent or a relative. If the adoptee is an adult or the petitioner is a stepparent or a relative, a preliminary home study may be required by the court for good cause shown. The department is required to perform the preliminary home study only if there is no licensed child-placing agency, child-caring agency registered under s. 409.176, licensed professional, or agency described in s. 61.20(2), in the county where the prospective adoptive parents reside. The preliminary home study must be made to determine the suitability of the intended adoptive parents and may be completed prior to identification of a prospective adoptive minor. A favorable preliminary home study is valid for 1 year after the date of its completion. Upon its completion, a signed copy of the home study must be provided to the intended adoptive parents who were the subject of the home study. A minor may not be placed in an intended adoptive home before a favorable preliminary home study is completed unless the adoptive home is also a licensed foster home under s. 409.175. The preliminary home study must include, at a minimum:

(a) An interview with the intended adoptive parents;

(b) Records checks of the department's central abuse registry and criminal records correspondence checks under s. 39.0138 through the Department of Law Enforcement on the intended adoptive parents;

(c) An assessment of the physical environment of the home;

(d) A determination of the financial security of the intended adoptive parents;

(e) Documentation of counseling and education of the intended adoptive parents on adoptive parenting;

(f) Documentation that information on adoption and the adoption process has been provided to the intended adoptive parents;

(g) Documentation that information on support services available in the community has been provided to the intended adoptive parents; and

(h) A copy of each signed acknowledgment of receipt of disclosure required by s. 63.085.

If the preliminary home study is favorable, a minor may be placed in the home pending entry of the judgment of adoption. A minor may not be placed in the home if the preliminary home study is unfavorable. If the preliminary home study is unfavorable, the adoption entity may, within 20 days after receipt of a copy of the written recommendation, petition the court to determine the suitability of the intended adoptive home. A determination as to suitability under this subsection does not act as a presumption of suitability at the final hearing. In determining the suitability of the intended adoptive home, the court must consider the totality of the circumstances in the home. A minor may not be placed in a home in which there resides any person determined by the court to be a sexual predator as defined in s. 775.21 or to have been convicted of an offense listed in s. 63.089(4)(b)2.

History.—s. 9, ch. 73-159; s. 5, ch. 75-226; s. 18, ch. 77-147; s. 5, ch. 78-190; s. 4, ch. 80-296; s. 3, ch. 82-166; s. 2, ch. 84-28; s. 1, ch. 85-189; s. 9, ch. 92-96; s. 126, ch. 98-403; s. 19, ch. 2001-3; s. 20, ch. 2003-58; s. 14, ch. 2004-371; s. 33, ch. 2006-86; s. 15, ch. 2008-151; s. 18, ch. 2012-81.

63.097   Fees.—

(1) When the adoption entity is an agency, fees may be assessed if they are approved by the department within the process of licensing the agency and if they are for:

(a) Foster care expenses;

(b) Preplacement and postplacement social services; and

(c) Agency facility and administrative costs.

(2) The following fees, costs, and expenses may be assessed by the adoption entity or paid by the adoption entity on behalf of the prospective adoptive parents:

(a) Reasonable living expenses of the birth mother which the birth mother is unable to pay due to unemployment, underemployment, or disability. Reasonable living expenses are rent, utilities, basic telephone service, food, toiletries, necessary clothing, transportation, insurance, and expenses found by the court to be necessary for the health and well-being of the birth mother and the unborn child. Such expenses may be paid during the pregnancy and for a period of up to 6 weeks postpartum.

(b) Reasonable and necessary medical expenses. Such expenses may be paid during the pregnancy and for a period of up to 6 weeks postpartum.

(c) Expenses necessary to comply with the requirements of this chapter, including, but not limited to, service of process under s. 63.088, investigator fees, a diligent search under s. 63.088, a preliminary home study under s. 63.092, and a final home investigation under s. 63.125.

(d) Court filing expenses, court costs, and other litigation expenses and birth certificate and medical record expenses.

(e) Costs associated with advertising under s. 63.212(1)(g).

(f) The following professional fees:

1. A reasonable hourly fee or flat fee necessary to provide legal representation to the adoptive parents or adoption entity in a proceeding filed under this chapter.

2. A reasonable hourly fee or flat fee for contact with the parent related to the adoption. In determining a reasonable hourly fee under this subparagraph, the court must consider if the tasks done were clerical or of such a nature that the matter could have been handled by support staff at a lesser rate than the rate for legal representation charged under subparagraph 1. Such tasks include, but need not be limited to, transportation, transmitting funds, arranging appointments, and securing accommodations.

3. A reasonable hourly fee for counseling services provided to a parent or a prospective adoptive parent by a psychologist licensed under chapter 490 or a clinical social worker, marriage and family therapist, or mental health counselor licensed under chapter 491, or a counselor who is employed by an adoption entity accredited by the Council on Accreditation of Services for Children and Families to provide pregnancy counseling and supportive services.

(3) Approval of the court is not required until the total of amounts permitted under subsection (2) exceeds:

(a) $5,000 in legal or other fees;

(b) $800 in court costs; or

(c) $5,000 in reasonable and necessary living and medical expenses.

(4) Any fees, costs, or expenses not included in subsection (2) or prohibited under subsection (5) require court approval prior to payment and must be based on a finding of extraordinary circumstances.

(5) The following fees, costs, and expenses are prohibited:

(a) Any fee or expense that constitutes payment for locating a minor for adoption.

(b) Any payment which is not itemized and documented on the affidavit filed under s. 63.132.

(c) Any fee on the affidavit which does not specify the service that was provided and for which the fee is being charged, such as a fee for facilitation, acquisition, or other similar service, or which does not identify the date the service was provided, the time required to provide the service, the person or entity providing the service, and the hourly fee charged.

(6)   Unless otherwise indicated in this section, when an adoption entity uses the services of a licensed child-placing agency, a professional, any other person or agency pursuant to s. 63.092, or, if necessary, the department, the person seeking to adopt the child must pay the licensed child-placing agency, professional, other person or agency, or the department an amount equal to the cost of all services performed, including, but not limited to, the cost of conducting the preliminary home study, counseling, and the final home investigation.

History.—s. 6, ch. 75-226; s. 1, ch. 77-174; s. 6, ch. 78-190; s. 2, ch. 84-101; s. 4, ch. 87-397; s. 1, ch. 90-55; s. 10, ch. 92-96; s. 20, ch. 2001-3; s. 21, ch. 2003-58.

63.102   Filing of petition for adoption or declaratory statement; venue; proceeding for approval of fees and costs.—

(1)   PETITION FOR ADOPTION.—A petition for adoption may not be filed until after the entry of the judgment or decree terminating parental rights unless the adoptee is an adult or the petitioner is a stepparent or a relative. After a judgment terminating parental rights has been entered, a proceeding for adoption may be commenced by filing a petition entitled, "In the Matter of the Adoption of " in the circuit court. The person to be adopted shall be designated in the caption in the name by which he or she is to be known if the petition is granted. Except for a joint petition for the adoption of a stepchild, a relative, or an adult, any name by which the minor was previously known may not be disclosed in the petition, the notice of hearing, the judgment of adoption, or the court docket as provided in s. 63.162 (3).

(2)   VENUE.—A petition for adoption or for a declaratory statement as to the adoption contract must be filed in the county where the petition for termination of parental rights was filed or granted or where the adoption entity is located. The circuit court in this state shall retain jurisdiction over the matter until a final judgment is entered on the adoption, either within or outside the state. The Uniform Child Custody Jurisdiction and Enforcement Act does not apply until a final judgment is entered on the adoption.

(3)   FILING OF ADOPTION PETITION REQUIRED.—Unless leave of court is granted for good cause shown, a petition for adoption shall be filed not later than 60 days after entry of the final judgment terminating parental rights.

(4)   CONFIDENTIALITY.—If the filing of the petition for adoption or for a declaratory statement as to the adoption contract in the county where the petitioner or minor resides would tend to endanger the privacy of the petitioner or minor, the petition for adoption may be filed in a different county, provided the substantive rights of any person will not thereby be affected.

(5)   PRIOR APPROVAL OF FEES AND COSTS.—A proceeding for prior approval of fees and costs may be commenced any time after an agreement is reached between the birth mother and the adoptive parents by filing a petition for declaratory statement on the agreement entitled "In the Matter of the Proposed Adoption of a Minor Child" in the circuit court.

(a)   The petition must be filed by the adoption entity with the consent of the parties to the agreement.

(b)   A contract for the payment of fees, costs, and expenses permitted under this chapter must be in writing, and any person who enters into the contract has 3 business days in which to cancel the contract unless placement of the child has occurred. To cancel the contract, the person must notify the adoption entity in writing by certified United States mail, return receipt requested, no later than 3 business days after signing the contract. For the purposes of this subsection, the term "business day" means a day on which the United States Postal Service accepts certified mail for delivery. If the contract is canceled within the first 3 business days, the person who cancels the contract does not owe any legal, intermediary, or other fees, but may be responsible for the adoption entity's actual costs during that time.

(c)   The court may grant approval only of fees and expenses permitted under s. 63.097. A prior approval of prospective fees and costs shall create a presumption that these items will subsequently be approved by the court under s. 63.132. The court, under s. 63.132, may order an adoption entity to refund any amounts paid under this subsection that are subsequently found by the court to be greater than fees, costs, and expenses actually incurred.

(d)   The contract may not require, and the court may not approve, any amount that constitutes payment for locating a minor for adoption.

(e)   A declaratory statement as to the adoption contract, regardless of when filed, shall be consolidated with any related petition for adoption. The clerk of the court shall only assess one filing fee that includes the adoption action, the declaratory statement petition, and the petition for termination of parental rights.

(f)   Prior approval of fees and costs by the court does not obligate the parent to ultimately relinquish the minor for adoption.

(6)   STEPCHILD, RELATIVE, AND ADULT ADOPTIONS.—Petitions for the adoption of a stepchild, a relative, or an adult shall not require the filing of a separate judgment or separate proceeding terminating parental rights pending adoption. The final judgment of adoption shall have the effect of terminating parental rights simultaneously with the granting of the decree of adoption.

History.—s. 10, ch. 73-159; s. 7, ch. 75-226; s. 5, ch. 87-397; s. 2, ch. 90-55; s. 11, ch. 92-96; s. 339, ch. 95-147; s. 21, ch. 2001-3; s. 22, ch. 2003-58; s. 9, ch. 2005-2, s. 16, ch. 2008-151.

63.112   Petition for adoption; description; report or recommendation, exceptions; mailing.—

(1)   The petition for adoption shall be signed and verified by the petitioner and filed with the clerk of the court and shall state:

(a)   The date and place of birth of the person to be adopted, if known;

(b)   The name to be given to the person to be adopted;

(c)   The date petitioner acquired custody of the minor and the name of the adoption entity placing the minor, if any;

(d)   The full name, age, and place and duration of residence of the petitioner;

(e)   The marital status of the petitioner, including the date and place of marriage, if married, and divorces, if applicable to the adoption by a stepparent;

(f)   A statement that the petitioner is able to provide for the material needs of the child;

(g)   A description and estimate of the value of any property of the person to be adopted;

(h)   The case style and date of entry of the judgment terminating parental rights or, if the adoptee is an adult or a minor relative or a stepchild of the petitioner, the address, if known, of any person whose consent to the adoption is required and, if such person has not consented, the facts or circumstances that excuse the lack of consent to justify a termination of parental rights; and

(i)   The reasons why the petitioner desires to adopt the person.

(2)   The following documents are required to be filed with the clerk of the court at the time the petition is filed:

(a)   A certified copy of the court judgment terminating parental rights under chapter 39 or under this chapter or, if the adoptee is an adult or a minor relative or stepchild of the petitioner, the required consent, unless such consent is excused by the court.

(b) The favorable preliminary home study of the department, licensed child-placing agency, or professional pursuant to s. 63.092, as to the suitability of the home in which the minor has been placed, unless the petitioner is a stepparent or a relative.

(c) A copy of any declaratory statement previously entered by the court pursuant to s. 63.102.

(d) Documentation that an interview was held with the minor, if older than 12 years of age, unless the court, in the best interest of the minor, dispenses with the minor's consent under s. 63.062(1)(c).

(3) Unless ordered by the court, no report or recommendation is required when the placement is a stepparent adoption or an adult adoption or when the minor is a relative of one of the adoptive parents.

History.—s. 11, ch. 73-159; s. 8, ch. 75-226; s. 19, ch. 77-147; s. 5, ch. 83-215; s. 12, ch. 92-96; s. 22, ch. 2001-3; s. 23, ch. 2003-58.

63.122   Notice of hearing on petition.—

(1) The hearing on the petition to adopt a minor may not be held sooner than 30 days after the date the judgment terminating parental rights was entered or sooner than 90 days after the date the minor was placed in the physical custody of the petitioner, unless good cause is shown for a shortening of these time periods. The minor must remain under the supervision of the adoption entity until the adoption becomes final. When the adoptee is an adult, the hearing may be held immediately after the filing of the petition. If the petitioner is a stepparent or a relative of the adoptee, the hearing may be held immediately after the filing of the petition if all persons whose consent is required have executed a valid consent and the consent has been filed with the court.

(2) Notice of hearing must be given as prescribed by the Florida Rules of Civil Procedure, and service of process must be made as specified by law for civil actions.

(3) Upon a showing by the petitioner or parent that the privacy, safety, or welfare of the petitioner, parent, or minor may be endangered, the court may order that the names of the petitioner, parent, minor, or all be deleted from the notice of hearing and from the copy of the petition attached thereto if the substantive rights of any person are not affected.

(4) Notice of the hearing must be given by the petitioner to the adoption entity that places the minor.

(5) After filing the petition to adopt an adult, the court may order an appropriate investigation to assist in determining whether the adoption is in the best interest of the persons involved and is in accordance with state law.

History.—s. 12, ch. 73-159; s. 9, ch. 75-226; s. 20. ch. 77-147; s. 13, ch. 92-96; s. 23, ch. 2001-3; s. 24, ch. 2003-58; s. 17, ch. 2008-151.

63.125   Final home investigation.—

(1) The final home investigation must be conducted before the adoption becomes final. The investigation may be conducted by a licensed child-placing agency or a professional in the same manner as provided in s. 63.092 to ascertain whether the adoptive home is a suitable home for the minor and whether the proposed adoption is in the best interest of the minor. Unless directed by the court, an investigation and recommendation are not required if the petitioner is a stepparent or if the minor is related to one of the adoptive parents within the third degree of consanguinity. The department is required to perform the home investigation only if there is no licensed child-placing agency or professional pursuant to s. 63.092 in the county in which the prospective adoptive parent resides.

(2) The department, the licensed child-placing agency, or the professional that performs the investigation must file a written report of the investigation with the court and the petitioner within 90 days after placement.

(3)   The report of the investigation must contain an evaluation of the placement with a recommendation on the granting of the petition for adoption and any other information the court requires regarding the petitioner or the minor.

(4)   The department, the licensed child-placing agency, or the professional making the required investigation may request other state agencies or child-placing agencies within or outside this state to make investigations of designated parts of the inquiry and to make a written report to the department, the professional, or other person or agency.

(5)   The final home investigation must include:

(a)   The information from the preliminary home study.

(b)   After the minor is placed in the intended adoptive home, two scheduled visits with the minor and the minor's adoptive parent or parents, one of which visits must be in the home, to determine the suitability of the placement.

(c)   The family social and medical history as provided in s. 63.082.

(d)   Any other information relevant to the suitability of the intended adoptive home.

(e)   Any other relevant information, as provided in rules that the department may adopt.

History.—s. 14, ch. 92-96; s. 24, ch. 2001-3; s. 25, ch. 2003-58.

63.132   Affidavit of expenses and receipts.—

(1)   Before the hearing on the petition for adoption, the prospective adoptive parent and any adoption entity must file two copies of an affidavit under this section.

(a)   The affidavit must be signed by the adoption entity and the prospective adoptive parents. A copy of the affidavit must be provided to the adoptive parents at the time the affidavit is executed.

(b)   The affidavit must itemize all disbursements and receipts of anything of value, including professional and legal fees, made or agreed to be made by or on behalf of the prospective adoptive parent and any adoption entity in connection with the adoption or in connection with any prior proceeding to terminate parental rights which involved the minor who is the subject of the petition for adoption. The affidavit must also include, for each legal or counseling fee itemized, the service provided for which the fee is being charged, the date the service was provided, the time required to provide the service if the service was charged by the hour, the person or entity that provided the service, and the hourly fee charged.

(c)   The affidavit must show any expenses or receipts incurred in connection with:

1.   The birth of the minor.

2.   The placement of the minor with the petitioner.

3.   The medical or hospital care received by the mother or by the minor during the mother's prenatal care and confinement.

4.   The living expenses of the birth mother. The living expenses must be itemized in detail to apprise the court of the exact expenses incurred.

5.   The services relating to the adoption or to the placement of the minor for adoption that were received by or on behalf of the petitioner, the adoption entity, either parent, the minor, or any other person.

The affidavit must state whether any of these expenses were paid for by collateral sources, including, but not limited to, health insurance, Medicaid, Medicare, or public assistance.

(2)   The court may require such additional information as is deemed necessary.

(3)   The court must issue a separate order approving or disapproving the fees, costs, and expenses itemized in the affidavit. The court may approve only fees, costs, and expenditures allowed under s.

63.097. The court may reject in whole or in part any fee, cost, or expenditure listed if the court finds that the expense is:

(a) Contrary to this chapter;

(b) Not supported by a receipt in the record, if the expense is not a fee of the adoption entity; or

(c) Not a reasonable fee or expense, considering the requirements of this chapter and the totality of the circumstances.

(4) This section does not apply to an adoption by a stepparent or an adoption of a relative or adult, the finalization of an adoption of a minor if the parental rights were terminated under chapter 39, or the domestication of an adoption decree of a minor child adopted in a foreign country.

History.—s. 13, ch. 73-159; s. 21, ch. 77-147; s. 15, ch. 92-96; s. 8, ch. 2000-151; s. 25, ch. 2001-3; s. 26, ch. 2003-58; s. 18, ch. 2008-151.

63.135   Information to be submitted to the court.—

(1) The adoption entity or petitioner must file an affidavit under the Uniform Child Custody Jurisdiction and Enforcement Act in the termination of parental rights proceeding in the first pleading or in an affidavit attached to that pleading.

(2) Each party has a continuing duty to inform the court of any custody proceeding concerning the child in this or any other state about which he or she obtained information during this proceeding.

History.—s. 6, ch. 87-397; s. 340, ch. 95-147; s. 27, ch. 2003-58; s. 19, ch. 2008-151.

63.142   Hearing; judgment of adoption.—

(1) APPEARANCE.—The petitioner and the person to be adopted shall appear either in person or, with the permission of the court, telephonically before a person authorized to administer an oath at the hearing on the petition for adoption, unless:

(a) The person is a minor under 12 years of age; or

(b) The appearance of either is excused by the court for good cause.

(2) CONTINUANCE.—The court may continue the hearing from time to time to permit further observation, investigation, or consideration of any facts or circumstances affecting the granting of the petition.

(3) DISMISSAL.—

(a) If the petition is dismissed, further proceedings, if any, regarding the minor must be brought in a separate custody action under chapter 61, a dependency action under chapter 39, or a paternity action under chapter 742.

(b) If the petition is dismissed, the court shall state with specificity the reasons for the dismissal.

(4) JUDGMENT.—At the conclusion of the hearing, after the court determines that the date for a parent to file an appeal of a valid judgment terminating that parent's parental rights has passed and no appeal, pursuant to the Florida Rules of Appellate Procedure, is pending and that the adoption is in the best interest of the person to be adopted, a judgment of adoption shall be entered. A judgment terminating parental rights pending adoption is voidable and any later judgment of adoption of that minor is voidable if, upon a parent's motion for relief from judgment, the court finds that the adoption substantially fails to meet the requirements of this chapter. The motion must be filed within a reasonable time, but not later than 1 year after the date the judgment terminating parental rights was entered.

History.—s. 14, ch. 73-159; s. 3, ch. 77-140; s. 26, ch. 2001-3; s. 28, ch. 2003-58; s. 20, ch. 2008-151.

63.152   Application for new birth record.—Within 30 days after entry of a judgment of adoption, the clerk of the court or the adoption entity shall transmit a certified statement of the entry to the

state registrar of vital statistics on a form provided by the registrar. A new birth record containing the necessary information supplied by the certificate shall be issued by the registrar on application of the adopting parents or the adopted person.

History.—s. 15, ch. 73-159; s. 5, ch. 90-309; s. 29, ch. 2003-58; s. 19, ch. 2012-81.

63.162   Hearings and records in adoption proceedings; confidential nature.—

(1)   All hearings held in proceedings under this act shall be held in closed court without admittance of any person other than essential officers of the court, the parties, witnesses, counsel, persons who have not consented to the adoption and are required to consent, and representatives of the agencies who are present to perform their official duties.

(2)   All papers and records pertaining to the adoption, including the original birth certificate, whether part of the permanent record of the court or a file in the office of an adoption entity are confidential and subject to inspection only upon order of the court; however, the petitioner in any proceeding for adoption under this chapter may, at the option of the petitioner, make public the reasons for a denial of the petition for adoption. The order must specify which portion of the records are subject to inspection, and it may exclude the name and identifying information concerning the parent or adoptee. Papers and records of the department, a court, or any other governmental agency, which papers and records relate to adoptions, are exempt from s. 119.07(1). In the case of an adoption not handled by the department or a child-placing agency licensed by the department, the department must be given notice of hearing and be permitted to present to the court a report on the advisability of disclosing or not disclosing information pertaining to the adoption. In the case of an agency adoption, the licensed child-placing agency must be given notice of hearing and be permitted to present to the court a report on the advisability of disclosing or not disclosing information pertaining to the adoption. This subsection does not prohibit the department from inspecting and copying any official record pertaining to the adoption that is maintained by the department or from inspecting and copying any of the official records maintained by an agency licensed by the department and does not prohibit an agency from inspecting and copying any official record pertaining to the adoption that is maintained by that agency.

(3)   The court files, records, and papers in the adoption of a minor shall be indexed only in the name of the petitioner, and the name of the minor shall not be noted on any docket, index, or other record outside the court file, except that closed agency files may be cross-referenced in the original and adoptive names of the minor.

(4)   A person may not disclose from the records the name and identity of a birth parent, an adoptive parent, or an adoptee unless:

(a)   The birth parent authorizes in writing the release of his or her name;

(b)   The adoptee, if 18 or more years of age, authorizes in writing the release of his or her name; or, if the adoptee is less than 18 years of age, written consent to disclose the adoptee's name is obtained from an adoptive parent;

(c)   The adoptive parent authorizes in writing the release of his or her name; or

(d)   Upon order of the court for good cause shown. In determining whether good cause exists, the court shall give primary consideration to the best interests of the adoptee, but must also give due consideration to the interests of the adoptive and birth parents. Factors to be considered in determining whether good cause exists include, but are not limited to:

1.   The reason the information is sought;

2. The existence of means available to obtain the desired information without disclosing the identity of the birth parents, such as by having the court, a person appointed by the court, the department, or the licensed child-placing agency contact the birth parents and request specific information;

3. The desires, to the extent known, of the adoptee, the adoptive parents, and the birth parents;

4. The age, maturity, judgment, and expressed needs of the adoptee; and

5. The recommendation of the department, licensed child-placing agency, or professional which prepared the preliminary study and home investigation, or the department if no such study was prepared, concerning the advisability of disclosure.

(5) The adoptee or other person seeking information under this subsection shall pay the department or agency making reports or recommendations as required hereunder a reasonable fee for its services and expenses.

(6) Subject to the provisions of subsection (4), identifying information regarding the birth parents, adoptive parents, and adoptee may not be disclosed unless a birth parent, adoptive parent, or adoptee has authorized in writing the release of such information concerning himself or herself. Specific names or identifying information must not be given in a family medical history. All nonidentifying information, including the family medical history and social history of the adoptee and the birth parents, when available, must be furnished to the adoptive parents before the adoption becomes final and to the adoptee, upon the adoptee's request, after he or she reaches majority. Upon the request of the adoptive parents, all nonidentifying information obtained before or after the adoption has become final must be furnished to the adoptive parents.

(7) The court may, upon petition of an adult adoptee or birth parent, for good cause shown, appoint an intermediary or a licensed child-placing agency to contact a birth parent or adult adoptee, as applicable, who has not registered with the adoption registry pursuant to s. 63.165 and advise both of the availability of the intermediary or agency and that the birth parent or adult adoptee, as applicable, wishes to establish contact.

History.—s. 16, ch. 73-159; s. 10, ch. 75-226; s. 2, ch. 77-140; s. 22, ch. 77-147; s. 2, ch. 77-446; s. 3, ch. 78-190; s. 5, ch. 80-296; s. 4, ch. 82-166; s. 3, ch. 84-101; s. 2, ch. 85-189; s. 2, ch. 87-16; s. 19, ch. 90-360; s. 16, ch. 92-96; s. 341, ch. 95-147; s. 23, ch. 96-406; s. 25, ch. 99-2; s. 27, ch. 2001-3; s. 30, ch. 2003-58; s. 20, ch. 2012-81.

63.165 **State registry of adoption information; duty to inform and explain.**—Notwithstanding any other law to the contrary, the department shall maintain a registry with the last known names and addresses of an adoptee and his or her parents whose consent was required under s. 63.062, and adoptive parents and any other identifying information that the adoptee, parents whose consent was required under s. 63.062, or adoptive parents desire to include in the registry. The department shall maintain the registry records for the time required by rules adopted by the department in accordance with this chapter or for 99 years, whichever period is greater. The registry shall be open with respect to all adoptions in the state, regardless of when they took place. The registry shall be available for those persons choosing to enter information therein, but no one shall be required to do so.

(1) Anyone seeking to enter, change, or use information in the registry, or any agent of such person, shall present verification of his or her identity and, if applicable, his or her authority. A person who enters information in the registry shall be required to indicate clearly the persons to whom he or she is consenting to release this information, which persons shall be limited to the adoptee and the birth mother, father whose consent was required under s. 63.062, adoptive mother, adoptive father, birth siblings, and maternal and paternal birth grandparents of the adoptee. Except as provided in this section, information in the registry is confidential and exempt from s. 119.07(1). Consent to the release of this information may be made in the case of a minor adoptee by his or her adoptive parents or by the

court after a showing of good cause. At any time, any person may withdraw, limit, or otherwise restrict consent to release information by notifying the department in writing.

(2)   The department may charge a reasonable fee to any person seeking to enter, change, or use information in the registry. The department shall deposit such fees in a trust fund to be used by the department only for the efficient administration of this section. The department and agencies shall make counseling available for a fee to all persons seeking to use the registry, and the department shall inform all affected persons of the availability of such counseling.

(3)   The adoption entity must inform the parents before parental rights are terminated, and the adoptive parents before placement, in writing, of the existence and purpose of the registry established under this section, but failure to do so does not affect the validity of any proceeding under this chapter.

History.—s. 5, ch. 82-166; s. 29, ch. 87-387; s. 3, ch. 91-99; s. 17, ch. 92-96; s. 85, ch. 97-237; s. 28, ch. 2001-3.

63.167   State adoption information center.—

(1)   The department shall establish a state adoption information center for the purpose of increasing public knowledge about adoption and promoting to adolescents and pregnant women the availability of adoption services. The department shall contract with one or more licensed child-placing agencies to operate the state adoption information center.

(2)   The functions of the state adoption information center shall include:

(a)   Providing a training program for persons who counsel adolescents, including, but not limited to, school counselors, county child welfare services employees, and family planning clinic employees.

(b)   Recruiting adoption services specialist trainees, and providing a training program for such specialists.

(c)   Operating a toll-free telephone number to provide information and referral services. The state adoption information center shall provide contact information for all adoption entities in the caller's county or, if no adoption entities are located in the caller's county, the number of the nearest adoption entity when contacted for a referral to make an adoption plan and shall rotate the order in which the names of adoption entities are provided to callers.

(d)   Distributing pamphlets which provide information on the availability of adoption services.

(e)   Promoting adoption through the communications media.

(f)   Maintaining a list of licensed child-placing agencies eligible and willing to take custody of and place newborn infants left at a hospital, pursuant to s. 383.50. The names and contact information for the licensed child-placing agencies on the list shall be provided on a rotating basis to the statewide central abuse hotline.

(3)   The department shall ensure equitable distribution of referrals to licensed child-placing agencies.

History.—s. 62, ch. 90-306; s. 4, ch. 2000-188; s. 31, ch. 2003-58; s. 21, ch. 2012-81; s. 22, ch. 2012-116.

63.172   Effect of judgment of adoption.—

(1)   A judgment of adoption, whether entered by a court of this state, another state, or of any other place, has the following effect:

(a)   It relieves the birth parents of the adopted person, except a birth parent who is a petitioner or who is married to a petitioner, of all parental rights and responsibilities.

(b)   It terminates all legal relationships between the adopted person and the adopted person's relatives, including the birth parents, except a birth parent who is a petitioner or who is married to a petitioner, so that the adopted person thereafter is a stranger to his or her former relatives for all purposes, including the interpretation or construction of documents, statutes, and instruments, whether executed before or after entry of the adoption judgment, that do not expressly include the adopted person by name or by some designation not based on a parent and child or blood relationship, except that rights of inheritance shall be as provided in the Florida Probate Code.

(c)   Except for rights of inheritance, it creates the relationship between the adopted person and the petitioner and all relatives of the petitioner that would have existed if the adopted person were a blood descendant of the petitioner born within wedlock. This relationship shall be created for all purposes, including applicability of statutes, documents, and instruments, whether executed before or after entry of the adoption judgment, that do not expressly exclude an adopted person from their operation or effect.

(2)   If one or both parents of a child die without the relationship of parent and child having been previously terminated and a spouse of the living parent or a close relative of the child thereafter adopts the child, the child's right of inheritance from or through the deceased parent is unaffected by the adoption and, unless the court orders otherwise, the adoption will not terminate any grandparental rights delineated under chapter 752. For purposes of this subsection, a close relative of a child is the child's brother, sister, grandparent, aunt, or uncle.

History.—s. 17, ch. 73-159; s. 11, ch. 75-226; s. 1, ch. 79-369; s. 1, ch. 87-27; s. 1, ch. 90-139; s. 18, ch. 92-96; s. 1, ch. 93-192; s. 342, ch. 95-147; s. 1, ch. 2001-226.

63.182   Statute of repose.—

(1)   Notwithstanding s. 95.031 or s. 95.11 or any other statute, an action or proceeding of any kind to vacate, set aside, or otherwise nullify a judgment of adoption or an underlying judgment terminating parental rights on any ground may not be filed more than 1 year after entry of the judgment terminating parental rights.

(2)(a)   Except for the specific persons expressly entitled to be given notice of an adoption in accordance with this chapter, the interest that entitles a person to notice of an adoption must be direct, financial, and immediate, and the person must show that he or she will gain or lose by the direct legal operation and effect of the judgment. A showing of an indirect, inconsequential, or contingent interest is wholly inadequate, and a person with this indirect interest lacks standing to set aside a judgment of adoption.

(b)   This subsection is remedial and shall apply to all adoptions, including those in which a judgment of adoption has already been entered.

History.—s. 18, ch. 73-159; s. 6, ch. 2000-188; s. 32, ch. 2003-58; s. 32, ch. 2003-154; s. 4, ch. 2006-265.

63.192   Recognition of foreign judgment or decree affecting adoption.—A judgment terminating the relationship of parent and child or establishing the relationship by adoption, or a decree granting legal guardianship for purposes of adoption, issued pursuant to due process of law by a court or authorized body of any other jurisdiction within or without the United States shall be recognized in this state, and the rights and obligations of the parties shall be determined as though the judgment or decree were issued by a court of this state. A judgment or decree of a court or authorized body terminating the relationship of a parent and child, whether independent, incorporated in an adoption decree, or incorporated in a legal guardianship order issued pursuant to due process of law of any other jurisdiction within or without the United States, shall be deemed to effectively terminate parental rights for purposes of a proceeding on a petition for adoption in this state. If a minor child has been made available for adoption in a foreign state or foreign country and the parental rights of the minor child's parent have been terminated or the child has been declared to be abandoned or orphaned, no

additional termination of parental rights proceeding need occur, and the adoption may be finalized according to the procedures set forth in this chapter.

History.—s. 19, ch. 73-159; s. 21, ch. 2008-151.

63.202   Authority to license; adoption of rules.—

(1)   The Department of Children and Families is authorized and empowered to license child placement agencies that it determines to be qualified to place minors for adoption.

(2)   No agency shall place a minor for adoption unless such agency is licensed by the department, except a child-caring agency registered under s. 409.176.

(3)   The department may adopt rules necessary to ensure that all child-placing agencies comply with this chapter to receive or renew a license.

History.—s. 20, ch. 73-159; s. 23, ch. 77-147; s. 7, ch. 78-190; s. 8, ch. 87-397; s. 12, ch. 97-101; s. 29, ch. 2001-3; s. 22, ch. 2012-81; s. 29, ch. 2014-19.

63.207   Out-of-state placement.—

(1)   Unless the parent placing a minor for adoption files an affidavit that the parent chooses to place the minor outside the state, giving the reason for that placement, or the minor is to be placed with a relative or with a stepparent, or the minor is a special needs child, as defined in s. 409.166, or for other good cause shown, an adoption entity may not:

(a)   Take or send a minor out of the state for the purpose of placement for adoption; or

(b)   Place or attempt to place a minor for the purpose of adoption with a family who primarily lives and works outside Florida in another state. If an adoption entity is acting under this subsection, the adoption entity must file a petition for declaratory statement pursuant to s. 63.102 for prior approval of fees and costs. The court shall review the costs pursuant to s. 63.097. The petition for declaratory statement must be converted to a petition for an adoption upon placement of the minor in the home. When a minor is placed for adoption with prospective adoptive parents who primarily live and work outside this state, the circuit court in this state may retain jurisdiction over the matter until the adoption becomes final. The prospective adoptive parents may finalize the adoption in this state.

(2)   An adoption entity may not counsel a birth mother to leave the state for the purpose of giving birth to a child outside the state in order to secure a fee in excess of that permitted under s. 63.097 when it is the intention that the child is to be placed for adoption outside the state.

(3)   When applicable, the Interstate Compact on the Placement of Children authorized in s. 409.401 shall be used in placing children outside the state for adoption.

History.—s. 12, ch. 75-226; s. 24, ch. 77-147; s. 8, ch. 78-190; s. 4, ch. 84-101; s. 9, ch. 87-397; s. 21, ch. 92-96; s. 30, ch. 2001-3; s. 34, ch. 2003-58.

63.212   Prohibited acts; penalties for violation.—

(1)   It is unlawful for any person:

(a)   To place or attempt to place a minor for adoption with a person who primarily lives and works outside this state unless all of the requirements of the Interstate Compact for the Placement of Children, when applicable, have been met.

(b)   Except an adoption entity, to place or attempt to place within the state a minor for adoption unless the minor is placed with a relative or with a stepparent. This prohibition, however, does not apply to a person who is placing or attempting to place a minor for the purpose of adoption with the adoption entity.

(c)   To sell or surrender, or to arrange for the sale or surrender of, a minor to another person for money or anything of value or to receive such minor child for such payment or thing of value. If a minor is being adopted by a relative or by a stepparent, or is being adopted through an adoption entity, this paragraph does not prohibit the person who is contemplating adopting the child from paying, under ss. 63.097 and 63.132, the actual prenatal care and living expenses of the mother of the child to be adopted, or from paying, under ss. 63.097 and 63.132, the actual living and medical expenses of such mother for a reasonable time, not to exceed 6 weeks, if medical needs require such support, after the birth of the minor.

(d)   Having the rights and duties of a parent with respect to the care and custody of a minor to assign or transfer such parental rights for the purpose of, incidental to, or otherwise connected with, selling or offering to sell such rights and duties.

(e)   To assist in the commission of any act prohibited in paragraphs (a)-(d). In the case of a stepparent adoption, this paragraph does not preclude the forgiveness of vested child support arrearages owed by a parent.

(f)   Except an adoption entity, to charge or accept any fee or compensation of any nature from anyone for making a referral in connection with an adoption.

(g)   Except an adoption entity, to place an advertisement or offer to the public, in any way, by any medium whatever that a minor is available for adoption or that a minor is sought for adoption; and, further, it is unlawful for any person purchasing advertising space or purchasing broadcast time to advertise adoption services to fail to include in any publication or fail to include in the broadcast for such advertisement the Florida license number of the adoption entity or The Florida Bar number of the attorney placing the advertisement.

1.   Only a person who is an attorney licensed to practice law in this state or an adoption entity licensed under the laws of this state may place a paid advertisement or paid listing of the person's telephone number, on the person's own behalf, in a telephone directory that:

a.   A child is offered or wanted for adoption; or

b.   The person is able to place, locate, or receive a child for adoption.

2.   A person who publishes a telephone directory that is distributed in this state shall include, at the beginning of any classified heading for adoption and adoption services, a statement that informs directory users that only attorneys licensed to practice law in this state and licensed adoption entities may legally provide adoption services under state law.

3.   A person who places an advertisement described in subparagraph 1. in a telephone directory must include the following information:

a.   For an attorney licensed to practice law in this state, the person's Florida Bar number.

b.   For a child-placing agency licensed under the laws of this state, the number on the person's adoption entity license.

(h)   To contract for the purchase, sale, or transfer of custody or parental rights in connection with any child, in connection with any fetus yet unborn, or in connection with any fetus identified in any way but not yet conceived, in return for any valuable consideration. Any such contract is void and unenforceable as against the public policy of this state. However, fees, costs, and other incidental payments made in accordance with statutory provisions for adoption, foster care, and child welfare are permitted, and a person may agree to pay expenses in connection with a preplanned adoption agreement as specified below, but the payment of such expenses may not be conditioned upon the transfer of parental rights. Each petition for adoption which is filed in connection with a preplanned adoption agreement must clearly identify the adoption as a preplanned adoption arrangement and must include a copy of the preplanned adoption agreement for review by the court.

(2) Any person who is a birth mother, or a woman who holds herself out to be a birth mother, who is interested in making an adoption plan and who knowingly or intentionally benefits from the payment of adoption-related expenses in connection with that adoption plan commits adoption deception if:

(a) The person knows or should have known that the person is not pregnant at the time the sums were requested or received;

(b) The person accepts living expenses assistance from a prospective adoptive parent or adoption entity without disclosing that she is receiving living expenses assistance from another prospective adoptive parent or adoption entity at the same time in an effort to adopt the same child; or

(c) The person knowingly makes false representations to induce the payment of living expenses and does not intend to make an adoptive placement.

Any person who willfully commits adoption deception commits a misdemeanor of the second degree, punishable as provided in s. 775.082 or s. 775.083, if the sums received by the birth mother or woman holding herself out to be a birth mother do not exceed $300, and a felony of the third degree, punishable as provided in s. 775.082, s. 775.083, or s. 775.084, if the sums received by the birth mother or woman holding herself out to be a birth mother exceed $300. In addition, the person is liable for damages caused by such acts or omissions, including reasonable attorney fees and costs incurred by the adoption entity or the prospective adoptive parent. Damages may be awarded through restitution in any related criminal prosecution or by filing a separate civil action.

(3) This section does not prohibit an adoption entity from charging fees permitted under this chapter and reasonably commensurate to the services provided.

(4) It is unlawful for any adoption entity to fail to report to the court, within a reasonable time period, the intended placement of a minor for purposes of adoption with any person not a stepparent or a relative, if the adoption entity participates in such intended placement.

(5) It is unlawful for any adoption entity to charge any fee except those fees permitted under s. 63.097 and approved under s. 63.102.

(6) It is unlawful for any adoption entity to counsel a birth mother to leave the state for the purpose of giving birth to a child outside the state in order to secure a fee in excess of that permitted under s. 63.097 when it is the intention that the child be placed for adoption outside the state.

(7) It is unlawful for any adoption entity to obtain a preliminary home study or final home investigation and fail to disclose the existence of the study or investigation to the court when required by law to do so.

(8) Unless otherwise indicated, a person who willfully and with criminal intent violates any provision of this section, excluding paragraph (1)(g), commits a felony of the third degree, punishable as provided in s. 775.082, s. 775.083, or s. 775.084. A person who willfully and with criminal intent violates paragraph (1)(g) commits a misdemeanor of the second degree, punishable as provided in s. 775.083; and each day of continuing violation shall be considered a separate offense.

History.—s. 21, ch. 73-159; s. 13, ch. 75-226; s. 25, ch. 77-147; s. 1, ch. 77-174; s. 9, ch. 78-190; s. 6, ch. 80-296; s. 5, ch. 84-101; s. 8, ch. 87-224; s. 10, ch. 87-397; s. 1, ch. 88-143; s. 3, ch. 90-55; s. 23, ch. 90-306; s. 22, ch. 92-96; s. 13, ch. 97-101; s. 31, ch. 2001-3; s. 35, ch. 2003-58; s. 22, ch. 2008-151; s. 23, ch. 2012-81; s. 20, ch. 2014-224.

63.213   Preplanned adoption agreement.—

(1) Individuals may enter into a preplanned adoption arrangement as specified in this section, but such arrangement may not in any way:

(a) Effect final transfer of custody of a child or final adoption of a child without review and approval of the court and without compliance with other applicable provisions of law.

(b)   Constitute consent of a mother to place her biological child for adoption until 48 hours after the birth of the child and unless the court making the custody determination or approving the adoption determines that the mother was aware of her right to rescind within the 48-hour period after the birth of the child but chose not to rescind such consent. The volunteer mother's right to rescind her consent in a preplanned adoption applies only when the child is genetically related to her.

(2)   A preplanned adoption agreement must include, but need not be limited to, the following terms:

(a)   That the volunteer mother agrees to become pregnant by the fertility technique specified in the agreement, to bear the child, and to terminate any parental rights and responsibilities to the child she might have through a written consent executed at the same time as the preplanned adoption agreement, subject to a right of rescission by the volunteer mother any time within 48 hours after the birth of the child, if the volunteer mother is genetically related to the child.

(b)   That the volunteer mother agrees to submit to reasonable medical evaluation and treatment and to adhere to reasonable medical instructions about her prenatal health.

(c)   That the volunteer mother acknowledges that she is aware that she will assume parental rights and responsibilities for the child born to her as otherwise provided by law for a mother if the intended father and intended mother terminate the agreement before final transfer of custody is completed, if a court determines that a parent clearly specified by the preplanned adoption agreement to be the biological parent is not the biological parent, or if the preplanned adoption is not approved by the court pursuant to the Florida Adoption Act.

(d)   That an intended father who is also the biological father acknowledges that he is aware that he will assume parental rights and responsibilities for the child as otherwise provided by law for a father if the agreement is terminated for any reason by any party before final transfer of custody is completed or if the planned adoption is not approved by the court pursuant to the Florida Adoption Act.

(e)   That the intended father and intended mother acknowledge that they may not receive custody or the parental rights under the agreement if the volunteer mother terminates the agreement or if the volunteer mother rescinds her consent to place her child for adoption within 48 hours after the birth of the child, if the volunteer mother is genetically related to the child.

(f)   That the intended father and intended mother may agree to pay all reasonable legal, medical, psychological, or psychiatric expenses of the volunteer mother related to the preplanned adoption arrangement and may agree to pay the reasonable living expenses and wages lost due to the pregnancy and birth of the volunteer mother and reasonable compensation for inconvenience, discomfort, and medical risk. No other compensation, whether in cash or in kind, shall be made pursuant to a preplanned adoption arrangement.

(g)   That the intended father and intended mother agree to accept custody of and to assert full parental rights and responsibilities for the child immediately upon the child's birth, regardless of any impairment to the child.

(h)   That the intended father and intended mother shall have the right to specify the blood and tissue typing tests to be performed if the agreement specifies that at least one of them is intended to be the biological parent of the child.

(i)   That the agreement may be terminated at any time by any of the parties.

(3)   A preplanned adoption agreement shall not contain any provision:

(a)   To reduce any amount paid to the volunteer mother if the child is stillborn or is born alive but impaired, or to provide for the payment of a supplement or bonus for any reason.

(b)   Requiring the termination of the volunteer mother's pregnancy.

(4)   An attorney who represents an intended father and intended mother or any other attorney with whom that attorney is associated shall not represent simultaneously a female who is or proposes to be a volunteer mother in any matter relating to a preplanned adoption agreement or preplanned adoption arrangement.

(5)   Payment to agents, finders, and intermediaries, including attorneys and physicians, as a finder's fee for finding volunteer mothers or matching a volunteer mother and intended father and intended mother is prohibited. Doctors, psychologists, attorneys, and other professionals may receive reasonable compensation for their professional services, such as providing medical services and procedures, legal advice in structuring and negotiating a preplanned adoption agreement, or counseling.

(6)   As used in this section, the term:

(a)   "Blood and tissue typing tests" include, but are not limited to, tests of red cell antigens, red cell isoenzymes, human leukocyte antigens, and serum proteins.

(b)   "Child" means the child or children conceived by means of a fertility technique that is part of a preplanned adoption arrangement.

(c)   "Fertility technique" means artificial embryonation, artificial insemination, whether in vivo or in vitro, egg donation, or embryo adoption.

(d)   "Intended father" means a male who, as evidenced by a preplanned adoption agreement, intends to assert the parental rights and responsibilities for a child conceived through a fertility technique, regardless of whether the child is biologically related to the male.

(e)   "Intended mother" means a female who, as evidenced by a preplanned adoption agreement, intends to assert the parental rights and responsibilities for a child conceived through a fertility technique, regardless of whether the child is biologically related to the female.

(f)   "Party" means the intended father, the intended mother, the volunteer mother, or the volunteer mother's husband, if she has a husband.

(g)   "Preplanned adoption agreement" means a written agreement among the parties that specifies the intent of the parties as to their rights and responsibilities in the preplanned adoption arrangement, consistent with the provisions of this section.

(h)   "Preplanned adoption arrangement" means the arrangement through which the parties enter into an agreement for the volunteer mother to bear the child, for payment by the intended father and intended mother of the expenses allowed by this section, for the intended father and intended mother to assert full parental rights and responsibilities to the child if consent to adoption is not rescinded after birth by a volunteer mother who is genetically related to the child, and for the volunteer mother to terminate, subject to any right of rescission, all her parental rights and responsibilities to the child in favor of the intended father and intended mother.

(i)   "Volunteer mother" means a female at least 18 years of age who voluntarily agrees, subject to a right of rescission if it is her biological child, that if she should become pregnant pursuant to a preplanned adoption arrangement, she will terminate her parental rights and responsibilities to the child in favor of the intended father and intended mother.

History.—s. 36, ch. 2003-58; s. 24, ch. 2012-81.

63.219   **Sanctions.**—Upon a finding by the court that an adoption entity has willfully violated any substantive provision of this chapter relative to the rights of the parties to the adoption and legality of the adoption process, the court is authorized to prohibit the adoption entity from placing a minor for adoption in the future in this state.

History.—s. 23, ch. 92-96; s. 32, ch. 2001-3; s. 37, ch. 2003-58.

63.222 Effect on prior adoption proceedings.—Any adoption made before July 1, 2012, is valid, and any proceedings pending on that date and any subsequent amendments thereto are not affected thereby unless the amendment is designated as a remedial provision.

History.—s. 22, ch. 73-159; s. 25, ch. 2012-81.

63.232 Duty of person adopting.—In order to protect the rights of all the parties involved in an adoption, any person adopting or attempting to adopt another person shall comply with the procedures established by this act.

History.—s. 23, ch. 73-159.

63.2325 Conditions for invalidation of a consent to adoption or affidavit of nonpaternity.—Notwithstanding the requirements of this chapter, a failure to meet any of those requirements does not constitute grounds for invalidation of a consent to adoption or revocation of an affidavit of nonpaternity unless the extent and circumstances of such a failure result in a material failure of fundamental fairness in the administration of due process, or the failure constitutes or contributes to fraud or duress in obtaining a consent to adoption or affidavit of nonpaternity.

History.—s. 33, ch. 2001-3; s. 26, ch. 2012-81; s. 10, ch. 2013-15.

63.233 Rulemaking authority.—The department shall adopt rules pursuant to ss. 120.536(1) and 120.54 to implement the provisions of this chapter.

History.—s. 11, ch. 87-397; s. 10, ch. 98-200.

63.235 Petitions filed before effective date; governing law.—Any petition for adoption filed before the effective date of this act shall be governed by the law in effect at the time the petition was filed.

History.—s. 37, ch. 2001-3; s. 38, ch. 2003-58.

63.236 Petitions filed before July 1, 2008; governing law.—A petition for termination of parental rights filed before July 1, 2008, is governed by the law in effect at the time the petition was filed.

History.—s. 23, ch. 2008-151.

Appendix E

Avoiding Adoption Scams

$\mathcal{A}$doption
$\mathcal{A}$dvocate

National Council For Adoption

ELISA ROSMAN, EDITOR
NICOLE M. CALLAHAN, EDITOR
CHUCK JOHNSON, EDITOR

NO. 36 • JUNE 2011   A PUBLICATION OF THE NATIONAL COUNCIL FOR ADOPTION

AVOIDING ADOPTION SCAMS

By Hal Kaufman[†]
June 2011

Editor's Note

NCFA is committed to protecting the best interests of and advocating for all members of the adoption triad: birthparents, adoptive parents, and children. While it is possible for birthparents to be defrauded, the author and NCFA agreed to focus this article specifically on prospective adoptive parents. Future Advocates will continue to focus on the protection and best interests of birthparents and children, as well.

Introduction

Most adoptions go well. The adoptive family has good intentions and works with adoption professionals who help address everyone's needs and legal rights. However, the fact remains that adoption fraud does indeed exist. Creating a legally binding family through adoption isn't always easy, and the existence of adoption fraud can make the process even more challenging.

It is important to note that not all unfortunate circumstances are the result of fraud. A finalized adoption may not occur even if adoption professionals provide all of the services for which a prospective adoptive family pays. An expectant mother may intend to place her child

with an adoptive family, then ultimately change her mind and decide to parent before the end of the legal risk period. These are difficult situations, but they are not necessarily the result of fraud.

When it comes to adoption fraud, the biggest factor working against prospective adoptive families is their strong, "I'll do whatever it takes" desire to adopt. Even when adoptive parents realize that something is amiss in a particular situation, their deep desire to adopt can sometimes override their instincts and logic and allow them to emotionally rationalize what is happening.

To decrease their chances of becoming victims of fraud, prospective adoptive parents must edu-

——————————— National Council For Adoption ———————————
225 N. Washington Street • Alexandria, VA 22314 • (703) 299-6633 • www.adoptioncouncil.org

1

Adoption Advocate

cate themselves about adoption scams, the common early warning signs that something is not right, and the actions they can take to help ensure a safe adoption.

While adoption fraud can certainly exist in international adoption, this *Adoption Advocate* focuses on domestic adoptions and the ways in which potential adoptive parents can recognize and avoid fraud.

Adoption Scams

An adoption scam occurs when an adoption professional, potential birth family, or prospective adoptive parent intentionally deceives another party for personal gain. The personal gain may be financial, but it may also be related to getting attention or experiencing a sense of power.

Here are just a few examples of fraudulent behavior:

- An adoption professional purposefully withholds medical information from an adoptive family to push an adoption through that the family would not otherwise pursue.
- An adoption professional promises an expectant mother that she will pay for her medical expenses, but then the professional reneges on the promise after parental rights are terminated.
- A woman pretends to be pregnant and leads a prospective adoptive family to believe that she is considering making an adoption plan with them.
- A pregnant woman promises to make an adoption plan with multiple families while accepting money for pregnancy-related expenses from all of them.
- A prospective adoptive family promises an open adoption to an expectant mother

so that she will make an adoption plan with them and then cuts off all contact after the adoption is finalized.

To avoid experiencing adoption fraud, prospective adoptive parents must pay close attention to the warning signs and practice due diligence when circumstances warrant.

While multiple types of adoption fraud unfortunately can and do occur, the remainder of this article focuses on fraud perpetrated against prospective adoptive parents.

Pay Attention to the Warning Signs

According to NCFA president Chuck Johnson, who spent 17 years working with hundreds of birthparents and adoptive families as the director of an adoption agency, "Many adoptive families that experience fraud recognize the seriousness of the warning signs only in hindsight. These families later acknowledge that they just didn't pay attention to the red flags or hoped that, by ignoring them, things would somehow work out. Unfortunately, it's impossible to get out of a bad situation or take steps to learn more if you cannot identify the red flags early on."

It's important to remember that a red flag or warning sign doesn't mean that a fraud will occur. It should be a trigger for adoptive families, however, to "dig deeper," further research the people with whom they are working, and proceed with caution.

Many adoptive families that experience fraud recognize the seriousness of the warning signs only in hindsight. These families later acknowledge that they just didn't pay attention to the red flags or hoped that, by ignoring them, things would somehow work out. Unfortunately, it's impossible to get out of a bad situation or take steps to learn more if you cannot identify the red flags early on.

Adoption Advocate

Warning Signs of Fraud by Adoption Professionals

Here are some of the more common warning signs of adoption professionals defrauding prospective adoptive parents:

- They are not responsive to calls or emails.
- They never send requested and promised documents.
- They pressure families inappropriately.
- They suggest atypical approaches or methods that conflict with previous commitments or written agreements. At their worst, they break the law.
- They don't take the necessary steps to learn about the expectant mother and biological father, thereby taking unnecessary risks due to lack of knowledge that the adoptive family must ultimately bear.
- They make guarantees about a situation or how quickly a prospective adoptive family will match and adopt.
- They find the adoptive family online and present them with just the "perfect" opportunity.

Warning Signs of Fraud by Potential Birthmothers

There are also warning signs related to birthmothers who may be attempting to commit adoption fraud:

- They continually make excuses for not sending proof of pregnancy, not responding to emails and messages, or missing scheduled calls or meetings.
- They immediately tell a prospective adoptive family how wonderful the family is without asking many questions or getting to know them at all.
- They avoid meeting with an adoption agency, pregnancy counselor, or attorney.
- They always seem like they are in the middle of multiple crises, and they try to pull the prospective adoptive family into their drama.
- They frequently ask the potential adoptive parents about paying for expenses.

Dig Deeper

Adoption scams existed long before the Internet, but the Internet does make it easier for scammers to find and take advantage of prospective adoptive parents. However, the Internet works both ways; prospective adoptive families can leverage technology to research both potential adoption professionals and potential birthparents.

Digging deeper isn't just about technology, however. Many low-tech methods may sound obvious when you read them here, yet some prospective adoptive parents spend thousands of dollars and make major life decisions without doing the proper due diligence.

Adoption scams existed long before the Internet, but the Internet does make it easier for scammers to find and take advantage of prospective adoptive parents. However, the Internet works both ways; prospective adoptive families can leverage technology to research both potential adoption professionals and potential birthparents.

Low-Tech Methods

Prospective adoptive families should interview the professionals with whom they are considering working and meet them in person. It's important to explore their values when it comes to adoption, as well as their expertise and ability to provide the required support for everyone involved. The decision to work with a particular adoption professional is too important to make without completing this basic step.

Families should also ask for references from adoption professionals and then do what many people fail to do – call them! Although the professionals will only offer satisfied clients as references, families can still ask important open-ended questions that can help provide insight into how the professional works. Make sure the references

Adoption Advocate

are from clients that have used the professional's services recently.

Families should also contact a state's bar association to research an attorney and contact a state's licensing specialist to research an agency. It's important to know whether others have made formal complaints against a particular professional.

High-Tech Methods

The Internet and technology in general can also play an important role in further researching potential adoption professionals and expectant parents. Here are just a few examples of what prospective adoptive families can do:

- Leverage adoption-related online forums to find families that have experience with a specific adoption professional.
- Publicly share non-identifying information about potential birth families (or identifying information on a one-to-one basis) to check whether the birth families are working with others or match the characteristics of prior scammers.
- Search online for past litigation against a particular adoption professional.
- Search for geotag data (latitude and longitude information) on digital picture files that potential birthparents send or identify a potential birthparent's general location from her Internet Protocol (IP) address to corroborate other statements that she has made.

Three Keys to Avoiding Adoption Fraud

There are many ways to substantially reduce the chances of being defrauded. Here are three of the most important tips:

1. Listen to your inner voice – your gut. If you sense that a particular situation is not quite right, follow your instincts and further research the situation or walk away.

2. Acquire *REAL* proof of pregnancy. Stories about doctor's appointments and how the baby is growing are not proof of pregnancy. An ultrasound image with the correct name and date on it is also not proof. Even "looking pregnant" is not proof. Prospective adoptive parents should seek written documentation from a doctor, and then follow up with the doctor's office to ensure its legitimacy.

3. Limit or eliminate the amount of cash provided to potential birth families. Sometimes it's legal to pay for pregnancy-related expenses as part of the adoption, but that doesn't mean that prospective adoptive parents have to provide the expectant mother with cash.[1] Instead, providers should be paid directly (e.g., pay the landlord directly to cover rent; pay the hospital or clinic directly to cover medical expenses; pay the utility company directly if the birthmother needs help paying her electric bill).

Finally, although it is important to be educated on this subject, prospective adoptive families should not lose sight of the fact that there are many more expectant parents genuinely exploring adoption as an option and many more ethical adoption professionals trying to help than there are people preying on hopeful adoptive parents.

Be Aware, But Not Paranoid

---

[1] For more information about what expenses potential adoptive parents can legally cover, please see information from the Child Welfare Information Gateway at: http://www.childwelfare.gov/systemwide/laws_policies/statutes/expenses.cfm

National Council
For Adoption

―――――――――Adoption Advocate―――――――

†**Hal Kaufman** is an adoptive father, open adoption advocate, and frequent speaker on the topic of adoption. Mr. Kaufman is also the founder of My Adoption Advisor (www.MyAdoptionAdvisor.com), an adoption education and consulting company that helps families adopt domestically more quickly and safely. My Adoption Advisor offers an on-demand adoption course called Identify Red Flags & Avoid Adoption Scams (www.MyAdoptionAdvisor.com/Adoption-Scams).

HELP US FUND THE *ADOPTION ADVOCATE*

National Council For Adoption is a non-profit organization supported by charitable donations.
To maintain our outstanding programs, we accept contributions of every size. To make a contribution,
please go to www.adoptioncouncil.org and click on "Contribute" or mail your check to
NCFA, 225 N. Washington Street, Alexandria, VA 22314. Thank you!

National Council
For Adoption

5

Appendix F

Selected Bibliography

Constitution:

U.S. Const. art. IV § 1.

Statutes:

21 C.F.R. § 1270 (2010).

25 U.S.C. § 1901 (2006).

25 U.S.C. § 1902 (2006).

25 U.S.C. § 1903 (2006).

25 U.S.C. § 1911 (2006).

25 U.S.C. § 1912 (2006).

25 U.S.C. § 1914 (2006).

25 U.S.C. § 1915 (2006).

123 U.S.C. 1616 (2006).

Ark. Code Ann. § 9-8-304(a).

Fla. Stat. § 63.042(3).

Miss. Code Ann. § 93-17-3(5).

N.C. Gen. Stat. § 48-2-301.

Utah Code Ann. § 78B-6-117(3).

Case Law:

Adoption of Tammy, 416 Mass. 205 (1993).

Allen v. Children's Servs., 567 N.E.2d 1346 (Ohio Ct. App. 1990).

Ann Marie N. v. City & County of S.F., 2001 WL 1261958 (2001).

Bottoms v. Bottoms, 249 Va. 410 (1995).

Burr v. Bd. of County Comm'rs, 491 N.E. 2d 1101 (Ohio 1986).

Caban v. Mohammed, 441 U.S. 380, 389 (1979).

C.O. v. Doe, 757 N.W.2d 343 (Minn. 2008).

Collier v. Krane, 763 F. Supp. 473 (D. Colo. 1991).

Davis v. Davis, 842 S.W.2d 588 (Tenn. 1992).

Finstuen v. Crutcher, 496 F.3d 1139 (10th Cir. 2007).

Fla. Dep't of Children & Families v. X.X.G., 45 So. 3d 79 (Fla. Dist. Ct. App. 2010).

Gibbs v. Ernst, 647 A.2d 882 (Pa. 1994).

Glona v. Am. Guarantee & Liab. Ins. Co., 391 U.S. 73 (1968).

Goodridge v. Dep't of Pub. Health, 798 N.E.2d 941 (Mass. 2003).

Griffith v. Johnston, 899 F.2d 1427 (5th Cir. 1990).

In re Adoption of Baby Boy L., 231 Kan. 199 (1982).

In re Adoption of Luke, 263 Neb. 365 (Neb. 2002).

In re Adoption of T.K.J., 931 P.2d 488 (Colo. Ct. App. 1996).

In re A.J.S., 204 P.3d 543 (Kan. 2009).

In re Baby M, 109 N.J. 396 (1988).

In re B.G.C., 496 N.W.2d 239 (Iowa 1992).

In re B.L.V.B., 628 A.2d 1271 (Vt. 1993).

In re Bridget R, 49 Cal. Rptr. 2d 507, 530 (Ct. App. 1996).

In re Jacob, 660 N.E.2d 397 (N.Y. 1995).

In re Petition of Doe, 638 N.E.2d 181 (Ill. 1994).

In re Santos Y, 112 Cal. Rptr. 2d 692, 699 (Ct. App. 2001).

J.A. v. St. Joseph's Children's & Maternity Hosp., 2001 WL 34644556 (2001).

Johnson v. Calvert, 19 Cal. Rptr. 2d 494 (1993).

Juman v. Louise Wise Servs., 678 N.Y.S.2d 611 (App. Div. 1st Dep't 1998).

Lassiter v. Dep't of Soc. Servs. of Durham County, 452 U.S. 18 (1981).

Lehr v. Robertson, 463 U.S. 248 (1983).

Levy v. Louisiana, 391 U.S. 68 (1968).

Lofton v. Sec'y of the Dep't of Children & Family Servs., 358 F.3d 804 (Fla. 11th Cir. Ct. 2004).

Mallette v. Children's Friend & Serv., 661 A.2d 67 (R.I. 1995).

Meracle v. Children's Servs. Soc., 437 N.W.2d 532 (Wis. 1989).

Michael H. v. Gerald D., 491 U.S. 110 (1989).

Michael J. v. L.A. County Dep't of Adoptions, 201 Cal. App. 3d 859 (1988).

Miss. Band of Choctaw Indians v. Holyfield, 490 U.S. 30 (1989).

Mohr v. Commonwealth, 653 N.E.2d 1104 (Mass. 1995).

Obergefell v. Hodges, 576 U.S. ___ (2015).

Quillon v. Walcott, 434 U.S. 246 (1978).

Roe v. Catholic Charities of the Diocese, 588 N.E.2d 354 (Ill. App. Ct. 1992).

Rowey v. Children's Friend & Serv., 2003 WL 23196347 (2003).

Russell v. Bridgens, 647 N.W.2d 56 (Neb. 2002).

Stanley v. Illinois, 405 U.S. 645 (1972).

York v. Jones, 717 F. Supp. 421 (E.D. Va. 1989).

Young v. Francis, 820 F. Supp. 940 (E.D. Pa. 1993).

Books:

Margot Gayle Backus, *"I am Your Mother; She Was a Carrying Case" Adoption, Class, and Sexual Orientation in Jeanette Winterson's Oranges Are Not the Only Fruit*, in Imagining Adoption: Essays on Literature and Culture (Marianne Novy, ed., The University of Michigan 2001).

Elizabeth Bartholet, *Family Bonds: Adoption and the Politics of Parenting* (Houghton Mifflin Co. 1993).

D. Marianne Blair, *Liability of Adoption Agencies and Attorneys for Misconduct in the Disclosure of Health-Related Information* in Adoption Law and Practice (LexisNexis 2004).

James B. Boskey & Joan Heifetz Hollinger, *Placing Children for Adoption* in Adoption Law and Practice (LexisNexis 2004).

Filis Casey & Marisa Catalina Casey, *Born in Our Hearts: Stories of Adoption* (Health Communications Inc., 2004).

E. Wayne Corp., ed., *Adoption in America: Historical Perspectives* (The University of Michigan 2005).

Kristina Fagan, *Adoption as National Fantasy in Barbara Kingsolver's Pigs in Heaven and Margaret Laurence's The Diviners*, in Imagining Adoption: Essays on Literature and Culture (Marianne Novy, ed., The University of Michigan 2001).

Madelyn Freundlich, *Wrongful Adoption: a Legal Remedy for Adoptive Parents*, Children's Rights.

John De Witt Gregory, Peter N. Swisher, & Sheryl L. Wolf, *Understanding Family Law* (2d ed., LexisNexis 2001).

Joan Heifetz Hollinger, *Adoption Law and Practice* (LexisNexis 2004).

Joan Heifetz Hollinger, *Adoption Procedure* in *Adoption Law and Practice* (LexisNexis 2004).

Joan Heifetz Hollinger, *Agreements and Court Orders for Post-Adoption Contact between Adoptive Families and Birth Parents or Other Birth Relatives* in *Adoption Law and Practice* (LexisNexis 2004).

Joan Heifetz Hollinger, *Consent to Adoption* in *Adoption Law and Practice* (LexisNexis 2004).

Joan Heifetz Hollinger, ed., *Uniform Adoption Act (1994)* in *Adoption Law and Practice* (LexisNexis 2004).

S. Randall Humm, Beate Anna Ort, Martin Mazen Anbari, Wendy S. Lader, & William Scott Biel, eds., *Child, Parent, and State: Law and Policy Reader* (Temple University Press, 1994).

Timothy P. Jackson, ed., *The Morality of Adoption: Social-Psychological, Theological and Legal Perspectives* (Wm. B. Eerdmans Publishing Co. 2005).

Cynthia R. Mabry & Lisa Kelly, *Adoption Law: Theory, Policy, and Practice* (2006)

National Council for Adoption, *Adoption Factbook V* (2011).

Adam Pertman, *Adoption Nation: How the Adoption Revolution is Transforming America* (Basic Books 2000).

Janet Leach Richards, *Mastering Family Law* (Carolina Academic Press 2009).

Dorothy Roberts, *Shattered Bonds: The Color of Child Welfare* (Basic Civitas Books 2002).

William M. Schur, *Attorney's Role in Private Agency Adoption*, in *Adoption Law and Practice* (LexisNexis 2004).

Sharon Vandivere & Karin Malm, *Adoption USA: A Chartbook Based on the 2007 National Survey of Adoptive Parents* (U.S. Dep't of Health & Human Services, Office of the Assistant Secretary for Planning & Evaluation, 2009).

Articles:

Daniel Albanil Adlong, *The Terminator Terminates Terminators: Governor Schwarzenegger's Signature, SB 678, and How California Attempts to Abolish the Existing Indian Family Exception an d Why Other States Should Follow*, 7 Appalachian, J.L. 109 (2007–2008).

Pamela K. Strom Amlung, *Conflicts of Interests in Independent Adoptions: Pitfalls for the Unwary*, 59 U. Cin. L. Rev. 169 (1990).

Annette Ruth Appell, *Reflections on the Movement toward A More Child-Centered Adoption*, 32 W. New Eng. L. Rev. 1 (2010).

Melinda Atkinson, *Aging Out of Foster Care: Towards A Universal Safety Net for Former Foster Care Youth*, 43 Harv. C.R.-C.L. L. Rev. 183 (2008).

Olga Batsedis, *Embryo Adoption: A Scientific Fiction or an Alternative to Traditional Adoption?*, 41 Fam. Ct. Rev. 565 (2003).

Alexia M. Baiman, *Cryopreserved Embryos as America's Prospective Adoptees: Are Couples Truly "Adopting" or Merely Transferring Property Rights?*, 16 Wm & Mary J. Women & L. 133 (2009).

Sarah Biehl, *Validating Oppression: Safe Haven Laws as Perpetuation of Society's Demonization of "Bad" Mothers*, 22 Children's Leg. Rights J. 17 (2002–2003).

John Francis Brosnan, *The Law of Adoption*, 22 Colum. L. Rev. 332 (1923).

Naomi Cahn, *Perfect Substitutes or the Real Thing?*, 52 Duke L.J. 1077 (2003).

Katie Caldwell & Nicole Ficere Callahan, *2010 Adoption Legislative Issues* 20 Adoption Advocate (newsltr. of National Council for Adoption) 1 (January 2010).

Jessica R. Caterina, *Glorious Bastards: The Legal and Civil Birthright of Adoptees to Access Their Medical Records in Search of Genetic Identity*, 61 Syracuse L. Rev. 145(2010).

Nell Clement, *Do "Reasonable Efforts" Require Cultural Competence? The Importance of Culturally Competent Reunification Services in the California Child Welfare System*, 5 Hastings Race & Poverty L. J. 397 (2008).

Christopher Colorado, *Tying the Braid of Second-Parent Adoptions—Where Due Process Meets Equal Protection*, 74 Fordham L. Rev. 1425 (2005).

M.E. Cooley & R.E. Petren, *Foster Parent Perceptions of Competency: Implications for Foster Parent Training*, Children & Youth Serv. Rev. (2011)

Sacha M. Coupet, *The Subtlety of State Action in Privatized Child Welfare Services*, 11 Chap. L. Rev. 85 (2007).

Susan L. Crocklin, *'What is an 'Embryo?': A Legal Perspective,"* 36 Conn. L. Rev. 1177 (Summer 2004).

Jack Darcher, *Market Forces in Domestic Adoptions: Advocating a Quantitative Limit on Private Agency Adoption Fees*, 8 Seattle J. for Soc. Just. 729 (2010).

Cynthia Dailard, *The Drive to Enact 'Infant Abandonment' Laws—A Rush to Judgment?*, The Guttmacher Report on Public Policy 1 (August 2000).

Evan B. Donaldson Adoption Institute, *Unintended Consequences: 'Safe Haven' Laws are Causing Problems, Not Solving Them*, Adoption Nation Education Initiative (March 2003).

Lauren M. Fair, *Shame on US: The Need for Uniform Adoption Records Legislation in the United States*, 48 Santa Clara L. Rev. 1039 (2008).

Mark R. Fletche, *Snowflake Adoption Raises Ethical Issues*, Hobbs News-Sun (Mar. 1, 2001), http://amarillo.com/stories/030101/bel_snowflake.shtml.

Madelyn Freundlich, *Expediting Termination of Parental Rights: Solving a Problem or Sowing the Seeds of a New Predicament?*, 28 Cap. U. L. Rev. 97 (1999).

Chris Guthrie & Joanna L. Grossman, *Adoption in the Progressive Era: Preserving, Creating, and Re-Creating Families*, 43 Am. J. Legal Hist. 235 (1999).

Cynthia Hawkins-Leon, *Adoption & Safe Families Act of 1997 ("ASFA"): A 5 Year Update—Solution or Panacea for the Foster Care Crisis?* (2003).

Jennifer S. Hendricks, *Essentially A Mother*, 13 Wm. & Mary J. Women & L. 429 (2007).

Joan Heifetz Hollinger & Naomi Cahn, *Forming Families by Law: Adoption in America Today*, 36-SUM Hum. Rts. 16 (Summer 2009).

Ruth-Arlene W. Howe, *Adoption Practice, Issues, and Laws 1958–1983*, 17 Fam. L.Q. 173 (1983).

Eileen P. Huff, *The Children of Homosexual Parents: The Voices The Courts Have Yet to Hear*, 9 Am. U. J. Gender Soc. Pol'y & L. 695 (2001).

Cheyanna Jeffke, *The "Existing Indian Family" Exception to the Indian Child Welfare Act: The States' Attempt to Slaughter Tribal Interests in Indian Children*, 66 La. L. Rev. 733 (2005–2006).

Lori L. Klockau, *A Primer on Adoption Law*, 31 WTR Fam. Advoc., 16 (Winter 2009).

Lynne Marie Kohm, Megan Lindsey & William Catoe, *An International Examination of Same Sex Parent Adoption*, 5 Regent J. Int'l L. 237 (2007).

Jason Kuhns, *The Sealed Adoption Records Controversy: Breaking Down the Walls of Secrecy*, 24 Golden Gate U. L. Rev. 261 (1994).

Heather Fann Latham, *Desperately Clinging to the Cleavers: What Family Law Courts Are Doing About Homosexual Parents*, 29 LAW & PSYCHOL. REV. 223 (2005).

Vanessa A. Lavey, *The Path to Recognition of Same Sex Marriage: Reconciling the Inconsistencies between Marriage and Adoption Cases*, 55 UCLA L. REV. 247 (2007).

Dan Lewerenz & Padraic McCoy, *The End of "Existing Indian Family" Jurisprudence: Holyfield at 20, In the Matter of A.J.S., and the Last Gasps of a Dying Doctrine*, 36 WM. MITCHELL. L. REV. 684 (2009–2010).

Margaret M. Mahoney, *Stepparents As Third Parties in Relation to Their Stepchildren*, 40 FAM. L.Q. 81 (2006).

Susan Vivian Mangold & Catherine Cerulli, *Follow the Money: Federal, State, and Local Funding Strategies for Child Welfare Services and the Impact of Local Levies on Adoptions in Ohio*, 38 CAP. U. L. REV. 349 (2009).

Mark T. McDermott, *Agency Versus Independent Adoption: The Case for Independent Adoption*, 3 Future of Children: Adoption 146 (1993).

Steve Mulligan, *Inconsistency in Illinois Adoption Law*, 39 LOY. U. CHI. L.J. 799 (2008).

Susan A. Munson, *Independent Adoption: In Whose Best Interest?*, 26 SETON HALL L. REV. 809 (1995–1996).

John E. B. Myers, *A Short History of Child Protection in America*, 42 FAM. L.Q. 449 (2008–2009).

National Adoption Information Clearinghouse, *State Regulation of Adoption Expenses: State Statutes Series 2003*, U.S. Department of Health & Human Services Administration for Children & Families (May 2003).

National Clearinghouse on Child Abuse and Neglect Information, *2003 Adoption State Statute Series Statute-at-a-Glance: Consent to Adoption*, National Adoption Information Clearinghouse (May 31, 2003).

National Clearinghouse on Child Abuse and Neglect Information, *2003 Adoption State Statute Series Statute-at-a-Glance: State Regulation of Adoption Expenses*, National Adoption Information Clearinghouse (May 31, 2003).

National Clearinghouse on Child Abuse and Neglect Information, *Openness in Adoption: A Fact Sheet for Families*, National Adoption Information Clearinghouse (Feb. 2003).

National Clearinghouse on Child Abuse and Neglect Information, *State Statutes Series 2004 — Infant Safe Haven Laws: Summary of State Laws* (National Adoption Information Clearinghouse 2004).

Laurence C. Nolan: *Unwed Children and Their Parents*, 28 Cap. U. L. Rev. 1 (1999).

Leigh Gaddie, *Open Adoption*, 22 J. Am. Acad. Matrim. Law. 499 (2009).

Susan L. Pollet, *Still A Patchwork Quilt: A Nationwide Survey of State Laws Regarding Stepparent Rights and Obligations*, 48 Fam. Ct. Rev. 528 (2010).

Mark W. Premo-Hopkins, *Between Organs and Adoption: Why Pre-Embryo Donors Should Not Be Allowed to Discriminate Against Recipients*, 2006 U. Chi. Legal F. 441 (2006).

Stephen B. Presser, *The Historical Background of the American Law of Adoption*, 11 J. Fam. L. 443 (1971–1972).

Sarah Ramsey, *The Honorable James R. Browning Symposium: Children & the Law: Symposium Article: Fixing Foster Care or Reducing Child Poverty: The PEW Commission Recommendations and the Transracial Adoption Debate*, 66 Mont. L. Rev. 21 (Winter 2005).

Spencer B. Ross, *Finstuen v. Crutcher: The Tenth Circuit Delivers a Significant Victory for Same Sex Parents With Adopted Children*, 85 Denv. U. L. Rev. 685 (2007–2008).

Elizabeth J. Samuels, *Time to Decide? The Laws Governing Mothers' Consents to the Adoption of Their Newborn Infants*, 72 Tenn. L. Rev. 509 (2005).

Vivek S. Sankaran, *Parens Patriae Run Amuck: The Child Welfare System's Disregard for the Constitutional Rights of Nonoffending Parents*, 82 Temp. L. Rev. 55 (2009).

Stacie Schmerling Perez, *Combating the Baby Dumping Epidemic: A Look at Florida's Safe Haven Law*, 33 Nova L. Rev. 245 (2008).

Somini Sengupta, *Criticism for Law Barring Foster Parents with Past Felonies*, N.Y. Times L39 (Feb. 27, 2000).

Amy Silberberg, *Open Adoption: Is it Legally Enforceable? Should it be?*, Adoptive Families 14 (November/December 1996).

Carol S. Silverman, *Regulating Independent Adoptions*, 22 Colum. J.L. & Soc. Probs., 323 (1989).

Krista Stone-Manista, *Parents in Illinois Are Parents in Oklahoma Too: An Argument for Mandatory Interstate Recognition of Same-Sex Adoptions*, 19 L. & Sexuality, 137 (2010).

Tiffany Woo, *When the Forever Family Isn't: Why State Laws Allowing Adoptive Parents to Voluntarily Rescind an Adoption Violate the Adopted Child's Equal Protection Rights*, 39 Sw. L. Rev. 569 (2010).

Barbara Bennett Woodhouse, *David C. Baum Memorial Lecture: The Courage of Innocence: Children as Heroes in the Struggle For Justice*, 2009 U. Ill. L. Rev. 1567 (2009).

Jamil S. Zainaldin, *The Emergence of a Modern American Family Law: Child Custody, Adoption, and the Courts, 1796–1851*, 73 Nw. U. L. Rev. 1038 (1978–1979).

Websites:

A Safe Haven for Newborns, http://www.asafehavenfornewborns.com/index.php?option=com_content&view=article&id=90&Itemid=171 (last accessed June 16, 2011).

Adopting.org, http://www.adopting.org/adoptions/legalized-abandonment-safe-havens-overview.html (last accessed June 16, 2011).

Bureau of Justice Statistics, http://bjs.ojp.usdoj.gov/content/homicide/children.cfm (last accessed June 16, 2011).

Center for the Future of Children, *The Future of Children*, http://www.princeton.edu/ futureofchildren/publications/docs/03_01_FullJournal.PDF (last accessed June 16, 2011).

Child Trends, *Child Welfare*, http://www.childtrends.org/_listAllPubs.cfm?LID=4D7366E5-AEF5-4F94-8B842104664487A6 (last accessed June 19, 2011).

Child Welfare Information Gateway, *Adam Walsh Child Protection and Safety Act of 2006 P.L. 109-248*, http://www.childwelfare.gov/systemwide/laws_policies/federal/index.cfm?event=federalLegislation.viewLegis&id=81 (last accessed June 16, 2011).

Child Welfare Information Gateway, *Adoption Promotion Act of 2003*, http://www.childwelfare.gov/systemwide/laws_policies/federal/index.cfm?event=federalLegislation.viewLegis&id=85 (last accessed June 16, 2011).

Child Welfare Information Gateway, *Adoption and Safe Families Act of 1997 P.L. 105-89*, http:// www.childwelfare.gov/systemwide/laws_policies/federal/index.cfm?event=federalLegislation.viewLegis&id=4 (last accessed June 16, 2011).

Child Welfare Information Gateway, *Child Abuse Prevention and Enforcement Act of 2000 P.O. 106-177*, http://www.childwelfare.gov/systemwide/laws_poli cies/federal/ index.cfm?event=federalLegislation.viewLegis&id=49 (last accessed June 16, 2011).

Child Welfare Information Gateway, *Child and Family Services Improvement Act of 2006 P.L. 109-288*, http://www.childwelfare.gov/systemwide/laws_poli cies/federal/index.cfm?event= federalLegislation.viewLegis&id=62 (last accessed June 16, 2011).

Child Welfare Information Gateway, *Foster Care Independence Act of 1999 P.L. 106-169*, http://www.childwelfare.gov/systemwide/laws_policies/federal/index .cfm?event=federalLegislation.viewLegis&id=48 (last accessed June 16, 2011).

Child Welfare Information Gateway, *Foster Care Statistics 2009*, http://www.child welfare.gov/pubs/factsheets/foster.cfm (last accessed May, 2011).

Child Welfare Information Gateway, *Fostering Connections to Success and Increasing Adoptions Act of 2008 P.L. 110-351*, http://www.childwelfare.gov/sys-temwide/laws_policies/ federal/index.cfm?event=federalLegislation.viewLegis &id=121 (last accessed June 16, 2011).

Child Welfare Information Gateway, *How the Child Welfare System Works*, http://www.childwelfare.gov/pubs/factsheets/cpswork.cfm (last accessed May, 2011).

Child Welfare Information Gateway, *Keeping Children and Families Safe Act of 2003 P.L. 108-36*, http://www.childwelfare.gov/systemwide/laws_policies/fed eral/ index.cfm?event=federalLegislation.viewLegis&id=45 (last accessed June 16, 2011).

Child Welfare Information Gateway, *Major Federal Legislation Index and Search*, http:// www.childwelfare.gov/systemwide/laws_policies/federal/ index.cfm ?event=federalLegislation.showForm (last accessed June 16, 2011).

Child Welfare Information Gateway, *Promoting Safe and Stable Families Amend-ments of 2001 P.L. 107-133*, http://www.childwelfare.gov/systemwide/laws_poli cies/federal/ index.cfm?event=federalLegislation.viewLegis&id=50 (last accessed June 16, 2011).

Child Welfare Information Gateway, *Safe and Timely Interstate Placement of Fos-ter Children Act of 2006 P.L. 109-239*, http://www.childwelfare.gov/sys-temwide/laws_policies/federal/ index.cfm?event=federalLegislation.viewLegis&id =82 (last accessed June 16, 2011).

Child Welfare Information Gateway, *Tax Relief and Health Care Act of 2006 P.L. 109-432*, http://www.childwelfare.gov/systemwide/laws_policies/fed eral/index.cfm?event=federal Legislation.viewLegis&id=61 (last accessed June 16, 2011).

Child Welfare League of America, *CAPTA Reauthorization Act of 2010*, http://www.cwla.org/advocacy/Capta.htm (last accessed June 16, 2011).

Embryos Alive, *embryosalive.com* (last accessed June 16, 2011).

Human Rights Campaign, *Adoption*, http://www.hrc.org/issues/parenting/adop tions/adoption_laws.asp (last accessed June 16, 2011).

Nightlight Christian Adoptions, nightlight.org (last accessed June 16, 2011).

National Adoption Information Clearinghouse, *Independent Adoptions in the U.S.*, (www.parentsoup.com) (last accessed December 7, 2004).

The National Conference of Commissioners on Uniform State Laws, *Legislative Fact Sheet — Adoption Act (1994)*, http://nccusl.org/LegislativeFact Sheet.aspx?title=Adoption Act (1994) (last updated 2010).

The PEW Commission on Children in Foster Care, *Fostering the Future: Safety, Permanence and Well-Being for Children in Foster Care*, http://www.pew fostercare.org/research/docs/ FinalReport.pdf (last accessed June 16, 2011).

Steven M. Kirsch, *Independent Adoption*, Adoptive Families Magazine (http://www.baby center.com/0_independent-adoption_1373616.bc) (last accessed June 16, 2011).

Uniform Law Commission, The National Conference of Commissioners on Uniform State Laws, *Legislative Fact Sheet — Adoption Act (1994)*, http://nc cusl.org/LegislativeFactSheet.aspx?title =Adoption Act (1994) (last accessed June 16, 2011).

U.S. Dep't of Health & Human Serv., Admin. for Children and Families, Admin. on Children, Youth & Families, Children's Bureau, *The AFCARS Report* (July 2010), www.acf.hhs.gov/programs/cb.

U.S. Dep't of Health & Human Serv., Admin. for Children and Families, Admin. on Children, Youth & Families, Children's Bureau, *The AFCARS Report* (June 2011), www.acf.hhs.gov/programs/cb.

U.S. Food and Drug Administration, *Tissue Guidances*, www.fda.gov/cber/tis sue/docs.htm (last accessed June 16, 2011).

Index

Pages with figures are indicated with "*fig.*". Pages with tables are indicated with "T".

National Survey of Children's Health (NSCH), 194–95

Native American children, transracial adoption of, 19–21, 73. *See also* Indian Child Welfare Act of 1978 (ICWA)

Native Village of Tununak v. State of Alaska Department of Health Services (2014), 122

Nebraska, adoption law in, 89, 131, 132–33, 151, 224T–225T

negligence, by adoption agencies, 175–77

　negligent failure to investigate, 177

　negligent misrepresentation, 175–76

　negligent nondisclosure, 176–77

neonaticide syndrome, 156, 160

Nevada, adoption law in, 90, 91, 130, 146, 225T

New Hampshire, adoption law in, 62, 90, 130, 152, 225T–226T

New Jersey, adoption law in, 226T

　embryos, legal characterization of, 169

　kinship care placement priority, 147

　open birth record policy, 66

　school enrollment, 139

　second parent/joint adoption, 90, 130

　transracial adoptions, 73

New Mexico, adoption law in, 90, 130, 152, 167–68, 226T–227T

New York, adoption law in, 227T

　adoption records, access to, 55, 67

　embryos, legal characterization of, 169

　kinship adoption, 147

　non-relative foster parent adoption, 151

　second parent/joint adoption, 90, 130

　statistics, grandparents, 140

　step-parent adoption, 131–32

　wrongful adoption tort, 178

New York Foundling Hospital, 7–10, 71–72

New York Foundling Hospital v. Gatti (1905), 9–10, 72

New York Society for the Prevention of Cruelty to Children, 14–15

Nielson v. Ketchum (2011), 121

Nightlight Christian (embryo) adoptions, 162–63, 169

non-agency adoption. *See* independent (non-agency) adoption

North American Council on Adoptable Children (NACAC), study by, 78–79

North Carolina, adoption law in, 227T–228T

　same sex adoption, 89, 131, 133–34

　school enrollment, 139

North Dakota, adoption law in, 152, 164, 228T–229T

NPFR, proposed, 50–51, 53

NSAP. *See* National Survey of Adoptive Parents (NSAP)

Obergefell v. Hodges (2015), 97, 110, 135

Ohio, adoption law in, 229T

　kinship care adoption priority, 151

　same sex adoption, 89, 97, 131

　school enrollment, 139

　wrongful adoption tort, 172–73, 178

Oklahoma, adoption law in, 94, 139, 146, 229T–230T

open adoption, 55–67

　for adoptees, benefits/risks of, 64

　for adoptive parents, benefits/risks of, 63–64

　agreements, forms of, 61–62

　beginning of, 17, 56–57

　for birth parents, benefits/risks of, 63

　birth parents' privacy interests, 59

　birth records, access to, 57–58

　completely open records, 62

　embryo adoptions, 165

　factors for successful open adoption relationships, 65–66

　record keeping of adoptions, 55–56

　record keeping of adoptions, public policies on, 66–67